Susanna Centlivre

The dramatic Works of the celebrated Mrs. Centlivre

Vol. III

Susanna Centlivre

The dramatic Works of the celebrated Mrs. Centlivre
Vol. III

ISBN/EAN: 9783337055974

Printed in Europe, USA, Canada, Australia, Japan

Cover: Foto ©ninafisch / pixelio.de

More available books at **www.hansebooks.com**

THE

DRAMATIC WORKS

OF THE CELEBRATED

MRS. CENTLIVRE,

WITH

A New Account of her Life.

COMPLETE IN THREE VOLUMES.

VOL. III.

LONDON:
JOHN PEARSON, 15, YORK ST., COVENT GARDEN.
1872

THE
WORKS

OF THE CELEBRATED

Mrs. CENTLIVRE.

VOLUME THE THIRD.

CONTAINING,

The WONDER.
The MAN BEWITCH'D.
GOTHAM ELECTION.
WIFE WELL MANAGED.
BICKERSTAFF'S BURIAL.
BOLD STROKE FOR A WIFE.
ARTIFICE.

LONDON:

Printed for J. KNAPTON, C. HITCH and L. HAWES,
J. and R. TONSON, S. CROWDER, W. BATHOE,
T. LOWNDS, T. CASLON, H. WOODGATE and S. BROOKS,
and G. KEARSLY.

M.DCC.LX.

THE
WONDER:
A
WOMAN keeps a SECRET.

A
COMEDY.

As it is ACTED at the

THEATRE-ROYAL in DRURY-LANE.

By His MAJESTY's Servants.

PROLOGUE

Spoken by Mr. MILLS.

*OUR Author fears the Criticks of the Stage,
Who, like Barbarians, spare nor Sex, nor Age ;
She trembles at those Censors in the Pit,
Who think good Nature shews a Want of Wit :
Such Malice, O ! what Muse can undergo it ?
To save themselves, they always damn the Poet.
Our Author flies from such a partial Jury,
As wary Lovers from the Nymphs of* Drury :
*To the few candid Judges for a Smile,
She humbly sues to recompense her Toil.
To the bright Circle of the Fair, she next
Commits her Cause, with anxious Doubts perplext.
Where can she with such Hopes of Favour kneel,
As to those Judges, who her Frailties feel ?
A few Mistakes, her Sex may well excuse,
And such a Plea, No* Woman *shou'd refuse :
If she succeeds, a* Woman *gains Applause,
What* Female *but must favour such a Cause ?
Her Faults,—whate'er they are—e'en pass 'em by
And only on her Beauties fix your Eye.
In Plays, like Vessels floating on the Sea,
There's none so wise to know their Destiny.
In this, howe'er, the Pilot's Skill appears,
While by the Stars his constant Course he steers :
Rightly our* Author *does her Judgment shew,
That for her Safety she relies on You.
Your Approbation, Fair ones, can't but move,
Those stubborn Hearts, which first you taught to love :
The Men must all applaud this Play of Ours,
For who dares see with other Eyes, than Yours.*

Dramatis Personæ.

MEN.

Don Lopez, a Grandee of *Portugal*. Mr. *Norris*.
Don Felix { his Son, in Love with *Violante*. } Mr. *Wilks*.
Frederick, A Merchant. - - - Mr. *Bickerstaff*.
Don Pedro, Father to *Violante*. - Mr. *Bullock*, Jun.
Col. *Britton*, A *Scotchman*. - - - Mr. *Mills*.
Gibby, His Footman. - - - Mr. *Bullock*, Sen.
Lissardo, Servant to *Felix*. - - Mr. *Pack*.

WOMEN.

Donna *Violante*, { Designed for a Nun by her Father, in Love with *Felix*. } Mrs. *Oldfield*.
Donna *Isabella*, Sister to *Felix*. - Miss *Santlow*.
Inis, Her Maid - - Mrs. *Cox*.
Flora, Maid to *Violante*. Mrs. *Saunders*.

Alguazil, Attendants, Servants, &c.

SCENE, *Lisbon*.

THE
WONDER.

ACT I. SCENE I.

Enter Don Lopez *meeting* Frederick.

Fred. Y Lord *Don Lopez.*
Don Lop. How d'ye *Frederick* ?
Fred. At your Lordſhip's Service, I am glad to ſee you look ſo well my Lord, I hope *Antonio* is out of danger.

D. Lop. Quite contrary ; his Fever increaſes, they tell me ; and the Surgeons are of Opinion his Wound is mortal,

Fred. Your Son *Don Felix* is ſafe I hope.

D. Lop. I hope ſo too, but they offer large Rewards to apprehend him.

Fred. When heard your Lordſhip from him ?

D. Lop. Not ſince he went ; I forbad him writing till the publick News gave him an Account of *Antonio*'s Health. Letters might be intercepted, and the Place of his Abode diſcovered.

Fred. Your Caution was good, my Lord ; tho' I am impatient to hear from *Felix*, yet his Safety is my chief Concern. Fortune has maliciouſly ſtruck a Bar between us in the Affairs of Life, but she has done me the Honour to unite our Souls.

D. Lop. I am not ignorant of the Friendship between my Son and you. I have heard him commend your Morals, and lament your want of noble Birth.

Fred. That's Nature's Fault, my Lord, 'tis some Comfort not to owe one's Misfortunes to one's self, yet 'tis impossible not to regret the want of noble Birth.

D. Lop. 'Tis pity indeed such excellent Parts as you are Master of, should be eclipsed by mean Extraction.

Fred. Such Commendation wou'd make me vain, my Lord, did you not cast in the Allay of my Extraction.

D. Lop. There is no Condition of Life without its Cares, and it is the Perfection of a Man to wear 'em as easy as he can; this unfortunate Duel of my Son's does not pass without Impression. But since 'tis past Prevention, all my Concern is now, how he may escape the Punishment; if *Antonio* dies, *Felix* shall for *England.* You have been there, what sort of People are the *English ?*

Fred. My Lord, the *English* are by Nature, what the ancient *Romans* were by Discipline, couragious, bold, hardy, and in love with Liberty. Liberty is the Idol of the *English,* under whose Banner all the Nation lists; give but the Word for Liberty, and straight more armed Legions wou'd appear, than *France,* and *Philip* keep in constant Pay.

D. Lop. I like their Principles; who does not wish for Freedom in all Degrees of Life? Tho' common Prudence sometimes makes us act against it, as I am now oblig'd to do, for I intend to marry my Daughter to *Don Guzman,* whom I expect from *Holland* every Day, whither he went to take Possession of a large Estate left him by his Uncle.

Fred. You will not sure sacrifice the lovely *Isabella* to Age, Avarice, and a Fool; pardon the Expression, my Lord; but my Concern for your beauteous Daughter transports me beyond that good Manners which I ought to pay your Lordship's Presence.

D. Lop. I can't deny the Justness of the Character, *Frederick?* but you are not insensible what I have suffered by these Wars, and he has two things which render him very agreeable to me for a Son-in-Law, he is rich and well born; as for his being a Fool, I don't conceive how that can be any

any Blot in a Hufband, who is already poffefs'd of a good Eftate.—A poor Fool indeed is a very fcandalous Thing, and fo are your poor Wits, in my Opinion, who have nothing to be vain of, but the Infide of their Skulls: Now for *Don Guzman* I know I can rule him, as I think fit; this is acting the politick Part, *Frederick*, without which, it is impoffible to keep up the Port of this Life.

Fred. But have you no Confideration for your Daughter's Welfare, my Lord?

D. Lop. Is a Hufband of twenty thoufand Crowns a Year, no Confideration? Now I think it a very good Confideration.

Fred. One way, my Lord. But what will the World fay to fuch a Match?

D. Lop. Sir, I value not the World a Button.

Fred. I cannot think your Daughter can have any Inclination for fuch a Hufband.

D. Lop. There I believe you are pretty much in the right, tho' it is a Secret which I never had the Curiofity to enquire into, nor I believe ever fhall.—Inclination, quotha! Parents would have a fine Time on't if they confulted their Childrens Inclinations! I'll venture you a Wager, that in all the garrifon Towns in *Spain* and *Portugal*, during the late War, there were not three Women, who have not had an Inclination to every Officer in the whole Army; does it therefore follow, that their Fathers ought to pimp for them? No, no, Sir, it is not a Father's Bufinefs to follow his Childrens Inclinations till he makes himfelf a Beggar.

Fred. But this is of another Nature, my Lord.

D. Lop. Look ye, Sir, I refolve fhe fhall marry *Don Guzman* the Moment he arrives; tho' I cou'd not govern my Son, I will my Daughter, I affure you.

Fred. This Match, my Lord, is more prepofterous than that which you propofed to your Son, from whence arofe this fatal Quarrel.—*Don Antonio*'s Sifter, *Elvira*, wanted Beauty only, but *Guzman* every thing, but—

D. Lop. Money—and that will purchafe everything, and fo Adieu. [*Exit.*

Fred. Monftrous! Thefe are the Refolutions which deftroy the Comforts of Matrimony——he is rich, and well born, powerful Arguments indeed! Could I but add them

The WONDER:

to the Friendſhip of *Don Felix*, what might I not hope? But a Merchant, and a Grandee of *Spain*, are inconſiſtent Names—*Liſſardo!* from whence came you?

Enter Liſſardo *in a Riding Habit.*

Liſſ. That Letter will inform you, Sir.
Fred. I hope your Maſter's ſafe.
Liſſ. I left him ſo; I have another to deliver which requires haſte—Your moſt humble Servant, Sir. *(bowing.*
Fred. To *Violante,* I ſuppoſe.
Liſſ. The ſame. [*Exit.*
Fred. (*Reads*) Dear *Frederick*, the two chief Bleſſings of this Life are a Friend, and a Miſtreſs; to be debarred the Sight of thoſe is not to live. I hear nothing of *Antonio*'s Death, therefore reſolve to venture to thy Houſe this Evening, impatient to ſee *Violante,* and embrace my Friend. Yours, *Felix.*
Pray Heaven he comes undiſcover'd.——Ha! Colonel *Britton.*

Enter Colonel Britton *in a Riding Habit.*

Col. Frederick, I rejoice to ſee thee.
Fred. What brought you to *Liſbon,* Colonel?
Col. La Fortune de la Guerre, as the *French* ſay, I have commanded theſe three laſt Years in *Spain,* but my Country has thought fit to ſtrike up a Peace, and give us good *Proteſtants* leave to hope for Chriſtian Burial, ſo I reſolve to take *Liſbon* in my Way home.
Fred. If you are not provided of a Lodging, Colonel, pray command my Houſe, while you ſtay.
Col. If I were ſure I ſhould not be troubleſome, I wou'd accept your Offer, *Frederick.*
Fred. So far from Trouble, Colonel, I ſhall take it as a particular Favour; what have we here?
Col. My Footman, this is our Country Dreſs, you muſt know, which for the Honour of *Scotland,* I make all my Servants wear.

Enter Gibby *in a* Highland *Dreſs.*

Gib. What mun I de with the Horſes, an like yer Honour, they will tack cold gin they ſtand in the Cauſeway.
Fred.

Fred. Oh! I'll take care of them, what hoa *Vafquez*, [*Enter* Vafquez. put thofe Horfes which that honeft Fellow will fhow you into my Stable, do you hear? and feed them well.

Vaf. Yes, Sir.—Sir, by my Mafter's Order, I am, Sir, your moft obfequious humble Servant. Be pleas'd to lead the Way. [*bowing.*

Gib. S'bled gang yer gat, Sir, and I fall follow ye: Ife tee hungry to feed on Compliments. [*Exit.*

Fred. Ha, ha, a comical Fellow.—Well, how do you like our Country, Colonel?

Col. Why Faith, *Frederick*, a Man might pafs his Time agreeable enough with-infide of a Nunnery, but to behold fuch Troops of foft, plump, tender, melting, wifhing, nay willing Girls too, thro' a damn'd Grate, gives us *Britons* ftrong Temptation to plunder. Ah *Frederick* your Priefts are wicked Rogues. They immure Beauty for their own proper Ufe, and fhow it only to the Laity to create Defires, and inflame Accompts, that they may purchafe Pardons at a dearer Rate.

Fred. I own Wenching is fomething more difficult here than in *England,* where Womens Liberties are fubfervient to their Inclinations, and Hufbands feem of no Effect but to take Care of the Children which their Wives provide.

Col. And does Reftraint get the better of Inclination with your Women here? No, I'll be fworn not one even in fourfcore. Don't I know the Conftitution of the *Spanifh* Ladies?

Fred. And of all Ladies where you come, Colonel, you were ever a Man of Gallantry.

Col. Ah *Frederick,* the *Kirk* half ftarves us *Scotchmen.* We are kept fo fharp at home, that we feed like Cannibals abroad. Hark ye, haft thou never a pretty Acquaintance now, that thou would'ft confign over to a Friend for half an Hour, ha?

Fred. Faith, Colonel, I am the worft Pimp in *Chriftendom,* you had better truft to your own Luck! the Women will foon find you out, I warrant you.

Col. Ay, but it is dangerous foraging in an Enemy's Country, and fince I have fome hopes of feeing my own again, I had rather purchafe my Pleafure, than run the Hazard of a *Stilletto* in my Guts. 'Egad, I think I muft e'en e'en marry, and facrifice my Body for the Good of my Soul wilt thou recommend me to a Wife then, one that is willing to exchange her *Moydores* for *Englifh* Liberty; ha Friend?

Fred. She muſt be very handſome, I ſuppoſe.

Col. The handſomer the better—but be ſure ſhe has a Noſe.

Fred. Ay, ay, and ſome Gold

Col. Oh, very much Gold, I ſhall never be able to ſwallow the Matrimonial Pill, if it be not well gilded.

Fred. Puh, Beauty will make it ſlide down nimbly.

Col. At firſt perhaps it may, but the ſecond or third Doſe will choak me——I confeſs *Frederick*, Women are the prettieſt Play-things in Nature; but Gold, ſubſtantial Gold, gives'em the Air, the Mien, the Shape, the Grace, and Beauty of a Goddeſs.

Fred. And has not Gold the ſame Divinity in their Eyes, Colonel?

Col. Too often.—Money is the very God of Marriage; the Poets drefs him in a Saffron Robe, by which they figure out the golden Deity, and his lighted Torch blazons thoſe mighty Charms, which encourage us to liſt under his Banner.

None marry now for Love, no, that's a Jeſt.
The ſelf ſame Bargain, ſerves for Wife, and Beaſt.

Fred. You are always gay, Colonel; come, ſhall we take a refreſhing Glaſs at my Houſe, and conſider what has been ſaid?

Col. I have two or three Compliments to diſcharge for ſome Friends, and then I ſhall wait on you with Pleaſure: Where do you live?

Fred. At yon Corner Houſe with the green Rails.

Col. In the Cloſe of the Evening I will endeavour to kifs your Hand. Adieu. [*Exit.*

Fred. I ſhall expect you with Impatience. [*Exit.*

Enter Iſabella *and* Inis *her Maid.*

Inis. For Goodneſs ſake, Madam, where are you going in this Pet?

Iſab. Any where to avoid Matrimony; the Thoughts of a Huſband is as terrible to me as the Sight of a Hobgoblin.

Inis.

Inis. Ay, of an old Hufband; but if you may chufe for yourfelf, I fancy Matrimony would be no fuch frightful thing to you.

Ifab. You are pretty much in the right, *Inis*; but to be forc'd into the Arms of an Ideot, a fneaking, fnivling, drivling, avaricious Fool, who has neither Perfon to pleafe the Eye, Senfe to charm the Ear, nor Generofity to fupply thofe Defects. Ah, *Inis!* what pleafant Lives Women lead in *England*, where Duty wears no Fetter but Inclination: The Cuftom of our Country inflaves us from our very Cradles, firft to our Parents, next to our Hufbands; and when Heaven is fo kind to rid us of both thefe, our Brothers ftill ufurp Authority, and expect a blind Obedience from us; fo that Maids, Wives, or Widows, we are little better than Slaves to the Tyrant Man; therefore to avoid their Power, I refolve to caft myfelf into a Monaftery.

Inis. That is, you'll cut your own Throat to avoid another's doing it for you. Ah, Madam, thofe Eyes tell me you have no Nun's Flefh about you; a Monaftery, quotha! Where you'll wifh yourfelf in the Green-Sicknefs in a Month.

Ifab. What care I, there will be no Man to plague me.

Inis. No, nor what's much worfe, to pleafe you neither—Ad'slife, Madam, you are the firft Woman that e'er defpair'd in a Chriftian Country——Were I in your Place——

Ifab. Why, what would your Wifdom do if you were?

Inis. I'd imbark with the firft fair Wind with all my Jewels, and feek my Fortune on t'other fide the Water; no Shore can treat you worfe than your own; there's ne'er a Father in *Chriftendom* fhould make me marry any Man againft my Will.

Ifab. I am too great a Coward to follow your Advice. I muft contrive fome way to avoid *Don Guzman*, and yet ftay in my own Country.

Enter Don Lopez.

Lop. Muft you fo, Miftrefs? but I fhall take Care to prevent you. (*Afide.*) *Ifabella*, whither are you going, my Child.

Ifab. Ha! my Father! to Church, Sir.

Inis.

Inis. The old Rogue has certainly over-heard her.
[*Aside.*
Lop. Your Devotion muſt needs be very ſtrong, or your Memory, very weak, my Dear; why, Veſpers are over for this Night; come, come, you ſhall have a better Errand to Church than to ſay your Prayers there. *Don Guzman* is arriv'd in the River, and I expect him aſhore To-morrow.
Iſab. Ha, To-morrow!
Lop. He writes me Word, That his Eſtate in *Holland* is worth 12000 Crowns a Year, which, together with what he had before, will make thee the happieſt Wife in *Liſbon.*
Iſab. And the moſt unhappy Woman in the World. Oh Sir! If I have any Power in your Heart, if the Tenderneſs of a Father be not quite extinct, hear me with Patience.
Lop. No Objection againſt the Marriage, and I will hear whatever thou haſt to ſay.
Iſab. That's torturing me on the Rack, and forbidding me to groan; upon my Knees I claim the Privilege of Fleſh and Blood. [*Kneels.*
Lop. I grant it, thou ſhalt have an Arm full of Fleſh and Blood To-morrow; Fleſh and Blood, quotha; Heaven forbid I ſhould deny thee Fleſh and Blood, my Girl.
Inis. Here's an old Dog for you. [*Aside.*
Iſab. Do not Miſtake, Sir; the fatal Stroke which ſeparates Soul and Body, is not more terrible to the Thoughts of Sinners, than the Name of *Guzman* to my Ear.
Lop. Puh, Puh; you lye, you lye.
Iſab. My frighted Heart beats hard againſt my Breaſt, as if it fought a Paſſage to your Feet, to beg you'd change your Purpoſe.
Lop. A very pretty Speech this; if it were turn'd into blank Verſe, it would ſerve for a *Tragedy*; why, thou haſt more Wit than I thought thou hadſt, Child.——I fancy this was all *extempore*, I don't believe thou did'ſt ever think of one Word on't before.
Inis. Yes, but ſhe has, my Lord, for I have heard her ſay the ſame Things a thouſand Times.
Lop. How, how? What do you top your ſecond-hand Jeſts upon your Father, Huſſy, who knows better what's good for you than you do yourſelf? remember 'tis your Duty to obey.
Iſab.

A Woman keeps a Secret. 15

Ifab. (*Rifing.*) I never difobey'd before, and wifh I had not Reafon now; but Nature has got the better of my Duty, and makes me loath the harfh Commands you lay.

Lop. Ha, ha, very fine! Ha, ha.

Ifab. Death itfelf wou'd be more welcome.

Lop. Are you fure of that?

Ifab. I am your Daughter, my Lord, and can boaft as ftrong a Refolution as yourfelf; I'll die before I'll marry *Guzman.*

Lop. Say you fo? I'll try that prefently. (*Draws.*) Here let me fee with what Dexterity you can breathe a Vein now (*offers her his Sword.*) The Point is pretty fharp, 'twill do your Bufinefs I warrant you.

Inis. Blefs me, Sir, What do you mean to put a Sword into the Hands of a defperate Woman?

Lop. Defperate, ha, ha, ha, you fee how defperate fhe is; what art thou frighted little *Bell?* ha!

Ifab. I confefs I am ftartled at your Morals, Sir.

Lop. Ay, ay, Child, thou hadft better take the Man, he'll hurt thee the leaft of the two.

Ifab. I fhall take neither, Sir; Death has many Doors, and when I can live no longer with Pleafure, I fhall find one to let him in at without your Aid.

Lop. Say'ft thou fo, my dear *Bell?* Ods, I'm afraid thou art a little Lunatick, *Bell.* I muft take care of thee Child, (*takes hold of her, and pulls out of his Pocket a Key*) I fhall make bold to fecure thee, my Dear: I'll fee if Locks and Bars can keep thee till *Guzman* comes; go, get you into your Chamber.

There I'll your boafted Refolution try,
And fee who'll get the better, you or I.

(*pufhes her in, and locks the Door.*

The WONDER:

ACT II.

SCENE, *a Room in* Don Pedro's *Houſe.*

Enter Donna Violante *reading a Letter, and* Flora *following.*

Flora. WHAT muſt that Letter be read again?
Vio. Yes, and again, and again, and again. a thouſand Times again ; a Letter from a faithful Lover can ne'er be read too often ; it ſpeaks ſuch kind, ſuch ſoft, ſuch tender Things—— *[Kiſſes it.*
Flo. But always the ſame Language.
Vio. It does not charm the leſs for that.
Flo. In my Opinion nothing charms that does not change; and any Compoſition of the four and twenty Letters, after the firſt Eſſay, from the ſame Hand, muſt be dull, except a Bank Note, or a Bill of Exchange.
Vio. Thy Taſte is my Averſion—(*Reads*) My all that's charming, ſince Life's not Life exil'd from thee, this Night ſhall bring me to thy Arms. *Frederick* and thee are all I truſt: Theſe ſix Weeks Abſence has been in Love's Accompt ſix hundred Years ; when it is dark, expect the wonted Signal at thy Window, till when, adieu, thine more than his own. *Felix.*
Flo. Who wou'd not have ſaid as much to a Lady of her Beauty, and twenty thouſand Pounds.—Were I a Man, methinks I could have ſaid a hundred finer Things ; I wou'd have compar'd your Eyes to the Stars, your Teeth to Ivory, your Lips to Coral, your Neck to Alabaſter, your Shape to——
Vio. No more of your Bombaſt, Truth is the beſt Eloquence in a Lover.—What Proof remains ungiven of his Love? When his Father threatned to diſinherit him, for refuſing *Don Antonio*'s Siſter, from whence ſprung this unhappy Quarrel, did it ſhake his Love for me ? And now, tho' ſtrict Enquiry runs thro' every Place, with large Rewards to apprehend him, does he not venture all for me?
Flo. But you know, Madam, your Father *Don Pedro* deſigns

designs you for a Nun, and says your Grandfather left you your Fortune upon that Condition.

Vio. Not without my Approbation, Girl, when I come to one and Twenty, as I am inform'd. But however, I shall run the Risk of that ; go call in *Liffardo*.

Flo. Yes, Madam ; now for a Thousand Verbal Questions. [*Exit, and enter with* Liffardo.

Vio. Well, and how do you do, *Liffardo?*

Liff. Ah, very weary, Madam—Faith thou look'st wondrous pretty, *Flora*. [*Aside to* Flora.

Vio. How came you ?

Liff. En Cavalier, Madam, upon a Hackney-Jade, which they told me formerly belong'd to an *English* Colonel. But I should have rather thought she had been bred a good *Roman Catholick* all her Life-time ; for she down on her Knees to every Stock and Stone we came along by. My Chaps waters for a Kiss, they do, *Flora*.
[*Aside to* Flora.

Flo. You'd make one believe you are wondrous fond, now.

Vio. Where did you leave your Master.

Liff. Od, if I had you alone House-Wife, I'd show you how fond I cou'd be——(*Aside to* Flora) at a little Farm-House, Madam, about five Miles off; he'll be at *Don Frederick's* in the Evening——Od, I will so revenge my-self of those Lips of thine. [*to* Flora.

Vio. Is he in Health ?

Flo. Oh, you counterfeit wondrous well. [*to* Liff.

Liff. No, every Body knows I counterfeit very ill.
[*to* Flora.

Vio. How say you ? Is *Felix* ill ? What's his Distemper ? Ha !

Liff. A pies on't, I hate to be interrupted——Love, Madam, Love —— In short, Madam, I believe he has thought of nothing but your Ladyship ever since he left *Lisbon*. I am sure he cou'd not, if I may judge of his Heart by my own. [*Looking lovingly upon* Flora.

Vio. How came you so well acquainted with your Master's Thoughts, *Liffardo?*

Liff. By an infallible Rule, Madam ; Words are the Pictures of the Mind, you know ; now to prove he thinks of nothing but you, he talks of nothing but you——for Example,

Example, Madam, coming from fhooting t'other Day, with a Brace of Partridges, *Liffardo*, faid he, go bid the Cook roaft me these *Violante's*——I flew into the Kitchin, full of Thoughts of thee, cry'd, here Cook, roaft me thfe *Florella's*. [*to* Flora.

Flo. Ha, ha, excellent —— You mimick your Mafter then it feems.

Liff. I can do every Thing as well as my Mafter, you little Rogue :— Another Time, Madam, the Prieft came to make him a Vifit, he call'd out haftily, *Liffardo*, faid he, bring a *Violante* for my Father to fit down on ;—— then he often miftook my Name, Madam, and call'd me *Violante* ; in fhort, I heard it fo often, that it became as familiar to me as my Prayers.

Vio. You liv'd very merrily then it feems.

Liff. Oh, exceeding merry, Madam. [*Kiffes* Flora's Hand.

Vio. Ha! exceeding merry; had you Treats and Balls?

Liff. Oh! Yes, yes, Madam, feveral.

Flo. You are mad, *Liffardo*, you don't mind what my Lady fays to you. [*Afide to* Liffardo.

Vio. Ha ! Balls——Is he fo merry in my Abfence ? And did your Mafter dance, *Liffardo ?*

Liff. Dance Madam ! Where Madam ?

Vio. Why, at thofe Balls you fpeak of.

Liff. Balls ! What Balls Madam ?

Vio. Why, fure you are in Love, *Liffardo* ; did not you fay, but now, you had Balls where you have been ?

Liff. Balls, Madam ! Od'slife, I afk your Pardon, Madam! I, I, I, had miflaid fome Wafh-Balls of my Mafter's t'other day ; and becaufe I could not think where I had laid them, juft when he afk'd for them, he very fairly broke my Head, Madam, and now it feems I can think of nothing elfe. Alas ! He dance, Madam ! No, no, poor Gentleman, he is as melancholy as an unbrac'd Drum.

Vio. Poor *Felix !* There, wear that Ring for your Mafter's Sake, and let him know, I fhall be ready to receive him. [*Exit* Vio.

Liff. I fhall Madam —(*puts on the Ring*) methinks a Diamond Ring is a vaft Addition to the little Finger of a Gentleman. [*admiring his Hand.*

Flo. That Ring muft be mine——Well *Liffardo!* What Hafte

Hafte you make to pay off Arrears now? Look how the Fellow ftands!

Liff. Egad, methinks I have a very pretty Hand—— and very white——and the Shape!——Faith, I never minded it fo much before!——In my Opinion it is a very fine fhap'd Hand——and becomes a Diamond Ring, as well as the firft Grandee's in *Portugal.*

Flo. The Man's tranfported! Is this your Love! This your Impatience!

Liff. (*Takes Snuff.*) Now in my Mind——I take Snuff with a very *Jantee* Air——Well, I am perfuaded I want nothing but a Coach, and a Title, to make me a very fine Gentleman. [*Struts about.*

Flo. Sweet Mr. *Liffardo,* (*curtefying*) if I may prefume to fpeak to you, without affronting your little Finger.——

Liff. Odfo Madam, I afk your Pardon——Is it to me, or to the Ring——you direct your Difcourfe, Madam?

Flo. Madam! Good lack! How much a Diamond Ring improves one!

Liff. Why, tho' I fay it——I can carry myfelf as well as any Body——But what wer't thou going to fay Child?

Flor. Why I was going to fay, that I fancy you had beft let me keep that Ring; it will be a very pretty Wedding-Ring, *Liffardo,* would it not?

Liff. Humph! Ah! But——but——but——I believe I fhan't marry yet a while.

Flo. You fhan't you fay——Very well! I fuppofe you defign that Ring for *Inis.*

Liff. No, no, I never bribe an old Acquaintance—— Perhaps I might let it fparkle in the Eyes of a Stranger a little, till we come to a right Underftanding—But then like all other mortal Things, it would return from whence it came.

Flor. Infolent——Is that your Manner of dealing?

Liff. With all but thee——Kifs me, you little Rogue you. [*Hugging her.*

Flor. Little Rogue! Prithee Fellow, don't be fo familiar, (*pufhing him away*) if I mayn't keep your Ring, I can keep my Kiffes.

Liff. You can, you fay! Spoke with the Air of a Chamber-maid.

Flor. Reply'd with the Spirit of a ferving Man.

Liff.

Liſſ. Prithee, *Flora,* don't let you and I fall out, I am in a merry Humour, and ſhall certainly fall in ſomewhere.
Flor. What care I, where you fall in.

Enter Violante.

Vio. Why do you keep *Liſſardo* ſo long, *Flora?* When you don't know how ſoon my Father may awake, his Afternoon Naps are never long.
Flor. Had *Don Felix* been with her, ſhe wou'd not have thought the Time long; theſe Ladies conſider no Body's Wants but their own.   [*Aſide.*
Vio. Go, go, let him out, and bring a Candle.
Flo. Yes, Madam.
Liſſ. I fly, Madam.   [*Exit* Liſſ. *and* Flora.
Vio. The Day draws in, and Night,——the Lover's Friend advances——Night more welcome than the Sun to me, becauſe it brings my Love.
Flor. (*Shrieks within*) Ah Thieves, Thieves! Murder, Murder!
Vio. (*Shrieks*) Ah! defend me Heaven! What do I hear? *Felix* is certainly purſu'd, and will be taken.

Enter Flora *running.*

Vio. How now! Why doſt ſtare ſo? Anſwer me quickly! What's the Matter?
Flo. Oh Madam! as I was letting out *Liſſardo,* a Gentleman ruſhed between him and I, ſtruck down my Candle, and is bringing a dead Perſon in his Arms into our Houſe.
Vio. Ha! a dead Perſon! Heaven grant it do's not prove my *Felix.*
Flor. Here they are, Madam.

Enter Colonel *with* Iſabella *in his Arms.*

Vio. I'll retire till you diſcover the Meaning of the Accident.   [*Exit.*
Col. (*Sets* Iſabella *down in the Chair, and addreſſes himſelfto* Flora.)
Madam, The Neceſſity this Lady was under, of being convey'd into ſome Houſe with Speed and Secrecy, will I hope excuſe any Indecency I might be guilty of, in preſſing ſo rudely into this——I am an entire Stranger to her Name

Name and Circumſtances; wou'd I were ſo to her Beauty too. (*Aſide*) I commit her Madam, to your Care, and fly to make her Retreat ſecure, if the Streets be clear; permit me to return and learn from her own Mouth, if I can be farther ſerviceable; pray Madam, how is the Lady of this Houſe call'd?

Flor. *Violante, Senior*——He is a handſome *Cavalier*, and promiſes well. [*Aſide.*

Col. Are you ſhe, Madam?

Flor. Only her Woman, *Senior.*

Col. Your humble Servant. Mrs. Pray be careful of the Lady——(*gives her two Moydores.*) [*Exit Col.*

Flor. Two Moydores! Well he is a generous Fellow. This is the only Way to make one careful; I find all Countries underſtand the Conſtitution of a Chamber-maid.

Enter Violante.

Vio. Was you diſtracted *Flora?* To tell my Name to a Man you never ſaw! Unthinking Wench! Who knows what this may turn to—What is the Lady dead! Ah! defend me Heaven, 'tis *Iſabella*, Siſter to my *Felix*, what has befal'n her? Pray Heaven he's ſafe——Run and fetch ſome cold Water, (*Exit* Flora, *and enters with Water*) *Iſabella*, Friend, ſpeak to me, Oh! ſpeak to me, or I ſhall die with Apprehenſion.

Flor. See, ſhe revives.

Iſab. Oh! hold my deareſt Father, do not force me, indeed I cannot love him.

Vio. How wild ſhe talks.——

Iſab. Ha! where am I?

Vio. With one as ſenſible of thy Pain as thou thyſelf canſt be.

Iſab. *Violante!* What kind Star preſerv'd, and lodg'd me here?

Flor. It was a Terreſtrial Star call'd a Man, Madam; pray *Jupiter* he proves a lucky one.

Iſab. Oh! I remember now, forgive me dear *Violante*, my Thoughts ran ſo much upon the Danger I eſcap'd, I had forgot.

Vio. May I not know your Story?

Iſab. Thou art no Stranger to one part of it; I have often told thee that my Father deſign'd to ſacrifice me to the

the arms of *Don Guzman*, who it feems is juft return'd from *Holland*, and expected afhore to-morrow, the Day that he has fet to celebrate our Nuptials ; upon my refufing to obey him, he lock'd me into my Chamber, vowing to keep me there till he arriv'd, and force me to confent. I know my Father to be pofitive, never to be won from his Defign ; and having no hope left me, to efcape the Marriage, I leap'd from the Window, into the Street.

Vio. You have not hurt yourfelf I hope.

Ifab. No, a Gentleman paffing by, by Accident caught me in his Arms ; at firft my Fright made me apprehend it was my Father, till he affur'd me to the contrary.

Flor. He is a very fine Gentleman I promife you, Madam, and a well bred Man I warrant him. I think I never faw a Grandee put his Hand into his Pocket with a better Air in my whole Life Time ; then he open'd his Purfe with fuch a Grace, that nothing but his Manner of prefenting me the Gold could equal.

Vio. There is but one common Road to the Heart of a Servant, and 'tis impoffible for a generous Perfon to miftake it.—But how came you hither *Ifabella ?*

Ifab. I know not, I defir'd the Stranger to convey me to the next *Monaftery*, but e'er I reach'd thy Door, I faw, or fancy'd that I faw, *Liffardo*, my Brother's Man, and the Thought that his Mafter might not be far off, flung me into a Swoon, which is all that I remember : Ha ! What's here (*takes up a Letter*) For Colonel *Britton, to be left at the Poft-Houfe in* Lifbon ; this muft be drop'd by the Stranger which brought me hither.

Vio. Thou art fallen into the Hands of a Soldier, take care he does not lay thee under Contribution, Girl.

Ifab. I find he is a Gentleman ; and if he be but unmarried I cou'd be content to follow him all the World over.—But I fhall never fee him more I fear. (*Sighs and Paufes.*)

Vio. What makes you figh, *Ifabella ?*

Ifab. The fear of falling into my Father's Clutches again.

Vio. Can I be ferviceable to you ?

Ifab. Yes, if you'll conceal me two or three Days.

Vio. You command my Houfe and Secrecy.

Ifab.

Ifab. I thank you *Violante,*—I wiſh you wou'd oblige me with Mrs. *Flora* a while.

Vio. I'll ſend for her to you—I muſt watch if Dad be ſtill aſleep, or here will be no room for *Felix.* [*Exit.*

Ifab. Well, I don't know what ails me, but methinks I wiſh I cou'd find this Stranger out.

Enter Flora.

Flor. Does your Ladyſhip want me, Madam?

Ifab. Ay, Mrs. *Flora,* I reſolve to make you my Confident.

Flor. I ſhall endeavour to diſchargè my Duty, Madam.

Ifab. I doubt it not, and deſire you to accept this as a Token of my Gratitude.

Flora. O dear *Senjora,* I ſhou'd have been your humble Servant, without a Fee.

Isab. I believe it—But to the Purpoſe—Do you think if you ſaw the Gentleman which brought me hither, you ſhou'd know him again?

Flor. From a Thouſand, Madam, I have an excellent Memory where a handſome Man's concern'd; when he went away he ſaid he would return again immediately, I admire he comes not.

Ifab. Here, did you ſay? You rejoice me—Tho' I'll not ſee him, if he comes, cou'd not you contrive to give him a Letter?

Flor. With the Air of a Duenna.—

Ifab. Not in this Houſe—You muſt veil and follow him —He muſt not know it comes from me.

Flor. What do you take me for a Novice in Love Affairs? Tho' I have not practis'd the Art ſince I have been in *Donna Violante'*s Service, yet I have not loſt the Theory of a Chamber-maid—Do you write the Letter, and leave the reſt to me—Here, here, here's Pen, Ink and Paper.

Ifab. I'll do't in a Minute. [*Sits down to write.*

Flor. So! This is Buſineſs after my own Heart; Love always takes care to reward his Labourers, and *Great Britain* ſeems to be his Favourite Country—Oh, I long to ſee the t'other two Moydores with a Britiſh Air—Methinks there's a Grace peculiar to that Nation in making a Preſent.

Ifab.

Ifab. So I have done, now if he does but find this Houfe again!

Flor. If he fhou'd not—I warrant I'll find him if he's in *Lifbon*. [*Puts the Letter into her Bofom.*

Enter Violante.

Vio. Flora, watch my Papa; he's faft afleep in his Study—If you find him ftir, give me Notice.—Hark, I hear *Felix* at the Window, admit him inftantly, and then to your Poft. [*Exit Flora.*

Ifab. What fay you *Violante?* Is my Brother come?

Vio. It is his Signal at the Window.

Ifab. (Kneels.) Oh! *Violante*, I conjure thee by all the love thou bear'ft to *Felix*—By thy own generous Nature —Nay more, by that unfpotted Vertue thou art Miftrefs of, do not difcover to my Brother I am here.

Vio. Contrary to your Defire, be affur'd I never fhall, but where's the Danger?

Ifab. Art thou born in *Lifbon*, and afk that Queftion? He'll think his Honour blemifh'd by my Difobedience, and wou'd reftore me to my Father, or kill me, therefore dear, dear Girl.

Vio. Depend upon my Friendfhip, nothing fhall draw thy Secret from thefe Lips, not even *Felix*, tho' at the Hazard of his Love; I hear him coming, retire into that Clofet.

Ifab. Remember *Violante*, upon thy Promife my very Life depends.

Vio. When I betray thee, may I fhare thy Fate.

Enter Flora *with* Felix.

Vio. My *Felix*, My everlafting Love. [*runs into his Arms.*

Fel. My Life, my Soul! My *Violante!*

Vio. What Hazards doft thou run for me; Oh, how fhall I requite thee?

Fel. If during this tedious painful Exile, thy Thoughts have never wander'd from thy *Felix*, thou haft made me more than Satisfaction.

Vio. Can there be room within this Heart for any but thyfelf. No, if the God of Love were loft to all the reft of Human Kind, thy Image wou'd fecure him in my Breaft,

A WOMAN *keeps a* SECRET.

Breaſt, I am all Truth, all Love, all Faith, and know no jealous Fears.

Fel. My Heart's the proper Sphere where Love reſides; cou'd he quit that he wou'd be no where found: And yet *Violante* I'm in doubt.

Vio. Did I ever give thee Cauſe to doubt, my *Felix.*

Fel. True Love has many Fears, and Fear as many Eyes as Fame; yet ſure I think they ſee no Fault in thee —— What's that? [*the Colonel pats at the Window without.*

Vio. What? I heard nothing. [*He pats again.*

Fel. Ha! What means this Signal at your Window?

Vio. Some Body perhaps, in paſſing by, might accidentally hit it, it can be nothing elſe.

Col. (*Within*) Hiſt, hiſt, *Donna Violante, Donna Violante.*

Fel. They uſe your Name by Accident too, do they, Madam? [*Enter* Flora.

Flo. There is a Gentleman at the Window, Madam, which I fancy to be him who brought *Iſabella* hither; ſhall I admit him? [*Aſide to* Violante.

Vio. Admit Diſtraction rather, thou art the Cauſe of this, unthinking Wretch! · [*Aſide to* Flora.

Fel. What has Miſtress *Scout* brought you freſh Intelligence? Death, I'll know the Bottom of this immediately!
[*offers to go.*

Flor. Scout, I ſcorn your Words, *Senior.*

Vio. Nay, nay, nay, nay, you muſt not leave me.
[*runs and catches hold of him.*

Fel. Oh! 'Tis not fair, not to anſwer the Gentleman, Madam. It is none of his Fault, that his Viſit proves unſeaſonable; pray let me go, my Preſence is but a Reſtraint upon you. [*ſtruggles to get from her.*
[*The Colonel pats again.*

Vio. Was ever Accident ſo miſchievous? [*Aside.*

Flor. It muſt be the Colonel, now to deliver my Letter to him. [*Exit.*

Fel. Hark, he grows impatient at your Delay—Why do you hold the Man, whoſe Abſence wou'd oblige you, pray let me go, Madam; conſider, the Gentleman wants you at the Window. Confuſion! [*ſtruggles ſtill.*

Vio. It is not me he wants.

Fel. Death, not you? Is there another of your Name in
B the

the Houſe? But, come on, convince me of the Truth of what you ſay: Open the Window, if his Buſineſs does not lye with you, your Converſation may be heard—— This, and only this, can take off my Suſpicion—What do you pauſe! Oh! Guilt! Guilt! Have I caught you, nay then I'll leap the Balcony. If I remember, this Way leads to it. [*breaks from her, and goes to the Door where Iſabella is.*]

Vio. Oh Heavens! Whall ſhall I do now? Hold, hold, hold, hold, not for the World —— You enter there —— Which way ſhall I preſerve his Siſter from his Knowledge? [*Aſide.*

Fel. What have I touch'd you; do you fear your Lover's Life?

Vio. I fear for none but you——for Goodneſs Sake, do not ſpeak ſo loud my *Felix.* If my Father hear you I am loſt for ever, that Door opens into his Apartment, What ſhall I do if he enters? There he finds his Siſter—If he goes out he'll quarrel with the Stranger —— Nay, do not ſtruggle to be gone, my *Felix.*——If I open the Window he may diſcover the whole Intrigue, and yet of all Evils we ought to chuſe the leaſt. Your Curioſity ſhall be ſatisfied. Whoe'er you are that with ſuch Inſolence dare uſe my Name, and give the Neighbourhood Pretence to reflect upon my Conduct: I charge you inſtantly be gone, or expect the Treatment you deſerve. [*goes to the Window, and throws up the Saſh.*

Col. I aſk your Pardon, Madam, and will obey; but when I left this Houſe to Night.

Fel. Good!

Vio. It is moſt certainly the Stranger, what will be the Event of this, Heaven knows. (*Aſide.*) you are miſtaken in the Houſe I ſuppoſe, Sir.

Fel. No, no, he is not miſtaken —— Pray Madam let the Gentleman go on.

Vio. Wretched Misfortune, pray be gone Sir, I know of no Buſineſs you have here.

Col. I wiſh I did not know it neither——But this Houſe contains my Soul, then can you blame my Body for hovering about it!

Fel. Excellent!

Vio. Diſtraction! He will infallibly diſcover *Iſabella.*
I tell

I tell you again you are miftaken; however, for your own Satisfaction, call To-morrow.

Fel. Matchlefs Impudence! An Affignation before my Face——No, he fhall not live to meet your Wifhes.
[*Takes out a Piftol and goes towards the Window; fhe catches hold of him.*

Vio. Ah! (*Shrieks*) hold I conjure you.

Col. To-morrow's an Age, Madam! May I not be admitted to Night?

Vio. If you be a Gentleman, I command your Abfence. Unfortunate! What will my Stars do with me? [*Afide.*

Col. I have done—Only this—Be careful of my Life, for it is in your keeping. [*Exit from the Window.*

Fel. Pray obferve the Gentleman's Requeft, Madam.
[*Walking off from her.*

Vio. I am all Confufion. [*Afide.*

Fel. You are all Truth. all Love, all Faith; Oh! thou all Woman!——How have I been deceiv'd! S'Death, cou'd not you have impos'd upon me for this one Night? Cou'd neither my faithful Love, nor the Hazard I have run to fee you, make me worthy to be cheated on?

Vio. Can I bear this from you? [*Weeps.*

Fel. (*Repeats*) When I left this Houfe to Night——to Night the Devil! Return fo foon.

Vio. Oh *Ifabella!* What haft thou involv'd me in!
[*Afide.*

Fel. (*Repeats*) This Houfe contains my Soul.

Vio. Yet I refolve to keep the Secret. [*Afide.*

Fel. (*Repeats*) Be careful of my Life, for 'tis in your keeping——Damnation!——How ugly fhe appears?
[*Looking on her.*

Vio. Do not look fo fternly on me, but believe me, *Felix,* I have not injur'd you, nor am I falfe.

Fel. Not falfe, not injur'd me! O *Violante,* loft and abandon'd to thy Vice! Not falfe, Oh monftrous!

Vio. Indeed I am not—There is a Caufe which I muft not reveal—Oh think how far Honour can oblige your Sex——Then allow a Woman may be bound by the fame Rule to keep a Secret.

Fel. Honour, what haft thou to do with Honour, thou that canft admit plurality of Lovers, a Secret? Ha, ha, ha, his Affairs are wondrous fafe, who trufts his Secret to a Woman's keeping, but you need give yourſelf no Trouble about clearing this Point, Madam, for you are become ſo indfferent to me, that your Truth, and Falſhood are the ſame?

Vio. My Love! [*Offers to take his Hand.*
Fel. My Torment! [*Turns from her.*

Enter Flora.

Flo. So I have deliver'd my Letter to the Colonel, and receiv'd my Fee. (*Aſide*) Madam, your Father bad me ſee what Noiſe that was—For Goodneſs ſake, Sir, why do you ſpeak ſo loud.

Fel. I underſtand my cue, Mſtreſs, my Abſence is neceſſary. I'll oblige you. (*going*) [*takes hold of him.*
Vio. Oh, let me undeceive you firſt!
Fel. Impoſſible!
Vio. 'Tis very probable if I durſt.
Fel. Durſt! Ha, ha, ha, durſt quotha.
Vio. But another Time I'll tell the all.
Fel. Nay, now or never.— —
Vio. Now it cannot be,
Fel. Then it ſhall never be—Thou moſt ungrateful of thy Sex, farewel. [*Breaks from her and Exit.*
Vio. Oh exquiſite Tryal of my Friendſhip! Yet not even this, ſhall draw the *Secret* from me,

*That I'll preſerve, let Fortune frown, or ſmile,
And truſt to Love, my Love to reconcile.* [*Exit.*

ACT III.

Enter Don Lopez.

Lop. WAS ever Man thus plagu'd! Odſheart, I cou'd ſwallow my Dagger for Madneſs; I know not what to think, ſure *Frederick* hád no Hand in her Eſcape—She muſt get out of the Window; and ſhe could not do that without a Ladder; and who cou'd bring it her, but him? Ay, it muſt be ſo. The Diſlike he ſhew'd to
Don

Don Guzman in our Difcourfe to Day, confirms my Sufpicion, and I will charge him home with it; fure Children were given me for a Curfe! Why, what innumerable Misfortunes attend us Parents, when we have employ'd our whole Care to educate, and bring our Children up to Years of Maturity? Juft when we expect to reap the Fruits of our Labour; a Man fhall in the tinkling of a Bell, fee one hang'd, and t'other whor'd.——This gracelefs Baggage ——But I'll to *Frederick* immediately. I'll take the Alguazil with me, and fearch his Houfe; and if I find her, I'll ufe her——by St. *Anthony*, I don't know how I'll ufe her. [*Exit.*

The Scene changes to the Street.

Enter Colonel *with* Ifabella's *Letter in his Hand, and* Gibby *following.*

Col. Well, tho' I cou'd not fee my fair *Incognita*, Fortune, to make me amends, has flung another Intrigue in my way. Oh! How I love thefe pretty, kind, coming Females, that won't give a Man the Trouble of wracking his Invention to deceive them.——Oh *Portugal!* Thou dear Garden of Pleafure——Where Love drops down his mellow Fruit, and every Bough bends to our Hands, and feems to cry come, Pull and Eat, how delicioufly a Man lives here without Fear of the Stool of Repentance?— This Letter I receiv'd from a Lady in a Veil—Some *Duenna!* Some necefary Implement of *Cupid?* I fuppofe the Stile is frank and eafy, I hope like her that writ it. (*Reads*) " Sir, I have feen your Perfon, and like it.—— *Very concife—"*And if you'll meet me at five o'Clock in " the Morning upon the *Terriero de paffa*, half an Hours " Converfation will let me into your Mind."——*Ha, ha, ha, a philofophical Wench: This is the firft Time I ever knew a Woman had any Bufinefs with the Mind of a Man.* " If your Intellects anfwer your outward Appearance, the " Adventure may not difpleafe you. I expect you'll not " attempt to fee my Face, nor offer any thing unbecom- " ing the Gentleman I take you for:"—Humph, the Gentleman fhe takes me for; I hope fhe takes me to be Flefh and Blood, and then I am fure I shall do nothing unbecoming a Gentleman. Well, if I muft not fee her

B 3 Face,

The WONDER:

Face, it fhall go hard if I don't know where fhe lives. ——*Gibby*.

Gib. Here, an lik yer Honour.

Col. Follow me at a good Diftance, do you hear, *Gibby?*

Gib. In truth dee I, weel eneugh, Sir.

Col. I am to meet a Lady upon the *Terreira de paſſa*.

Gib. The Deel an mine Eye gin I kenn her, Sir.

Col. But you will when we come there, Sirrah.

Gib. Like eneugh, Sir; I have as fharp and Eyn tul a bony Lafs, as ere a Lad in aw *Scotland*; and what mun I dee wi her, Sir?

Col. Why, if fhe and I part, you muft watch her home, and bring me Word where fhe lives.

Gib. In troth fal I, Sir, gin the Deel tak her not.

Col. Come along then, 'tis pretty near the Time.——I like a Woman that rifes early to purfue her Inclination.

Thus we improve the Pleaſures of the Day,
Whilſt taſtleſs Mortals ſleep their Time away. [*Exit.*

Scene changes to Frederick's *Houſe.*

Enter Inis *and* Liffardo.

Liſſ. Your Lady ran away, and you not know whither? Say you?

Inis. She never greatly car'd for me after finding you and I together; but you are very grave, methinks, *Liſ-fardo*.

Liſſ. (*Looking upon the Ring*) Not at all——I have fome Thoughts indeed of altering my Courfe of living; there is a critical Minute in every Man's Life, which, if he can but lay hold of, he may make his Fortune.

Inis. Ha! What, do I fee a Diamond Ring! Where the Deuce had he that Ring? You have got a very pretty Ring there, *Liſſardo*.

Liſſ. Ay, the Trifle is pretty enough——But the Lady which gave it me is a *Bona Roba* in Beauty, I affure you

[*Cocks his Hat and ſtruts.*

Inis. I can't bear this——The Lady! What Lady, pray?

Liſſ. Oh fy! There's a Queftion to afk a Gentleman.

Inis.

Inis. A Gentleman! Why, the Fellow's fpoil'd! is this your Love for me? Ungrateful Man, you'll break my Heart, fo you will. [*Burſts into Tears.*
Liſſ. You tender-hearted Fool.——
Inis. If I knew who gave you that Ring, I'd tear her Eyes out, fo I wou'd. [*Sobs.*
Liſſ. So, now the Jade wants a little Coaxing; why, what doſt thou weep for now, my Dear? Ha!
Inis. I fuppofe *Flora* gave you that Ring; but I'll—
Liſſ. No, the Devil take me if fhe did, you make me fwear now——So, they are All for the Ring, but I ſhall bob 'em: I did but joke, the Ring is none of mine, it is my Maſter's; I am to give it to be new fet, that's all; therefore, prithee dry thy Eyes, and kifs me, come.
[*Enter* Flora.
Inis. And do you really fpeak Truth now?
Liſſ. Why do you doubt it?
Flo. So, fo, very well! I thought there was an Intrigue between him and *Inis*, for all he has forfworn it fo often. [*Aſide.*
Inis. Nor han't you feen *Flora* fince you came to Town.
Flo. Ha! How dares fhe name my Name?]*Aſide.*
Liſſ. No, by this Kifs I han't. [*Kiſſes her.*
Flo. Here's a diſſembling Varlet. [*Aſide.*
Inis. Nor don't you love her at all?
Liſi. Love the Devil; why did not I always tell thee fhe was my Averfion?
Flo. Did you fo, Villain? [*Strikes him a Box on the Ear.*
Liſſ. Zounds, fhe here! I have made a fine Spot of Work on't. [*Aſide.*
Inis. What's that for? Ha. [*Bruſhes up to her.*
Flo. I ſhall tell you by and by, Mrs. *Frippery,* if you don't get about your Bufinefs.
Inis. Who do you call *Frippery,* Mrs. *Trollop!* Pray get about your Bufinefs: If you go to that, I hope you pretend to no Right and Title here.
Liſſ. What the Devil do they take me for, an Acre of Land, that they quarrel about Right and Title to me?
[*Aſide.*
Flo. Pray what Right have you, Miſtrefs, to aſk that Queſtion?

Inis. No matter for that, I can fhow a better Title to him than you, I believe.

Flo. What, has he given thee nine Months earneft for a living Title? Ha, ha.

Inis. Don't fling your flaunting Jefts at me, Mrs. *Bold-face*, for I won't take 'em, I affure you.

Liff. So! Now am I as great as the fam'd *Alexander*. But my dear *Statira* and *Roxana*, don't exert yourfelves fo much about me: Now, I fancy, if you wou'd agree lovingly together, I might, in a modeft Way, fatisfy both your Demands upon me.

Flo. You fatisfy! No, Sirrah, I am not to be fatisfy'd fo foon as you think, perhaps.

Inis. No, nor I neither——What, do you make no Difference between us?

Flo. You pityful Fellow, you; what, you fancy, I warrant, that I gave myfelf the trouble of dogging you, out of Love to your filthy Perfon; but you are miftaken, Sirrah—It was to deteƈt your Treachery.—How often have you fworn to me that you hated *Inis*, and only carried fair for the good Chear fhe gave you; but that you could never like a Woman with crooked Legs, you faid.

Inis. How, how, Sirrah, crooked Legs! Ods; I cou'd find in my Heart. [*Snatching up her Petticoat a little.*

Liff. Here's a lying young Jade now! Prithee, my Dear, moderate thy Paffion. [*Coaxingly.*

Inis. I'd have you to know, Sirrah, my Legs was never —your Mafter, I hope, underftands Legs better than you do, Sirrah. [*paffionately.*

Liff. My Mafter, fo,fo. [*Shaking his Head and winking.*

Flo. I am glad I have done fome Mifchief, however. [*Afide.*

Liff. (*To Inis.*) Art thou really fo foolifh to mind what an enrag'd Woman fays? Don't you fee fhe does it on purpofe to part you and I? (*runs* to Flora) cou'd not you find the Joke without putting yourfelf in a Paffion! You filly Girl you? why I faw you follow us plain enough, Mun, and faid all this, that you might not go back with only your Labour for your Pains—But you are a revengeful young Slut tho'. I tell you that, but come kifs, and be Friends.

Flo. Don't think to coax me hang your Kiffes.

Fel.

A WOMAN *keeps a* SECRET.

Fel. (Within) Liffardo.
Liff. Odſheart, here's my Maſter ; the Devil take both theſe Jades for me, what ſhall I do with them ?
Inis. Ha ! 'Tis *Don Felix*'s Voice ; I wou'd not have him find me here, with his Footman, for the World.
[*Aſide.*
Fel. (Within) Why, *Liffardo, Liffardo !*
Liff. Coming Sir, What a Pox will you do ?
Flo. Bleſs me, which Way ſhall I get out !
Liff. Nay, nay, you muſt e'en ſet your Quarrel aſide, and be content to be mew'd up in this Cloaths Preſs together, and ſtay where you are, and face it out——there is no help for it !
Flo. Put me any where, rather than that ; come, come, let me in. [*He opens the Preſs, and ſhe goes in.*
Inis. I'll fee her hang'd, before I'll go into the Place where ſhe is.—— I'll truſt Fortune with my Deliverance : Here us'd to be a Pair of back Stairs, I'll try to find them out. [*Exit.*

Enter Felix *and* Frederick.

Fel. Was you aſleep, Sirrah, that you did not hear me call ?
Liff. I did hear you, and anſwer'd you, I was coming, Sir.
Fel. Go get the Horſes ready, I'll leave *Liſbon* to Night, never to ſee it more.
Liff. Hey dey ! What's the Matter now ? [*Exit.*
Fred. Pray tell me, *Don Felix !* What has ruffled your Temper thus ?
Fel. A Woman—Oh Friend, who can name Woman, and forget Inconſtancy !
Fred. This from a Perſon of mean Education were excuſable, ſuch low Suſpicions have their Source from vulgar Converſation ; Men of your politer Taſte never raſhly cenſure.—Come, this is ſome groundleſs Jealouſy—Love raiſes many Fears.
Fel. No, my Ears convey'd the Truth into my Heart, and Reaſon juſtifies my Anger : *Violante*'s falſe, and I have nothing left, but thee, in *Liſbon*, which can make me wiſh ever to ſee it more, except Revenge upon my Rival, of whom I am ignorant. Oh, That ſome Miracle would reveal

veal him to me, that I might thro' his Heart punifh her Infidelity.

Enter Liffardo.

Liff. Oh! Sir, here's your Father *Don Lopez* coming up.

Fel. Does he know that I am here?

Liff. I can't tell, Sir, he afk'd for *Don Frederick.*

Fred. Did he fee you?

Liff. I believe not, Sir, for as foon as I faw him, I ran back to give my Mafter Notice.

Fel. Keep out of his Sight then.—And dear *Frederick*, permit me to retire into the next Room, for I know the old Gentleman will be very much difpleafed at my Return without his Leave.   [*Exit.*

Fred. Quick, quick, be gone, he is here.

Enter Don Lopez, *fpeaking as he enters.*

Lop. Mr. *Alguazil*, wait you without till I call for you. *Frederick*, an Affair brings me here—which—requires Privacy—So that if you have any Body within Ear-fhot, pray order them to retire.

Fred. We are private, my Lord, fpeak freely.

Lop. Why then Sir, I muft tell you, that you had better have pitch'd upon any Man in *Portugal* to have injur'd, than myfelf.

Fel. (*Peeping*) What means my Father?

Fred. I underftand you not, my Lord!

Lop. Tho' I am old, I have a Son.—Alas! Why name I him? He knows not the Difhonour of my Houfe.

Fel. I am confounded! The Difhonour of his Houfe.

Fred. Explain yourfelf my Lord! I am not confcious of any difhonourable Action to any Man, much lefs to your Lordfhip.

Lop. 'Tis falfe! you have bebauched my Daughter.

Fel. Debauch'd my Sifter! Impoffible! He cou'd not, durft not be that Villain.

Fred. My Lord I fcorn fo foul a Charge.

Lop. You have debauch'd her Duty at leaft, therefore, inftantly reftore her to me, or by St. *Anthony* I'll make you.

Fred. Reftore her my Lord! Where fhall I find her?

Lop. I have thofe that will fwear fhe is here in your Houfe.   *Fel.*

Fel. Ha! In this Houfe?
Fred. You are mifinform'd, my Lord, upon my Reputation I have not feen *Donna Ifabella*, fince the Abfence of *Don Felix*.
Lop. Then, pray Sir——If I am not too inquifitive, what Motive had you for thofe Objections you made againſt her Marriage with *Don Guzman* Yeſterday?
Fred. The Difagreeablenefs of fuch a Match, I fear'd, wou'd give your Daughter caufe to curfe her Duty, if ſhe comply'd with your Demand, that was all, my Lord!
Lop. And fo you help'd her thro' the Window to make her difobey.
Fel. Ha, my Siſter gone! Oh Scandal to our Blood!
Fred. This is infulting me, my Lord, when I aſſure you I have neither feen, nor know any thing of your Daughter——If ſhe is gone, the Contrivance was her own, and you may thank your Rigour for it.
Lop. Very well, Sir; however, my Rigour ſhall make bold to fearch your Houfe: Here, call in the Alguazil.—
Flo. (*Peeping*) The Alguazil? What in the Name of Wonder will become of me!
Fred. The Alguazil! My Lord, you'll repent this.

Enter Alguazil *and Attendants.*

Lop. No Sir, 'tis you that will repent it, I charge you, in the King's Name, to affiſt me in finding of my Daughter. —Before you leave no Part of the Houfe unfearch'd; come, follow me. [*Goes towards the Door where* Felix *is;* Frederick *draws, and plants himſelf before the Door.*
Fred. Sir, I must fiıſt know by what Authority you pretend to fearch my Houfe, before you enter here.
Alg. How! Sir, dare you prefume to draw your Sword upon the Reprefentative of Majeſty! I am, Sir, I am his Majeſty's *Alguazil*, and the very Quinteffence of Authority——therefore put up your Sword, or I ſhall order you to be knock'd down——for know, Sir, the Breath of an *Alguazil*, is as dangerous as the Breath of a *Demy-Culverin*.
Lop. She is certainly in that Room, by his guarding the Door——if he difputes your Authority, knock him down, I ſay.

Fred.

Fred. I shall show you some Sport first! The Woman you look for is not here, but there is something in this Room, which I'll preserve from your Sight at the Hazard of my Life.

Lop. Enter, I say, nothing but my Daughter can be there—Force his Sword from him. [Felix *comes out and joins* Frederick.

Fel. Villains, stand off! Assassinate a Man in his own House.

Lop. Oh, oh, oh, *Misericordia*, what do I see my Son!

Alg. Ha, his Son! Here's five hundred Pounds good, my Brethren, if *Antonio* dies, and that's in the Surgeon's Power, and he's in love with my Daughter, you know—*Don Felix!* I command you to surrender yourself into the Hands of Justice, in order to raise me and my Posterity, and in Consideration you lose your Head to gain me five hundred Pounds, I'll have your Generosity recorded on your Tomb-stone——at my own proper Cost and Charge—I hate to be ungrateful.

Fred. Here's a generous Dog now——

Lop. Oh that ever I was born—Hold, hold, hold.

Fred. Did I not tell you, you wou'd repent, my Lord. What ho! Within there (*Enter Servants*) Arm yourselves, and let not a Man in, nor out, but *Felix*——Look ye, *Alguazil*, when you wou'd betray my Friend for filthy Lucre, I shall no more regard you as an Officer of Justice, but as a Thief and Robber thus resist you.

Fel. Generous *Frederick!* Come on, Sir, we'll show you Play for the five hundred Pounds.

Alg. Fall on, seize the Money right or wrong, ye Rogues. [*They fight.*

Lop. Hold, hold, *Alguazil!* I'll give you the five hundred Pounds, that is, my Bond to pay it upon *Antonio*'s Death, and twenty Pistoles however Things go, for you and these honest Fellows to drink my Health.

Alg. Say you so, my Lord! Why look ye, my Lord, I bear the young Gentleman no ill Will, my Lord, if I get but the five hundred Pounds, my Lord — Why, look ye, my Lord——'Tis the same Thing to me whether your Son be hanged or not, my Lord.

Fel. Scoundrels.——

Lop. Ay, well, thou art a good-natur'd Fellow, that is

is the Truth on't——Come then, we'll to the Tavern, and sign and seal this Minute : Oh *Felix!* be careful of thyself, or thou wilt break my Heart.   [*Exit* Lopez, Alguazil *and Attendants*,

Fel. Now *Frederick*, tho' I ought to thank you for your Care of me, yet, till I am satisfied about my Father's Accusation, I can't return the Acknowledgments I owe you: Know you aught relating to my Sister?

Fred. I hope my Faith and Truth are known to you —And here by both I swear, I am ignorant of every Thing relating to your Father's Charge.

Fel. Enough, I do believe thee! Oh Fortune! Where will thy Malice end!

Enter Servant.

Ser. Sir, I bring you joyful News; I am told that *Don Antonio* is out of Danger, and now in the Palace.

Fel. I wish it be true, then I'm at Liberty to watch my Rival, and pursue my Sister? Prithee *Frederick*, inform thyself of the Truth of this Report.

Fred. I will this Minute——Do you hear, let no body in to *Don Felix* till my Return. [*Exit.*

Ser. I'll observe, Sir. [*Exit.*

Flo. (*Peeping*) They have almost frighted me out of my Wits—I'm sure—Now *Felix* is alone, I have a good Mind to pretend I came with a Message from my Lady; but then how shall I say I came into the Cupboard. [*Aside.*

Enter Servant, seeming to oppose the Entrance of somebody.

Ser. I tell you, Madam, *Don Felix* is not here.

Vio. (*Within*) I tell you, Sir, he is here, and I will see him. (*breaks in*) You are as difficult of Access, Sir, as a first Minister of State.

Flo. My Stars! My Lady here! [*Shuts the Press close.*

Fel. If your Visit was designed to *Frederick*, Madam, he is abroad.

Vio. No, Sir, the Visit is to you.

Fel. You are very punctual in your Ceremonies, Madam.

Vio. Tho' I did not come to return your Visit, but to take that which your Civility ought to have brought me.

Fel.

Fel. If my Ears, my Eyes and my Underſtanding ly'd, then I am in your Debt, elſe not, Madam.

Vio. I will not charge them with a Term ſo groſs, to ſay they ly'd, but call it a Miſtake, nay, call it any thing to excuse my *Felix*—Cou'd I, think ye, cou'd I put off my Pride ſo far, poorly to diſſemble a Paſſion which I did not feel? Or ſeek a Reconciliation, with what I did not love? Do but conſider, if I had entertain'd another, ſhou'd I not rather embrace this Quarrel, pleas'd with the Occaſion that rid me of your Viſits, and gave me Freedom to enjoy the Choice which you think I have made; have I any Intereſt in thee but my Love? Or am I bound by aught but Inclination to ſubmit and follow thee——No Law whilſt ſingle binds us to obey, but you by Nature and Education, are oblig'd to pay a Deference to all Woman-kind.

Fel. Theſe are fruitleſs Arguments. 'Tis moſt certain thou wert dearer to theſe Eyes than all that Heaven e're gave to charm the Sense of Man; but I wou'd rather tear them out, than ſuffer 'em to delude my Reason, and enſlave my Peace.

Vio. Can you love without Eſteem? And where is the Eſteem for her you ſtill ſuſpect? Oh *Felix!* There is a Delicacy——in Love, which equals even a religious Faith; true Love n'eer doubts the Object it adores, and Scepticks there, will diſbelieve their Sight.

Enter Serant.

Fel. Your Notions are too refin'd for mine, Madam. How now, what do you want?

Ser. Only my Maſter's Cloak out of this Preſs, Sir, that's all——Oh! the Devil, the Devil.   [*Opens the Preſs, ſees* Flora, *and roars out.*

Vio. Ha, a Woman conceal'd! Very well, *Felix!*

Flo. Diſcover'd! Nay then Legs befriend me. [*runs out.*

Fel. A Woman in the Preſs!   [*Enter* Liſſardo. How the Devil came a Woman there, Sirrah.'

Liſſ. What ſhall I ſay now?

Vio. Now *Liſſardo* ſhew your Wit to bring your Maſter off.

Liſſ. Off Madam! Nay, nay, nay, there, there needs no

no great Wit to, to, to, bring him off Madam, for she did, and she did not come as, as, as, as, a, a, Man may say directly to, to, to, to speak with my Master, Madam.

Vio. I see by your Stammering, *Lissardo*, that your Invention is at a very low Ebb.

Fel. 'Sdeath, Rascal! speak without Hesitation, and the Truth too, or I shall stick my Stilletto in your Guts.

Vio. No, no, your Master mistakes, he wou'd not have you speak the Truth.

Fel. Madam, my Sincerity wants no Excuse.

Liss. I am so confounded between one and the other, that I can't think of a Lye.— [*Aside.*

Fel. Sirrah, fetch me this Woman back instantly, I'll know what Business she had here!

Vio. Not a step; your Master shan't be put to the Blush ——Come a Truce, *Felix!* Do you ask me no more Questions about the Window, and I'll forgive this.

Fel. I scorn Forgiveness where I own no Crime, but your Soul, conscious of its Guilt, would fain lay hold of this Occasion to blend your Treason with my Innocence.

Vio. Insolent! Nay, if instead of owning your Fault you endeavour to insult my Patience, I must tell you, Sir, you don't behave yourself like that Man of Honour you wou'd be taken for, you ground your Quarrel with me upon your own Inconstancy; 'tis plain you are false yourself, and wou'd make me the Aggressor——It was not for nothing the Fellow oppos'd my Entrance——This last Usage has given me back my Liberty, and now my Father's Will shall be obey'd without the least Reluctance. [*Exit.*

Fel. Oh, stubborn, stubborn Heart, what wilt thou do? Her Father's Will shall be obey'd; Ha, That carries her to a Cloyster, and cuts off all my Hopes at once——By Heaven she shall not, must not leave me! No she is not false, at least my Love now represents her true, because I fear to lose her: Ha! Villain, art thou here: (*turns upon* Lissardo) tell me this Moment whom this Woman was, and for what Intent she was here conceal'd——Or

Liss. Ah, good Sir, forgive me, and I'll tell you the whole Truth. (*falls on his Knees.*

Liss. It, it, it, was Mrs. *Flora,* Sir, *Donna Violante's* Woman——you must know, Sir, we have had a sneaking
Kind-

Kindnefs for one another a great while—She was not willing you fhould know it, fo when fhe heard your Voice, fhe ran into the Cloaths-Prefs; I wou'd have told you this at firft, but I was afraid of her Lady's knowing it; this is the Truth, as I hope for a whole Skin, Sir.

Fel. If it be not, I'll not leave you a whole Bone in it, Sirrah——fly, and obferve if *Violante* goes directly home.

Liff. Yes, Sir; yes.

Fel. I muft convince her of my Faith: Oh! how irrefolute is a Lover's Heart! My Refentment cool'd when hers grew high—Nor can I ftruggle longer with my Fate; I cannot quit her, no I cannot, fo abfolute a Conqueft has fhe gain'd——Woman's the greateft fovereign Power on Earth.

In vain Men ftrive their Tyranny to quit,
Their Eyes command, and force us to fubmit.
So have I feen a mettled Courfer fly,
Tear up the Ground, and tofs his Rider high,
Till fome experienc'd Mafter found the Way,
With Spur and Rein to make his Pride obey.

Scene the Terreiro de paffa.

Enter Colonel *and* Ifabella *veil'd.*
Gibby *at a Diftance.*

Col. Then you fay, it is impoffible for me to wait of you home, Madam.

Ifab. I fay it is inconfiftent with my Circumftance, Colonel, and that Way impoffible for me to admit of it.

Col. Confent to go with me then——I lodge at one *Don Frederick*'s a Merchant juft by here, he is a very honeft Fellow, and I dare confide in his Secrecy.

Ifab. Ha, does he lodge there? Pray Heaven I am not difcover'd. [*Afide.*

Col. What fay you, my Charmer? fhall we breakfast together; I have fome of the beft Bohea in the Univerfe.

Ifab. Pu! Bohea! Is that the beft Treat you can give a Lady at your Lodgings—Colonel!

Col. Well hinted——No, no, no, I have other Things at thy Service, Child.

Ifab. What are thofe Things pray,

Col.

Col. My Heart, Soul, and Body into the Bargain.

Ifab. Has the laſt no Incumbrance upon it; can you make a clear Title, Colonel?

Col. All Freehold, Child, and I'll afford thee a very good Bargain. [*embraces her.*

Gib. Au my Sol, they mak muckle Wards about it, Iſe ſeer weary with ſtanding, Iſe e'en tak a Sleep.
[·*Lies down.*

Ifab. If I take a Leaſe it muſt be for Life, Colonel.

Col. Thou ſhalt have me as long, or as little Time as thou wilt; my Dear, come, let's to my Lodging, and we'll Sign and Seal this Minute.

Ifab. Oh, not ſo faſt, Colonel, there are many Things to be adjuſted before the Lawyer and the Parſon comes.

Col, The Lawyer, and Parſon! No, no, ye little Rogue, we can finiſh our Affairs without the Help of the Law— or the Goſpel.

Ifab. Indeed, but we can't, Colonel.

Col. Indeed! Why haſt thou then trappan'd me out of my warm Bed this Morning for nothing! Why, this is ſhowing a Man half famiſh'd a well furniſh'd Larder, then clapping a Padlock on the Door, till you ſtarve him quite.

Ifab. If you can find in your Heart to ſay Grace, Colonel, you ſhall keep the Key.

Col. I love to ſee my Meat before I give Thanks, Madam, therefore uncover thy Face, Child, and I'll tell thee more of my Mind.——If I like you——

Isab. I dare not riſk my Reputation upon your Ifs, Colonel,—and ſo Adieu. [*Going.*

Col. Nay, nay, nay, we muſt not part.

Ifab. As you ever hope to ſee me more, ſuſpend your Curioſity now; one Step farther loſes me for ever.—— Show yourſelf a Man of Honour, and you ſhall find me a Woman of Honour. [*Exit.*

Col. Well, for once, I'll truſt to a blind Bargain, Madam.——(*Kiſſes her Hand and parts.*) But I ſhall be too cunning for your Ladyſhip, if *Gibby* obſerves my Orders: Methinks theſe Intrigues, which relate to the Mind, are very inſipid.——The Converſation of Bodies is much more diverting.——Ha! What do I ſee, my Raſcal aſleep? Sirrah,

Sirrah, did I not charge you to watch the Lady? And is it thus you obferve my Orders, ye Dog. [*Kicks him all this while, and he fhrugs, and rubs his Eyes, and yawns.*

Gib. That's true, and lik your Honour; but I thought that when ence ye had her in yer awn Honds, yee mite a orderd her yer fal weel eneugh without me, en ye keen, and lik her Honour.

Col. Sirrah, hold your impertinent Tongue, and make hafte after her; if you don't bring me fome Account of her, never dare to fee my Face again. [*Exit.*

Gib. Ay! This is bony Wark indeed, to run three hundred Mile to this wicked Town, an before I can weel fill my Wem, to be fent a Whore-hunting after this black fhee Devil.—What fal I gang to fpeer for this Wutch now? Ah, for a ruling Elder——or the Kirk's Treaferer ——or his Mon——Id gar, my Mafter make twa oh this; —But I'm feer ther's na fike honeft People here, or there wou'd na be fo muckle Sculdudrie *.

[*Enter an* Englifh *Soldier paffing along.*

Gib. Geud Mon, did ye fee a Woman, a Lady, ony gate her away enow?

Eng. Man. Yes, a great many. What kind of a Woman is it you enquire after.

Gib. Geud. troth, fhe's ne Kenfpekle, fhe's aw in a Clowd.——

Eng. Man. What! it's fome High-land Monfter which you brought over with you, I fuppofe, I fee no fuch, not I, kenfpekle quotha!

Gib. Huly, huly, Mon, the Deel pike out yer Eyn, and then you'll fee the bater, ye *English* bag Pudin Tike.

Eng. Man. What fays the Fellow? [*Turning to* Gibby.

Gib. Say! I fay I am a better Fellow than e'er ftude upon yer Shanks—an gin I heer meer a yer din, deal a my Sol, Sir, but Ife crak your Crown.

Eng. Man. Get you gone, you *Scotch* Rafcal, and thank your Heathen Dialect, which I don't underftand, that you han't your Bones broke.

Gib. Ay! an ye do no underftond a *Scots* Man's Tongue

---

* *Fornication.*

— Ife

A WOMAN keeps a SECRET.

—Ife fe gin ye can underftond a *Scots* Man's Gripe: Wha's the batter Man now, Sir?
[*Lays hold of him, ftrikes up his Heels, and gets aftride over him.*

Here Violante *croffes the Stage,* Gibby *jumps up from the Man, and brufhes up to* Violante.

Gib. I vow, Madam, but I am glad that yee and I are foregather'd.

Vio. What wou'd the Fellow have?

Gib. Nothing, away Madam, wo worth yer Heart, what a muckle deel a Mifchief had yee like to bring upon poor *Gibby*.

Vio. The Man's drunk.——

Gib. In troth am I not.——An gin I had not fond ye, Madam, the Laird knows when I fhou'd; for my Mafter bad me nere gang Heam, without Tydings of yee, Madam.

Vio. Sirrah, get about your Bufinefs, or I'll have your Bones drubb'd.

Gib. Geud Faith, my Mafter has e'en dun that te yer Honds, Madam.

Vio. Who is your Mafter, Friend?

Gib. Mony e'en Spiers the gat, they ken right weel— It is no fo long fen yee parted wi' him, I wifh he ken yee haafe as weel as yee ken him.

Vio. Pugh, the Creature's mad or miftakes me for fome Body elfe; and I fhou'd be as mad as he, to talk to him any longer. [*Exit.*

Enter Liffardo *at the upper end of the Stage.*

Liff. So, fhe's gone Home, I fee. What did that *Scotch* Fellow want with her? I'll try to find it out, perhaps I may difcover fomething that may make my Mafter friends with me again.

Gib. Are ye gaune Madam, a deel fcope in your Company, for I'm as weefe as I was; but I'll bide and fee whafe Houfe it is, gin I can meet wi ony Civil Body to fpier at.——Weel of aw Men in the Warld, I think our *Scots* men the greateft Feuls, to leave their weel favour'd honeft Women at Heam, to rin walloping after a Pack of Gyrcarlings here, that fhame to fhow their Faces, and

peer

peer Men, like me, are forc'd to be their Pimps; a Pimp! Godfwarbit, *Gibby*'s ne'er be a Pimp——And yet in troth it is a Threving Trade; I remember a Countryman aw mi ean, that by ganging a fike like Errants as I am now, come to gat Preferment: My Lad, wot yee wha lives here?   [*Turns and sees* Liffardo.
Liff. Don Pedro de Mendofa.
Gib. An did ye fee a Lady gang in but now?
Liff. Yes I did.
Gib. An dee ken her te?
Liff. It was *Donna Violante* his Daughter; what the Devil makes him fo inquifitive? Here is fomething in it, that's certain. 'Tis a cold Morning, Brother, what think you of a Dram?
Gib. In troth, very weel, Sir.
Liff. You feem an honest Fellow, prithee let's drink to our better Acquaintance.
Gib. Wi aw my Heart, Sir; gang yer gat to the next House, and Ife follow ye.——
Liff. Come along then.   [*Exit.*
Gib. Don Pedro de Mendosa——*Donna Violante* his Daughter; that's as right as my Leg now——Ife need na meer, I'll tak a Drink, an then to my Master.——
Ife bring him News will mak his Heart full Blee;
Gin he rewards it not, Deel pimp for me.   [Exit.

ACT IV.
SCENE, Violante's *Lodgings.*

Enter Ifabella *in a gay Temper, and* Violante *out of Humour.*

Isab. MY Dear, I have been feeking you, this half Hour, to tell you the moft lucky Adventure.
Vio. And you have pitched upon the moft unlucky Hour for it, that you cou'd poffibly have found in the whole four and Twenty.
Isab.

Isab. Hang unlucky Hours, I won't think of them; I hope all my Misfortunes are paſt.
Vio. And mine all to come.
Isab. I have ſeen the Man I like.
Vio. And I have ſeen the Man I cou'd wiſh to hate.
Isab. And you muſt aſſiſt me in diſcovering whether he can like me, or not.
Vio. You have aſſiſted me in ſuch a Diſcovery already, I thank ye.
Isab. What ſay you, my Dear?
Vio. I ſay I am very unlucky at Diſcoveries, *Isabella*; I have too lately made one pernicious to my Eaſe; your Brother is falſe.
Isab. Impoſſible!
Vio. Moſt true.
Isab. Some Villain has traduc'd him to you.
Vio. No, *Isabella*, I love too well to truſt the Eyes of others; I never credit the ill-judging World, or form Suspicions upon vulgar Cenſures; no, I had ocular Proof of his Ingratitude.
Isab. Then I am moſt unhappy: my Brother was the only Pledge of Faith betwixt us; if he has forfeited your Favour, I have no Title to your Friendſhip.
Vio. You wrong my Friendſhip, *Isabella*; your own Merit intitles you to every Thing within my Power.
Isab. Generous Maid——But may I not know what Grounds you have to think my Brother falſe.
Vio. Another time—But tell me, *Isabella*, how can I ſerve you?
Isab. Thus then——The Gentleman that brought me hither, I have ſeen and talk'd with upon the *Terreiro de paſſa* this Morning, and find him a Man of Senſe, Generosity, and good Humour; in ſhort, he is every Thing that I cou'd like for a Huſband, and I have diſpatch'd Mrs. *Flora* to bring him hither; I hope you'll forgive the Liberty I have taken.
Vio. Hither, to what Purpoſe?
Isab. To the great univerſal Purpose, Matrimony.
Vio. Matrimony! Why do you deſign to ask him?
Isab. No, *Violante*, you muſt do that for me.
Vio. I thank you for the Favour you deſign me, but deſire

fire to be excus'd : I manage my own Affairs too ill, to be trufted with those of other People ; befides. if my Father fhou'd find a Stranger here, it might make him hurry me into a *Monaftery* immediately ; I can't for my Life admire your Conduct, to encourage a Person altogether unknown to you.——'Twas very imprudent to meet him this Morning, but much more fo, to fend for him hither, knowing what Inconveniency you have already drawn upon me.

Isab. I am not infenfible how far my Misfortunes have embarraft you ; and, if you please, facrifice my Quiet to your own.

Vio. Unkindly urg'd—Have I not preferr'd your Happinefs to every Thing that's dear to me ?

Isab. I know thou haft——Then do not deny me this laft Requeft, when a few Hours perhaps, may render my Condition, able to clear thy Fame, and bring my Brother to thy Feet for Pardon.

Vio. I wifh you don't repent of this Intrigue. I fuppose he knows you are the fame Woman that he brought in here last Night.

Isab. Not a Syllable of that ; I met him veil'd, and to prevent his knowing the Houfe, I order'd Mrs. *Flora* to bring him by the back Door into the Garden.

Vio. The very Way which *Felix* comes; if they fhould meet, there would be fine Work——Indeed, my Dear, I can't approve of your Defign.

Enter Flora.

Flor. Madam, the Colonel waits your Pleafure.

Vio. How durft you go upon fuch a Meffage, Miftrefs, without acquainting me ?

Isab. 'Tis too late to difpute that now, dear *Violante*, I acknowledge the Rafhnefs of the Action—But confider the Neceffity of my Deliverance.

Vio. That is indeed a weighty Confideration ; well, what am I to do?

Isab. In the next Room I'll give you Inftructions ; in the mean time, Mrs. *Flora*, fhow the Colonel into this.

[*Exit* Flora *one Way, and* Isab. *and* Vio. *another.*

Re-enter Flora *with the* Colonel.

Flo. The Lady will wait on you prefently, Sir. [*Exit.*

Col.

Col. Very well——This is a very fruitful Soil. I have not been here quite four and twenty Hours, and I have three Intrigues upon my Hands already, but I hate the Chafe, without partaking the Game. (*Enter* Violante *veil'd*) Ha, a fine fized Woman—Pray Heaven fhe proves handfome—I am come to obey your Ladyfhip's Commands.

Vio. Are you fure of that, Colonel?

Col. If you be not very unreafonable indeed, Madam; a Man is but a Man.   [*Takes her Hand and kiffes it.*

Vio. Nay, nay, we have no Time for Compliments, Colonel

Col. I underftand you, Madam——*Montre moy votre Chambre.*   [*Takes her in his Arms.*

Vio. Nay, nay, hold Colonel, my Bed-chamber is not to be enter'd without a certain Purchafe.

Col. Purchafe! Humph: This is fome kept Miftrefs, I fuppofe, who induftrioufly lets out her leifure Hours. (*Afide*) Look ye, Madam, you muft confider we Soldiers are not over-ftocked with Money.—But we make ample Satisfaction in Love; we have a World of Courage upon our Hands now, you know:—Then prithee ufe a Confcience, and I'll try if my Pocket can come up to your Price.

[*Puts his Hand into his Pocket.*

Vio. Nay, don't give yourfelf the Trouble of drawing your Purfe, Colonel, my defign is level'd at your Perfon, if that be at your own Difpofal.

Col. Ay, that it is Faith, Madam, and I'll fettle it as firmly upon thee——

Vio. As Law can do it.

Col. Hang Law in Love affairs; thou fhalt have Right and Title to it out of pure Inclination——A matrimonial Hint again! Gad, I fancy the Women have a Project on Foot to tranfplant the Union into *Portugal.*

Vio. Then you have an Averfion to Matrimony, Colonel; did you ever fee a Woman, in all your Travels, that you cou'd like for a Wife?

Col. A very odd Queftion—Do you really expect that I fhou'd fpeak Truth now?

Vio. I do, if you expect to be fo dealt with, Colonel.

Col. Why then——Yes.

Vio. Is fhe in your own Country, or this?

Col.

Col. This is a very pretty kind of a Catechifm; but I don't conceive which Way it turns to Edification : In this Town I believe, Madam.

Vio. Her Name is———

Col. Ay, how is fhe call'd, Madam?

Vio. Nay, I afk you that, Sir.

Col. Oh, oh, why fhe is call'd—Pray, Madam, how is it you fpell your Name?

Vio. Oh, Colonel, I am not the happy Woman, nor do I wifh it.

Col. No, I am forry for that.—What the Devil does fhe mean by all thefe Queftions? [*Afide.*

Vio. Come, Colonel, for once be fincere.——Perhaps you may not repent it.

Col. Faith, Madam, I have an Inclination to Sincerity, but I'm afraid you'll call my Manners in Queftion : This is like to be but a filly Adventure, here's fo much Sincerity required. [*Afide.*

Vio. Not at all : I prefer Truth before Compliment in this Affair.

Col. Why then, to be plain with you, Madam, a Lady laft Night wounded my Heart by a Fall from a Window, whofe Perfon I cou'd be contented to take, as my Father took my Mother, till Death us doth part.——But whom fhe is, or how diftinguifh'd, Whether Maid, Wife, or Widow, I can't inform you ; perhaps you are fhe.

Vio. Not to keep you in Sufpence, I am not fhe, but I can give you an Account of her : That Lady is a Maid of Condition, has ten thoufand Pounds; and if you are a fingle Man, her Perfon and Fortune are at your Service.

Col. I accept the Offer with the higheft Tranfports ; but fay, my charming Angel, art thou not fhe? (*offers to embrace her*) This is a lucky Adventure. [*Afide.*

Vio. Once again, Colonel, I tell you I am not fhe— But at Six this Evening you fhall find her on the *Terreira de paffa*, with a white Handkerchief in her Hand ; get a Prieft ready, and you know the reft.

Col. I fhall infallibly obferve your Directions, Madam.

Enter Flora *haftily, and whifpers* Violante, *who ftarts and feems furprised.*

Vio. Ha, *Felix* croffing the Garden, fay you, what fhall I do now? *Col.*

Col. You feem furpriz'd, Madam.

Vio. Oh, Colonel, my Father is coming hither, and if he finds you here, I am ruin'd !

Col. Od'slife, Madam, thruft me any where ; can't I go out this Way?

Vio. No, no, no, he comes that Way ; how fhall I prevent their Meeting ? Here, here, ftep into my Bedchamber and be ftill, as you value her you love ; don't ftir till you've Notice, as ever you hope to have her in your Arms.

Col. On that Condition I'll not breathe. [*Exit*.

Enter Felix.

Fel. I wonder where my Dog of a Servant is all this while——But fhe is at home I find——How coldly fhe regards me——You look, *Violante,* as if the Sight of me were troublefome.

'Vio. Can I do otherwife, when you have the Affurance to approach me, after what I faw to Day.

Fel. Affurance, rather call it good Nature, after what I heard laft Night ; but fuch regard to Honour have I in my Love to you, I cannot bear to be fufpected, nor fuffer you to entertain falfe Notions of my Truth, without endeavouring to convince you of my Innocence, fo much good Nature have I more than you *Violante.*——Pray give me Leave to afk your Woman one Queftion ; my Man affures me fhe was the Perfon you faw at my Lodgings.

Flo. I confefs it, Madam, and afk your Pardon.

Vio. Impudent Baggage, not to undeceive me fooner ? what Bufinefs cou'd you have there ?

Fel. Liffardo and fhe, it feems, imitate you and I.

Flo. I love to follow the Example of my Betters, Madam.

Fel. I hope I am juftify'd——

Vio. Since we are to part, *Felix*, there needed no Juftification.

Fel. Methinks you talk of parting as a Thing indifferent to you ; can you forget how you have lov'd ?

Vio. I wifh I could forget my own Paffion ; I fhou'd with lefs Concern remember yours——But for Mrs. *Flora*——

Fel. You muft forgive her ;——Muft, did I fay ? I fear I have

The WONDER:

I have no Power to impofe, tho' the Injury was done to me.

Vio. 'Tis harder to pardon an Injury done to what we love than to ourfelves; but at your Requeft, *Felix*, I do forgive her; go watch my Father, *Flora*, left he fhou'd awake and furprize us.

Flo. Yes, Madam. [*Exit* Flora.

Fel. Doft thou then love me, *Violante?*

Vio. What need of Repetition from my Tongue, when every Look confeffes what you afk?

Fel. Oh! let no Man judge of Love but thofe who feel it; what wondrous Magic lies in one kind Look.——One tender Word deftroys a Lover's Rage, and melts his fierceft Paffion into foft Complaint. Oh the Window, *Violante*, would'ft thou but clear that one Sufpicion!

Vio. Prithee, no more of that, my *Felix*, a little Time fhall bring thee perfect Satisfaction.

Fel. Well, *Violante*, on that Condition you think no more of a Monaftery.——I'll wait with Patience for this mighty Secret.

Vio. Ah, *Felix*, Love generally gets the better of Religion in us Women: Refolutions made in Heat of Paffion, ever diffolve upon Reconciliation.

Enter Flora *haftily.*

Flo. Oh, Madam, Madam, Madam! my Lord your Father has been in the Garden, and lock'd the back Door, and comes muttering to himfelf this Way.

Vio. Then we are caught: Now, *Felix*, we are undone.

Fel. Heavens forbid, this is moft unlucky! let me ftep into your Bed-chamber, he won't look under the Bed; there I may conceal myfelf. [*runs to the Door, and pufhes it open a little.*

Vio. My Stars! If he goes in there he'll find the Colonel.——No, no, *Felix*, that's no fafe Place, my Father often goes thither; and fhou'd you cough, or fneeze, we are loft.

Fel. Either my Eyes deceiv'd me, or I faw a Man within; I'll watch him clofe——She fhall deal with the Devil, if fhe conveys him out without my Knowledge. (*Afide*) What fhall I do then?

Vio. Blefs me, how I tremble!

Flo.

Flo. Oh, Invention! Invention!—I have it, Madam; here, here, here, Sir, off with your Sword, and I'll fetch you a Difguife. [*Runs in and fetches out a Riding-Hood.*
Fel. Ay, ay, any thing to avoid *Don Pedro.*
Vio. Oh! Quick, quick, quck, I fhall die with Apprehenfion. [Flora *puts the Riding-Hood on* Felix.
Flo. Befure you don't fpeak a Word!
Fel. Not for the *Indies.*——But I fhall obferve you clofer than yon imagine. [*Afide.*
Pedro (*Within.*) *Violante,* where are you Child? (*Enter* Don Pedro.) Why, how came the Garden Door open? Ha! How now; who have we here?
Vio. Humph, he'll certainly difcove*e* him. [*Afide.*
Flo. 'Tis my Mother, and pleafe you, Sir.
[*She and* Felix *both curtefy.*
Pedro. Your Mother! By St. *Anthony* fhe's a Strapper; why, you are a Dwarf to her.—How many Children have you, good Woman?
Vio. Oh! if he fpeaks we are loft. [*Afide.*
Flo. Oh! Dear *Senior,* fhe can't hear you; fhe has been deaf thefe twenty Years.
Pedro. Alas, poor Woman.——Why you muffle her up as if fhe were blind too.
Fel. Wou'd I were fairly off. [*Afide.*
Pedro. Turn up her Hood.
Vio. Undone for ever.——St. *Anthony* forbid: Oh, Sir, fhe has the dreadfulleft unlucky Eyes.——Pray don't look upon them; I made her keep her Hood fhut on purpofe.——Oh, oh, oh!
Pedro. Eyes! Why what's the Matter with her Eyes?
Flo. My poor Mother, Sir, is much afflicted with the Cholick; and about two Months ago fhe had it grievoufly in her Stomach, and was over-perfuaded to take a Dram of filthy *Englifh Geneva.*——Which immediately flew up into her Head, and caus'd fuch a Defluxion in her Eyes, that fhe cou'd never fince bear the Day-light.
Pedro. Say you fo—Poor Woman!—Well, make her fit down, *Violante,* and give her a Glafs of Wine.
Vio. Let her Daughter give her a Glafs below, Sir; for my part fhe has frighted me fo, I fhan't be myfelf thefe two Hours. I am fure her Eyes are evil Eyes.
Fel. Well hinted.

Pedro Well, well, do fo; evil Eyes, there is no evil Eyes, Child. [*Exit* Felix *and* Flora.

Vio. I am glad he's gone.

Pedro. Haſt thou heard the News, *Violante?*

Vio. What News, Sir?

Pedro. Why, *Vaſquez* tells me, that *Don Lopez*'s Daughter *Iſabella*, is run away from her Father; that Lord has very ill Fortune with his Children.——Well, I'm glad my Daughter has no Inclination to Mankind; that my Houſe is plagu'd with no Suitors. [*Aſide.*

Vio. This is the firſt Word I ever heard of it; I pity her Frailty.———

Pedro. Well faid, *Violante.*——Next week I intend thy Happineſs ſhall begin. [*Enter* Flora.

Vio. I don't intend to ſtay ſo long, I thank you Papa. [*Aſide.*

Pedro. My Lady *Abbeſs* writes Word ſhe longs to ſee thee, and has provided every Thing in order for thy Reception.—Thou wilt lead a happy Life, my Girl.—Fifty Times before that of Matrimony; where an extravagant Coxcomb might make a Beggar of thee, or an ill-natur'd ſurly Dog break thy Heart.

Flo. Break her Heart! She had as good have her Bones broke as to be a Nun; I am ſure I had rather of the two.———You are wondrous kind, Sir; but if I had ſuch a Father, I know what I would do.

Pedro. Why, what wou'd you do Minx, ha?

Flo. I wou'd tell him I had as good Right and Title to the Laws of Nature, and the End of the Creation, as he had.———

Pedro. You wou'd, Miſtreſs'; who the Devil doubts it? A good Aſſurance is a Chamber-maid's Coat of Arms; and lying, and contriving, the Supporters.——Your Inclinations are on the Tip-toe it ſeems—If I were your Father, Houſewife, I'd have a Pennance enjoyn'd you, ſo ſtrict that you ſhould not be able to turn you in your Bed for a Month——You are enough to ſpoil your Lady, Houſewife, if ſhe had not abundance of Devotion.

Vio. Fye, *Flora*; Are not you aſham'd to talk thus to my Father? You faid, Yeſterday, you wou'd be glad to go with me into the Monaſtery.

Pedro. She go with thee! No, no, ſhe's enough to debauch

bauch the whole Convent—— Well, Child, remember what I faid to thee ; next Week——

Vio. Ay, and what am I to do this too.—— (*Afide.*) I am all Obedience, Sir ; I care not how foon I change my Condition.

Flo. But little does he think what Change fhe means.
[*Afide.*

Pedro. Well faid, *Violante*——I am glad to find her fo willing to leave the World, but it is wholly owing to my prudent Management ; did fhe know that fhe might command her Fortune when fhe came at Age, or upon the Day of Marriage, perhaps fhe'd change her Note.——
But I have always told her that her Grandfather left it with this Provifo, That fhe turned Nun ; now a fmall Part of this twenty thoufand Pounds provides for her in the Nunnery, and the reft is my own ; there is nothing to be got in this Life without Policy. (*Afide.*) Well, Child, I am going into the Country for two or three Days, to fettle fome Affairs with thy Uncle.——And then——Come help me on with my Cloak, Child.

Vio. Yes, Sir.   [*Exit* Pedro *and* Violante.
Flo So now for the Colonel.   (*Goes to the Chamber-Door.*) Hift, hift, Colonel.   [*Colonel peeping.*
Col. Is the Coaft clear?
Flo. Yes, if you can climb ; for you muft get over the Wafh-Houfe, and jump from the Garden-Wall into the Street.
Col. Nay, nay, I don't value my Neck if my Incognita anfwers but thy Lady's Promife. [*Exit* Col. *and* Flora.

Re-enter Pedro *and* Violante.

Pedro. Good by, *Violonte*, take care of thyfelf, Child.
Vio. I wifh you a good Journey, Sir.—Now to fet my Prifoner at Liberty.   [*Enter* Felix *behind* Violante.
Fel. I have lain perdue under the Stairs, till I watch'd the old Man out.
Vio. So, Sir, you may appear.   [*Goes to the Door.*
Fel. May he fo, Madam?—I had Caufe for my Sufpicion, I find, treacherous Woman.
Vio. Ha, *Felix* here ! Nay, then, all's difcover'd.
Fel. (Draws.) Villain, whoe'er thou art, come out I charge thee, and take the Reward of thy adulterous Errand.

Vio. What shall I say?——Nothing but the Secret which I have sworn to keep can reconcile this Quarrel.
[*Aside.*
Fel. A Coward! Nay, then I'll fetch you out, think not to hide thyself; no, by St. *Anthony*, an Altar should not protect thee, even there I'd reach thy Heart, tho' all the Saints were arm'd in thy Defence.]*Exit.*
Vio. Defend me Heaven! What shall I do? I must discover *Isabella*, or here will be Murder.——

Enter Flora.

Flo. I have help'd the Colonel off clear, Madam.
Vio. Say'st thou so, my Girl? then I am arm'd.

Re-enter Felix.

Fel. Where has the Devil in Compliance to your Sex convey'd him from my just Resentments?
Vio. Him, who do you mean, my dear inquisitive Spark? Ha, ha, ha. will you never leave these jealous Whims?
Fel. Will you never cease to impose upon me?
Vio. You impose upon yourself, my Dear; do you think I did not see you? Yes, I did, and resolved to put this Trick upon you; I knew you'd take the Hint, and soon relapse into your wonted Error: How easily your Jealousy is fired? I shall have a blessed Life with you.
Fel. Was there nothing in it then, but only to try me?
Vio. Won't you believe your Eyes?
Fel. No, because I find they have deceived me; well, I am convinc'd that Faith is as necessary in Love as in Religion; for the Moment a Man lets a Woman know her Conquest, he resigns his Senses, and sees nothing but what she'd have him.
Vio. And as soon as that Man finds his Love return'd, she becomes as errant a Slave, as if she had already said after the Priest.
Fel. The Priest, *Violante* would dissipate those Fears which cause these Quarrels; when wilt thou make me happy?
Vio. To-morrow, I will tell thee; my Father is gone for two or three Days to my Uncle's, we have Time enough to finish our Affairs——But prithee leave me now, for I expect some Ladies to visit me.
Fel.

Fel. If you command it.—Fly fwift ye Hours, and bring To morrow on.—You defire I wou'd leave you, *Violante.*
Vio. I do at prefent.
Fel. So much you reign the Sovereign of my Soul,
That I obey without the leaft Controul. [Exit.

Enter Ifabella.

Ifab. I am glad my Brother and you are reconcil'd, my Dear, and the Colonel efcap'd without his Knowledge ; I was frighted out of my Wits when I heard him return.—I know not how to exprefs my Thanks, Woman—for what you fuffer'd for my Sake, my grateful Acknowledgments fhall ever wait you ; and to the World proclaim the Faith, Truth, and Honour of a Woman.———
Vio. Prithee don't compliment thy Friend, *Ifabella.*—You heard the Colonel, I fuppofe?
Ifab. Every Syllable, and am pleas'd to find I do not love in vain.
Vio. Thou haft caught his Heart, it feems; and an Hour hence may fecure his Perfon.—Thou haft made hafty Work on't, Girl.
Ifab. From hence I draw my Happinefs, we fhall have no Accounts to make up after Confummation.

She who for Years, protracts her Lover's Pain,
And makes him wifh, and wait, and figh in vain,
To be his Wife, when late fhe gives Confent,
Finds half his Paffion was in Courtfhip fpent;
Whilft they who boldly all Delays remove,
Find every Hour a frefh Supply of Love.

ACT V.
SCENE, Frederick's *Houfe.*

Enter Felix *and* Frederick.

Fel. THIS Hour has been propitious, I am reconcil'd to *Violante,* and you affure me *Antonio* is out of Danger.
Fred. Your Satisfaction is doubly mine.

Enter

Enter Liffardo.

Fel. What Hafte you made, Sirrah, to bring me Word if *Violante* went home?

Liff. I can give you very good Reafons for my Stay, Sir—Yes, Sir, fhe went home.

Fred. O! Your Mafter knows that, for he has been there himfelf, *Liffardo*.

Liff. Sir, may I beg the Favour of your Ear?

Fel. What have you to fay? [*Whifpers, and* Felix *feems uneafy*.

Fred. Ha, *Felix* changes Colour at *Liffardo's* News. What can it be?

Fel. A *Scots* Footman, that belongs to Colonel *Britton*, an Acquaintance of *Frederick's*, fay you? the Devil! If fhe be falfe, by Heaven I'll trace her. Prithee, *Frederick*, do you know one Colonel *Britton*, a *Scotsman*?

Fred. Yes, why do you afk me?

Fel. Nay, no great Matter; but my Man tells me that he has had fome little Difference with a Servant of his, that's all.

Fred. He is a good harmlefs innocent Fellow, I am forry for it; the Colonel lodges in my House, I knew him formerly in *England*, and met him here by Accident laft Night, and gave him an Invitation home; he is a Gentlemen of a good Eftate, befides his Commiffion; of excellent Principles, and ftrict Honour, I affure you.

Fel. Is he a Man of Intrigue?

Fred. Like other Men, I fuppofe, here he comes —— [*Enter* Colonel.

Colonel, I began to think I had loft you.

Col.—And not without fome Reafons, if you knew all.

Fel. There's no Danger of a fine Gentleman's being loft in this Town, Sir.

Col. That Compliment don't belong to me, Sir. But I affure you I have been very near being run away with.

Fred. Who attempted it?

Col. Faith, I know her not—Only that fhe is a charming Woman, I mean as much as I faw of her.

Fel. My Heart fwells with Apprehension.—Some accidental Rencounter.

Fred. A Tavern, I fuppofe, adjufted the Matter.—

Col. A Tavern! No, no, Sir, fhe is above that Rank,

I af-

I affure you; this Nymph fleeps in a Velvet Bed, and Lodgings every Way agreeable.

Fel. Ha, a Velvet Bed!—I thought you faid but now, Sir, you knew her not.

Col. No more I don't, Sir.

Fel. How came you then fo well acquainted with her Bed?

Fred. Ay, ay, come, come, unfold.

Col. Why then you muft know, Gentlemen, that I was convey'd to her Lodgings, by one of Cupid's Emiffaries, call'd a Chambermaid, in a Chair, thro' fifty blind Alleys, who, by the help of a Key, let me into a Garden.

Fel. S'Death, a Garden, this muft be *Violante's* Garden. [*Afide.*

Col. From thence conducted me into a fpacious Room, then dropt me a Courtesy, told me her Lady would wait on me prefently; fo, without unvailing, modeftly withdrew.

Fel. Damn her Modefty; this was *Flora*. [*Afide.*

Fred. Well, how then Colonel?

Col. Then Sir, immediately from another Door iffued forth a Lady, arm'd at both Eyes; from whence fuch Showers of Darts fell round me, that had I not been cover'd with the Shield of another Beauty, I had infallibly fall'n a Martyr to her Charms; for you muft know I juft faw her Eyes: Eyes, did I say? No, no, hold, I faw but one Eye, tho' I fuppofe it had a Fellow, equally as killing.

Fel. But how came you to fee her Bed, Sir? S'Death, this Expectation gives a thoufand Racks. [*Afide.*

Col. Why, upon her Maid's giving Notice her Father was coming, fhe thrust me into the Bed-Chamber.

Fel. Upon her Father's coming?

Col. Ay, fo fhe faid; but putting my Ear to the Key-hole of the Door, I found it was another Lover.

Fel. Confound the jilt! 'Twas fhe without Difpute. [*Aside.*

Fred. Ah poor Colonel, ha, ha, ha.

Col. I difcover'd they had had a Quarrel, but whether they were reconcil'd or not, I can't tell, for the fecond Alarm brought the Father in good earneft, and had like to have made the Gentleman and I acquainted, but ſhe found ſome other Stratagem to convey him out.

Fel. Contagion ſeize her, and make her Body ugly as her Soul. There's nothing left to doubt of now,—'Tis plain 'twas ſhe——Sure he knows me, and takes this Method to inſult me ; S'Death, I cannot bear it.   [*Aſide.*

Fred. So, when ſhe had diſpatched her old Lover, ſhe paid you a Viſit in her Bed-Chamber, ha, Colonel?

Col. No, Pox take the impertinent Puppy, he ſpoil'd my Diverſion, I ſaw her no more.

Fel. Vory fine ; give me Patience, Heaven, or I ſhall burſt with Rage.   [*Aſide.*

Fred. That was hard.

Col. Nay, what was worſe, the Nymph that introduced me convey'd me out again over the Top of a high Wall, where I ran the Danger of having my Neck broke, for the Father, it ſeems, had lock'd the Door by which I enter'd.

Fel. That Way I miſs'd him :——Damn her Invention. (*Aſide*). Pray Colonel, was this the ſame Lady you met upon the *Terriero de paſſa* this Morning?

Col. Faith I can't tell, Sir, I had a Deſign to know who that Lady was, but my Dog of a Footman, whom I had order'd to watch her home, fell faſt aſleep—I gave him a good beating for his Neglect, and I have never ſeen the Raſcal ſince.

Fred. Here he comes.

Enter Gibby.

Col. Where have you been, Sirrah?

Gib. Troth Iſe been ſeeking yee an like yer Honour theſe twa Hoors an meer, I bring yee glad Teedings, Sir.

Col. What have you found the Lady?

Gib. Geud Faite ha I, Sir—an ſhee's called *Donna Violante,* and her Parent *Don Pedro de Mendoſa,* an gin yee wull gang wa mi, an't like ye'r Honour, Iſe mak you ken the Huſe right weel.

Fel. O Torture ! Torture !   [*Aſide.*

Col. Ha ! *Violante* ! That's the Lady's Name of the Houſe where my Incognita is, ſure it could not be her, at leaſt it was not the ſame Houſe I'm confident.   [*Aſide.*
Fred.

Fred. Violante ! 'Tis falſe, I wou'd not have you credit him, Colonel.

Gib. The Deel burſt my Blader, Sir, gin I lee.

Fel. Sirrah, I ſay you do lye, and I'll make you eat it, you Dog. (*kicks him*) And if your Maſter will juſtify you.——

Col. Not I, faith Sir,—I anſwer for no body's Lyes but my own, if you please, kick him again.

Gib. But gin he dus, Ife ne take it, Sir, gin he was a thousand *Spaniards*. [*walks about in a Paſſion.*

Col. I ow'd you a beating, Sirrah, and I'm oblig'd to this Gentleman for taking the Trouble off my Hands; therefore say no more, d'ye hear, Sir ? [*Aſide to* Gibby.

Gib. Troth de I Sir, and feel tee.

Fred. This muſt be a Mistake, Colonel, for I know *Violante* perfectly well, and I'm certain ſhe would not meet you upon the *Terriero de paſſa.*

Col. Don't be too positive, *Federiek*, now I have ſome Reaſons to believe it was that very Lady.

Fel. You'd very much oblige me, Sir, if you'd let me know theſe Reasons.

Col. Sir.

Fel. Sir, I ſay I have a Right to enquire into those Reaſons yon ſpeak off.

Col. Ha, ha, really Sir I cannot conceive how you, or any Man can have a Right to enquire into my Thoughts.

Fel. Sir, I have a Right to every Thing that relates to *Violante*—And he that traduces her Fame, and refuſes to give his Reaſons for't, is a Villain. [*Draws.*

Col. What the Devil have I been doing ; now Bliſters on my Tongue, by Dozens. [*Aſide.*

Fred. Prithee *Felix* don't quarrel, till you know for what ; this is all a Miſtake I'm positive.

Col. Look ye, Sir, that I dare draw my Sword I think will admit of no Dispute—But tho' fighting's my Trade, I'm not in Love with it, and think it more honourable to decline this Buſineſs, than pursue it. This may be a Miſtake ; however, I'll give you my Honour never to have any Affair directly or indirectly with *Violante*, provided ſhe is your *Violante* ; but if there ſhou'd happen to be another of her Name, I hope you wou'd not engroſs all the *Violantes* in the Kingdom.

Fel.

Fel. Your Vanity has given me fufficient Reasons to believe I'm not miftaken ; I'm not to be impos'd upon, Sir.

Col. Nor I bully'd, Sir.

Fel. Bully'd ! S'Death, fuch another Word, and I'll nail thee to the Wall.

Col. Are you sure of that, *Spaniard.* [*Draws.*

Gib. (*Draws*] Say ne meer Mon, aw my Sol here's Twa to Twa, donna fear Sir, *Gibby* ftonds by ye for the Honor a *Scotland.* [*Vapours about.*

Fred. By St. *Anthony* you fhan't fight (*interposes*) on bare Suspicion, be certain of the Injury, and then.——

Fel. That I will this Moment, and then, Sir—I hope you are to be found.——

Col. Whenever you pleafe, Sir. [*Exit* Felix.

Gib. S'Bleed, Sir, there neer was *Scotsman* yet that fham'd to fhew his Face. [*ftrutting about.*

Fred. So, Quarrels fpring up like Mufhrooms, in a Minute : *Violante*, and he, was but juft reconcil'd, and you have furnifh'd him with frefh Matter for falling out again, and I am certain, Colonel, *Gibby* is in the Wrong.

Gib. Gin I be Sir, the Mon that tald me leed, and gin he dud, the Deel be my Landlard, Hell my Winter Quarters, and a Rope my Winding Sheet, Gin I dee no lik him as lang as I can hold a Stick in my Hond, now see yee.

Col. I am forry for what I have faid, for the Lady's Sake, but who could divine, that fhe was his Miftress ; prithee who is this warm Spark ?

Fred. He is the Son of one of our Grandees, nam'd *Don Lopez de Pementell*, a very honeft Gentleman, but fomething paffionate in what relates to his Love—He is an only Son, which perhaps may be one Reason for indulging his Paffion.

Col. When Parents have but one Child, they either make a Madman, or a Fool of him.

Fred. He is not the only Child, he has a Sifter ; but I think, thro' the Severity of his Father, who would have married her againft her Inclination, fhe has made her Efcape, and notwithstanding he has offer'd five hundred Pounds, he can get no Tydings of her.

Col. Ha ! How long has fhe been miffing ?

Fred.

Fred. Nay, but since last Night, it seems.
Col. Last Night! The very Time! How went she?
Fred. No body can tell, they conjecture thro' the Window.
Col. I'm transported! This must be the Lady I caught; what sort of a Woman is she?
Fred. Middle siz'd, a lovely brown, a fine, pouting Lip, Eyes that roul and languish, and seem to speak the exquisite Pleasure that her Arms could give!
Col. Oh! I'm fir'd with his Description—'Tis the very she—What's her Name?
Fred. Isabella—You are transported, Colonel.
Col. I have a natural Tendency in me to the Flesh, thou know'st, and who can hear of Charms so exquisite, and yet remain unmov'd? Oh, how I long for the appointed Hour! I'll to the *Terriero de passa*, and wait my Happiness; if she fails to meet me, I'll once more attempt to find her at *Violante's* in spite of her Brother*'s* Jealousy. (*Aside*) Dear *Frederick*, I beg your Pardon, but I had forgot, I was to meet a Gentleman upon Business at Five, I'll endeavour to dispatch him, and wait on you again as soon as possible.——
Fred. Your humble Servant, Colonel. [*Exit.*
Col. Gibby, I have no Business with you at present
[*Exit Colonel.*
Gib. That's weel—naw will I gang and seek this Loon, and gar him gang with me to *Don Pedro's* Huse——Gin he'll no gang of himsel, Ise gar him gang by the Lug, Sir; Godswarbit *Gibby* hates a Lear. [*Exit.*

Scene changes to Violante*'s* Lodgings.

Enser Violante *and* Isabella.

Isab. The Hour draws on, *Violante*, and now my Heart begins to fail me, but I resolve to venture for all that.
Vio. What does your Courage sink, *Isabella*.
Isab. Only the Force of Resolution a little retreated, but I'll rally it again for all that.

Enter Flora.

Flo. Don Felix is coming up, Madam.
Isab. My Brother! Which Way shall I get out—Dispatch

patch him as foon as you can, dear *Violante*. [*Exit
into the Closet.*
Vio. I will. (*Enter* Felix *in a surly Pofture.*) *Felix,*
what brings you back fo foon, did not I fay toemorrow?
Fel. My Paffion choaks me, I cannot fpeak, oh, I fhall
burft! (*Afide.*)   [*Throws himfelf into a Chair.*
Vio. Blefs me! are you uot weil, my *Felix*?
Fel. Yes,—No,—I don't know what I am.
Vio. Hey Day! What's the Matter now? Another jealous Whim!
Fel. With what an Air fhe carries it.——I fweat at her
Impudence.   [*Afide.*
Vio. If I were in your Place, *Felix*, I'd chufe to flay
at home, when thefe Fits of Spleen were upon me, and
not trouble fuch Perfons as are not oblig'd to bear with
them.   [*Here he affects to be carelefs of her.*
Fel. I am very fenfible, Madam, of what you mean:
I difturb you no doubt, but were I in a better Humour, I
fhou'd not incommode you lefs. I am but too well convinc'd, that you could eafily difpense with my Vifit.
Vio. When you behave yourfelf as you ought to do, no
Company fo welcome—But when vou referve me for your
ill Nature, I wave your Merit, and confider what's due
to myfelf—And I muft be fo free to tell you, *Felix,* that
thefe Humours of yours will abate, if not abfolutely deftroy, the very Principles of Love.
Fel. (*Rifing*) And I muft be so free to tell you, Madam,
that fince you have made fuch ill Returns to the Refpect
that I have paid you, all you do fhall be indifferent to me
for the Future, and you fhall find me abandon your Empire with fo little Difficulty, that I'll convince the World
your Chains are not fo hard to break as your Vanity would
tempt you to believe——I cannot brook the Provocation
you give.
Vio. This is nòt to be born—Infolent! You abandon!
You! Whom I have fo often forbad ever to fee me more!
Have you net fall'n at my Feet? Implor'd my Favour
and Forgivenefs—Did you not trembling wait, and wifh,
and figh, and fwear yourfelf into my Heart? Ingrateful
Man! If my Chains are fo eafily broke as you pretend,
then you are the filliest Coxcomb living, you did not
break 'em leng ago; and I muft think him capable of
brooking

brooking any thing on whom such Usage could make no Impression.

Isab. (*Peeping.*) A Duce take your Quarrels, she'll never think on me.

Fel. I always believed, Madam, my Weakness was the greatest Addition to your Power, you would be le(s imperious, had my Inclination been less forward to oblige you—You have indeed forbad me your Sight, but your Vanity even then assured you I would return, and I was Fool enough to feed your Pride.——Your Eyes, with all their boasted Charms, have acquired the greatest Glory in conquering me.——And the brightest Passage of your Life is, wounding this Heart with such Arms as pierce but few Persons of my Rank. [*Walks about in a great Pet.*

Vio. Matchless Arrogance! True Sir, I should have kept Measures better with you, if the Conquest had been worth preserving, but we easily hazard what gives us no Pain to lose——As for my Eyes, you are mistaken if you think they have vanquished none but you; there are Men above your boasted Rank who have confess'd their Power, when their Misfortune in pleasing you made them obtain such a disgraceful Victory.

Fel. Yes, Madam, I am no Stranger to your Victories.

Vio. And what you call the brightest Passage of my Life, is not the least glorious Part of yours.

Fel. Ha, ha, do'nt put yourself into a Passion, Madam, for I assure you, after this Day, I shall give you no Trouble—You may meet your Sparks on the *Terriero de Passa* at Four in the Morning, without the least Regard of mine——For when I quit your Chamber, the World shan't bring me back.

Vio. I am so well pleas'd with your Resolution, I don't care how soon you take your Leave.—But what you mean by the *Terriero de Passa* at Four in the Morning, I can't guess.

Fel. No, no, no, not you——You was not upon the *Terriero de Passa* at Four this Morning.

Vio. No, I was not; but if I ;was, I hope I may walk where I please, and at what Hour I please, without asking you Leave.

Fel. Oh, doubtless, Madam! And you might meet Colonel *Brittou* there, and afterwards send your Emissary to
fetch

fetch him to your Houfe———And upon your Father's coming in, thruft him into your Bed-Chamber — without afking my Leave. 'Tis no Bufinefs of mine if you are expofed among all the Footmen in Town—Nay, if they Ballad you, and cry you about at a Halfpenny a-piece——— They may, without my Leave.

Vio. Audacious ! Don't provoke me—don't ; my Reputation is not to be fported with (*Going up to him*) at this Rate———No. Sir, it is not. (*burfts into Tears*) Inhuman *Felix!* Oh, *Ifabella*, what a Train of Ills haft thou brought on me? [*Afide.*

Fel. Ha ! I cannot bear to fee her weep—A Woman's Tears are far more fatal than our Swords. (*Afide.*) Oh, *Violante*—S'Death ! what a Dog am I ? Now have I no Power to ftir ;—Doft not thou know fuch a Person as Colonel *Britton ?* Prithee telt me, didft not thou meet him at Four this Morning upon the *Terriero de Paſſa ?*

Vio. Were it not to clear my Fame, I would not anfwer thee, thou black Ingrate !—But I cannot bear to be reproach'd with what I even blufh to think of, much lefs to act ; by Heaven, I have not feen the *Terriero de Paſſa* this Day.

Fel. Did not a *Scots* Footman attack you in the Street neither, *Violante ?*

Vio. Yes, but he miftook me for another, or he was drunk, I know not which.

Fel. And do not you know this *Scots* Colonel ?

Vio. Pray afk me no more Queftions, this Night fhall clear my Reputation, and leave you without Excufe for your bafe Sufpicions ; more than this I fhall not fatisfy you, therefore pray leave me.

Fel. Didft thou ever love me, *Violante ?*

Vio. I'll anfwer nothing.—You was in Hafte to be gone juft now, I fhould be very well pleas'd to be alone, Sir.

[*She fits down, and turns afide.*

Fel. I fhall nct long interrupt your Contemplation. — Stubborn to the laft. [*Afide.*

Vio. Did ever Woman involve herfelf as I have done ?

Fel. Now would I give one of my Eyes to be Friends wit her ; for fomething whifpers to my Soul fhe is not guilty.—(*He paufes, then pulls a Chair, and fits by her at a little Diftance, looking at her fome time without fpeaking—*

Then

A Woman keeps a Secret. 65

Then draws a little nearer to her.) Give me your Hand at Parting, however *Violante*, won't you, (*Here he lays his open upon her Knee several times.*) won't you—won't you—won't you!

Vio. (*Half regarding him*) Won't I do what?

Fel. You know what I would have, *Violante*. Oh, my Heart!

Vio. (*Smiling.*) I thought my Chains were eafily broke. (*Lays her Hand into his.*)

Fel. (*Draws his Chair clofe to her, and kiffes her Hand in a Rapture.*) Too well thou knoweft thy Strength.—Oh my charming Angel, my Heart is all thy own. Forgive my hafty Paffion ; 'tis the Tranfport of a Love fincere!

Don Pedro *within.*

Pedro. Bid *Sancho* get a new Wheel to my Chariot prefently.

Vio. Blefs me ! My Father return'd ! What fhall we do now, *Felix?* We are ruin'd, paft Redemption.

Fel. No, no, no, my Love ; I can leap from thy Clofet Window. [*Runs to the Door where* Ifabella *is, who claps too the Door, and bolts it within fide.*

Ifab. (*Peeping.*) Say you fo : But I fhall prevent you.

Fel. Confufion ! Some Body bolts the Door withinfide ; I'll fee who you have conceal'd here, if I die for't : Oh *Violante!* haft thou again facrific'd me to my Rival? [*Draws.*

Vio. By Heaven thou haft no Rival in my Heart, let that fuffice——Nay, fure you will not let my Father find you here——Diftraction !

Fel. Indeed but I fhall—except you command this Door to be open'd, and that Way conceal me from his Sight.

[*He ftruggles with her to come to the Door.*

Vio. Here me, *Felix*—Though I were fure the refufing what you afk would feparate us for ever, by all that's powerful you fhall not enter here. Either you do love me, or you do not ; convince me by your Obedience.

Fel. That's not the Matter in debate—I will know who is in this Clofet, let the Confequence be what it will. Nay, nay, nay, you ftrive in vain ; I will go in.

Vio. You fhall not go in——

Enter

Enter Don Pedro.

Ped. Hey day! What's here to do? I will go in, and you fhan't go in—and, I will go in—Why, who are you, Sir?

Fel. 'Sdeath! What fhall I fay now!

Ped. Don. Felix, pray, what's your Bufinefs in my Houfe? Ha, Sir?

Vio. Oh Sir, what Miracle return'd you home fo foon? Some Angel 'twas that brought my Father back to fuccour the diftrefs'd——This Ruffian he, I cannot call him Gentleman——has committed fuch an uncommon Rudenefs, as the moft profligate Wretch would be afham'd to own——

Fel. Ha, what the Devil does fhe mean! [*Afide.*

Vio. As I was at my Devotion in my Clofet, I heard a loud knocking at our Door, mix'd with a Woman's Voice, which feem'd to imply fhe was in Danger.——

Fel. I am confounded! [*Afide.*

Vio. I flew to the Door with utmoft Speed, where a Lady vail'd rufh'd in upon me; who, falling on her Knees, begged my Protection, from a Gentleman, who, fhe faid, purfued her: I took Compaffion on her Tears, and locked her into his Clofet; but in the Surprize having left open the Door, this very Perfon whom you fee, with his Sword drawn, ran in, protefting, if I refus'd to give her up to his Revenge, he'd force the Door.

Fel. What in the Name of Goodnefs does fhe mean to do! Hang me! [*Afide.*

Vio. I ftrove with him till I was out of Breath, and had you not come as you did, he muft have enter'd—But he's in Drink, I fuppofe, or he could not have been guilty of fuch an Indecorum. [*Leering at* Felix.

Ped. I'm amazed!

Fel. The Devil never fail'd a Woman at a Pinch: What a Tale has fhe form'd in a minute——In Drink, quotha; a good hint: I'll lay hold on't to bring myfelf off. [*Afide.*

Ped. Fie *Don Felix*! No fooner rid of one Broil, but you are commencing another.—To affault a Lady with a naked Sword, derogates much from the Character of a Gentleman, I affure you.

Fel. (*Counterfeits Drunkenefs*) Who, I affault a Lady, ——upon

—upon Honour the Lady affaulted me, Sir; and would have fciz'd this Body Politick upon the King's Highway —— let her come out, and deny it if fhe can—pray, Sir, command the Door to be open'd, and let her prove me a Lyar if fhe knows how——I have been drinking right *French* Claret, Sir, but I love my own Country for all that.

Ped. Ay, ay, who doubts it, Sir?——Open the Door, *Violante*, and let the Lady come out. — Come, I warrant thee, he fhan't hurt her.

Fel. Ay, now which Way will fhe come off?

Vio. (*Unlocks the Door*) Come forth, Madam, none fhall dare to touch your Veil—I'll convey you out with Safety, or lofe my Life—I hope fhe underftands me   [*Afide.*

Enter Ifabella *veil'd, and croffes the Stage.*

Ifab. Excellent Girl!   [*Exit.*
Fel. The Devil! A Woman! I'll fee if fhe be really fo.
    [*Offers to follow her.*
Ped. (*Draws*) Not a Step, Sir, till the Lady be paft your Recovery—I never fuffer the Laws of Hofpitality to be violated in my Houfe, Sir.——I'll keep *Don Felix* here till you fee her fafe out, *Violante.*

Vol. Get clear of my Father, and follow me to the *Terriero de paffa*, where all Miftakes fhall be rectified. (*Afide to* Felix.)   [*Exit* Violante.

Ped. Come, Sir, you and I will take a Pipe and a Bottle together.

Fel. Damn your Pipe, Sir, I won't fmoke——I hate Tobacco——Nor I, I, I, I won't drink, Sir—No, nor I won't ftay, neither, and how will you help yourfelf?

Ped. As to fmoking, or drinking, you have your Liberty, but you fhall ftay, Sir.   [*Gets between him and the Door*, Felix *ftrikes up his Heels and Exit.*

Fel. Shall I fo, Sir——But I tell you, old Gentleman, I am in hafte to be married——And fo God be with you.

Ped. Go to the Devil—In hafte to get married, quotha, thou art in a fine Condition to get married, truly!

Enter a Servant.

Ser. Here's *Don Lopez de Pementel* to wait on you Senior.

Ped.

Ped. What the Devil does he want? Bring him up, he's in purfuit of his Son, I fuppofe.

Enter Don Lopez.

Lop. I am glad to find you at Home, *Don Pedro*, I was told you was feen upon the Road to —— this Afternoon.

Ped. That might be, my Lord; but I had the Misfortune to break the Wheel of my Chariot, which oblig'd me to return—What is your Pleafure with me, my Lord?

Lop. I am inform'd that my Daughter is in your Houfe, *Don Pedro.*

Ped. That's more than I know, my Lord; but here was your Son juft now as drunk as an Emperor.

Lop. My Son drunk! I never saw him drunk in my Life; where is he, pray, Sir?

Ped. Gone to be married.

Lop. Married! To whom? I don't know that he courted any Body.

Ped. Nay, I know nothing of that——Within there! (*Enter Servant.*) bid my Daughter come hither, fhe'll tell you another Story, my Lord.

Ser. She's gone out in a Chair, Sir.

Ped. Out in a Chair! What do you mean, Sir?

Ser. As I fay, Sir; and *Donna Ifabella* went in another juft before her.

Ser. And *Don Felix* follow'd in another; I overheard them all bid the Chairs go to *Terriero de paſſa.*

Ped. Ha! What Bufinefs has my Daughter there? I am confounded, and know not what to think.——Within there. [*Exit.*

Lop. My Heart mifgives me plaguily —— Call me an *Alguazil*, I'll purfue them ftrait.

SCENE *changes to the Street before* Don Pedro's *Houfe.*

Enter Liffardo.

Liſſ. I wifh I cou'd fee *Flora*——Methinks I have an hankering Kindnefs after the Slut—We muft be reconcil'd.

Enter Gibby.

Gibb. Aw my Sol, Sir, but Ife blithe to find yee here now. *Liſſ.*

Liff. Ha! Brother! Give me thy Hand, Boy.

Gib. Not fe faft, fe ye me—Brether me ne Brethers, I fcorn a Lyar as muckle as a Theife, fe ye now, and yee muft gang intul this Houfe with me, and juftifie to *Donna Violante's* Face, that fhe was the Lady that gang'd in here this Morn, fe yee me, or the Deel ha my Sol, Sir, but ye and I fhall be twa Folks.

Liff. Juftify it to *Donna Violante's* Face, quotha, for what? Sure you don't know what you fay.

Gib. Troth de I, Sir, as weel as ye dee; therefore come along, and mak no meer Words about it.

[*Knocks haftily at the Door.*

Liff. Why, what the Devil do you mean? Don't you confider you are in *Portugal?* Is the Fellow mad?

Gib. Fallow! Ife none of your Fallow, Sir, and gin this Place were Hell, id gar ye dee me Juftice, (*Liff. going*) nay, the Deel a Feet ye gang. [*Lays hold of him, and knocks again.*

Enter Don Pedro.

Ped. How now! what makes you knock fo loud?

Gib. Gin this be *Don Pedro's* Houfe, Sir, I wou'd fpeak with *Donna Violante*, his Daughter.

Liff. Ha! *Don Pedro* himfelf! I wifh I were fairly off.
[*Afide.*

Ped. Ha! what is it you want with my Daughter, pray?

Gib. An fhe be your Doughter, and lik yer Honour, command her to come out, and anfwer for herfelf now, and either juftify or difprove what this Child told me this Morn.

Liff. So, here will be a fine Piece of Work. [*Afide.*

Ped. Why, what did he tell you ha?

Gib. Be me Sol, Sir, Ife tell you aw the Truth; my Mafter got a pratty Lady upon the how de yec call't— *Paffa* here at Five this Morn, and he gar me watch her heam—And in Troth I lodg'd her here, and meeting this ill-favoured Theife, fe ye me, I fpierd wha fhe was—And he told me her Name was *Donna Violante, Don Pedro de Mendofa's* Daughter.

Ped. Ha! My Daughter with a Man abroad at Five in the Morning: Death, Hell, and Furies; by St. *Anthony* I'm undone. [*Stamps.*

Gib.

Gib. Wunds, Sir, ye put yer Saint intul bony Company.

Ped. Who is your Mafter, you Dog you? Adfheart, I fhall be trick'd of my Daughter, and my Money too, that's worft of all.

Gib. Ye Dog you! 'Sblead, Sir don't call Names—I won't tell you wa my Mafter is, fe ye me now.

Ped. And who are you, Rafcal, that knows my Daughter fo well? Ha! [*Holds up his Cane.*

Liff. What fhall I fay to make him give this *Scots* Dog a good beating? (*Afide.*) I know your Daughter, *Senior*. Not I, I never faw your Daughter in all my Life.

Gib. (*Knocks him down with his Fift.*) Deel ha my Sol, Sar, gin ye get no your Carich for that Lye now.

Pedro. What hoa! Where are all my Servants? (*Enter Servants on one Side*, Colonel, Felix, Ifabella, *and* Violante *on the other Side.*) Raife the Houfe in purfuit of my Daughter.

Serv. Here fhe comes, *Senior*.

Col. Hey Day! What is here to do?

Gib. This is the Loon lik Tik, and lik yer Honor, that fent me Heam with a Lye this Morn.

Col. Come, 'tis all well, *Gibby*, let him rife.

Pedro. I am Thunder ftruck——and have not Power to fpeak one Word.

Fel. This is a day of Jubilee, *Liffardo*; no quarrelling with him this Day.

Liff. A Pox take his Fifts.——Egad, thefe *Britons* are but a Word and a Blow.

Enter Don Lopez.

Lop. So, have I found you, Daughter; then you have not hang'd yourfelf yet, I fee.

Col. But fhe is married, my Lord.

Lop. Married! Zounds, to whom?

Col. Even to your humble Servant, my Lord. If you pleafe to give us your Bleffing [*Kneels.*

Lop. Why, hark ye, Miftrefs, are you really married?

Ifab. Really fo, my Lord.

Lop. And who are you, Sir?

Col. An honeft *North Briton* by Birth, and a Colonel by Commiffion, my Lord.

Lop.

Lop. A Heretick ! The Devil [*Holds up his Hands.*
Pedro. She has plaid you a flippery Trick indeed, my Lord—Well, my Girl, thou haft been to fee thy Friend married.—Next Week thou fhalt have a better Hufband, my Dear. (*To* Violante.)
Fel. Next Week is a little too foon, Sir, I hope to live longer than that.
Pedro. What do you mean, Sir ? You have not made a Rib of my Daughter too, have you ?
Vio. Indeed but he has, Sir ; I know not how, but he took me in an unguarded Minute,——when my Thoughts were not over ftrong for a *Nunnery*, Father.
Lop. Your Daughter has play'd you a flippery Trick too, *Senior*.
Pedro. But your Son fhall be never the better for't, my Lord ; her twenty Thoufand Pounds was left on certain Conditions, and I'll not part with a Shilling.
Lop. But we have a certain Thing call'd Law, fhall make you do Juftice, Sir.
Pedro. Well, we'll try that,——my Lord, much good may it do you with your Daughter-in Law. [*Exit.*
Lop. I wifh you much Joy of your Rib. [*Exit.*

Enter Frederick.

Fel. Frederick, welcome !—I fent for thee to be Witnefs of my good Fortune, and make one in a Country Dance.
Fred. Your Meffenger has told me all, and I fincerely fhare in all your Happinefs.
Col. To the Right about, *Frederick*, wifh thy Friend Joy.
Fred. I do with all my Soul ;——and, Madam, I congratulate your Deliverance.—Your Sufpicions are clear'd now, I hope, *Felix.*
Fel. They are, and I heartily afk the Colonel Pardon, and wifh him happy with my Sifter ; for Love has taught me to know, that every Man's Happinefs confifts in chufing for himfelf.
Liff. After that Rule I fix here. [*To* Flora.
Flo. That's your Miftake ; I prefer my Lady's Service, and turn you over to her that pleaded Right and Title to you to Day.

Liff.

Liff. Chufe, proud Fool ; I fhan't afk you twice.

Gib. What fay you now, Lafs ; will ye ge yer Maidenhead to poor *Gibby.*——What fay you, will ye dance the Reel of Bogye with me ?

Inis. That I may not leave my Lady,—I take you at your Word,—and tho' our Wooing has been fhort, I'll by her Example love you dearly. [*Mufic plays.*

Fel. Hark ! I hear the Mufick ; fomebody has done us the Favour to fend them ; call them in.

A Country Dance.

Gib. Waunds, this is bonny Mufick.—How caw ye that Thing that ye pinch by the Craig, and tickle the Weam, ont make it cry *Grum, Grum.*

Fred. Oh ! that's a Guittar, *Gibby.*

Fel. Now, my *Violante,* I shall proclaim thy Vertues to the World.

No more let us thy Sex's Conduct blame,
Since thou'rt a Proof to their eternal Fame,
That Man *has no Advantage but the Name.*

EPILOGUE.

Spoken by Mifs *SANTLOW*.

Written by MR. PHILIPS.

*Cuſtom with all our Modern Laws combin'd,
Has given ſuch Power deſpotic to Mankind,
That We have only ſo much Vertue now,
As they are pleas'd in favour to allow.
Thus like Mechanic Work we're us'd with Scorn,
And wound up only, for a preſent Turn ;
Some are for having our whole Sex enſlav'd,
Affirming* we've no Souls,* *and* can't be ſav'd ;
*But were the Women all of my Opinion,
We'd ſoon ſhake off this falſe uſurp'd Dominion ;
We'd make the Tyrants own, that we cou'd prove,
As fit for other Buſineſs as for Love.
Lord! What Prerogative might we obtain,
Could we from Yielding, a few Months refrain!
How fondly wou'd our dang'ling Lovers doat!
What Homage wou'd be paid to Petticoat!
'Twou'd be a Jeſt to ſee the Change of Fate,
How we might all of Politicks debate ;
Promiſe and Swear, what we ne'er meant to do,
And what's ſtill harder,* Keep our Secrets too.
Ay Marry! Keep a Secret, *ſays a Beau,
And ſneers at ſome ill-natur'd Wit below ;
But faith, if we ſhou'd tell but half we know,*

---

* Alluding to an ironical Pamphlet tending to prove that *Women* had *no Souls.*

EPILOGUE.

There's many a spruce young Fellow in this Place,
Would never more presume to show his Face;
Women *are not so weak, whate'er* Men *prate;*
How many tip top Beaus have had the Fate,
T'enjoy from Mamma's Secrets *their Estate.*
Who, if her early Folly had made known,
Had rid behind the Coach, that's now their own.
But here, the wond'rous Secret *you discover;*
A Lady *ventures for a* Friend,——*a* Lover.
Prodigious. For my Part I frankly own,
I'ad spoiled the Wonder, *and the* Woman *shown.*

The MAN's bewitch'd;

OR,

The Devil to do about Her.

A

COMEDY.

As it is ACTED at the

NEW-THEATRE in the HAY-MARKET,

By Her MAJESTY's Servants.

THE
PREFACE.

I *Shou'd not have troubled my courteous Reader with a Preface, had I not lain under the Necessity of clearing myself of what some People have been pleased to charge me with*, viz. *of being the Author of a Paper call'd*, The Female Tatler, *consequently of a Paragraph in that of the* 14th *Instant, relating to this Comedy ; tho' I think no reasonable Person will believe I could be guilty of so much Folly. Tho' Vanity is said to be the darling Vice of Womankind; yet nothing but an Idiot would express themselves so openly ; and I hope the World won't think me guilty of printing, what I must blush to read, nor imagine it wrote even by any Friend of mine, for two Reasons :* First, *the Grossness of the Flattery;* Secondly, *the Injury it must of course do me, in the Run of my Play, by putting those People out of Humour, whose Action was to give Life to the Piece. I suppose these Reasons are sufficient to convince the judicious Part, that I was no ways concerned in those Reflections, but own I was treated with all the seeming Civility in the World, till the second Night of my Comedy. I willingly submitted to Mr.* Cibber's *superior Judgment in shortening the Scene of the Ghost in the last Act, and believed him perfectly in the Right, because too much Repetition is tiresome. Indeed, when Mr. Estcourt sliced most of it out, I could not help interposing my Desires to the contrary, which the rest readily complied with ; and I had the Satisfaction to see I was not deceived in My Opinion, of its pleasing. This Passage I happen'd to mention among my Acquaintance; for 'tis natural to have a kind of a Tender for our own Productions, but especially if they have the Fortune to divert others. Now, if from this the Author of the* Tatler *gather'd his Accounts, I am guilty of speaking, but not designedly ; for who they are that write that Paper, or how distinguish'd, I am perfectly ignorant, and declare I never was concerned, either in writing, or publishing any of the* Tatlers.

I never

The PREFACE.

I never had the Vanity to think, much less to publish, that any thing I am capable of doing, could support the Stage, tho' I have had the good Fortune to please, or to find the Town willing to be pleased; tho', at present, it seems, a certain Author has enter'd a Caveat against all Plays running to a sixth Night, but his own. Tho' an Opera interfer'd with this Comedy, yet brought above Forty Pounds the second Night, which shew'd it had some Merit; for I have known a Play kept up, that fail'd of half that Money the second Night. Now, by the Rules of the House, it ought to have been play'd on: But who can secure the Life of a Play, when that of a Man is often sacrificed to the Malice of Parties? This Play met with a kind Reception in general, and notwithstanding the Disadvantages it had to struggle with, by raising the Prices the first Day, and the Nearness of Christmas, *it would have made its way to a sixth Night, if it had had fair Play. Mistake me not, I do not mean from the Representation; for I must do the Players Reason: Had I searched all the Theatres in the World, I could not have selected a better Company, nor had more Justice done me in the Action, tho' they have not dealt honourably by me in my Bargain; for they ought not to have stop'd the Run, upon any Pique whatever. 'Tis small Encouragement to write for the Stage, when the Actors, according to the Caprice of their Humours, maugre the Taste of the Town, have power to sink the Reputation of a Play; for if they resolve not to act it, the Town can't support it.*

Well, if there is any Merit in suffering wrongfully, I shall find my Account in't one time or another; in the mean while I entreat the Female Tatler *to be witty no more at my Expence. I desire I may not be rank'd in the Number of those that support the Stage, since the Stage is become a Noun Substantive, and resolves to shew it is able to stand by itself.*

PRO-

PROLOGUE.
By a GENTLEMAN.
Spoken by Mr. WILKS.

*OUR Female Author trembling stands within,
    Her Fear arises from another's Sin;
One of her Sex has so abus'd the Town,
That on her Score she dreads your angry Frown:
Tho' I dare say, poor Soul, she never writ
Lampoon, or Satyr on the Box or Pit;
A harmless hum'rous Play is her Extent of Wit.
Tho' Bickerstaff's vast Genius may engage,
And lash the Vice and Follies of the Age;
Why shou'd tender Delia tax the Nation;
Stickle, and make a Noise for Reformation,
Who always gave a Loose, herself, to Inclination?
Scandal and Satyr's thrown aside to-day,
And Humour the sole Business of our Play,
Beaux may dress on to catch the Ladies Hearts,
And good Assurance pass for mighty Parts:
The Cits may bring their Spouses without Fear,
We shew no Wife that's poaching for an Heir,
Nor teach the Use of fine Gauze Handkerchier.
Cowards may huff, and talk of mighty Wonders,
And Jilts set up—for Twenty thousand Pounders.
Our Author, even tho' she knows full well,
Is so good-natur'd, she forbears to tell
What Colonels, lately, have found out the Knack
To muster Madam, still, by Ned, or Jack,
To keep their Pleasures up; a frugal Way,
They give her—Subaltern's Subsistence for her Pay.
In short, whate'er your Darling Vices are,
They pass untouch'd in this Night's Bill of Fare.
But if all this can't your Good-Nature wake,
Tho' here and there, a Scene should fail to take,
Yet spare her for the* Busie-Body's *sake.*

D 4   EPI-

EPILOGUE.

Spoken by Mrs. OLDFIELD.

Written by Mr. CIBBER.

A Porter delivers a Letter juſt as ſhe is going to ſpeak.

WHAT's this? a Billet-Doux? from Hands unknown?
'Tis new to ſend it thus 'fore all the Town:
But ſince the poor Man's Paſſion's ſo agog,
I'll read it out by way of Epilogue.

Reads, Madam,
  Permit a Wretch to let you know,
  That he's no more in *Statu Quo*.
  My Ruin from this Night commences,
  Unleſs your Smiles refund my Senſes;
  For with one Thruſt of *Cupid*'s Dart,
  You've whip'd your Slave quite thro' the Heart:
  Therefore, I beg you, caſt your Eye
  O'er Boxes, Pit and Gallery,
  In Pity of my Pains and Doubt,
  And try if you can find me out.

Poor Soul! He ſeems indeed in diſmal Plight;
Let's ſee! it can't be, ſure! from th' upper Flight;
No, no—that's plain—for—None of them can Write:
Nor can I think it from the Middle fell;
For I'm afraid——as few of them can Spell:
Beſide, their haggling Paſſions never gain,
Beyond the Paſſage-walking Nymphs of Drury-Lane:
And then the Pit's more flock'd with Rakes and Rovers,
Than any of theſe ſenſeleſs, whining Lovers.
The Backs o' th' Boxes too ſeem moſtly lin'd
With Souls, whoſe Paſſion's to themſelves confin'd.
In ſhort, I can't perceive, 'mongſt all you Sparks,
The Wretch diſtnguiſh'd by theſe bloody Marks.
                                              But

Dramatis Personæ.

MEN.

Sir Jeffrey Conſtant, *Father to Captain* Conſtant.	*Mr.* Bowman.
Captain Conſtant, *in Love with* Belinda.	*Mr.* Mills.
Lovely, *Friend to Captain* Conſtant.	*Mr.* Huſband.
Faithful, *a Gentleman of Fortune in Love with* Laura.	*Mr.* Wilks.
Sir David Watchum, *Guardian to* Laura.	*Mr.* Johnſon.
Truſty, *Steward to Sir* Jeffrey. —	*Mr.* Eſtcourt.
Num, *A Country Squire in Love with* Belinda.	*Mr.* Dogget.
Slouch, *Servant to* Num. —	*Mr.* Crofs.
Clinch, *Servant to Captain* Conſtant.	*Mr.* Pinkeman.
Roger, *Farmer to Sir* Jeffrey. —	*Mr.* Bullock.
Manage, *Servant to* Faithful. —	*Mr.* Cibber.
Coachman. — — —	*Mr.* Harris.
Sam———	
Another Servant.	

WOMEN.

Belinda, *Suppos'd Daughter to* Truſty.	*Mrs.* Oldfield.
Laura, *An Heireſs in Love with* Faithful.	*Mrs.* Crofs.
Maria, *A Gentlewoman of Fortune.*	*Mrs.* Porter.
Dorothy, *Belind's Maid.* — — —	*Mrs.* Saunders.
Lucy, *Laura's Maid.* — — — —	*Mrs.* Bicknell.

SCENE, *the* Minſter-yard *in* Peterborough.
The Hour, Six in the Morning.

EPILOGUE.

*But since the Town has heard your kind Commands, Sir,
The Town shall e'en be Witness my Answer.
First then, beware you prove no Spark in Red,
With empty Purse, and regimental Head;
That thinks no Woman can refuse t' engage in't,
While Love's advanc'd with offer'd Bills on Agent;
That swears he'll settle from his Joy's commencing,
And make the Babe, the Day he's born, an Ensign.
Nor cou'd I bear a titl'd Beau, that steals
From fasting Spouse her matrimonial Meals;
That Modish sends next Morn to her Apartment,
A civil How d'ye—for alas! from th' Heart meant:
Then powder'd for th' ensuing Day's Delights,
Bows thro' his Croud of Duns, and drives to* White's.
*Nor cou'd I like the Wretch, that all Night plays,
And only takes his Rest on winning Days;
Then sets up from a lucky Hit, his Rattler,
Then's traced from his Orig'nal—in the* Tattler.
*To tell you all that are my fixt Aversion,
Wou'd tire the Tongue of Malice, or Aspersion.
But if I find 'mongst All one generous Heart,
That deaf to Stories takes the Stage's Part;
That thinks that Purse deserves to keep the Plays,
Whose Fortune's bound for the Support of Opera's;
That thinks our Constitution here is justly fixt,
And now no more with Lawyers Brawls perplext:
He, I declare, shall my whole Heart receive;
And (what's more strange) I'll love him while I live.*

The MAN'S bewitch'd;
OR,
The Devil to do about Her.

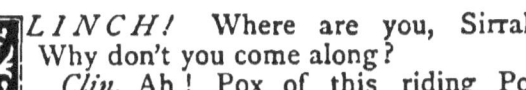

ACT I.

SCENE I. *The Minſter-Yard in* Peterborough.

Enter Captain Conſtant, *and* Clinch *in Mourning, with Riding-Habit over it.*

Capt. *CLINCH!* Where are you, Sirrah? Why don't you come along?
Clin. Ah! Pox of this riding Poſt. ——Look ye, Captain; if you have threeſcore Miles farther to go, I am your humble Servant.
Capt. No, Sirrah, I am at my Journey's End——This Town of *Peterborough* is the Bound of all my Wiſhes.
Clin. Say you ſo, Sir! Pray be pleas'd to make it mine too.
Capt. Why? What is your Wiſh?
Clin. Why, with Submiſſion, Sir, to know the Reaſon of your Expedition, and Gravity of Habit: Have you a mind to ſet up the Buſineſs of an Undertaker here in the Country?
Conſt. No, *Clinch*, my Buſineſs is with the Living, not with the Dead, I'll aſſure you.
Clin. Then can't I for my Blood imagine why you are thus dreſs'd; your Father, nay, your whole Family are well; not ſo much as a Nephew, or ſecond Couſin dead; nay, nor no fear of Peace——Then why the Devil are we in black? You laugh——Can theſe Clothes cauſe

Joy,

Joy, without the Perquifite that belongs to it? 'Tis a mournful Equipage, and fhocks my Soul, I am fure.

Conft. Perquifite! Why what Perquifite does Mourning bring with it to cause Joy? ha!

Clin. Oh, Sir, feveral:——As when a Wife buries her Hufband, fhe has Sorrow in one Hand, and Joy in t'other; a fhort Widowhood cures fuch a Grief.——Or a rich Heir at the laft Gafp of his Parent, where there is a Year's Rent in the Steward's Hands——But, Sir, to the Point; either let me into the Secret, or difcharge me.

Conft. Ha, ha, ha! Why then if I muft tell thee; this Habit, if Fortune favours me, will be worth to me two thoufand Pounds.

Clin. Say you fo, Sir; and pray how much will it be worth to me? For I am drefs'd like you——If I have not the fame Privilege, why fhould I be confin'd to the fame Garb?

Conft, Oh! you fhall have your Part, *Clinch*, never fear.

Clin. Ay, Sir, but there are fome Parts I don't care for——I hope you have no Defign to rob upon the Highway.

Conft. Rascal!

Clin. Nay, ben't angry, Sir; if there fhould be Peace, 'tis what many an honeft Gentleman muft come to: I have no Averfion for the Name; but I have for the Punifhment——I'll not ftrike a Stroke——therefore what good can I do you?

Conft. Ha, ha, ha! I fhall have more Occafion for your Eyes than your Arm—You can weep, Sirrah, can't you?

Clin. Ay, Sir, I fhall weep, that's certain, to fee you come to the Gallows——

Conft. Ye Dog you, I tell you there is no Danger.

Clin. No Danger——Why then fhall I weep for Joy, Sir.——But how, Sir, how; muft I roar, or fhed Tears?

Conft. So you do but counterfeit well, no matter which.

Clin. Ah, let me alone for counterfeiting. I defy a Woman to outdo me in that.—Look ye, Sir, you fhall hear—hem, hem. [*Roars out.*

Conft. Very well——be fure when I weep——

Clin. I'll make terrible Faces——What think you, Sir, is not my Pipe very mufical for weeping?

Conft. Oh! Excellent.

Clin. But what does this fignify? Where lies the Mystery?

Conft.

The Devil to do about her.

Conſt. Well then.—Since you muſt know it; You are not infenfible how my Father has treated me, ever fince I refus'd to marry Mrs. *Homebred*, whofe Manners fuited with her Name, and her Face was coarfer than either; and becaufe I drew a Bill upon him for fifty Pounds laſt Campaign, he threatens to difinherit me; nay, and fwears, that if for the future I don't make it appear I live upon half my Pay, he'll make my Serjeant his Heir, who was once his Footman. In ſhort, I can bear his ill Ufage no longer.

Clin. Ah! Sir, had you married that Lady with twenty thoufand Pounds, you need not have drawn upon him for fifty.

Conſt. If ſhe had twenty Times as much, I ſhou'd refufe her for *Belinda*'s Sake.

Clin. But Sir *Jeffry* refolves againſt that Match——You muſt not marry his Steward's Daughter.

Conſt. I hope to prove you a Lyar, Sir; and by this Drefs to carry my Defign; which is to perfuade *Truſty*, that my Father dy'd of an Apoplexy. by which means he muſt account with me for the half Year's Rent, he fent the old Gentleman Word was ready for him. Two thoufand Pound, *Clinch*——This Letter I furpriz'd by an Accident; 'tis from my Father to him. [*Reads.*

Mr. *Truſty*, " The feveral Sums which you have re-
" turn'd me without any Receipt, amount to eight hun-
" dred Pounds; there remains behind two thoufand two
" hundred Pounds, which you tell me is ready for me;
" don't give yourfelf any Trouble about remitting that,
" for I defign to be down myfelf in a Fortnight; and then
" the Leafes which you mention'd, ſhall be renewed."
You need write no more, till you fee
            Your real Friend, Jeffrey Conſtant.

Clin. Excellent, Sir! Why here may be a pretty Penny towards, if the Devil don't crofs it. But, Sir, if my old Maſter ſhould take a Maggot, and write to *Truſty*, to return his Money after all——His Letter and our Story wou'd have fmall Connexion; we ſhou'd bo oblig'd to alter our Note. I wou'd advife you to take the old Steward to the Tavern, and ſtay as little in his House as you can,

can, for fear of difcovery : Befides, Sir, a Glass of Wine and a Fowl, makes Bufiness go on chearfully, Sir.

Conft. Chearfully, Sirrah !——You don't consider that it is not my Bufiness to be chearful——I admire *Faithful* ftays fo long.

Clin. Perhaps he can't find Mr. *Lovely*, Sir.

Conft. I directed him to the Coffee-houfe, where he feldom fails to be at this Time of the Morning.

Clin. Poor Gentleman ! I warrant he's ruminating upon his Misfortunes. Well! 'tis fometimes a Bleffing to want Money——You 'fcap'd the Highway-men, Sir !

Conft. What am I the better for that, Sirrah ? My Pockets are as empty as my Friends, who fell into their Hands : But here comes my fellow Traveller—and *Lovely* with him ; he has found him at laft——Dear *Lovely*, how is't ?

Enter Lovely, Faithful, *and* Manage *in riding Habit.*

Lov. Captain *Conftant,* welcome ! Who expected to fee you here? Why did not you fend me Word of your coming?

Clin. He hardly knew it himfelf two Hours before he got on Horfeback, Sir ; nay, I much queftion if he knows it yet.

Conft. My Journey indeed was fomething precipitate.

Clin. Ay, Sir ; don't you fee we are in Mourning?

Lov. Mr. *Faithful* has inform'd me of every Particular ; and I wifh I cou'd really give thee Joy of fix thousand a Year, Boy.

Clin. At the rate of half a Year's Rent you may——If Fortune proves not an errant Jilt indeed, Sir.

Lov. Come, Gentlemen ; what think you of my Houfe? I'll get fomething for Breakfaft, whilft you change your Linnen.

Conft. 'Tis near Six——I have a mind to fee if *Belinda* comes to Church this Morning.

Lov. She feldom fails—

Faith. Prithee, *.Lovely* ; can you inform me, if a young Lady that lives at Sir *David Watchum*'s will be here, too ?

Lov. Mrs. *Laura Wealthy,* your Miftress, you mean.

Faith. The same.

Lov. We have heard of the Lady; but I believe nobody

body in *Peterborough* has feen her, except his own Servants.

Conft. What kind of a Temper is the old Fellow of?

Lov. The moft peevifh, fplenetick, miftruftful, ill-natur'd Wretch in the whole County : He comes to the Coffee-houfe every Morning in an old rufty Chariot for hafte, the longeft Journey he takes in the Year. He feldom comes to Church ; nay, fince that Lady came, he has not once been feen there ; we fancy he dare not ftay two Hours from home, for fear fhe fhould be ftol'n away.

Man. Ah, Sir ! This Account is msft uncomfortable in our Affairs.———

Faith. It gives me more chagrin, than the Rogues did, when they ftripp'd me of my Money this Morning—— Which way fhall I give *Laura* Notice of my being in Town?

Conft. Have Courage, *Faithful* ; I warrant we profper.

Lov. Nothing like a good Heart ; you fhall not want a fmall Sum of Money, Sir.

Faith. I thank you, Sir.

Conft. I'll be as diligent in thy Affairs, as in my own ——If any lucky Opportunity offers, I'll be ready to ferve thee.

Lov. I'll be the fame to both.

Conft. I know it ; and when I am able, I hope, if my Defign fucceeds, thou fhalt meet Returns in me.

Faith. I am oblig'd to both.—But who have we here?

Several People crofs the Stage to Church.

Lov. Here comes *Belinda*, and with her my Tyrant *Maria*.

Faith. Well, Gentlemen, you'll beft entertain your Miftreffes alone ; I'll back to the Coffee-houfe, and over a Difh of Tea think what course to steer.———

Conft. Mind if the *Courant* be there, wherein I got my Father's Death inferted, the better to favour my Plot.

Faith. I will, Captain, and be fure to confirm the News. [*Exit* Faith. *and* Manage.

Lov. We'll call on you prefently.———

The Bell rings.

Conft. But is *Maria* obdurate ftill, *Lovely?*

Lov.

Lov. Not in reality, *Conſtant*——But ſhe has ſo much of the Woman in her, to keep up her Rule till the laſt.

Enter Belinda *and* Maria.

Conſt. Ladies, good Morrow ! The Sound of the Saint's Bell brings Angels abroad. [*Salutes 'em.*
Bel. Conſtant ! and in Mourning ! Pray who's dead ?
Conſt. One for whom I ought to grieve, did it not ſmooth a Paſſage to *Belinda's* Arms, through the Hearts of our inexorable Parents.
Bel. Your Father ! Sir.
Clin. The fame, Madam ! He's as dead as a Herring, I promiſe you———
Mar. Now don't I know, whether I had beſt ſay I'm ſorry for your Loſs, or wiſh you much Joy of your Gain.
Clin. I dare ſwear, Madam, he can't tell you yet.
Conſt. Peace, Blockhead.
Mar. Mr. *Lovely,* are you for Prayers ?
Conſt. You are the Shrine he kneels to, Madam ; if you'll vouchſafe to hear him, he can pray moſt devoutly.
Mar. And diſſemble moſt fervently———
Lov. No faith, Madam, that Quality does not belong to us——that is the Womens Prerogative.
Bel. And do you never encroach upon our Privileges, ſweet Sir ?
Lov. Yes, yes, faith ; I have encroach'd upon ſome of the Sex's Privileges in my Time, I muſt own. Curioſity —Madam, ſeldom leads us to put on maſking Habits ; but a Lady cannot dreſs without 'em ; Diſſimulation is as neceſſary as her Patches.
Bel. Ay ! How do you prove that ?
Lov. Why thus : When you wou'd gain a Man you like, you appear what you are not——We believe you Angels, but don't always find you ſo.
Mar. We always find you Angels, but of the fal'n Kind.
Conſt. 'Tis impoſſible to be otherwiſe, whilſt Beauty keep her Court below ; you charm our Eyes, and all our Senſes wait you.
Lov. Pride and Vanity predominate in your Sex, and like Centinels relieve one another ; Pride has made a Lady ſwear ſhe has hated ſuch a Man, tho' ſhe was dying for
the

the Sight of him.——And Vanity made her carefs a Fop, that at the fame Time fhe wifh'd at the Devil.

Mar. And are not you even with us? Will not you figh, ogle, cringe, flatter, fwear, kneel, nay, give it under your Hand, you love to Defperation? But let the poor miftaken Nymph once yield, and you'd give Bond and Judgment to that old Gentleman you nam'd but now, in two Days to take her off your Hands.

Conft. I hope you don't include the whole Sex, Madam?

Lov. That fhe does not, I'm fure; for fhe knows I never fwore any thing to her, but what I'm ready to make good——And if fhe be not the moft unconfcionable Woman, fhe will own I love her heartily.

Conft. That I dare witnefs for thee, *Lovely.*

Bel. Ay! Why, what Proofs has he given?

Lov. Proofs! Why I talk of her all Day—And dream of her all Night——When fhe's absent, figh for her; and am tranfported when I fee her. If thefe be not Proofs of Love, let the Parfon fay Grace, and I'll give her better.

Bel. All this may be done without one Grain of Love, may it not, Captain?

Conft. Not when you are the Object, Madam; and you are too well acquainted with my Heart, to afk that Queftion out of fcruple, I'm certain.

Mar. Thefe are no Proofs; you muft grow lean and meagre——Eat little, and fleep lefs——Write fifty Letters in a Day. and burn them all again——Then ftart up, and draw your Sword; hold it to your Breaft; then throw it away again——Then take your Pen and write your laft Farewel——Difpatch it to your Miftrefs——Then take a Turn by fome melancholy purling Stream, with Hat pull'd o'er your Eyes, in deep Contemplation refolve thro' what Door to let in Death, if the Meffenger return without Succefs——When I fee you do this, I'll write Lover upon your Brow.

Lov. When I do, you fhall write Fool on my Forehead.

Hang this whining Way of wooing,
Loving was defign'd a Sport, &c.   [*Sings.*

Conft. Come, come, Madam, a Truce; you know he loves you.

Lov. As well as I know fhe loves me; we were born
for

for one another, Child ; no Man in the Kingdom fhall have thee but myfelf——Then if you will eat Chalk, and die of the Pip, I can't help it : Ha, ha, ha !

Mar. Be not fo pofitive, *Lovely.*—One Sect of Philofophers tells us, we ought to doubt of every Thing.

Lov. But the Topic was not a Woman in that Affertion ; but if it were, Women in their Days were no more like Women in ours, than a Clodhopper is to a Captain o'Foot. Our Ladies are like two Negatives, to be underftood in the Affirmative ; ha, ha ! Madam, does not my Friend here look like one of thofe Lovers you defcrib'd ? Faith, I think a Woman cannot wifh a fimpler Figure—— Now has he a thoufand Things to fay to *Belinda* alone.

Conft. You guefs right, *Lovely*——I am going to your Father's, Madam, to fettle our Accounts ; I hope you'll return as foon as Prayers are over.

Bel. Directly——

Conft. Oh *Belinda!*

Now is the Crifis of our good or ill ;
Turn for me, Fate, or let thy Wheel ftand ftill.

Lov. You'll remember us in your Prayers, Ladies.—

Mar. Amongft *Jews, Turks* and *Infidels.* [*Exit.*

Lov. Come, now for my Houfe——We'll call on *Faithful.*

Conft. Lead on—I'll change my Linen, and to *Trufty*'s immediately——But hold——*Clinch,* hark ye.

Clin. Sir——

Const. I had no Opportunity to inform *Belinda* of my Project ; you muft away to *Trufty*'s and let her Maid into the Secret, I wou'd not impofe upon her—The Man that truly loves, cannot deceive the Object of his Vows.

He never felt the Force of Cupid's Dart,
Who lets his Tongue run counter to his Heart ;
Or ever can deferve the charming Maid,
That is by Falfhood to his Arms betray'd.
For mutual Paffions in all States agree,
And lines the Yoke with true Felicity.
She fhall my Project with my Love compare,
If fhe approves it, I'm indeed an Heir.

Clin. *Or at the worft, we are but as we were.*

Enter

The Devil to do about her. 91

Enter 'Squire Num *and his Man* Slouch.

Num. What think you *Slouch!* Had we beſt go into the *Minſter,* or tarry here whilſt Mrs. *Belinda* comes out; for her maid ſays ſhe's here: Lord, Lord, how religious Folks are in this Town! Why they riſe as early to Church here, as our Parſon's Wife does to milking, I think—— Well, but what had we beſt to do, ha?

Slou. Why go in, I think—or tarry here; which you will, Maſter.

Num. Nay, nay, mun, I don't know which is beſt, that makes me aſk you; for I know, *Slouch,* you underſtand Breeding and Haviours; for you have been at *London* with fat Bullocks, and ſo was never I; but I reſolve to go next time, ha! *Slouch!*

Slou. Ay, Maſter; but and you marry this ſame Mrs. *Belinda,* as ſure as your nane is *'Squire Num,* ſhe'll not let you budge a Step.

Num. Marry her! Nay, nay, I ſhall marry her, that's ſure enough, I think; and yet I'll ſee *London* for all that ——Why, what doſt thou think I'll be ty'd to a Wife's Tail all the Days of my Life? No, no; the Family of the *Nums* won't be Wife rid, *Slouch*—But hark ye, an her Father ſhou'd chop up the Wedding to D'ay, before my new Clothes are made; for he likes me woundily, mun.

Slou. Od, well thought on, Maſter! Don't go into the Church, I ſay; who knows but when the Parſon has done his Prayers, but he may begin your Plagues, Maſter, ha!

Num. Od, that's ſmart now——Ha, ha; huſh, huſh, *Slouch,* they are here—Now ſhow your Manners——

Enter Truſty, Belinda *and* Maria. *Several others croſs the Stage as from Church.*

Tru. I have met a Report in the Church, that the News ſays *Jeffrey Constant* is dead; if it be true, there's a better Huſband for *Belinda* than this Fool——Od! I'll for *London* as ſoon as I have din'd; my Heart akes; pray Heaven he ſettled his Affairs before he died: I have no Receipt for the Money I paid him.

Num. Sir, your Servant; Father has ſent me agen to ſee Mrs. *Belinda,* and bid me tell you, That he wou'd come over himſelf, I think, next Week, and do what you wou'd have him to do, I think——And ſo, I ſuppoſe, we are

agreed

agreed, Forsooth——Only I muſt deſire you to ſtay till my new Clothes are made. Father bought the Cloth laſt *Sturbich* Fair; and the Taylor comes To-morrow, don't he, *Slouch?*

Slou. Ay, and his Man *Staytape*, too; and he works like a Dragon——My Maſter will ſoon be fit, Forſooth.

Mar. Fit, quotha! for what? ha, ha.

Num. For what! Nay, nay, let me alone for that, an I don't ſhow her for what, when I have her once, I'll be flea'd.

Mar. Heaven defend me from the Trial!

Tru. Sir, ſince I ſaw you laſt, I have conſider'd my Daughter is no proper Match for you; and therefore I deſire you to return with all poſſible Speed, and acquaint your Father, that he may not undertake any unneceſſary Journey.

Bel. Ten thousand Bleſſings on that Voice.

Num. Hey-day: What's the Matter now! Why you don't pretend to make a Fool of me, do ye?

Mar. No, thou art made to his Hands——ha, ha, ha——

Num. Who ſpeaks to you. Miſtreſs; I was not made for you, I'm ſure.

Mar. No, I thank my Stars!

Num. I'll not be chous'd at this rate, mun: Did you not tell me, if my Father would ſettle ſo, and ſo, that I ſhou'd have her——And now you come with a conſider—when it has coſt me the Lord knows what in Journeys, as *Slouch* can teſtify.

Slou. Yes with a ſafe Conſcience, I can ſwear it has coſt my Maſter—and me, above thirty Shillings upon you.

Bel. What, did you club with your Maſter then, Mr. *Slouch?*

Slou. Now and then, for a Flaggon of Ale, and it pleaſe you.

Bel. Oh you ſhall be no Loſer, Friend—There's ſomething to defray your Expences.   [*Gives him Money.*

Slou. Thank you kindly, Forſooth——Od, this 'tis to be ſharp——Now wou'd I give Six-pence to know if this be a good Guinea, or a Counter——   [*Aſide.*

Tru. As to your Charges Mr. *Num*——if you pleaſe
to

The Devil to do about her. 93

to give me a Bill they fhall be difcharg'd—But for my Daughter, I have defign'd her otherways.

Num. A Bill! I fcorn your Words; I'm as well able, do you fee, to fpend thirty Shillings as you, for ought I knows; yet I'm not angry neither; only what makes me mad, is, that you fhou'd think me fuch a Fool to be fob'd off I know not how —— Why mun, all our Town knows that I'm to have her, and they have promis'd me the Bells fhou'd ring a whole Day——And now you'd have me go home with a Tale of a Tub, like a Dog that has lost his Ears——What did you come bouncing to our Houfe for! and fay I fhou'd have your Daughter—— I did not come after her, nor you neither, mun.

Tru. What I faid I thought at that Time, Sir; but no Man can blame me for changing my Miud to Advantage in difpofing of my Child——I have a better Profpect both in Birth and Eftate, than you, or your Father can offer. Therefore I fay, without any Paffion, I defire you'd give yourfelf no farther Trouble about this Matter, Nr. *Num.*

Bel. Birth, and Eftate! What means my Father? How I tremble!

Mar. He has certainly heard of Sir *Jeffrey*'s Death, and defigns to make thee happy.

Bel. Impoffible! he was in the *Minfter* before us.

Num. Birth, and Eftate! *Slouch*, come hither, Sirrah! Han't my Father a Thousand a Year?

Slou. Yes, that he has, an more too: He has ten Hundred, I'll fwear it.

Num. I believe he has, as you fay, *Slouch*.

Om. Ha, ha, ha, ha, ha!

Num. And I am all the Children he has, am I not *Slouch*?

Slou. Ay, all that he dares own, Sir.

Num. Look ye there, now! An I'll hold you a Bottle of Cyder that I'm as well born as he; my Father's Churchwarden, and Captain of the Militia, as 'tis known very well; and I'm call'd the young Captain, fo I am.

Slou. Aye, that every body knows.

Tru. Sir, I have nothing to say to that, and am your humble Servant——Come *Belinda*.

Bel. I wifh you a good Journey, Sir.

Mar. Captain, your Servant. [*Exit.
Num.*

Num. A murrain take your Fleer——
Slou. You may go to *London*, now, Sir.
Num. Go to *London*, go to the Devil! 'Slife I'll follow them mun, may hap he do's but joke; and Father will break my Head, becaufe I did not underſtand a Joke—Therefore come along, *Slouch*. [*Exeunt.*

ACT II.

SCENE, *Sir* David Watchum's *Houſe.*

Enter Sir David *into a Garden before the Door.*

Sir *Dav.* I HAVE furvey'd my Houſe round and round to Night, from Door to Door, and Gate to Gate——He that wou'd keep a handſome Woman of twenty thouſand Pound, muſt learn the Gameſter's Art, to live without Sleep——Methought, from my Garret-Window, I faw a Man fauntring about my Ground, and ſeem'd to pry too narrowly into my Houſe—It may be a Rogue——I would not loſe Mrs. *Laura*; for, if poſſible, ſhe ſhall fill no Arms but mine. I have kept her from the Sight of Man theſe twelve Months; and now I deſign to offer her Liberty, provided ſhe'll conſent to be my Wife; if ſhe refuſes, I'll have the Lights quite ſtop'd up, and ſhe ſhall not ſo much as fee the Sun——Ha! who's here! Ho, 'tis *Lucy*, her Maid: I wiſh I cou'd make this Jade of my Intereſt——What the Vengeance does ſhe do up ſo early?

Enter Lucy.

Lucy. This old Fellow is certainly the Devil—One can go no where, but one is ſure to meet him.

Sir *Dav.* What makes you here, ha, Miſtreſs?—Now am I afraid of venturing to the Coffee-houſe, tho' my Coach is at the Door.

Lucy. Too much Sleep is unwholeſome, you know, Sir, by your own Rule; ſo hearing the Door open, I came down to breathe the Morning Air

Sir *Dav.* That you might have done at your Window;
no,

The Devil to do about her. 95

no, no, you have fome Plot in Hand now, I warrant! Where's your Miftrefs?

Lucy. In her Chamber,: Where fhou'd fhe be?

Sir *Dav.* In her Bed wou'd be a fitter Place —— Women of Virtue, that have no Intrigues, are faft afleep in their Beds at this Time a-day.

Lucy. Afleep! That's impoffible in this Houfe — Pray how can any body fleep, as long as you are awake; are you not rambling all Night; up Stairs, down Stairs, locking one Door, and opening another; hemming, coughing, fpitting, fneezing, yawning, ftamping, mutt'ring? — One no fooner fhuts one's Eyes——but flap goes a Door, clatter goes a Key—down tumbles a Stool, bow-wow goes the Dog——This is the conftant Mufick you make, Sir; 'Slife, if one were a Slave in *Turkey,* one fhould fometimes reft in quiet.

Sir *Dav.* Good lack, good lack, all this I get for my Care——Why all this is your Lady's Good, *Lucy.*

Lucy. Nay, if you call this Good! Then pray, Sir, employ your Study for the future, to do her ill Offices; for nothing can be more difagreeable, than your prefent Treatment both to my Lady and me.

Sir *Dav.* Say you fo! What, you don't like your way of living then? ha.

Lucy. Not at all, I affure you, Sir—Living! d'ye call it ——We wou'd have Liberty, Sir.

Sir *Dav.* You fhall have Liberty, if your Lady is not her own Enemy—and for your Part, if you pleafe, you may ferve yourfelf and her by being ferviceable to me.

Lucy. Which Way, pray Sir? For there are not many Things I wou'd refufe to procure my Lady her dear, dear Liberty; pray inform me, I'm impatient tn know it.

Sir *Dav.* Why thus—I have a very cordial Affection for Mrs. *Laura,* out of pure confideration of her Youth— I wou'd not have a young Woman fall into ill Hands at firft; therefore I defign to marry her myfelf.

Lucy. Heaven forbid! That would be falling into ill Hands, indeed. [*Afide.*

Sir *Dav.* Now I wou'd have you break this Matter to her; and fecond it with all the Force of Argument you are capable of——When we are married, you fhall take what Liberty you pleafe.

Lucy.

Lucy. Why, fure a Perfon of your experienc'd Years, wou'd not be guilty of fuch a Folly.

Sir Dav. What do you call Folly? I had no Children by my laſt Wife, and I wou'd willingly have an Heir to keep up my Name——and do you call this Folly?

Lucy. Heirs! Why, do you hope for an Heir of your own getting, Sir?

Sir Dav. Why not, pray?

Lucy. What, upon fuch a fine Woman as fhe is——In my Confcience, were I in your Place, I fhou'd dread being the erranteſt, you know what, in Chriſtendom.

Sir Dav. Oh Mrs. Pert! that's not your Bufinefs, I fhall dread no fuch Thing—All I defire of you, is to tell her, my Eſtate, Prudence, Wifdom and Temperance, outweighs Youth, Folly, Titles and Debauchery.

Lucy. Yes, for one that is in love with her Grave. Certainly, Sir, you are not in your right Senfes—Why, your Requeſt is fo abominable, fo vile, fo ridiculous, and fo unjuſt; that I wou'd not be concern'd in it for a thoufand Pounds———Indeed, you have pitch'd upon the wrong Perfon, Sir.

Sir Dav. Say you fo! Good lack——So I have pitch'd upon the wrong Perfon you fay! ha! If I had defir'd you to fay your Prayers, I'll be hang'd if I had not pitch'd upon the wrong Perfon too, Goffip prate-a-pace ——but I'll hamper ye, I warrant you; I'll crofs your Defigns, till I have finifh'd my own—go, get out of my Sight.

Lucy. Well, furely this Life won't laſt always. [*Exit.*

Enter Manage.

Man. My Maſter ſtays at the Coffee-houfe, and has fent me to furvey this Dome, and try to give Mrs. *Laura's* Maid Notice of his Arrival; but how far I may be ferviceable to him, I know not——Ha! who have we yonder! The old Guardian himfelf, I doubt——So, he has found me——What the Duce muſt I pretend now?

Sir Dav. What do you want, Friend, ha?

Man. Good-morrow, Sir.

Sir Dav. Well, Good-morrow; what more?

Man. I hope you are well, Sir.

Sir Dav. Yes, thank Heaven, Sir! What then?

Man.

The Devil to do about her. 97

Man. Why, then I'm very glad of it, Sir.

Sir Dav. You are very glad of it, Sir! Why, what a Pox, is my Health to you? Who are you? What are you? And from whence come you, ha, Sir?

Man. Faith, Sir, your Queſtions are ſo copious, that they require a conſiderable Study to anſwer: Let me recollect a little—I have gone through ſo many Trades, that without my Diary (which I have not about me at preſent) I can't remember half of them; nor indeed can I tell how to ſtile myſelf otherwiſe than an univerſal Man——The World is my Country; and for want of an Eſtate, I live by my Wits.

Sir Dav. A Rogue, I warrrant him. [*Aſide.*

Man. Sometimes an honeſt Man, ſometimes a Knave; juſt as Occaſions fall out.

Sir Dav. Ay! and you oftener happen to be Knave, than an honeſt Man, I doubt, Friend.

Man. Why look ye, Sir, that is juſt as I abound, or want Money; for my preſent Profeſſion is Phyſick—Now, when my Pockets are full, I cure a Patient in three Days; when they are empty, I keep him three Months.

Sir Dav. An excellent Principle, truly—But pray, what is your Buſineſs at my Houſe?——We are all in a good State of Health at preſent.

Man. Nay, no very great Buſineſs, only I look'd in as I paſs'd by, Sir, that's all.

Sir Dav. Now in my Opinion you have another Reaſon; for you have the Aſpect of thoſe Sparks that come in at a Window, or down a Chimney at two in the Morning.——

Man. Have a care what you ſay, Sir, I'm known very well not far off.

Sir Dav. Ay, too well, perhaps! Zounds, Sir, what Buſineſs have you here? ſpeak.

Man. A queer old Duke this—Why, Sir, if you muſt know, I am in ſearch of ſome Simples, which I have occaſion for.——

Sir Dav. Simples!

Man. Yes, Sir.

Sir Dav. Simples! A very ſimple Excuſe, Faith——

Man. Sir, I have many Years practis'd Chymiſtry, and there's ſcarce any Diſeaſe incident to Humanity, but I have

have cur'd ; Stone, Gravel, Spleen, Vapours, Fits of the Mother, and fo forth———

Sir Dav. Rather Fits of the Father, I fancy.

Man. I had attained fuch Perfection in the Chymical Art, that I wanted but one Degree of Heat to reach the Philofopher's Stone.

Sir Dav. That Habit, methinks, does not anfwer this mighty Skill.

Man. Oh ! Sir, Skill does not lie in Clothes—And the moft ingenious are not always the moft fortunate—I have had many Croffes in my Time—which has reduc'd me much below my Birth, I affure you—I ferve an Officer at prefent, in the Quality of a *Valet de Chambre*, whofe Life I fav'd at the Battle of *Audenard*, when he was fhot thro' with a Cannon-ball.

Sir Dav. How ! fhot through with a Cannon-ball.

Man. Yes, Sir ; what, do you wonder at that ? Why, Sir, I have a Water, that if your Head were off, I'd but wafh it with that, and clap it upon your Shoulders again, and you fhou'd grow as perfectly well in Half an Hour, as ever you was in your Life ; I have made the Experiment upon Thoufands ; my Mafter's Brother was one of them.———

Sir Dav. If you were in Petticoats, I fhou'd take you for the *Kentifh* Miracle——What is this Officer's Name, Friend, that you ferve ?

Man. Captain *Bounce*, Sir.

Sir Dav. Bounce! I fancy you are related to him ; are you not, Friend ?

Man. No, Sir, not at all ; indeed he ufes me more like a Relation, than a Servant, for the Reafon before-mentioned.

Sir Dav. Ha ! and where is he, pray ?

Man. At the *Talbot*, Sir ; if you pleafe I'll fetch him hither ?

Sir Dav. By no means, Sir ; but what Bufinefs have you here in *Peterborough ?*

Man. We have been raifing Recruits, Sir——A Pox of this old Dog ; how many impertinent Queftions does he afk ?—Here's no Hopes of feeing *Lucy*.——

Sir Dav. Well, Sir, I defire you'd look your Simples, elfe

The Devil to do about her.

elfewhere; for I don't like you, notwithstanding your fair Pretences.

Man. Sir I shall obey you——but pray who does this House belong to?

Sir *Dav.* Why, this House belongs to——its Master.

Man. Indeed, Sir——Pray who is the Master, if I may be so bold as to ask?

Sir *Dav.* Why that Master is——a Man, Friend.

Man. Really Sir! your answers are so concise and so ingenious, that it is impossible to quit your Company—— We design for *Cambridge* to-night, pray what Time do you think we shall get in?

Sir *Dav.* The Town Clock will tell you when you come there.

Man. Is it possible!—I humbly thank you, Sir—one Thing more I wou'd gladly be resolv'd——I have a Brother bound for *Portugal*, pray is the Wind fair, Sir.

Sir *Dav.* What do you take me for, a Weather-cock, Sirrah? Hark ye, the Wind will blow you no good, if you don't get about your Business; remember that, and so farewel. [*Exit.*

Man. Very well——this must be Sir *David* his own-self——'Egad he has all his Paces, it will be hard to bring Matters about here; I'm just as wise as when I came ——and have told fifty Lyes to no Purpose——Ha! his Coach at the Door, I'll watch whither he goes, I'm resolv'd.——

Re-enter Sir David.

Sir *Dav.* What, are you not gone yet, Sirrah? I'll have you laid by the Heels, if you don't get off my Ground this Moment.

Man. Sir, I am going this Moment——A Pox of his Leathern Jaws——Well, I'll inform my Master what has pass'd, and leave him to think on what's to come.—— [*Exit.*

Sir *Dav.* So, he is gone——I don't like the Countenance of this Fellow——*Sam*——

Enter Servant.

Sam. Sir.

Sir *Dav.* Lock my Doors, dy'e hear; till I return from the Coffee-house, let no Body in or out.——

Sam.

Sam. I shall observe, Sir. [*Ex. Severally.*

SCENE changes to the *Coffee-house*; Lovely, Constant, and Faithful.

Faith. I have confirm'd the whole Town in the Belief of my Father's Death.

Const. Then thou hast done me Service—Come, you'll both go with me to *Trusty's*——

Faith. No, I have a Mind to stay here; to see if Sir *David* comes; this Morning I will try to get acquainted with him; perhaps my being a Stranger, he may invite me to Dinner.

Lov. Ha, ha! he would as soon give thee his Estate.

Enter Manage.

Faith. Ha! *Manage*, what News? Hast thou seen *Lucy?*
Man. No, Sir, but I have seen the Knight.
Faith. Well, and what have you discover'd?
Man. That it was not worth your while to come Post from *London*, to return the same Way——Ah! Pox of the last Horse I rid; what a cursed fall had I in *Stangate-hole* ——don't you remember, Sir, how I lay over Head and Ears in Mire; whilst the Gentlemen of the Pad disburthen'd you of a hundred Pounds?

Faith. Hang your unseasonable Memory, Sirrah; leave fooling, and tell me——You saw Sir *David*, did you speak to him?

Man. Yes, Sir, but he answer'd me with a damn'd sour Air; and I assure you it will require Cannon to reduce his Citadel.

Faith. Love has taught me to surmount all Difficulties.
Man. But here the Knight will be immediately; for I heard him give Orders to lock up the Doors, till he return'd from the Coffee house.

Lov. Ay, that's right, Sir *David*! ha, ha.
Faith. Lock up the Doors! Ah, poor *Laura*! how shall I give thee Notice of my being here?—

Const. I have a Thought in my Head, if it cou'd be put in practice——Hark, I hear the Coach——ha! here's no body in the Room to discover the Trick——Let us pretend a Quarrel——Draw, *Faithful*.

Faith. To what Purpose?

Const.

The Devil to do about her.

Conſt. You ſhall know inſtantly——*Lovely*, do you ſeem to part us; he's here—Damn you, Sir, you lye. (*draws.*) I have not loſt, nor will I pay———
Faith. Take your Lye back, Sir. [*ſeem to fight.*

Enter Sir David.

Lov. Why Gentlemen, Gentlemen, what do you mean?
Faith. Damn you, Sir, you ſhall pay me———
Conſt. There is the Money then, you have it——pretend to be wounded with that Thrust, *Faithful.*
 [*Aſide to him.*
Faith. I am wounded—pray help to lead me home.
Lov. Oh Friend! what have you done?
Sir *Dav.* What's here, Murder?
Conſt. I hope the Wound's not mortal——Curſe on my unlucky Arm; how doſt thou, *Ned?*
Sir *Dav.* Do quotha! if the Gentleman is wounded, I muſt ſecure you, Sir.
Const. Secure me, Sir! Alas! Sir, I don't intend to fly; a Pox of all Wagers, I ſay.
Faith. Pray lead me to my Inn, for I feel my ſpirits very faint.
Lov. Lead you! Alas, I doubt you cannot walk ſo far.
Conſt. What, is there not a Chair or Coach to be got?
Lov. Sir *David* has a Coach at the Door, if you could prevail with him to lend it you a little.
Const. Sir, pray oblige us with your Coach, it ſhall return immediately.
Sir *Dav.* With all my Heart.——[*Goes to the Door, and ſpeaks to his Coachman aloud.*
Tom, here, carry this Gentleman home——d'ye hear, and make Haſte back again.
Faith. Oh! Friend, I underſtand you now; my Soul dances with the bare Idea.
Conſt. It has succeeded to my Wish—*Lovely*, help, lead him to the Coach.
Sir *Dav.* If there be any Danger, Mr. *Lovely*, take care to ſecure the Murderer.
Lov. Oh! they are intimate Friends, Sir *David*, he won't flinch, I know.

Sir *Dav.* Well, well, look you to that.——
[*Ex. into the House.*
Conſt. Manage! Come you along with us, I have ſome inſtructions for you. [*Exeunt.*

SCENE *changes to the Outside of* Truſty's *House.*

Enter Lovely, Conſtant, Clinch, *and* Manage.

Lov. He'll certainly get Admittance to his Miſtreſs by this ſtratagem; but if the Knight ſhou'd find him there, how will he come off?

Conſt. Nay, let him look to that——but *Manage* ſhall take *Clinch*'s great Coat, 'tis like a Livery.—Sweet Sir, can you condeſcend to wear a Livery an Hour or two?

Man. To ſerve my Maſter's Amour I will, Sir—elſe I ſcorn a Livery—I muſt have that black Wig too.

Conſt. Well, well! Here *Clinch*, change, change with him. [*They change Clothes.*

Clin. So Sir! Now I am your *Valet de Chambre.*

Man. Well, Sir, what am I to do now?

Conſt. Why, go watch about Sir *David*'s Door, and as you fee occaſion, employ your Wits.

Man. Very well, Sir, let me alone for that; your humble Servant, Gentlemen. [*Exit.*

Enter Dolly, *one of the Houſe.*

Dolly. Oh! Are you come, Captain; I have told my Miſtreſs every Particular—Pleaſe to walk in, Sir, I'll inform my Maſter you are here. [*They go in.*

The SCENE *draws, and diſcovers them in a room.*

Lov. 'Tis an admirable Projeƈt, Captain, if you are not diſcover'd; but your Father will certainly know it in a little Time.

Conſt. If poſſible, I'll marry the Woman to-night.

Lov. I fear Sir *Jeffrey* will reſent the Trick.

Conſt. I hope to convince him the Trick was upon *Truſty*; for he may recover the Money of him, if he pleaſes, and with me it may paſs for his Daughter's Portion: but rather than fail, I'll give the Steward my Bond, when 'tis diſcover'd, to refund the Money, when I become Maſter

of

The Devil to do about her. 103

of my Father's Eſtate ; for without *Belinda*, nothing can make me happy.

Clin. Ah, Sir, you'll ſcarce find a Man in the Army of your Mind—Prefer a Woman to Money ! Why, Sir, Money is the very Hinge the whole World turns upon——A Soldier, and not love Money ! Money has Power to alter all Conſtitutions, and in ſpite of Cuſtom, ſtamp what Form it pleaſes—'Twill make an honeſt Man a Knave ; nay, 'twill make a Knave an honeſt Man—'twill make a Coward valiant—an old Woman young—a young Woman a Saint— a Lawyer juſt—a Stateſman loyal—and a Courtier keep his Word.

Lov. Ha, ha, *Clinch* is a Wit.

Clin. Faith, I always thought ſo by my Poverty.

Conſt. Well hinted *Clinch*—I'm in thy Debt—
[*gives him half a Guinea.*

Clin. Oh Sir, I am yours in all Reſpects—Oh ! this dear Colour !

What can there be that this dear Coin can't buy?
For thee Men toil and ſweat, ſwear, cheat and lye ;
For thee does Friend his deareſt Friend betray,
And Women give their very Souls away.
Join but Ambition to this glitt'ring Evil.
And in an Inſtant Man is made a Devil.

Conſt. Ha, ha, ha !

Lov. Ha, ha, ha !

Conſt. Ad's-heart, Sir, ſet your weeping Face in order—Here comes the Steward—

Enter Truſty.

Tru. Captain *Conſtant*, your Servant ! you are welcome into the Country. What, you are in want of Men ; I warrant you are going to raiſe Recruits.

Conſt. Not at this Time, Sir ; 'tis a more unwelcome Accident that brought me down. [*Takes out a Handkerchief, and ſeems to weep.*

Truſt. Good lack ! the News is really true then, Sir *Jeffrey* is dead.

Clin. Ay, poor Gentleman, he's laid low——

Truſt. I confeſs I heard ſo, but I hop'd it might be Report only ; I did deſign to have ſet out for *London* as ſoon as I had din'd——My Heart akes——Bleſs me ! What have

The Man's bewitch'd; or,

have I paid without any Receipt?——I lov'd Sir *Jeffrey* like a Brother: truly I am very much troubled——
[*ſeems to weep.*
Clin. Grief is very catching, I find; it makes me weep too——Be comforted, Sir, (*To* Conſtant.) Fathers muſt go as well as Sons——Why do you afflict yourself at this rate, Sir? Since Death is Death, who can help it?
Lov. Pray be comforted, Sir *John*——   [*To* Conſtant.
Truſt. Pray of what Diſtemper did he die?
Clin. Ah! Deuce on't! What was that hard Word? Now can't I think on't, as I hope to be Great—
Lov. Of an Apoplexy—A Pox on the Doctors, for giving Death ſo many ſtrange Names.   [*Aſide.*
Clin. Right, Sir——He died of an Apoplexy, Sir.
Tru. Of an Apoplexy! Why then I doubt he died ſuddenly.
Conſt. In a Moment's Time, Sir, he was alive and dead——
Clin. Ay, without ever ſpeaking one Word, Sir—
Tru. (*Roars out*) Oh, oh, oh. Did he ſettle his Affairs in his Health? Did he make any Will?——
Conſt. Not any, Sir.
Clin. No, Sir; he has left all Sixes and Sevens.
Tru. Oh, oh, oh——   [*faints.*
Lov. Ha! Help, *Clinch*, I hope he is not dead.
Clin. No, no, he breathes, thank Heaven; pray you look up, Sir.
Conſt. Why are you thus concern'd?
Lov. You really encrease Sir *John*'s Grief, Sir.
Tru. Oh! what have I loſt?
Conſt. I know you have loſt a Friend in my Father; but you ſhall find him again in me.
Tru. Oh, but he has left all Things at fixes and ſevens, *Clinch* ſays—Did he ſay nothing to you about me before he dy'd?
Conſt. Not a Syllable—But I ſuppoſe your Concern proceeds from having paid him Money without any Thing to ſhow for it under his Hand.
Tru. Ay, Sir, there's my Misfortune—Oh, oh.
Clin. 'Tis the Money, not the Man—Let not that trouble, you, Sir, my young Maſter has been inform'd to a Farthing what it was—Tell him, tell him, Sir, your Father

The Devil to do about her. 105

ther appear'd, and let me alone to clinch it. [*Aſide to Conſtant.*

Tru. Inform'd!

Conſt. Yes, Mr. *Truſty*; my Father cou'd not reſt till he had diſclos'd your Affair.

Clin. Ah, good honeſt Soul! feeing he was ſnatch'd away fo ſuddenly, he has ſeveral Times appeared.

Tru. How! appear'd, ſay you?

Clin. Aſk my Maſter elſe.

Conſt. Moſt certain, Sir.——

Clin. He haunted us ſix Days like the Devil; ſometimes like a ſhag Dog——Sometimes like a white Pidgeon—At laſt he took his own Shape. *Clinch*, ſaid he, don't you know me? Then addreſſing himſelf to my Maſter, don't be afraid, ſaid he, I come to tell you, that at ſeveral Times, I have received from Mr. *Truſty*———

Tru. Ah dear Ghoſt, dear Ghoſt; how much did he ſay?

Conſt. Eight hundred Pound.

Tru. Right to a Penny; look ye there now, fee what it is to deal with honeſt Men; one loſes nothing by them tho' in their Graves.

Clin. Oh, the Dead, Sir, are always generous; they value Money no more than that— [*Snapping his Fingers.*

Tru. Poor Gentleman, that he ſhou'd take a Journey from the other World upon my Account.

Clin. Ah, Sir, the Dead ride Poſt upon the Winds—He charg'd me to tell you, for your Satisfaction, he wou'd come and give you an Acquittance himſelf.

Tru. By no means, I am content; let the Dead viſit who they will for me.

Conſt. O, fear not, Sir, he'll not trouble you; but to our Buſineſs, Sir, what you have paid I will diſcount.

Tru. And the reſt of the Money is at your Service, and my Daughter too, Sir *John*, if you have not loſt the Remembrance of her.

Conſt. To ſhow you that I have not, Mr. *Truſty*, I aſſure you ſhe will be the welcomeſt Preſent of the two.

Lov. Thy Buſineſs is done, *Constant*.

Tru. Say you ſo, Sir *John*! Well, I'll fetch the Writings, and diſpatch ſome Affairs, and then I'll carry you to

E 5   my

106   *The Man's bewitch'd; or,*

my Daughter—But upon fecond Thoughts, pleafe to walk into my Study, 'tis more convenient.

Conft. With all my Heart, I'll follow you——
                                                    [*Exit* Trufty.

Lov. Matters go as you cou'd wifh ; you'll be married to-night, Captain.

Conft. I with 'twere over ; Egad I'd rather fight half a dozen Men, than defcend to this rafcally Way of Lying, were there any Help for it ; it is beneath a Soldier.—

A Soldier fcorns the whining Lover's Art;
His Courage takes Poffeffion of the Heart:
Difdains by Treachery to raife his Name,
But boldly owns the bright ambitious Flame,
And courts his Miftrefs as he courts his Fame.

ACT III.

SCENE, Trufty *in his Study, with* Conftant, Lovely *and* Clinch. *Papers and Money upon the Table.*

Trufty. THERE, Sir *John,* there are in thefe Bags Two and twenty hundred Pounds, which, with the Eight hundred I remitted Sir *Jeffrey,* is juft Three thousand Pound ; if you pleafe, you may count it, 'tis moft in Gold.

Conft. No, I'll take your Word for't ; here, *Clinch,* carry it to *Drive* the Carrier, he is juft now going to *London* order him where to pay it in, d'ye hear?

Clin. Yes, Sir——   [*Exit with the Bags.*

Lov. He is loaden with it ; ha, ha, ha.——

Tru. Poor Sir *Jeffrey,* reft his Soul, did promife to bate me twenty Pound a Year ; for I have paid him two hundred Pounds a Year thefe fixteen Years, for that Land which is not worth an Hundred and four-fcore.

Lov. Say you fo, Mr. *Trufty?* Then you muft perform your Father's Promife, Sir *John.*

Conft, Ay, when he has paid me as much as he has my Father.

Lov, Come, fhall I fettle Matters between you? Advance

vance Sir *John* a hundred Pounds ; you know he has been kept fhort, and doubtlefs has Occafion for ready Money, and he fhall bate you twenty Pound a Year.

Tru. Oh, that's all one, Mr. *Lovely*—I can't do that.

Conft. Nay, fince Mr. *Lovely* has propos'd it, if you won't do that———

Tru. Well, but Sir *John*, perhaps you'll expect a large Fortune with my Daughter ; I can't tell you how to———

Conft. I afk you for none, Sir.

Tru. Why then there's the hundred Pound ; but you muft fignify at the Bottom of this Leafe our Bargain.

Enter Roger, *a Farmer.*

Conft. Give it me, I'll do't.——— [*fits down to write.*

Rog. Morrow, Landlord, I ha' brought you a little Rent, and in troth 'tis but a little neither ; for we ha' had but a' forry Crop of Barley, and the Crows, a Murrain take 'em, ha' eat up all my Beans, I think.

Tru. But you have a new Landlord, *Roger.* Old Sir *Jeffrey* is dead, and there's his Son.

Rog. Say you fo ; Mafter ! Blefs you, Sir, I did not know your Father, not I, tho' I have paid him many a fair Pound———Nor I dan't know you ; but an you be my Landlord, I'm an honeft Man ; and tho' I fay it, pay my Rent as well as any body.

Conft. I don't doubt it, Friend—I am forry your Harveft has not prov'd fo good as you expcted.

Rog. I hope, Mafter, for Luck's fake now, you'll 'bates me fomething of my Rent.

Conft. I can't do that, *Roger*—For taxes takes away all my Money———

Rog. Nay, as you fay, Mafter, thefe Taxes are fad Things, that's the Truth on't—Od they find out ftrange Ways ; they had got a Trick here once to make one pay for one's Head—Mercy on us, I was afraid they wou'd make one pay for one's Tail too—My Neighbour *What de call um*———fays it coft him the Lord knows what in Buryings and Chriftnings———Adod 'tis a fore Thing, a Man muft pay for lying with his own Wife.

Lov. Ha, ha, ha, 'tis a Grievance indeed ; but Taxes can't be help'd fo long as the Wars continue.

Rog. Wars ! Why what need there be any Wars?

Can't

Can't People live peaceably and quietly among themfelves —If they will fquabble and play the Rogue, let 'em go to Law ; can't they fet the Lawyers to work ! I warrant they'll quickly make them as quiet as Lambs.

Conft. Ha, ha, ha ; but we are at Wars with a Prince that cares for no Laws but his own ; nay, he breaks them too, when 'tis his Intereft.——

Rog. Why then Mercy upon us, I say—Well an how ! may one wifh you much Joy ? Ha, you got a Wife, Landlord ? By the Mefs you are a pretty Man.——

Conft. I'm not fo happy yet, *Roger.*

Rog. Say you fo? Good lack, I'm forry for't.—Why now here's Mafter *Trufty* has a good fweatly look'd Genlewoman to his Daughter—What think you of her, Landlord ?—Od, and all Parties was agreed, fhe'd make a rare Bedfellow, I perfuaded.

Lov. I believe Sir *John* is of your Mind ; have you any Intereft with her Father?

Rog. Not I, in troth, Mafter *Lovely*—but the Gentlewoman is of a fweet Temper.

Lov. Do you think you cou'd perfuade her to run away with him.

Rog. Wou'd I cou'd. Sir——for a pretty Woman is the beft Luggage in the World—for when a Man is weary, he may reft upon it ; ha, ha.

Conft. You are waggifh, *Roger.*

Trusty. Yes, yes, *Roger* will joke ; there's your Acquittance, if Sir *John* pleafe to fign it.——

Conft. 'Tis the fame Thing if you fign it, Mr. *Trusty.*

[*Signs the Note.*

Trusty. I find my Daughter ftands fair in your Opinion, *Roger.*

Rog. Look ye, Sir—I hope you arn't angry ! I meant no harm———I fpoke as I thought ; an I had a hundred Daughters———my Landlord, and Mr. *Lovely* fhould have them all, an they wou'd ; ha, ha.

Conft. I am obliged to you truly.

Lov. Oh ! a hundred wou'd be too many.

Conft. Prithee haft thou never a fingle one at present?

Rog. Not that I know of, in troth, Sir ; but an you'll do me a small Kindnefs, Sir, I may chance to get you one about fourteen Years hence.

Lov.

The Devil to do about her. 109

Lov. That will be fomething too long to ftay.

Conft. But what can I ferve thee in, *Roger*?

Rog. Why, Mrs. *Belinda* has a kind of a Maid called *Dorothy* ; I have had a hankering Mind after her thefe two Years ; but the fliving Baggage will not come to a Resolution yet.

Tru. You muft apply yourfelf to my Daughter, *Roger*, fhe'll be the beft Advocate ; but I doubt fhe's too fine for you.

Rog. Too fine ! nay, nay, I'll never quarrel with her for that ; and fhe can win Gold, as the Saying is, e'en let her wear it.

Tru. But I doubt you are not fine enough for her.

Rog. Mayhap fo, as you fay ; indeed, I have not fuch gay Clothes as thefe Gentlefolk have, becaufe I can't afford it, de ye fee ? elfe I fhou'd like 'em well enough—— In troth, I believe I have fome Seeds of a Gentleman in me ; for methinks now I like broad Cloath better than my Leathern Breeches ; and a Holland Shirt, far before a Hempen one—adod methinks, I, I, I, cou'd be well enough contented with a Bottle of Wine every Day——I am mainly inclin'd to ftrong Beer—and don't care a Farthing if I never were to drink any fmall.

Lov. Oh ! extraordinary Symptoms of a Gentleman, I'll affure you—Well, we'll fpeak to *Dolly* for you.

Tru. Ay, ay, we'll all fpeak for you ; go, go into the Cellar then, and drink thy Belly full.

Con. Be fure to drink *Dolly's* Health.

Rog. Thank you kindly, Sir—Ay, ay, Mafter, that I will, I promife you, in a full Horn—So, Landlord, good-by to you with all my Heart. [*Exit.*

Tru. Now, Sir *John*, I'll fend my Daughter to keep you Company, till I look for fome Leafes your Father order'd me to get drawn, which, if you think fit to fign——

Con. If the Tenants are able Men, with all my Heart.

Tru. Oh ! very fufficient Men, Sir *John*. [*Ex.* Trufty.

Lov. Well, thou haft fecured the Money, *Conftant* ; and my Advice is to difpatch the Woman, as faft as you can, and find fome Pretence to defer thefe Leafes for two or three Days—Sir *Jeffrey* is whimfical, and if he fhou'd alter his Mind, and come down.———

Con.

Con. Here wou'd be no ſtaying for me, if he ſhou'd ; therefore I deſign to be as quick as poſſible——but here comes the Star that guides me to Happineſs

Enter Belinda *and* Maria.

Lov. And my Pilot——
Mar. What Voyage are you for, pray?
Lov. The everlaſting Voyage of Matrimony, Child :— And your Eyes are two ſuch dangerous Rocks, that nothing but your Tongue can ſteer me into Harbour.
Mar. But any of my Sex can ſteer you out ; you'll be for cruſing from Port to Port, to make that everlaſting Voyage agreeable.
Lov. No, Faith, where I drop my Anchor, there my Veſſel is moor'd for Life.——Well, *Conſtant*, what ſays the Eady? will ſhe let thy *Habeas Corpus* remove her?
Bel. Out of one Priſon into another, is it not ſo, *Con-ſtant*?
Lov. Interrogating ! Nay, then 'tis proper to be alone ; there is a very pretty Collection of Prints in the next Room, Madam, will you give me leave to explain them to you?
Mar. Any Thing that may divert your Love-Subject.
[*Exit*
Con. Can *Belinda* term my Arms a Priſon?
Bel. But Marriage is a Fetter, *Conſtant*.
Con. I'll not make it one ; I'm a true *Britiſh* Subject, I'm for Liberty and Property.——
Bel. And Self-Intereſt, for they are inſeparable.
Con. I hope our Intereſts are the ſame, and when link'd, will be the ſtronger. Come, Madam, conſider our Opportunity may be ſhort, we ought to be quick, to prevent Diſcovery ; I have your Father's Conſent,
Bel. Diſcovery ! why, what is it you fear? 'tis but reaſonable I be let into the Secret, if I'm in Danger of ſharing the Puniſhment, Sir *John*.
Con. Why that Sir *John, Belinda?* I know you are inform'd of all, then do not ridicule my ardent Paſſion ; 'twas my Love for you that firſt inſpir'd me with this Stratagem ; then prithee come, my deareſt.——
[*Taking her Hand.*
Bel.

The Devil to do about her.

Bel. Not a ſtep, ſweet Servant—I'll know upon what Terms I capitulate, e'er I ſurrender.

Con. Terms! Madam! Has not *Dolly* told you of the Plot?

Bel. Yes, upon your Father and mine, Captain, but I don't think it ſafe to join in it! Suppoſe my Father be oblig'd to pay back this Money; may not that be Provocation enough to diſown me? and if your's ſhou'd for this Trick diſinherit you?——What Jointure can you make me?

Con. My Heart, Madam.

Bel. Pſhaw! that is the ſlippery'ſt Piece in all Fortune's Treaſure—we never can be certain of that——

Con. Then my Soul.

Bel. Where ſhall I find it? The Learned can't agree where to place it; therefore I'll have no Trouble about that.

Con. Then take my Body for Bail, that I'm ſure is forth-coming.

Bel. Ay, but there's No — *Ne exeat Regnum* in Love's Court——

Con. To cut off all Objeᴄtions, I ſettle this Money upon you; and either put it out to Intereſt, or purchaſe ſome pretty Retirement; where if *Belinda* loves but half ſo well, as I flattere'd myſelf ſhe did, I can forſake all Courts and Company — and prefer a Grott with her, before all the Trappings of the Fools of Fortune——

Bel. Generouſly ſaid! I have try'd thee, *Conſtant*; and find thy Nature like thy Name; there take my Hand—my Heart was thine before.

Con. *'Tis Sympathy of Souls that joins us two,*
Death only shall our Gordion Knot undo.

Bel. *Until that Hour,* Belinda *will be true.*

Re-enter Lovely *and* Maria.

Lov. Joy to thee, my Friend; and you, Madam, we over-heard your Proteſtations——

Con. Prithee let's fetch the Parſon this Minute.

Lov. To chuſe—Ladies, we'll return inſtantly. [*Exit.*

Mar. Proſperity to *Belinda*!

Bel. Dare not you bear me Company, Girl? Have you the Heart to let me run this Hazard alone?

Mar.

Mar. Why, what wou'd you have me do?

Bel. Even what I defign to do—Marry—for I'm sure thou lov'ft that handfome young Fellow.

Mar. I find you uńderftand your own Conftitution, *Belinda*.

Bel. So well; that if you follow my Example, you'll act as refolutely.

Mar. Thine is a rafh Venture, if Sir *Jeffrey* fhou'd not forgive him.

Bel. The more honourable; we have Love, and that's the beft Eftate in a married Life.

Mar. True, but what can we poor Women do, whofe Parents are not inclin'd to grant our Wifhes;——you know mine are fet againft the Match———

Bel. Pugh, Parents will relent in Time——If not, Mr. *Lovely* has Fortune enough to make you happy—You love him, and he loves yon; were I in your Place, I'd fain fee a third fhou'd part us.

Mar. True, I do love him—but will not marry him, without a Portion; he fhall never throw that in my Difh, I refolve.

Bel. An admirable Refoluticn truly——Then you'll go on; hang your Head, crofs your Arms, figh your Soul into the Air—fit up all Night like a Watch-Candle, and diftil your Brains through your Eye-lids——for fo I have done——no, no, Girl, e'en let us fave our Tears, till we are married.

Mar. What, you think like moft Wives, we fhall have Occafion for them then, ha, ha.

Bel. As it may fall out——Then let us marry whilft we are young, that we may be able to bear it with the better Courage.——But here's my Father over Head and Ears in Papers; I tremble though, to think what he will fay when he finds the Cheat.

Enter Trufty, *with Papers in his Hand.*

Mar. And fee who is behind him—— [*Enter* Num *and* Slouch.

Bel. I have a fudden Thought how to divert my Father's Anger; when all's difcover'd, I'll put it in practice. ———Sir, your humble Servant.

Num.

The Devil to do about her.

Num. Od, fhe fpeaks, *Slouch*——Nay, Madam, I'm your humble Servant.

Tru. Ha! what's that?—Why, Sir, I admire—hey-day, where are the Gentlemen, Daughter?

Num. Gentlemen, Sir, why here is one Gentleman; indeed I can't fay much for *Slouch*——

Tru. Why don't you anfwer me, ha?

Bel. I know not, Sir, they went out foon after we entered.

Mar. They whifper'd, Sir, and left the Room.

Tru. Ah! I don't like that——

Slou. May-hap they are gone to fight for Mrs. *Belinda*. An fhe'd marry you, Mafter, now, how rarely they'd be chous'd, ha, ha.

Num. Od, fo they wou'd, as you fay, *Slouch*—— Madam, what fay you? Mr. *Trufty*, fhall we make an end on't? I know you are a merry Man, and did but joke wi' me.

Tru. Say you fo! I doubt you won't find it fo, Sir.

Num. No! Why I verily believe the Gentlewoman has a Kindnefs for me, by her Looks; how fay you, Miftrefs? fpeak the Truth, and fhame the Devil, as the Saying is— han't you?

Bel. Well, if I muft fpeak the Truth, 'Squire, I have as much Kindnefs for you as for anybody; my Father commanded me to love.

Trufty. Ay! why what fay you to Sir *John Conftant?* Don't you like him better?

Bel. I did once, Sir, but I don't remember I ever had your Confent in that.

Trufty. You have it now then—'Tis time enough; it is good to know what one has to truft to.

Bel. Your Leave now, Sir, comes too late, he may have chang'd his Mind.

Trufty. No, no, you fhall be married to-Night, he fhan't have time to think of Change.

Num. Look ye, Sir, fair and foftly—he shall not have her to Night, may-hap—for all your hafte; *Slouch*, ftand by me.

Slou. That I will, Mafter, in any Ground in *England*.

Mar Humph! I guefs her drift——

Bel. Then 'tis time for me to think on't Sir.

Trufty.

Trusty. Hey-day, what's here now?
Bel. I don't like Matches huddled up in haste; and I learn't from your Instructions, Sir, to consult my future Happiness in a marry'd State.
Num. Good again, I'faith, ha, ha.
Trusty. Your future Happiness! Why, what can cross your future Happiness, Mistress?
Num. What, will they quarrel about me now, *Slouch*, ha?
Slou. The Woman has a woundy Mind to you, I see that, Master.
Bel. Sir *John*'s Carriage is more loose and familiar than formerly——from which I draw this Conclusion, Sir; that he thinks his Quality may now command, and when a Lover loses Respect, his Sincerity quickly follows. I like not the Method of our Quality—The Name of Husband without the Fondness, is like a Title without an Estate, of no value with the Wife.
Mar. I am of her Opinion, Sir.
Num. And I too, Faith——Od, she talks rarely; I shall have her, I find——In my Conscience I love her ten times the better, because I see she loves me——and let me tell you, Sir, your Daughter is honester than you are— Why shou'd you pretend to cross her Will? You plainly see, she has a Mind to no body but me——Mun——
Tru. I plainly see you are a Fool, and she's another—
Num. Look ye, say what you will o' me, but don't affront her; for all you are her Father, I won't let my Wife be call'd Names, de ye see.
Tru. Zounds, get out of my Doors.
Num. Ay, but who is the Fool then?
Bel. Pray be calm; since you once lik'd the Squire for a Son-in-law, I hope I shan't disoblige you in preferring him before Sir *John* for a Husband.
Num. Disoblige him! who cares if it does, Madam: Come along——
. *Mar.* Ha, ha. If thy Father shou'd take thee at thy Word, *Belinda*?
Bel. My Stars forbid———
Tru. Did you ever see such a provoking Creature?
Enter Constant *and* Lovely.
Oh, Sir *John*, 'tis well you are come——Where have you

The Devil to do about her.

you been; You are in Danger of lofing your Miftrefs here.
Con. I hope, Sir, I have taken the beft Way to fecure her.
Lov. If the Parfon can do it, for we have got him in the next Room.
Bel. To Conftant.] Humour what I fay——
Tru. Now Miftrefs, you had beft bring your Objections again, and fpoil your Fortune.
Bel. To Num.] If you dare maintain your Claim to me, I am yours--I fay again, Sir, I like the Squire beft.
Num. Dare ! od, I, I, I, I, dare a, a.
Con. What dare you do, Sir ?
Num. What a Plague do you ftare at fo ?
Con. What was that you mutter'd ! What dare you do ?
Num. I dare do as much as you dare do——What a Pox, I'm not to be frighted wi' Looks, mun.
Slo. Od, take heed, Mafter, he has a woundy long Sword.
Num. A Sword ! I care not a——for his Sword, nor him neither.   [*Walks about in a Heat.*
Mar. Ha, ha, ha.
Bel. Ha, ha, ha, Sir *John*, this Gentleman is a Perfon whom I efteem.
Num. Ay, Sir, and one that fhe intends to marry too.
Con. Marry ! when, Sir?
Num. When fhe pleafes, Sir ; now, an you'll lend us your Parfon ?
Lov. Ay, 'tis fit you afk him Leave indeed !
Con. I'll lend you my Sword in your Guts firft.
Num. Your Sword in my Guts——*Slouch*, give me your Cudgel   [*Snatches his Stick.*
Slou. Ads Blead, clear the Way, clear the Way ; I'll turn the 'Squire loofe to any Man in *Zomerfetfhire.*
Num. Come, out with your Spit, mun——Wounds, and I don't make ye put it up again, I'll ne'er ftrike ftroke more.
Con. The Devil, he'll knock me down. [*Lays his Hand on his Sword.*
Tru. Oh don't draw, Sir *John*——Lay down your Stick, Sir, and get you about your Bufinefs, or you'll oblige me to ufe you worfe than I am willing to do.
Mar. Excellent Sport, ha, ha.   *Lov.*

Lov. Incomparable, ha, ha.

Bel. Who cou'd have thought the Lout fo courageous —Oh pray let us have no fighting.

Tru. You have had your Anfwer, Sir, therefore pray be gone quietly.

Bel. You 'fright me out of my Wits, 'Squire ; pray go out of my Father's Houfe peaceably; if you love me, do, we'll find fome other Way.

Num. Love ye, yes, I do love you ; or what makes me in fuch a Paffion, think you ? Well, well, I will go out——Look ye, Sir, an you be a Man, follow me ; I'll box fairly with you now for half a Crown, and this Gentleman fhall hold Stakes, and fee fair Play——If you dare now?

Lov. Fie, fie, 'Squire, Gentlemen don't ufe to box.

Con. Box, ye Blockhead, ha, ha, ha.

Num. Blockhead ! ——Zounds, I'll learn you to call Names. [*Strips off his Coat.*

Slou. Come on Sirrah, I'll fight with you at the fame Time—(*begins to ftrip.*) I'll ftand by my Mafter, for the Honour of *Zomerfetfhire.*

Clin. Death, you fhamble ham'd Dog ! I'll beat your Head off—— [*Give him a Box of the Ear.*

Num. Ay ! are you there ? Faith, come on—come on. [*Falls foul upon* Clinch.

Lov. Hold, hold, two to one is odds. [*Parts them.*

Clin. Let me alone, Sir, egad I'll fight 'em both.

Bel. Ha, ha, ha, what do you do, 'Squire, fight with a Footman ! Pray leave off, or you'll difoblige me for ever.

Tru. Oh Lord, oh Lord ! What fhall I do ?

Num. What care I.

Mar. What don't you care for your Miftrefs ?

Num. Yes, yes, but I won't be made a Fool on ; but I will go——an I were fure you wou'd not be forc'd to marry this fame Spark——I won't leave you in the Lurch, Madam.

Bel. No, no, 'Squire, they fhall not force me, I [promife you.

Num. Then I go——but look to't, an I catch you out of this Houfe, by the Mafs I'll rib you. [*Exit.*

Om. Ha, ha, ha.

Tru.

The Devil to do about her. 117

Tru. Adod, I was out of all Patience with the Fool—Come, take her by the Hand, Sir *John*, you fhall be married this Minute, we'll fettle Bufinefs afterward.
Bel. Indeed, Sir, you'll repent this hafty Match.
Con. What means *Belinda* ?
Bel. You fhall know within.
Tru. Get along——In my Soul, I think the whole Compofition of Women is Contradiction. [*Ex. omnes.*

SCENE *Sir* David's *Houfe.*

Enter Faithful *and* Coachman.

Faith. There, honeft Coachman, drink my Health; but pray can't I fpeak with the Gentlewoman of the Houfe?
Coach. Sir *David* has no Wife, Sir; but here is a young Lady, I'll call her Maid; Mrs. *Lucy*, Mrs. *Lucy*, here is a Gentleman wou'd fpeak with your Miftrefs——

Enter Lucy.

Lucy. A Gentleman ! blefs me, how came you to let a Man in, *Thomas*, in Sir *David*'s Abfence ?
Coach. Sir *David* bid me himfelf, or you may be fure I had not done it——I thank you, Sir. [*Ex Coachman.*
Lucy. What do I fee ? Mr. *Faithful.*
Faith. The fame ! How fares my Love, my deareft *Laura* ? Quick bring me to her, I am impatient till I fee her.
Lucy. Nay, nay, fhe wou'd be as impatient as you, if fhe knew you were here——But by what Miracle did you prevail with Sir *David*?
Faith. Prithee afk no Queftions—I'll inform thy Lady; hafte, my Time's but fhort, therefore muft improve it.
Lucy. Well, follow me then. [*Exit.*

The SCENE *draws, and difcovers Mrs.* Laura *at her Spinet.*

After the Song, enter Lucy *and* Faithful.

Lau. What did that Blockhead bawl fo for, *Lucy* ?
Lucy. To have an Acquaintance of yours admitted, Madam.

Lau.

Lau. An Acquaintance of mine!—Ha! my dear *Faithful*! Am I awake? and is it really he?

Faith. My deareſt Love—(*Run into one another's Arms.*) Oh let me hold thee here for ever, for ever taſte the Nectar on theſe Lips——There is ſtill the ſame Fragrancy, as when we parted laſt.

Lau. Oh! it was a fatal Parting—Say, my Love, how cam'ſt thou here? for the old Monſter allows no Mortal to viſit me.

Faith. By Stratagem, my Dear; he ſent me hither in his Coach, yet knows not I am come; thou ſhalt have the Story at more convenient Leiſure; but now let us employ our Time to advantage.

Lau. Heavens! how I tremble! He'll ſoon be back, for he's never out above half an Hour.—*Lucy*, watch below. [*Exit.*] What can this ſhort Interview avail us? which Way ſhall I get out of his Power? The nauſeous Goat told *Lucy* he deſigned to marry me himſelf—and caſts ſuch loving Looks every time he ſees me, that I am half diſtracted, leſt he ſhould give his horrid Paſſion vent.

Faith. Ha! Confound his Paſſion with himſelf—Conſent to fly with me to a Friend's Houſe in Town, where we'll be married, and put it out of his Power to confine thee.

Lau. With all my Heart——My Priſon is ſo odious to me, I need but ſmall Intreaties to make me quit it—— This is the Cloſet he keeps my Writings in; if we cou'd contrive to get them along with us, or he'll give us Trouble enough to get 'em out of his Hand; here—don't you think one might wrinch it open?

Faith. So he may proſecute us for a Robbery.

Lau. Let him, I'll meddle with nothing of his.

Enter Lucy *haſtily.*

Lucy. Oh Madam! there's Sir *David* in a violent Paſſion, beating all the Servants in before him.

Lau. Undone! What ſhall I ſay? what will become of thee?

Faith. Sink the Villain——Have Patience, my deareſt, take no Thought for me; ſeem not to know me; pretend Surprize, and beg me to be gone; leave the reſt to me.

Enter

The Devil to do about her.

Enter Sir David, *beating his Men in upon the Stage.*
Sir *Dav.* Ye Dogs, what have you done, ha?
Coach. What do you beat me for? Did you not bid me carry him home?
Sir *Dav.* Zounds, not to my Home, you Rafcal. [*Beats him.*
Faith. What do you mean, Madam, by faying you don't know me? 'Sdeath, did not I lodge here laſt Night?
Sir *Dav.* How's this? how's this?
Lau. No indeed, Sir, I never faw you before; neither do we let Lodgings, then pray be anfwer'd.
Faith. A very pretty Trick, faith! What, have you a Mind to cheat me of my Horfes, and Portmanteau—— Look ye, Madam, this won't pafs upon me.
Sir *Dav.* No, nor upon me, neither, Sir.
Faith. Sir, your humble Servant; I think I have had the Honour to fee you fomewhere. I am in difpute with this Gentlewoman here; fhe'd fain perfuade me I have miſtook my Inn——and that I did not lie here laſt Night.
Sir *Dav.* Lie here! Why, do you take this Lady for an Hoſteſs, Sir?
Faith. Nay, Sir, fhe is very handfome—but why the Devil muſt Beauty make her deny her Calling?——Ad, you Country Gentlemen do fo kifs and flatter your Land-ladies, that egad, they don't know where their Tails hang ——but we make them know themfelves in *London*—— Once more, will you call your Servants?
Sir *Dav.* Oh the Devil! ye Dogs, I'll be reveng'd on you. [*Beats his Servants, they run off.*
Sam. The Fault's not mine, Sir; *Thomas* bid me let him in.
Faith. What, no Attendance yet? So, ho, Tapſter, Chamberlain——Pray Sir, fit down——I warrant I'll make fomebody hear—Heark ye, you Miſtreſs—You are not above your Bufinefs too, are you? [*To* Lucy.
Sir *Dav.* Oh, oh, oh, I fhall go diſtraƈted.
Lucy. Pray, Sir, know your way out, don't think I am one of your Wenches.
Faith. Good lack; ha, ha, what are you a fine Lady too? The Devil! Sure this is a Bawdy-houfe——
Sir *Dav.* I dare fwear you'd make it one, if you cou'd—
Faith. Sir, I take this for an extraordinary Inn—Pray do

do me the Favour to fit——I'll beat the Chamber down, but I'll make fomebody come up. So, ho, the Houfe here—— [*Stamps*.

Sir Dav. A plague fplit you, what do you make all this Noife for? Oh, oh.

Lau. Pray, Sir *David*, humour the Gentleman, for I fancy he is a little befide himfelf.

Sir Dav. Humour the Devil! Hell and Furies! This muft be fome Rogue——Here, where are you, Rafcals?

Enter Servants.

Faith. Ay, Scoundrels, where are you? Ye Dogs, what is the Reafon we can have no Attendance? (*Strikes one of them.*) Fetch us a Bottle of Claret, Sirrah, and bring us Word what we can have to eat——

Sir Dav. Bring a Bottle of Claret! bring a Halter—— What do you ftrike my Servants for? ha, Sir.

Faith. Your Servants, Sir! They are my Servants, as long as I pay for what I call for——Ho! I find you are the Landlord of this well-govern'd Inn—Make your People more tractable, do you hear, Sir? Or I fhall not only beat them, but you too——Death, ye Villains, why don't you ftir? [*Strikes another.*

Lau. What will be the End of this? All my Comfort lies in his Affurance.——

Sir Dav. Zounds, let him ftir if he dares——Get out of my Houfe, Sirrah, or I'll lay you by the Heels; don't put your Shams upon us——Don't bully here; I thought you was wounded when I lent you my Coach—But I find you are a Rogue, and either defigned to rob my Houfe, or ravifh this Lady—Fetch me a Conftable quickly; the Devil! I'll box with you, if you're for Boxing——Get into that Room, *Laura*, I'll deal with him I warrant ye—
[*Puts* Laura *in.*

Lau. Oh unfortunate! How fhall I ever fee him again?

Faith. I'll be here about an Hour hence before this Door. [*To* Lucy.

Lucy. Ah! but to what Purpofe?

Sir Dav. I thought you were wounded when I lent you my Coach.

Faith. Wounded, Sir! why fo I am, and my Wounds bleed

bleed afreſh with vexation——Was it your Coach? I find I was miſtaken then, you are not my Landlord; I aſk your Pardon, Sir.

Enter Manage, *running.*

Sir *Dav.* Rot your Pardon—How now, who the Devil are you, Sir?

Man. I am this Gentleman's Servant—Bleſs me, Sir, what do you do here? Why Sir *John* and Mr. *Lovely* have been ſearching all the Town for you; they brought a Surgeon to the *Talbot*, and not finding you there, nor no where elſe, ſent me to aſk this Gentleman's Coachman where he drove you to, and ſwear if you be not found preſently, they'll indict the Coachman for your Murther.

Sir *Dav.* I wou'd you were all hang'd for Company; why, what a plaguy Miſtake was here?—

Faith. Ha! A lucky Hint——Bleſs me, Sir, I am under the greateſt Confuſion imaginable; can you forgive me, Sir? Upon my Honour, I thought I had been in my Inn; I aſk a thouſand Pardons, pray excuſe me to the Lady.

Sir *Dav.* Oh, Sir, never trouble your Head about the Lady.

Faith. Why, Sir, I'm a Gentleman.

Sir *Dav.* A Gentleman, Sir! and what then, Sir?

Faith. And am Maſter of an Eſtate to ſupport that Character, Sir.

Sir *Dav.* Zounds, was ever Man ſo plagu'd, to have his Servants kick'd about like Foot-balls, his Houſe thunder'd about his Ears like a common Inn, then to be told impudently, I'm a Gentleman, and have an Eſtate to ſupport that Character?

Faith. I aſk your Pardon agen, Sir, for the unlucky Accident, in miſtaking your Houſe; but cannot apprehend what Crime I have committed in my Apology.

Sir *Dav.* Sir, without any manner of Apology, I wou'd be very proud to wait on you down Stairs.

Faith. By no means, Sir—I muſt not permit that.

Sir *Dav.* Death and the Devil, begone without it, then.

Faith. That I will, Sir; but intreat the Favour of ſeeing the Lady firſt; upon Honour I was never ſo concern'd in my Life; I wou'd not for five hundred Pound quit the Houſe

House, till I have convinc'd her of my Error, and made my Acknowledgment upon my Knees.

Sir *Dav.* Zounds, here's the Devil to do about her—Which Way shall I get rid of him?

Faith. Pray Mistress, inform the Lady of my Resolution. [*So* Lucy.

Sir *Dav.* Hark ye, Huswife, stir out of this Place, and I'll break your Neck down Stairs.

Faith. Why then I must be guilty of a second Rudeness to acquit myself of the first, I think that's the Room the Lady went into, Sir. [*Going towards the Door.*

Sir *Dav.* Hold, hold, hold, Sir; where the Devil are you going?—Zounds, advance one Step farther, and I'll indict you for a Robbery.

Faith. Well, since you are so positive, Sir, I will be gone; but pray, Sir, is the Lady your Grand-daughter, Daughter, Niece, Cousin, or, or——

Sir *Dav.* 'Tis my Wife, my Wife, my Wife, my Wife, Sir, do you hear that and tremble.

Faith. Ods my Life, Sir, I beg your Pardon with all my Heart and Soul——Your most Obedient, humble Servant. [*Exit.*

Sir *Dav.* The Devil go with you.

Man. (*To* Lucy) My Master has not a Souse of Money, else you wou'd not want your Fee. We were robb'd coming down. [*Exit.*

Sir *Dav.* Zounds, Sir, what do you loyter here for? Why don't you go after your Master? Goe troop.

[*Turns him out.*

Sir *Dav.* What do you sauntring here, get in to your Mistress! What, does your Chops water at the Sight of a Man, ha?

Lucy. I'm sure you are the worst Sight I cou'd have seen at present. [*Exit.*

Sir *Dav.* I don't understand this Mistake tho'——He is a strapping young Dog; I wish *Laura* had not seen him—But I'll go see if he is gone, lest there should be more Roguery at the Bottom. [*Exit.*

ACT

ACT IV.

Enter on one Side Faithful *and* Manage ; *on the other* Conſtant *and* Clinch.

Con. Faithful, well met, I was going in ſearch of thee ; my Affairs are ended, what Hopes of thine. Did the Project turn to thy Advantage?

Faith. It gave me Entrance to the charming Fair, who receiv'd me with equal Tranſport ; but juſt as ſhe conſented to come away with me, the old Fox return'd—A Curſe of his Diligence——

Man. I came timely to my Maſter's Reſcue, Sir ; and when his Pockets are repleniſh'd, I hope he'll own it.

Faith. That I will, *Manage.*

Con. 'Tis now in my Power to lend thee Twenty Pieces, Friend——There they are—— [*Gives Money.*

Faith. I thankfully accept them ; and next the finiſhing my own Wiſhes, I am pleas'd thou haſt gain'd thine ; but after what Method to purſue mine, Heaven knows ; I told *Lucy* I wou'd be about the Door in an Hour, but I know not if 'twill be in *Laura's* Power to get out, or what can diſguiſe me ; Sir *David* will certainly know me again, if he ſees me——The Time is well nigh expir'd.

Man. I have a Thought !——Cou'd you procure my Maſter a red, or blue Coat, in this Town, think you, Sir?

Con. I have my Regimental Surtout I rid down in, you know.

Man. Right, that will do ; I told him I ſerv'd an Officer ; I warrant we'll paſs upon him—Come, ſtrip *Clinch*, ſtrip ; give me my Cloaths again——(*Strips and changes with* Clinch *again.*) But 'tis neceſſary, Sir, that you change your Wig too.

Con. And what if you put a Patch croſs your Cheek, like a Scar?

Faith. With all my Heart—I muſt, and will redeem her, or cut his Throat.

Con. Nay, Twenty thouſand Pound gives an Edge to Invention.

Clin. So now I am in *Statu quo.*

Faith. Were ſhe not Miſtreſs of a Groat, I ſhou'd prefer her before the moſt celebrated Beauty in the Kingdom ;

our

124 *The Man's bewitch'd; or,*

our Infant Years firſt ſowed the Seeds of Love, which, as we grew, ripen'd to a perfect Paſſion; her Parents dying, left her to the Care of mine; oh, in what Pleaſure have we paſt the Day, and quarrell'd with the Night that call'd us from each other! Whilſt I made the Campaign with you, Captain, my Father died! Oh fatal Thought, her Friends remov'd her to this Sir *David Watchum*'s, 'tis twelve Months ſince, during which Time, 'till now, I never cou'd find Means to ſee or hear from her.

Con. I know the Story perfectly well, and wiſh thou may'ſt ſucceed with all my Soul; but I find he is upon his Guard——

Faith. If he cou'd ſummon Hell to guard her, I will by Pclicy or Force releaſe her.

Man. Why then, pray reſolve upon which immediately; ſhall we lay open Siege, or blockade his Citadel. The Head muſt always work before the Hand——Now, tis neceſſary. e'er we attempt, to know the weakeſt and ſtrongeſt Parts; then we open our Trenches and cannonade the Place, ruin their Ramparts, make a Breach, and then give the Aſſault, take the old Rogue by the Throat, plunder his Caſtle, and carry off the Booty——Which is the Lady, Sir?——

Con. Ha, ha, ha, *Manage* talks like a Soldier.

Faith. Ah, if we cou'd do that *Manage!* I have good Intereſt in the Town——And they have Notice of my coming——

Man. So much the better; the more Friends we have in the Garriſon, the ſooner we ſhall become Maſters of it ——Well. as I am chief Engineer, and have the Artillery, I muſt ſurvey the Ground to find the moſt convenient Place to raiſe my Battery. But away, away, Sir, and diſguiſe yourſelf; the Drum beats—leave the reſt to Fortune, ſhe cannot always run againſt us——I have known the Sun riſe upon a private Centinel——who before his Setting was a Captain of Foot—Nothing like Diligence and Courage to nick the fickle Jade.

Con. Come, thou ſhalt be dreſs'd in a moment, [*Ex. omn.*

SCENE, *The Out-ſide of Sir* David's *Houſe; Sir* David *in the Garden before his Door.*

Sir *Dav.* I remember a Saying of a certain Philoſopher,

The Devil to do about her. 125

pher, That nothing is harder to keep than a Secret: but I think 'tis ten Times harder to keep a handfome Woman ——I am ſtrangely affected with this laſt Accident; and then the t'other Rogue that was here in the Morning, that ſerves an Officer——A Pox on thefe Officers——for they have more Stratagems in their Heads, than all the Kingdom befides. But I have order'd the Smith to barricade my Windows, from the Cellar to the Garret; he'll be here immediately, but *Laura* muſt not fee him——Poor Girl, ſhe's terribly frighted at my Dog of a Coachman's Miſtake; I have invited her into the Garden, here ſhe and her Maid comes.

Enter Laura *and* Lucy.

Lau. What favourable Devil, *Lucy*, has procur'd us this Liberty? It happens as I wou'd have it, if *Faithful* be but here now.

Lucy. I'm amaz'd—For 'tis the firſt freſh open Air you have breath'd thefe twelve Months, Madam. But ſuppofe Mrs. *Faithful* ſhou'd be here! Yonder's the old *Argus*, he refolves to watch you, I fee.

Lau. Nay then!

Sir *Dav.* Well, Madam, how do you after your Fright? I ſent for you into the Garden, to take the Air——The Air is good after a Fright——

Lau. Ay, if one cou'd change the Place too, Sir *David*; but the Air of my Chamber and this is much the ſame—But let me be where I will, if you are there, I find no Difference in the Air—I know not what ails me, but when I fee you, I ſigh as often as I draw Breath.

Sir *Dav.* Ha! ſhe loves me. Oh happy *David*—— Indeed, Madam! And are thofe Sighs pleafant or painful, pray?

Lau. Oh, very painful, Sir——

Sir *Dav* Then you muſt have a Huſband to cure thofe Sighs, Child.

Faithful *and* Manage *appear between the Scenes.*

Faith. She's here? Oh the charming Maid—but that old Monſter is with her.

Sir *Dav.* What think you of a married Life, *Laura?*

Lau. Of nothing better—I might diffemble like many of my Sex; exclaim againſt Marriage and Mankind;

F 3   profefs

The Man's bewitch'd; or,

profefs to die in a Cloyfter, or a Maid at large—Mafk my real Inclinations, feign Indifference to Love, and place all my Happinefs in my own Sex——but I have a Heart too fincere; and therefore frankly own, that the utmoft of my Ambition is to be a Wife.

Faith. To me, fhe means——Oh, how fhall I deliver her!

Lucy. Well faid, Madam; why fhou'd a Lady lofe the Prime of her Youth, when fhe may do fo much in her Generation? I refolve to follow your Example to a Hair.

Sir *Dav.* Good Wits jump——I refolve to marry too; I have every Day frefh Offers, very advantageous Offers, but my Heart is prepoffefs'd, dear *Laura*, for I will own it now, I love you exceedingly.

Lucy. So, now 'tis out.

Sir *Dav.* More, if poffible, than you love me.

Lau. That's very poffible, truly.

Faitth. Love her! Oh the rank old Goat; Death! that Confeffion has made me lofe all Patience.

Man. Hold, hold, Sir, pray be content a little.

Sir *Dav.* Come, don't blufh *Laura*, thy Sighs betray'd thy Love, but I'm difcreet.

Faith. Now do I long to tell him he lyes in his Throat.

Man. 'Egad, Sir, you had better lofe your Longings at this Time.

Lau. What do you fay, Sir——that I love you! your Opinion is fmall Proof of your Difcretion.

Sir *David.* Why fo, Child?

Lau. Becaufe you never was more miftaken in your Life; for inftead of loving you I hate you mortally.

Faith. Oh, bleffed Sound!

Sir *Dav.* Really! but why fo, prithee?

Lau. Nay, you love without Reafon; and perhaps I hate by the fame Rule.

Lucy. Well, Sir, if her Declaration be not fo kind as you wou'd have it, it is not the lefs fincere.

Sir *Dav.* Is it not, Gilflirt, after what I have done for her?

Lau. Yes, you have done for me, I thank you, Sir.

Lucy. Nay, pray be not angry, but ftate the Cafe right.

Lau. If Love has render'd me charming in your Eyes, confider how he has drawn you in mine.

Lucy.

The Devil to do about her. 127

Lucy. She's amiable, you ugly—She's gay, you morofe—She's generous, you a Mifer—She's fixteen, you fixty,—She has the fineſt Teeth in the World, you but one in your Head, and that ſhakes ; and the firſt fit of Coughing, good-by to it.

Man. A Deviliſh Wench. She has drawn him to a Hair.

Lau. Mark *Lucy's* Defcription, and then tell me if thefe be not irrefiſtible Charms, for one of my Age and Conſtitution.

Lucy. What Woman do you think, Sir, on this fide fourscore, would have fuch a Bedfellow?

Sir *Dav.* She fhall, Miſtrefs, or ſhe fhall have nobody, mark that ; and your Witticifms, Mrs. *Frippery*, fhall get you nothing——How now ! who do you want ?

[Faithful *and* Manage *come forward.*

Lau. My dear *Faithful!* I know him in all Difguifes ; how fhall I forbear running into his Arms?

Lucy. Have a care, Madam, if you difcover you know him, you'll never fee him more ; *Manage* has fome Plot in his Head, by his winking.

Sir *Dav.* What is it you look at, Sir ! why don't you fpeak ?

Man. Be calm, Sir, and take no notice of the Lady.

Faith. I was fo charm'd with the Finenefs of the Profpeƈt in that Moment you fpoke, Sir, I was not Maſter of my Tongue.

Sir *Dav.* And now you are Maſter of it, Sir, what have you to fay ?

Faith. Nothing, Sir ; only having the Misfortune to break my Chariot—I took a Walk this Way, till it is put in order again ; and coming by this Houfe, my Man told me that you entertain'd fome hard Thoughts of him, from fome Difcourfe that pafs'd between you to-day—So I prefum'd to call, to clear his Reputation.

Sir *Dav.* This is the Officer ! A Rogue in red now ; and the Simple-hunter with him—I don't like 'em——As for that, Sir, you need not give yourfelf farther Trouble, for I have nothing to do with his Reputation, nor yours neither.

Faith. I hope 'tis no Offence to look about me a little ; this Houfe is finely fituated——'Tis the beſt Air I have breath'd this Twelve-month.

F 4 Sir

Sir *Dav.* Pox o' your Compliment—That's your Miftake, Sir; 'tis the worſt Air in the Univerſe——Let me adviſe you to get out of it as faſt as you can; for 'tis very fatal to Strangers.

Lau. He tells you Truth, Sir; for ever ſince I breath'd this Air, I have neither eat, drank, or ſlept with Eaſe.

Faith. I am ſorry for that, Madam; but I find a quite contrary Effect; methinks I feel new Life, and I have a ſtrong Hope to carry off the Health I wiſh.

Sir *Dav.* I wiſh, Sir, your Legs would be pleas'd to carry off your Body.

Faith. Sir, I will not be troubleſome——but I deſire you wou'd give me leave to take a view of your Gardens; I have bought me a ſmall Seat in a Country Village, and I deſign to have a pretty Garden made.

Sir *Dav.* Ah! wou'd you were buried in the Garden—go, get in, Gentlewoman, go—he has no Buſineſs with you, you don't belong to the Garden.

Man. (*To* Lucy.) Find ſome Way to bring your Lady down again; do you hear? let her pretend——

[*Whiſpers to* Lucy.

Lucy. Yes, yes, I hear; but how to put it in Practice, I know not.

Lau. I am diſtracted! Oh Invention! where art thou? Help me Brains, or ceaſe to think.

Sir *Dav.* What do you loiter for, ha? get in—

Lucy. Sir *David*, you uſe us like Slaves; ſend us in and out at Pleaſure——Is my Lady a Perſon to be treated ſo by her Guardian? Theſe twelve Months we have not ſeen the Shadow of any Hat but yours—I'm ſure nothing that's Male has reach'd our Eyes.

Sir *Dav.* Why, how now, Mrs. Prate-a-pace? if you don't like your living, troop off. Go—There are more Servants to be had.

Faith. I ſhall certainly diſcover myſelf, if he goes on at this Rate——Sir, I had rather quit this Place immediately, than you ſhou'd incommode the Ladies.

Lau. Pray, Sir *David*, mind your own Servants, you ſhall never have any Power over mine. Let me adviſe you to tarry till to-morrow; 'tis dangerous travelling too late; let me intreat you to ſtay in this Town till to-morrow.——What ſaid *Manage* to you, *Lucy?*

Lucy

Lucy. Ay, pray take my Lady's Advice, Sir. You ſhall know within; take Courage, Madam.

Sir Dav. Zounds, get in, I believe you want to lie with him all night, you are ſo concern'd for his Stay.

Lucy. I hope ſome brave Man will attempt the Reſcue of my Miſtreſs. [*He puſhes 'em in.*

Faith. My Heart ſwells at theſe Indignities, and I cou'd ſhake his detcſted rotten Soul out of his wither'd ſapleſs Carcaſe.

Man. Be eaſy, Sir, Paſſion will do us no good—I have something in my Head may hit, perhaps.

Faith. I am ſorry, Sir, I ſhou'd be the Cauſe of your being angry with your Daughter.

Sir Dav. My Daughter?

Faith. I aſk your Pardon, Sir, may be 'tis your Wife.

Sir Dav. She ſhall be e'er long, Sir.

Faith. You ſhall be Worm's Meat firſt. [*Aſide.* I had better knock him down, and fetch her out this Moment.

Man. And the next Moment fetch you to Goal. Indeed, Sir, you had better keep your Temper—You have made a very excellent Choice, Sir; wou'd all Huſbands manage their Wives ſo, we ſhould not have ſo many Coquets abroad.

Sir Dav. I don't deſign my Wife ſhall follow the Way of the World.

Man. Second him, Sir; keep him in Talk a little——

Faith. You do well, Sir, 'tis below a man to let his Wife rule, and rattle where ſhe pleaſes; to viſit, and be viſited by half the Fops of the Nation; for my Part, had I a Wife, I ſhou'd follow your Method.

Sir Dav. Egad, I believe I was miſtaken in this Gentleman. I wiſh, Sir, I had this Lecture read to ſome that blame me for my Conduct.

Man. If you pleaſe, Sir, I'll go into your Houſe, and write it down this Moment! it ſhan't coſt you a Farthing, Sir.

Sir Dav. I'll not give you the trouble, Sir, I ſhall remember it.

Enter Lucy *haſtily.*

Lucy. Oh! undone, undone; help, help; oh Sir *David!* what have you brought upon us?

Sir *Dav.* What the Devil do you bawl fo for?

Lucy. Oh! the faddeft Accident has befallen my poor Lady!——

Faith. Ha! her Lady, faid fhe?

Man. Peace, Sir, and mind the Plot——
[*Afide to* Faithful.

Sir *Dav.* What accident, ha? You roar as if fhe had broke a Leg, or an Arm.

Lucy. Worfe, Sir, worfe, much worfe; fhe's mad, Sir———

Sir *Dav.* Mad!

Lucy. Ay, diftracted, Sir——When you thruft us in, fhe found the Smith barricading her Windows; as foon as ever fhe laid her Eyes upon the Iron Bars, her Looks grew wild; her fudden Starts and broken Speeches convince me of her Brain being turn'd——When, before I was aware——fhe catch'd up an Iron Bar, and broke the Blackfmith's Pate; fhe beat her Head againft the Wall— runs, fkips, fings, dances, ftamps, raves, and throws all the Things about the Room——I wou'd have fhut her in, but fhe fet up fuch a Roar, that I left the Door open, and fled for my life——Make the beft of your Plot, *Manage*——— [*Afide.*

Man. Ay, ay, let me alone.

Sir *Dav.* Mercy on us; what fhall I do?

Lucy. Here fhe comes, oh my poor Lady!---with your great Bafe Viol in her hand; oh, oh, oh!

Sir *Dav.* Oh the Devil! if fhe breaks my Bafe, I had rather lofe five Pounds: Oh, oh, oh.

Man. Have Patience, Sir, I may be ferviceable to you in this Affair, as little Opinion as you had of my Skill to-day.

Enter Laura, *with a Bafe and Papers; her Clothes aukwardly hanging.*

Lau.   Give me Liberty and Love,
        Give me Love and Liberty,
        From an Iron Grate,
        And the Man I hate,
        Dear Fortune fet me free.

Faith. What Defign you by this, *Manage?*

Man.

The Devil to do about her.

Man. To put you in Poffeffion of your Miftrefs, before I have done, Sir, if you'll be quiet.

Lau. What, are you a Blackfmith? [*To Sir* David.

Sir *Dav.* Oh, pox o' the Blackfmith, how fhe harps upon him!——

Lau. Ho! now I know you, your are a Singing-mafter.

Sir *Dav.* A Singing mafter! good lack, good lack—

Lau. Here is a Piece of Mufick, which I have juft now received from *London*: 'tis Part of the laft new Opera—there, there, there's a Part for you. (*Gives Sir* David *a Paper.*) Ha! are not you the new Eunuch? Ay, 'tis he! here, here, here's your Part. [*Gives* Faithful *a Letter.*

Faith. A Letter, Oh! for an Opportunity to read it.
[*Draws off by degrees.*

Lau. *Give me Liberty and Love,*
   Give me Love and Liberty———Come, why don't you fing. (*To Sir* David.) [*She beats Time all this while, with her Hand upon his Head, and with her Foot upon his Toes.*

Sir *Dav.* Poor *Laura*, I can't fing. Child——Zounds, Death and the Devil, fhe has kill'd my Toe.

Lau. What, won't you fing, I'll break the Fiddle then.

Lucy. Pray, Sir *David*, humour her.

Man. Let me advife you to comply with her, Sir; fhe's poffefs'd, and with a very mifchievous Dæmon.

Lau. Come, begin. *Give me Liberty and Love.*

Sir *Dav.* }
Lucy.   } *Give me Liberty and Love.* [*They all fing*
Man.   }   *whilft* Faithful *reads.*

Faith. (Reads.) *Dear* Faithful, *find fome Way to deliver me, or what I now act in jeft, will follow in earneft; I have all my Jewels and Writings about me; for I have broke the old Man's Clofet for them, and I'll find a Way to get Money prefently. Yours entirely,* Laura. Yes, I will deliver thee, or die for it. *Manage,* read that.
[*Gives him the letter.*

Man. Recommend me for a white Witch to Sir *David*; let me alone for the reft.

Faith. Poor Lady! I am extremely concern'd for her, Sir; pray confult my Servant about her Diftemper; in my Opinion fhe's bewitch'd.

Sir Dav. I doubt fo too, Sir; has he really Skill in thefe Matters?

Faith. No Man in the Kingdom more, I affure you; he has cur'd feveral, to my Knowledge, both in *Spain* and *Flanders*.

Lau. Why do you look at me fo? Did you never fee an old Woman before? I'd have you to know, Miftrefs, I have been as handfome as you——but age alters every body——I have been the Mother of fixteen Children—— all Boys——Hark ye, let me counfel you—don't marry an old Fellow.

Lucy. No, why fo, pray?

Lau. Becaufe your Youth will renew his Age——and you'll be plagu'd with him to Eternity—I married an old fufty Guardian, becaufe I could not get out of his Hands; which is the Reafon why you fee fo many Wrinkles in my Face, ha, ha, ha. In my Confcience there he ftands— What, can I go no where, but you muft follow me—you old crippling Cuckold you—Look ye how angry he is now at being call'd Cuckold——Yet he wou'd marry a young Wife——ha, ha, ha.

Sir Dav. Mercy upon us! how do fuch Things come in her Head?

Faith. The Wildnefs of her Fancy.

Enter Manage.

Man. I'll do your Bufinefs for you, Sir; I have confulted the Stars, and find fhe is bewitch'd by an old Woman.

Sir Dav. By an old Woman! Ay, indeed, fhe talks of an old Woman.

Man. It is a very troublefome Spirit that is in her, and muft be charm'd out into another, or fhe can't be cur'd, ——Tell me, Sir, can you procure any body for that Purpofe?

Sir Dav. Here's her Maid, won't fhe do?

Lucy. What! Do you think I'd have the Devil put into me, Sir, I afk you Pardon for that.

Lau. Hark! there's my Drum beating up for Volunteers——What fay you, my Lads, are you for the Wars? Her Majefty has honour'd me with a Colonel's Commiffion; I'm juft now raifing my Regiment——you fhall all

ferve

The Devil to do about her.

ferve under me, Come——hold, now I think on't, I want a hundred Guineas to raife Men with——Hark ye, won't you lend me a hundred Guineas? [*To Sir* David.

Sir *Dav.* Lack-a-day, it makes me weep, to fee how many forts of Madneffes poffefs her.

Man. A good Thought for fome Money——Humour her, Sir, whatever fhe afks for, let her have.

Lau. Lend me a hundred Guineas, I fay, or my Soldiers fhall batter your Houfe about your Ears.

Lucy. For Heaven's fake, Sir, give 'em her, you'll have them again fafe.

Faith. I wou'd advife you to let her have 'em, Sir.

Sir *Dav.* Well, be fure you take care of them; there, there is threefcore in that Purfe, you may tell her there is a hundred; but take care I have them again. [*To* Lucy.

Man. Ay, when we have nothing elfe to do with 'em. [*Afide.*

Lau. Give it me—fo, now my Boys will you ferve the Queen.

Man. Ay, with all my Heart, under you, Sir.

Lau. There then, there's Gold for you, Sirrah; (*Gives him a Guinea.*) and what fay you, you are a handfome proper Fellow, fix Foot high——I'll make you Serjeant of the Grenadiers——What fay you, will you ferve under me?

Man. Humph! He wou'd rather ferve her another Way, I dare fwear. [*Afide.*

Faith. And know no Joy beyond it; ferve ye!——by Heaven, that I will, with my Life; command me, Colonel, I'll follow you through all Difficulties and Danger; and die by your Side, or bring you off fafe.

Lau. Then there's Money, my Hero, to forward our Defigns. [*Gives him the Purfe.*

Sir *Dav.* Hold, hold, *Laura*, you muft not give away your Money? *Lucy* take care on't. I hope, Sir, you'll return the Money.

Faith. Certainly, Sir.

Lucy. I'll fee to that, Sir.

Lau. Return the Money, to whom? They are my Soldiers, and the Money mine——I borrow'd it of the moft confounded old Rogue in *Peterborough*; tell him I fay fo
—but

—but you look like an honeſt Man, I'll make you a Corporal——Come, let me fee you exercife, Serjeant.

Sir Dav. Oh Lord, oh Lord !

Lau. Serjeant take heed ; to the right and left by half Flanks——form Files upon the Flanks of the Battalion— March——ha, ha, you are curfed dull, Serjeant——

Faith. I am a little aukward at firſt, Colonel, but I fhall learn. [*Stamps.*

Sir Dav. Oh, Oh, Oh !

Lau. Well, well, I'll teach you then——Silence, Join your right Hand to your Firelock——Cock your Firelock ——Prefent ; Fire——Excellent.

    Give me Liberty and Love,
    Give me Love and Liberty. [*Sings.*

Sir Dav. Oh fad, oh fad ! what fhall I do ? Pray Sir defire your Man to try his fkill.

Faith. Manage, the Gentleman implores your Aid.

Man. I am ready, if he can find any body to make the Experiment ; it muſt be a Man, Sir——will you endure it yourfelf.

Sir Dav. No, faith and troth not I !

Faith. Well, Sir, to do you and the Lady fervice, I'll venture——but take care, *Manage,* that you bring the Devil out of me again——

Man. Yes, Sir, that I can eafily ; for he is not half fo hard to get out of a Man, as he is out of a Woman.

Sir Dav. Good lack ! what fhou'd the Reafon of that be, I wonder ! (*Afide.*) Sir, I thaṅk you heartily———— a very worthy Gentleman this——Well, what muſt I do, Sir ?

Man. Stand ſtill, I charge you——And do you fetch us an eafy Chair, Miſtrefs.—— [*To* Lucy.

Lucy. Yes, Sir. [*Exit.*

Man. Stay, I muſt limit your Bounds ; there Sir, you muſt not for your Life crofs this Circle.

Sir Dav. Well, Sir, I fhall obferve you.

    Enter Lucy *with a Chair.*

Lucy. Here, Sir.

Man. Very well ; pray, Madam, be pleas'd to ſit dcwn.

Lau. Sit down ! why, is Dinner coming ?——Ho, cry
                                                             a Mer

The Devil to do about her.

a Mercy! you are a Barber; hold, hold, you shall shave my Corporal first, to try your Razor.

Sir Dav. Oh Lord, oh Lord! what shall I say to her?

Man. Keep your Place, Sir——No, no, Sir, I am a Shoe-maker, and if I fit your Foot, and pleafe you, I defire your Honour wou'd let me have the Bufinefs of your Regiment.

Lau. With all my Heart.

Man. Then pray fit down, Sir, that I may take Meafure. (*She fits down.*) Now for you, Sir, you muft kneel right before her—clofer——clofer yet; there, look full in her Eyes——Clafp both her Hands in yours. [*Manage pulls a Book out of his Pocket, and looks on't.*

Lau. Give me Liberty and Love,
Give me Love and Liberty. [*Sings.*

Faith. My charming Angel! Oh, let me kneel here for ever, for ever gaze on thofe dear Eyes; how I have languifh'd for thee, Heaven only knows.

Lau. And what I have born for thee, Hell cannot match! Oh, if *Manage* fail in his Plot, I'm undone for ever.

Faith. Fear not, my Love, he is lucky at Contrivance.

Sir Dav. What are they doing?

Man. Alpha, Beta, Gamma, Delta.

Sir Dav. Blefs me, what are thofe the Names of the Spirits?

Man. Philo fe en pafias, gloffais, kai en to panti poto, kai en to panti topo—Now do you be well, Madam; and do you feem to be mad, Sir, quick, quick——

Sir Dav. Why, what a many Devils there are! certainly fhe has a Legion in her.

Lau. Where am I, *Lucy*? Methinks I wake from fome untoward Dream.

Lucy. She recovers, Sir. How do you, Madam?

Sir Dav. I'm glad on't. How doft thou do, *Laura*?

Lau. Pretty well.

Man. Death, Sir, keep your Place, or you'll fpoil all.

Faith. Ha! my Brain-pan fplits——I'm all a-flame, my Blood boils o'er, give me Room, I'll fcale the Region of the Air, and pull the Winds down head-long on us all.

Sir *Dav.* Oh, oh, oh, he's ftark mad! What fhall we do with him now?
Man. We fhall do well enough with him; but keep your Place, for he's very defperate.
Lau. Defend me Heaven, what ails the Gentleman?
Lucy. He'll kill us; the Man's bewitch'd.
Man. Here, here, Ladies, ftand in this Circle, and don't crofs it for your Lives. [*Sets 'em in a Circle.*
Sir *Dav.* Oh, pray Sir, read again——
Faith. What's here, old *Belzebub!* No, 'tis his Squib and Cracker; I'll fet fire to it and blow it up——Ho, lo, where are you Scoundrels, Dogs, Rogues, Cooks, the Devil wants his Dinner, and you muft fpit this Swine, Hell dines on Hog's Flefh to-day. [*Draws his Sword.*
Man. Undone, undone; the Spirit grows too ftrong for my Art! Fly, fly, Sir, for Life——
Sir *Dav.* Oh, oh, oh, fave me, fave me. [*Runs in and flaps the Door.*
Man. Now, now, make your Efcape; he has flap'd the Door after him——Quick, quick——
Faith. My Life, my Soul!
Lau. My Angel, my All. [*Embraces.*
Man. Oh, the Devil! Don't ftand Lifeing and Dearing now, but make Hafte to Mr. *Trufty*'s, I'll bring the Parfon after you.
Lucy. Ay, good Madam, be quick.
Lau. Any where, good *Manage.*
Faith. Fly *Manage*, and bring *Lovely* with thee too, to be Witnefs of my good Fortune, this Hour makes thee mine for ever:

Now in thy Arms immortal Joys I'll tafte,
And quite forget our anxious Sorrows paft,

Lucy. Now Heav'n be prais'd, we've Liberty at laft.
Exeunt.
Sir David *above.*

Sir *Dav.* Oh, I'm robb'd, ravifh'd, dead and buried—My Clofet is broke open, and all my Writings gone; Mr. *Conjurer*, Mr. *Conjurer*, can you help me to the Thief? Ha! no body to be feen! Blefs me——*Lucy*——*Laura*, why *Laura?* Ah! Murder, Murder, Thieves, Thieves. [*Cries out till he comes down.*
Enter

The Devil to do about her.

Enter Sir David.

Here, where are all my Servants? (*Enter Servants.*) Run fome one Way, fome another; make Enquiry thro' he whole Town for Mrs. *Laura*, fhe is carry'd away by wo Rogues or Devils, I know not which, run run——

Serv. Why, if the devil has carry'd her away, Sir, where can we run?

Sir *Dav.* To Hell, ye Dog, do you ftand to prate?—
 [*Beats him.*

Serv. Marry, look her there yourfelf an you will——
 [*Exit.*

Sir *Dav.* Oh, that I fhou'd believe thefe Conjuring, foldierng Rafcals; but I'll find 'em, if they are above Ground; and if they are mortal, I'll hang 'em, that's my Comfort. [*Exit.*

ACT V.

S C E N E, *The Street before Mr.* Trufty's *Door*; Roger *comes out of the Houfe with a Pitchfork on his Shoulder, and a Lanthorn in his Hand.*

Rog. I T will be very dark e'er I get home——Od, I'm main merry. Mafter *Trufty*, keeps rare nappy Ale, and *Dick* the Butler is an honeft Fellow; Lord, Sirs, how bravely thefe Gentlefolk live——Methinks I like it hugely; and I'm perfuaded, I was defign'd for a Gentleman, but was fpoil'd in the making; nay, nay, I was made well enough too, that's the Truth on't; but 'tis that damn'd Jade *Fortune* that has fpoil'd me; for an I had an Eftate now, I know how to live like a Gentleman——I cou'd fcorn the Poor, and fcrew up my Tenants, and wou'd fooner give Ten Pound to a Wench, than Twopence for Charity; I cou'd quickly turn——my Cart into a Coach, and my Man *Plod* into a Coachman——I cou'd hurry into the Tradefmen's Books——Wear fine Clothes, and never pay for them—Lie with their Wives, and make my Footmen beat their Hufbands, when they come to afk me for Money. Get drunk with Lords, and break the
 Watch-

Watchmen's Heads——Scour the Streets, and fleep in a Bawdy-houfe——Sell my Lands, and pay no Debts—— Get a Charge of Baftards for the Parifh to maintain —— Then, by the help of Commiffion, tranfport myfelf out of their Reach.——

Enter Sir Jeffrey Conftant, *in a riding Habit.*

Sir Jeff. Do you hear, Friend?

Rog. Mayhap I do——And mayhap I do not; What then, Sir?

Sir Jeff. Nay, the Matter's not great——Do you live at that Houfe?

Rog. I did a little while ago——When I was in the Cellar.

Sir Jeff. A comical Fellow. Then you don't ferve Mr. *Trufty?*

Rog. No, Sir, I ferve his Mafter, tho' as moft Farmers do their Landlords.

Sir Jeff. I underftand you: You rent one of the Knight's Farms?

Rog. Ay, and a plaguy dear one too——

Sir Jeff. Say you fo! That's a Pity; I'll fpeak a good Word for thee—Is Mr. *Trufty* at home?

Rog. I thank you heartily. Yes, Sir, he's at home. (*Runs to the Door and knocks.* Trufty *opens the Door and fhrieks out and throws it to again.*) Wookers, what's the Matter now?

Sir Jeff. Was not that Mr. *Trufty?*

Rog. Yes, Sir, I think fo.

Clin. (*Within.*) Oh undone, undone; (Clinch *peeps out as affrighted.*) here's my old Mafter.

Sir Jeff. What's that?

Rog. Nay, I heard a Noife, but can't tell what they faid ——But an you pleafe to come wo'me, Sir, I'll carry you in the Back-way.

Sir Jeff. The Back-way——What can be the Meaning of this? Why fhou'd he ftart at fight of me? There muft be fomething more in it than I can fathom; and yet I think he's an honeft Man. I never found any Thing to the contrary. Prithee, Friend, knock again.

[Roger *knocks, then liftens.*

Rog.

Rog. They are all afleep, Sir——For I cannot fo much as hear a Moufe ftir——

Sir *Jeff.* Afleep! That's impoffible—But come, Friend, fhew me the Back-door you fpoke of——

Rog. Ay, Sir: But upon fecond Thoughts—I muft be a little wary too. Are not you fome Rogue, that comes to rob the Houfe with half a dozen Piftols about you? For look ye, I'm an honeft Man, and won't be drawn in for a Halter.

Sir *Jeff.* You Rafcal, do I look like a Thief?

Rog. Nay, nay, as for Looks——That's no Matter, do ye fee—I have known many a Rogue with as good a Countenance——No Difparagement in your's, I promife you. So that I fhall not ftir one Step without you'll ftand fearch——

Sir *Jeff.* I fhall break your Head, Sirrah, if you provoke me, I tell you but that.

Rog. And what muft I be doing in the mean Time—Ha! old Gentleman? Break my Head, quotha!——You are miftaken—We don't ufe to take broken Heads in our Country, mun——Ha, ha, I won't fhew you the Back-door now, and how will you help youfelf?——

Sir *Jeff.* I know all the Doors of this Houfe as well as you—And can fhew myfelf in—— [*Going.*

Rog. Can you fo—but I'll watch you—I wonder who this old Fellow is.

Sir *Jeff.* Sure fome Madnefs has feiz'd the Family; for certainly I'm not chang'd—Without Difpute, *Trufty* knows me; but I'll find the Caufe prefently. [*Exit.*

Rog, And fo will I.—— [*Exit.*

Enter out of the Houfe, Captain Conftant, Lovely *and* Clinch.

Clin. So, Sir, here's Mufick to your Wedding, with a Witnefs. What do you intend to do now?——Do you think it poffible to perfuade your Father too, that he died of an Apoplexy.

Lov. I fear, *Clinch*, that's beyond the Art of thy Impudence to do——

Clin. Nay, this Plot was none of my Impudence's contriving, that's my Comfort—I'm but a Servant; my Mafter told me, he was in Mourning for his Father——And, Faith

Faith, I refolve not to believe the Father to the contrary : Such an entire Deference have I for all your Commands, Sir.

Conft. Why thou can'ft not fure have the Confidence to ftand it out to his Face.

Clin. Never fear me, Sir—You don't know what I can do—What fay you, Sir? Shall we perfuade the old Gentleman into a Ghoft ; or will you own your Fault, and refund the Money?

Conft. Neither, *Clinch*—I have more Duty, than to attempt the one ; and more Neceffity, than to fubmit to the other.———

Clin. Nay, if you be fo divided—What do you propofe?

Conft. I know not what to do—I'm glad the Ceremony was over, before he came.

Lov. And the Money fent away—What think you of my Houfe, till the Heat of the Difcovery be over? 'Tis my Opinion your Prefence won't be proper—I warrant Sir *David* will be in Purfuit of Mrs. *Laura* prefently too —But we have feen her fairly married ; fo that *Faithful* is out of Danger ; we'll leave him here.———

Conft. Shall I not take *Belinda* with us? I fear as much for her, as for myfelf———

Clin. So there's no-body fears for me, I find—(*Afide.*) I am like to have my Part, truly.

Lov. No, truft to her Management——She turn'd the Act upon her Father, you know, and made him impofe her own Choice upon her. Let *Clinch* ftay and ufe his own Difcretion—If he can banter Sir *Jeffrey*, and fave his Bones, let him : But be fure to give us Notice of all that paffes.

Clin. What if my Bones are broke?————I thank you heartily for your Love, Sir.

Conft. No, no, *Clinch* ; take Heed you keep out of the Reach of his Cane.

Clin. Or he'll make me feel he's Flefh and Blood.— Hark, I hear him coming, Good-bye to you, Sir————
[*Runs in.*
Lov. 'Tis Time for us to fly———   [*Exeunt.*
Enter Dolly.

Dolly. Well, I'm glad my Lady's marry'd ; for if this old

old Spark had come three Hours sooner, I wou'd not have ventur'd Two to Ten of the Match—I can't imagine where the Bridegroom's gone—Nor what he will do, when my Master comes to have a right Understanding; but I resolve to keep him ignorant as long as I can. Ho, here he comes.

Enter Trusty.

Oh, Sir, I am frighted out of my Wits; I went to serve my Lady's *Italian* Greyhound, and I found a great swinging Dog, as large as an Ox, with two great Eyes, as big as Bushels; and before I could call out—Whip it was vanish'd————

Trust. Mercy upon us—'Twas certainly Sir *Jeffrey*—— *Clinch.* [*Enter* Clinch.

Clin. Sir, did you call————

Trust. Did not you say your old Master appear'd in the Shape of a Dog?

Clin. Ay, Sir, several Times.

Dolly. In a huge great Dog?

Trust. As big as an Ox.

Clin. Ay, Sir, as big as an Elephant.

Dolly. Ah! then it was certainly him I saw. Oh dear, oh dear, if the House be haunted, I must leave it. I cannot live in't, if I might have a thousand Pounds; and may be, he'll appear to no body but me——I am sure I never did him any Harm; 'tis true, I did not love him, because he was something stingey——He never gave me a Farthing in his Life————

Trust. Nay, for that Matter, I have got many a fair Pound by him, and yet he appeared to me to-day

Clin. Indeed, Sir! In what Shape, pray?

Dolly. Like an Ox, or an Elephant.

Trust. No, in his own Shape; but I wish I may never see him more, for I was horribly scar'd.

Clin. What, had he a cloven Foot, Sir, did you mind?

Trust. Nay, for my Part,—I know not whether he had any Feet or no————Ha! bless me, defend me,—protect me————Avoid, Satan————(*Retreating all this while.*) I never wrong'd that Form, which thou hast ta'en; so tell him—And for my Money, I have accounted for that! and all Things are rectify'd———— [*Exit.*

Enter

The Man's bewitch'd; or,

Enter Sir Jeffrey, *amaz'd.*

Dolly. Oh! ſhield me ye Stars. [*Runs in.*
Clin. O Legs! ſave me, ſave me. [*Runs in.*

Enter Roger.

Sir *Jeff.* What! Am I become a Monſter? Do I affright all I come near? What can be the Reaſon of this? The Doors are all barricaded; and when I knock, none will anſwer—Prithee, Friend, aſk ſomebody the Cauſe of theſe Diſorders?

Rog. No! Sir, I'll not budge a Foot; for I dan't know what to ſay to you. The Family were all well and in their right Senſes, when I left them; and now, upon Sight of you, they are all diſtracted, I think—I wiſh you be'n't a Conjurer, or hark ye, Sir,——Is not your Name *Emmes*—Rais'd by the *French* Prophets to Life again?

Sir *Jeff.* Sirrah, I believe you are the Devil: This Fellow will make me mad. This muſt be ſome Stratagem to abuſe me; and this Rogue is in their Intereſt. Why don't you go about your Buſineſs, Sirrah? What do you hanker after me for?

Rog. Nay——an you go to ·that, what do you lounge about this Houſe for?—Oh! *Dolly,* are you there; here's an old Gentleman is quite out of Patience.

Dolly. (*Trembling above.*) Oh, oh, oh, oh——

Rog. Hey day! What have you got the Palſy?

Sir *Jeff.* What ails you, to tremble ſo, Sweetheart? Is Mr. *Truſty* within?

Dolly. I, I, I, I, I, o, o, o, o, *Roger*—Ha, ha, have a care, ca, care——Don't yo, yo, you come near him—Nor let him to, to, to, touch you, even with his little Finger——

Sir *Jeff.* Bleſs me! What ails the Wench?

Rog. No, why what's the Matter? He has not the Plague about him, has he? Or is he a Spy from the King of *France*—Od an he be, I'll maul him——

Dolly. Oh, oh,——'tis a, a, Ghoſt.

Rog. The Devil it is—— [*Takes his Pitchfork off his Shoulder, and holds it out at Sir* Jeffrey.

Sir *Jeff.* A Ghoſt, where?—Who—What's a Ghoſt? Death, what means ſhe?

Rog.

The Devil to do about her.

Rog. Od's flefh, my Hair ftands an end. Look ye—Keep off Mr. *Belzebub,* or—or——

Sir Jeff. Look ye, Sweetheart, what Frenzy has poffefs'd you, I know not——But if you take me for a Ghoft——you are deceiv'd. Therefore look well at me ——Do I not appear like Flefh and Blood?

Dolly. Ay, bo, bo, bo, but we, we, we know yo, yo, you a, a, a, a, are not fo, Sir.

Sir Jeff. Zounds, will they perfuade me out of my Life? See, Friend——Do I walk like a Spirit? Do the Dead move, and talk as I do?

Rog. When I am dead,——if you ask me, I'll refolve you, if I can.

Sir Jeff. Why! Feel me, feel me.

Rog. Feel the Devil——Mercy upon me——Keep off, I fay—will ye——Or I'll ftick your Ghoftfhip thro' the Guts

Sir Jeff. What fhall I do?——Nay, prithee, Friend.

Rog. Friend me no Friends——Look ye, I am not to be coax'd by the Devil, when I know 'tis the Devil. Indeed, when you are got into a Lawyer, or an handfome Woman, one may be trapan'd.

Sir Jeff. Why will you be fo pofitive? Has any body impos'd upon you?——Pray who told you I was dead?

Dolly. Thofe that knew very well, Sir.

Enter Clinch.

But I am not able to bear the fight of you any longer ——Now let *Clinch* take his Part.

Sir Jeff. Go to be hang'd——Hell and Furies! Ha, what do I fee——My Son's Man! Sirrah, Sirrah, what makes you here?——

Clin. Mercy upon me——

Sir Jeff. What do you ftare at, Rafcal, ha?

Clin. But that I believe you are dead, Sir, or I fhou'd fwear you are alive——

Sir Jeff. You believe I am dead, Rogue——How dare you believe fuch an impudent Lye? Where's the Rake, your Mafter? I find now who has rais'd this Report. Sirrah, what's your Bufinefs here?

Clin. To wait on my Mafter, Sir——

Sir Jeff. To wait on your Mafter———And where is your Mafter, pray?

Clin. Nay, for my Part, Sir, I am not qualify'd to anfwer a Spirit———There's Mr. *Anthem,* the Afternoon Lecturer, within. He has juft marry'd Mr. *Faithful* to a great Heirefs, which he brought in juft now———*Roger* here may ftep and call him out a little.

Rog. With all my Heart———If there be any Thing that troubles his Mind, I'll go this Minute———

Sir Jeff. Sirrah———I'll qualify you for an Hofpital ———I will, ye Dog——— [*Runs after him.*

Clin. Oh, oh, oh.

Rog. Well run, *Clinch*; well run, Ghoft!———Ad, 'tis a plaguy malicious Spirit, tho'.

Clin. Oh, oh, oh. [*Runs in.*

Rog. I'll venture to fpeak to it once more———In the Name of Goodnefs—What is it that difturbs your Reft? Pray tell me; and as I'm an honeft Man, I'll do you Juftice as far as Twenty Pounds a Year Free-Land, and all the Crops of my Farm goes———For I perceive you was my Landlord, whilft you was living; and tho' your Son feems to be a very honeft Gentleman, yet I don't know what he may prove for a Landlord———Then pray fpeak, can I ferve you?

Sir Jeff. 'Tis in vain to be angry———I muft feem to comply with this Fellow—Yes, Friend, it is in thy Power to ferve me; if thou canft procure me the Sight of Mr. *Trufty,* 'tis with him my Bufinefs is.

Rog. I'll do my beft Endeavours, Sir———but keep your Diftance———(*He goes a little Way, then turns back.*) But hark ye, Sir, fuppofe he won't come out, can't I tell him your Mind?

Sir Jeff. No, no, I muft fpeak with him myfelf——— Death———

Rog. Good lack———what, perhaps—your Soul won't reft elfe———

Sir Jeff. Heaven give me Patience!

Rog. (*Going, turns back.*) But after you have fpoken with him, will you be quiet, and haunt this Houfe no more? that's the Queftion, look ye!

Sir Jeff. A Pox of thy impertinent Interrogations; no———

Rog.

The Devil to do about her. 145

Rog. That's enough!——but hold, muſt he come out, or ſpeak to you through the Window?

Sir Jeff. Any Way, ſo I do but ſpeak to him——
Oh, oh!————

Rog. Very well, very well. (*Going.*) But hark ye, Sir Ghoſt—you'll be here——or Mr. *Truſty* will be woundy angry with me.

Sir Jeff. Oh Patience, Patience; or I ſhall burſt. (*Aſide.*) Ay, ay, I'll not ſtir.

Rog. Well, I'll take your Word (*Going.*) Hold, hold, one Thing more, and I ha' done—Pray tell me the Nature of a Ghoſt—do you troubled ſpirits fly in the Air, or ſwim in the Water, pray?

Sir Jeff. Oh! the Devil————

Rog. Mercy upon us! what are you the Devil, ſay you? Oh, Heaven help you! Well, then, are you ſure he will ſee you? for every body can't ſee a Ghoſt, they ſay, eſpecially if the Devil be in't.

Sir Jeff. Zounds, I tell you, he'll ſee me as plain as you ſee me.

Rog. Nay, nay, that's plain enough—Well, I'll knock, but, but, but don't you come an Inch nearer me, I charge you. [*Knocks.*

Sir Jeff. Wou'd I had been an hundred Miles off, when I firſt ſaw thee. What has my gracelefs ſon been doing?

Dolly. Who's there? [*Speaks within.*

Rog. 'Tis I, *Dolly*, prithee tell Maſter *Truſty* that he muſt ſpeak to this Ghoſt, or there's nothing to be done—

Dolly. I doubt he will not be perſuaded to it.

Rog. Why, let him ſpeak to it through the Window, or from the Top of the Houſe—ſo he does but ſpeak to it; but in ſhort, it muſt be ſpoke to, and by him, for it is a confounded ſullen Spirit, and will tell its Mind to nobody elſe—He ſmells curſedly of Brimſtone—Look ye, if Maſter will come out, it ſhan't hurt him—for I'll keep it off with my Fork, ſo tell him, *Dolly*.

Dolly. I'll inform him.

Truſty *opens the Window.*

Rog. So, I have done it, you ſee————Here's Maſter *Truſty.* [*Going towards the Window.*

Sir

Sir Jeff. I thank you.

Truſt. I am not able to ſtand, if it comes near me—— Why are you thus diſturb'd, Sir *Jeffrey*?———I aſſure you, your Son has done every Thing very juſtly.

Sir Jeff. Why are you thus impos'd upon, Mr. *Truſty*, to believe I am dead?———My Son, quotha!———Oh that I had never got that Son——— [*Weeps.*

Truſt. I know not what to think; ſure 'tis no Ghoſt.

Rog. Well, this Thing is the likeſt Fleſh and Blood, that ever I ſaw———

Sir Jeff. Pray do but touch me, Mr. *Truſty*—'tis very odd, you will not be perſuaded to touch me.

[*Puts out his Hand towards the Window.*

Rog. Take Heed, Mr. *Truſty.*

Truſt. Why ſhou'd I fear, I never wrong'd him—I'll venture; but firſt—(*Holds up his Hand as if he pray'd.*) now—ha! 'tis a real Hand,—He's living;—Sir, I am convinc'd.

Rog. Say you ſo———why then if you are alive, the Fright's over, and I'm glad on't with all my Heart.

Truſt. I aſk your Pardon, Sir; I have been abus'd— groſly abus'd; Sir *Jeffrey*, your Son, came down in Mourning, and aſſur'd me you was dead.

Sir Jeff. I'll make him mourn for ſomething, I warrant you.

Truſt. Ah! that he does already, Sir, for I have paid him all the rents in my Hands.

Sir Jeff. Have you ſo?——'Tis the laſt Rents he ſhall ever take for any Land of mine———I'll diſinherit him this Day.

Truſt. Oh! undone, undone for ever——Oh, oh, oh!

[*Weeps.*

Rog. Here's ſmall Mirth towards, as far as I can find. I'll e'en take t'other Horn of Ale, and t'other Buſs of *Dolly*—— [*Ex. into the Houſe.*

(Clinch *liſtening.*)

Sir Jeff. What has that Rogue's Extravagance coſt me? But if he ſtarves for the future, I care not; he never ſhall get a Groat from me.

Clin. Nay, then we may all go for Soldiers. [*Aſide.*

Sir Jeff. Where is he?

Truſt. Oh, oh, oh! I know not; but wherever he is—

I am

I am wretched, he has made me miserable, I'm sure. Oh, oh, oh!

Sir Jeff. No, Mr. *Trusty*; though you have us'd me dirtily, in making me the Jest of your Family; for you might have discover'd the Imposture with less Precaution; yet I'll not take that Advantage which the Laws allow. You have serv'd me long, and I believe you honest. I'll discharge you from what you have paid my undutiful Child——Let him take what he has got, and make the best on't.

Clin. That's something, however. [*Aside.*

Trust. You are generous, Sir *Jeffrey*, even, beyond my Hopes: But Oh! there is yet a greater Offence behind, which cuts me deeper than the Money———Alas! my Daughter———

Sir Jeff. What of her?

Trust. Is married to your Son; Oh; oh, oh!

Sir Jeff. Then he is compleatly wretched——A Wife, and no Estate; ha, ha, ha; I'm glad on't with all my Heart.

Clin. There's a kind Father now———I must give my Master Notice of his good Fortune. [*Exit.*

Trust. Oh! say not so, Sir; be not glad of my Child's Ruin; had I known you liv'd, the Match had never been.

Sir Jeff. Go; you are not the Man I took you for—you are but a Knave. You ought to have been as just to my Heir, as to myself———What, was your Blood fit to be popt into my Estate? Ha! or have you been really a Steward, and cheated me out of a Fortune for your Daughter?

Trust. Sir, what I am Master of, I got fairly under you, Part, and Part under my Lord *Belville* in *Ireland*, whom I serv'd twenty Years in the same Post I do you; when he died, he trusted me with a Secret, which yet I have divulged to no Man; and when I do, the World will say I am an honest Man. Love first join'd their Hearts, and my Ignorance their Hands; use me as you please, but pardon them.

Enter Lovely, *&c.*

Lov. I must become an Intercessor in that too, Sir *Jeffrey*; Love is the great Cementer of the Marriage-State; it reconciles all Differences—it bends the Stubborn---and it it tames the Bold, it wins the Haughty, foftens the Savage, and reclaims the Libertine ! then will you caft off your Son for a Vertue, you ought rather to prize him for?

Sir *Jeff.* That Love can never be a Vertue, Mr. *Lovely*, that teaches a Child to trick his Parents.

Lov. Stratagems ever were allow'd of in Love and War; Sir, you muft forgive him.

Enter Captain Conftant, Belinda *and* Maria.

Mar. And I muft fecond Mr. *Lovely*, Sir; the Captain has married a virtuous Woman, and I believe you'll confefs a handfome one too.

Sir *Jeff.* Nay, I have nothing to fay againft her Virtue, nor her Beauty neither; fhe's a pretty Woman, that's the Truth on't; if fhe had married any body's Son but mine, I fhou'd have wifh'd her Joy with all my Heart— Oh thou gracelefs Wretch, get out of my Sight

Con. (*Kneeling.*) I confefs, Sir, I am unworthy of your Mercy, but throw myfelf wholly upon your Good-Nature and fatherly Affection, with this Refolution, never to attempt aught againft your Pleafure more.

Sir *Jeff.* No, Sir, nothing you can do for the future, fhall either pleafe, or difpleafe me; mark that.

Bel. Give us but your Bleffing, Sir, and we fhall never quarrel with Fortune for her Favours : Love fhall fupply that Defect; my chief Concern fhall be to fhew my Duty, and by my Care to pleafe you, prove the entire Affection I have for your Son ! and that Way make up the Inequality of my Birth and Fortune.

Sir *Jeff.* You fhall never make up any Thing with me, I promife you, Madam, whilft he is your Father———— Death, marry my Slave?

Truft. The Name of Slave belongs not to us free-born People, Sir *Jeffrey*; but were I your Slave, fhe is not; for fince the Truth muft out, fhe is no Child of mine, but Daughter to my Lord *Belville*; which I have brought up ever fince fhe was three Days' old; her Mother dying in her Labour, and her Marriage being private, becaufe fhe was much below my Lord's Quality; and he at that Time under the Tuition of a Father : He never made it publick, but put her into my Hands to breed up as my own. When he came to his Eftate, he purchas'd a thoufand

The Devil to do about her.

fand Pounds a Year, and fettled it on her; which I have manag'd ever fince, and now will deliver it up to Captain *Conſtant*. This I had told in the Infancy of their Loves; but that I ſaw your Son was not well with you, and did not then think him a Match good enough for her; but fince he has over-reach'd me, I hope you'll prove a Father.

Sir *Jeff.* Is it poſſible! Od, Madam, I wiſh you Joy with all my Soul, Faith I do; and if this is Matter of Fact, you ſhall find me a Father: *Jack*, you ſhall go to *Flanders* no more.

Lov. Dear *Conſtant*, I congratulate thy good Fortune—

Mar. And I your's, Madam, fince I no more muſt call you Couſin.

Bel. Still let me hold that Name; for fince I never knew my Father, I ſhall acknowledge this good Man as ſuch.

Mar. Sir *Jeffrey*, I was poſitive you wou'd not repent.

Sir *Jeff.* You, that are fo poſitive in thefe Matters; why don't you and Mr. *Lovely* ſtrike up a Bargain? he has follow'd you a considerable Time.

Lov. That Queſtion is à propos, Sir *Jeffrey*. What can you fay, Madam? muſt I dangle after you two or three Years longer? Faith, I wiſh I hold out.

Truſt. Give him thy Hand, Girl; I'll engage to reconcile thy Father, or give thee a Portion myſelf.

Sir *Jeff.* Why, what Objections can he make againſt Mr. *Lovely*.

Truſt. Only Principles: Her Father's a violent Tory, and this honeſt Gentleman's a Whig, that's all.

Sir *Jeff.* Ha, ha, a ſtrong Reaſon, Faith.

Truſt. I'll bring him over, I warrant thee, Girl.

Mar. Upon that Condition, there's my Hand.

Lov. And here's my Heart. [*Embrace.*

Sir *Jeff.* Why, that's well faid—we only want the Man in Black now.

Enter Faithful *and* Laura, Lucy *and* Manage.

Faith. We have juſt done with ours; he is within ſtill.

Tru. Dear Mr. *Faithful*, I wiſh thee Joy with all my Heart; and you, Madam.

Om. We all do the fame.

Faith. I thank you all, and heartily return the fame to
each

each of you ; I wou'd have the whole Race of Mankind blefs'd, now I am fo.

Lau. There cannot be a Joy beyond what I am pof-fefs'd of.

Bel. I hope, Madam, we fhall be better acquainted for the Future.

Lau. I fhall be very ambitious of the Honour.

Enter Sir David.

Sir *Dav.* Ho ! have I found you. Villains ? I charge you all in the Queen's Name, to affift me in fecuring this Couple.

Truft. Why Faith, Sir *David*, they are fecure enough, for they are lawfully link'd in the Chains of Matrimony, I'm witnefs.

Sir *Dav.* Marry'd ! the Devil they are.

Mar. Yes, Sir, I'll fwear to it, if occafion be.

Lucy. So will I too, Sir *David.*

Lau. And with my own Confent, I affure you——You may barricade your Windows now, Sir *David*, I fhall run mad no more ; Ha, ha, ha !

Faith. I fhall trouble your Houfe no more, Sir, I am difpoffefs'd, Sir *David*, you need not run from me now ; ha, ha, ha !

Con. And he will know his Inn for the future ; ha, ha, ha !

Faith. And am perfectly recover'd of my Wound, Sir ; and fhall have no Occafion to borrow your Coach again ; without you'll do me the Favour to let it carry my Wife to *London.*

Sir *Dav.* Carry her to Hell——Here's a fhuffling cutting Rafcal in all his Tropes and Figures : Zounds, how I am trick'd ! But you have robb'd me, Miftrefs.

Lau. Of nothing but my Writings, Sir, mark that.

Sir *Dav.* The Law fhall tell you that ; and fo, may the Itch of Variety feize you, and the Curfe of Cuckoldom fall on him ; Arrefts and Poverty on you all. [*Exit.*

Truft. Ha, ha, ha ! now *Lovely*, for the Parfon.

Enter 'Squire Num *and* Slouch.

Num. Hold ! I forbid the Banns ; you fhan't have her, mun, for all you are fo cock-fure.

Si

The Devil to do about her.

Sir Jeff. What Banns do you forbid, Friend?
Num. Why, Mr. *Trusty*'s Daughter's Banns.
Om. Ha, ha, ha, ha!
Lov. Alas! 'Squire, you come too late; fhe that was Mr. *Trusty*'s Daughter, is marry'd; and I'm juft going to't.
Num. That was! What do you mean?
Lov. Why, I mean that Mrs. *Belinda,* that has fnapt your Heart, 'Squire, proves to be a Lord's Daughter, and not Mr. *Trusty*'s, as you believe; and now is Captain *Constant*'s Wife, here.
Num. A Lord's Daughter! Nounds, I'm glad I'm rid of her—Captain, I wifh you much Joy with all my Heart ——Od, I'll engage fhe fhakes your Commiffion for you; ha, ha.
Om. Ha, ha, ha, ha!
Num. Why, what Luck have I had, *Slouch!* Mercy on us; what a Ruin had I brought upon all our Country Gentlemen innocently? For fhe wou'd have corrupted all their Wives; the Devil a one wou'd have made her own Butter, after being acquainted with her.
Bel. Oh! you miftake, 'Squire, I am an excellent Houfewife; ha, ha, ha!
Num. Yes, yes, fome in our Country know by woful Experience, what Houfewives you Quality make; Nounds, 'twou'd undo the High Sheriff of the County to find you in clean Cards; then your plaguy outlandifh Liquors, your Coffee and Tea, fucks up the Cream of a whole Dairy, and your Suppers and Dinners for your Goffips wou'd confound all the Eggs and Pullen; and the Money you game away, wou'd ruin a Lord of a Manor. No, no, no Quality Breed for us Country Gentlemen; 'egad, that wou'd be worfe than double Taxes; ha, ha.
Con. Ha, ha! Well then, 'Squire, I have done you a Piece of Service; I hope all Animofities are forgot.
Num. They are i'faith, Sir; and if you'll give me Leave, I'll be heartily merry with you.
Truft. You fhall be heartily welcome, 'Squire; I fent for the Mufick—Hark, I hear them tuning their Inftruments.
Num. Mufick! 'Egad, if they can play my Tune, I'll give you a Jig.
Truft. Come, let's in then, and begin. [*Exit.*

SCENE

SCENE, *The Inside of the House, and discovers them dancing.*

Enter Roger *and* Dolly.

Rog. Save you all—Master and Landlord that was, and Master and Landlord that is, I'm glad to hear all is over, with all my Soul——I hope you'll not forget your Promise tho' to your poor Tenant *Roger*—which was to speak to Master——no, no, speak to yourself now, Sir——My Farm is woundly dear.

Trust. You are wondrous merry, *Roger*.

Rog. So is every body you know, Sir, when they are prepared for the Parson; are they not, Mrs. *Belinda?* I hope I shall have your Consent; for I have got *Dolly* in the Mind at last.

Bel. I wish you Joy with all my Heart, *Roger*.

Con. I'm glad to see you follow your Lady's Example, Mrs. *Dorothy*.

Dolly. She set too good a Pattern, not to imitate, Sir.

Con. Here remains three to be provided for yet; which is *Clinch, Lucy* and *Manage*.

Lucy. The best Provision I desire, is to wait on my Lady still, Sir.

Man. And I on my Master; who knows but Time may chop up a Wedding between you and I, Child? [*To* Lucy

Faith. Your Desires are granted; what says *Clinch ?*

Clin. I had a kind of a Tender for *Dolly*; but since she's dispos'd of, I'll stand as I do.

Const. Then we are all agreed.

Sir *Jeff.* Well, honest *Roger*, if thou'lt give us a Song to your Dance now, I'll be as good as my Word, and make thy Farm easy in the Rent for the next Year.

Rog. Say you so? I thank you heartily, Master, I'll do my best, I can't sing like your *Londoners*—But 'tis a new Ballad, and 'twas made at *London*, by a very honest Country Gentleman, last Sessions of Parliament. Hum, hum.
[*Sings.*

Slouch. Ads Blead, you sing, Sir, and the 'Squire by, that's more than any Man in *Zomersetshire* will venture to do; Master, Ods Wounds, hold your own, Master.

A SONG

The Devil to do about her.

A SONG, *by the* Author, *and sung by* Mr. Dogget.

Wou'd you chuse a Wife for a happy Life,
Leave the Court, and the Country take ;
Where Dolly and Sue, young Molly and Prue,
Follow Roger and John, whilst Harvest goes on,
   And merrily, merrily rake.

Leave the London Dames, be it spoke to their Shames,
To lig in their Beds till Noon ;
Then get up and stretch, then paint too and patch,
Some Widgeon to catch, then look on their Watch,
   And wonder they rose up so soon.

Then Coffee and Tea, both Green and Bohea,
Is serv'd to their Tables in Plate ;
Where their Tattles do run, as swift as the Sun,
Of what they have won, and who is undone,
   By their gaming, and sitting up late.

The Lass give me here, tho' brown as my Beer,
That knows how to govern her House ;
That can milk her Cow, or farrow her Sow ;
Make Butter, or Cheese, or gather green Pease,
   And values fine Clothes not a Louse.

This, this is the Girl, worth Rubies and Pearl ;
This the Wife that will make a Man rich :
We Gentlemen need no Quality Breed,
To squander away what Taxes would pay,
   In truth we care for none such.

Con. Now I am happy———
Belinda *mine, and you my faults forgive ;*
'Tis from this Moment I begin to live.
Love sprang the Mine, and made the Breach in Duty,
No Cannon-Ball can execute like Beauty,
But I'll no more in search of Pleasures rove,
Since every Blessing is compriz'd in Love. [*Exeunt.*

G 5   A. GO.

A

GOTHAM

ELECTION.

Dramatis Perſonæ.

M E N.

TICKUP, *a Candidate for* Gotham.
Sir John Worthy, *another Candidate talk'd on, but not ſeen.*
Friendly, *an Agent for Sir* Roger Truſty.
Score-double, *an Inn-keeper.*
Watt Waſhball, *a Barber.*
The Mayor *of* Gotham.
Mallet, *a Carpenter, and his Son.*
Scruple, *a Quaker.*
A Cobler.
A Miller.
Ben Blunt.
Gregory Gabble.
Roger Sly.
Timothy Shallow.

W O M E N.

Lady Worthy,
Goody Gabble.
Goody Shallow.
Goody Sly.
Midwife, and other Women,

SCENE, *Gotham.*

A

A GOTHAM ELECTION.

ACT I. SCENE I.

Enter on one Side Mr. Friendly.
On the other, Scoredouble, *an Inn-keeper.*

Friend. A! Landlord, I'm glad to fee you.
Score. Mr. *Friendly,* you are welcome.
Friend. I hope Mrs. *Scoredouble* and your pretty Daughter's well.
Score. Yes, yes, Sir, the Women are in good Cafe; my Wife, as the old Zaying is, *is better in Health than good Condition.* In troth I'm glad to zee you; pray, what brought you to *Gotham* an I may be fo bold to afk you? Elections, I warrant you?
Friend. Something like it, Landlord; pray what fort of a Man is your Mayor?
Score. Why, his Worfhip is a huge Admirer of the *French*; nay, 'tis whifper'd by zome, that his Zon is with the Knight of the *Dragon,* for he has never been zeen zince the Duke of what d'e call him went away.
Friend. Say you fo!
Score. Ay, an he has a Daughter, a weighty Girl, I promife you: Od wou'd you had her, Mr. *Friendly.*; fhe has Five Thoufand Pound, and a right Lover of her Country.
Friend. Five Thoufand Pound! a-gad, a fudden Thought comes into my Head, I'll purfue it; who knows but I may make fome lucky Difcovery: I thank you for your kind Wifhes, Landlord, but I can never hope for such a Fortune:

tune : His Son with the Knight of the *Dragon*, fay you, why then your Mayor is a *Jacobite*.

Score. Nay, he is fhrewdly fufpeƈted by zome to be a down-right *Papift* in his Heart ; but to zay Truth of him, he does go to Church conftantly, he does, indeed ; he does go to Church.

Friend. A pretty Fellow, for the Head of a Corporation.

Score. What do you pleafe to drink, Sir?

Friend. Why, bring us the beft your Houfe affords.

Score. The beft my houfe affords, ha, ha, ha, that is as you think it, Sir ;——now moft of our Gentry, for this laft vour Years, d'ye mind, will touch nothing but *French* Claret,—there are zome that like your *Port* Wines ftill, but very few, and thofe of the poorer Zort too, as my Barboard can witnefs.

Friend. Come, bring fuch as you like yourfelf.

Score. Why then, Mafter, we'll have a bottle of white *Lifbon.*——Here, *Sam*, bring a Bottle of the beft white *Lifbon*, d'ye hear.

Friend. Withal my Heart.—Well, Landlord, and how will Eleƈtions go with you in *Gotham* ?

Score. Why here is old tugging vort :——Here has been zuch roafting of Oxen : Zuch Veafting, and zuch Caballing, as you ne'er zaw the like! Here's one Squire *Tickup*, a *Londoner*, I think puts up for one ;——he's over Head and Ears in Debt, they zay, and zo has a Mind to get above the Law, and pay no Body.

Friend. That's one Way, indeed, to ferve himfelf ; but he that has not Honefty enough to pay his own Debts, may eafily be brought to give up the Debts of the Nation.——I hope he has no confiderable Number of Votes fecur'd, has he?

Score. He has zome——Here has happen'd an unfortunate Squabble between Sir *John Worthy*, and his Lady.

Friend. Sir *John Worthy!* Does not he put up too?

Score. Ay, and he and his Family has reprefented this zame Burrough of *Gotham* thefe vorty Years, and yet I believe he will lofe it now ; I am forry vor't, vor he's a very honeft Gentleman.

Friend. How fo, prithee?

Score. Why you muft know his Lady is a what d'ye call it,——

A GOTHAM *Election*. 159

it,——a High-flyer,——and nothing zo great as our Parſon's Wife and ſhe; now you muſt know, the Parſon had given my Lady a game Cockeril,——and, as the Devil would have it, a Diſſenter's Dog happen'd to worry this zame Cockeril,——and becauſe Sir *John* wou'd not go to Law with him for his Dog's Fault, my Lady zwears he's a Rebel, and would pull down the Church.

Friend. Ha, ha, excellent; but how does this effect Sir *John*'s Election?

Score. Why, my Lady being plaguy cunning de mind, ——ſhe reſerv'd to herſelf a Thouſand Pound when ſhe married Sir *John*; now ſhe ſwears ſhe'll ſpend every Groat on't, but ſhe'll fling Sir *John* out of his Election; and under the Roſe, d'ye zee, they zay that ſhe, and this zame Squire *Tickup*, are mainly well acquainted; zo ſhe veaſts the good Wives, d'ye mind, and ſo ſecures all thoſe Huſbands Votes, whoſe Wives wear the Breeches, ha, ha, ha.

Friend. Ha, ha, come my Service to you, and to all thoſe honeſt Fellows not under Petticoat Government.

Score. With all my Heart; hang Petticoat Government I zay; Zooks I love to wear my own Breeches.

Friend. Here's ſtrange Juggling it ſeems.

Score. Ha, ha, but now you talk of Juggling, we had rare Juggling here not long ſince; we had like to have had all the Money in the Country juggled away.

Friend. As how!

Score. Why, here was a Trickſter came down to *Gotham*——

Enter Wat Waſhball.

Ho, *Wat Waſhball*! Come in, come in mun; this zame Man can teſtify what I am going to zay: He is a very honeſt Freeholder, of vour Pounds a Year, zo he is,—— a Barber here by; with your Leave, Maſter, I'll drink to him.

Friend Pray do, you are welcome, Friend.

Wat. Thank you, Sir.

Score. Come pull a Chair *Wat*, and zit down; I was telling Maſter *Friendly* here, of the Trickſter that chang'd the Cards zo, you know, *Wat*, in the Town-Hall.

Wat. Ay, that was a bitter Dog, I believe we ſhant forget him in Haſte.

Friend. Why, what did he do?

Score.

Score. Why, you muſt know, Sir, he play'd ſeveral Tricks but his greateſt Skill lay in changing the Cards, —— He had a plaguy Nack at that ; —— don't you remember, *Wat*,——how he dealt a Card round the Hall, ——when our High Sheriff had got the Ace of Hearts, you know?

Wat. Ay, as plain an Ace of Hearts are ever I zaw in all my born Days.

Score. Ay, and what does this zame Trickſter but with one——Whif, conjures away this zame Ace of Hearts,—and claps the Knave of Clubs in its Place.

Friend. Ha, ha, ha.

Score. When my Neighbour *Waſhball* and I zaw that, we wou'd have had the Mayor made his Mittimuſs, and zent him to a Gaol.

Wat. No, no, not for that, not for that, Landlord, it was for changing an *Engliſh* Guinea into a *French* Piſtole, you know.

Score. Right, right, zo it was ; *Wat*, zo it was ; and you know the Mayor said the Piſtole was the better Gold, and wou'd not meddle with him vor't.

Friend. But there was Four Shillings loſt by that Change ; what cou'd your Mayor ſay for that?

Wat. Zay! Why he pretended to prove by Logick, I think he call'd it,——that Seventeen and Six-pence was more than One and Twenty and Sixpence.

Friend. Pretty Sophiſtry truly, for a Mayor of a Corporation ;——and what is become of this Juggler?

Score. Gone to the Devil, vor ought I know.

Friend. From whence came he?

Wat. Why zome zay from one Part, zome another ; but thoſe that pretend to know beſt, zay he came from zome Part of the Zouth-Zeas.

Friend. I rather believe the South-Seas came from him.

Wat. Pray what is this zame Zouth-Zeas? A Shire, Town, Burrough, or Market-Town.

Friend. It was a Market, and once had a very great Trade for Flumery and Leeks.

Score. Well, of all Garden Stuff, I hate those zame Leeks.

Wat. They leave a plaguy Stink behind them.

Enter.

A GOTHAM *Election*.

Enter Drawer.

Drawer. Dinner's upon Table, Sir.

Score. Mafter *Friendly*, will you eat a Slice of Buttock of Beef and Carrots?

Friend. With all my Heart,——and after Dinner I fhou'd be glad if you'd bring me acquainted with fome of the honeft Fellows of *Gotham*; I'll try if I can recommend a worthy Gentleman to them, one that has Gold enough, and owes no Man a Groat; is as generous as a Prince, and loves his Country as he loves his Wife.

Score. Ha, ha, ha, troth Mafter, that may be little enough, vor what as I do know——pray, who is he?

Friend. Sir *Roger Trufty*.

Score. Sir *Roger*! I fhall be glad to zee him with all my Heart, Blood and Guts, as they zay. [*Exeunt.*

SCENE changes to a Room in a Tavern.

Enter Lady Worthy, *Mr.* Tickup, *Goody* Gabble, *and Goody* Shallow.

Lady. Never fear, my dear *Tickup*,——as far as my Thoufand Pound goes I'll ftand by you; I'll fpend it every Shilling but carry my Point; I hate a Whig fo much, that I'll throw my Hufband out of his Election, or throw my-felf out of the World! a Parcel of canting Rogues; they have always Moderation in their Mouths,——rank Refift-ance in their Hearts,——and hate Obedience even to their lawful Wives,——and then they bear a mortal Hatred to Three Pound Fourteen and Fippence?

Tick. Ay, they hate all Coin that won't take their Im-preffion.

Lady. Why there's my Brute of a Hufband now, he hates the *French* fo much, that he won't let poor *Fanny* learn to dance.

Good G. Nay, my Hufband is a little poifon'd that Way too;——will you believe it, Madam, he had the Impu-dence to forbid me Dancing with your Honour's Worfhip laft Night;——he faid Dancing was a bold Recreation, and that was an Inlet to Sin;——but I pluck'd up a Spi-rit, and told him, I wou'd do it; that I wou'd dance, and dance again, fo I wou'd,——od my Gentleman was foon fnub'd, fnub'd, for he knew, an he rais'd my Paffion once, he wou'd have enough to do to get it down again.

Good S. Well, an I zay but one Word to *Timothy Shallow,* down goes Thimble and Shears,——and up he takes Gloves and Stick, and away goes he.——Ah, you're a happy Woman, Goody *Gabble;* your Hufband is a Man every Inch of him, I'll zay that for him.

Good G. You'll fay that for him ; Pray how come you to know what Man my Hufband is, Goody *Shallow?* Have you found him a Man for your Bufinefs, ha?

Good S. I, I found your Hufband a Man for my Bufinefs, I have a Hufband as fit for Bufinefs as yours;—— and tho' I zay it, that fhou'd not zay it, there is not a better Workman in the Parifh.

Tick. Ay, ay, they are both good Workmen enough in their Way ; fhe only jefted with you, that's all.

Lady. Ay, ay, Neighbours, nothing elfe,—well, you'll ufe your Endeavours with your Hufbands to give their Votes for Mr. *Tickup.*

G. Gab. That I fhall fure, Madam,——your Worfhip promifes me I fhall nurfe the young Squire, as foon as he is born.

Tick. That you fhall.

G. Gab. And I am to have Twenty Pounds a Year.

Lady. Ay, I'll pafs my Word for't.

G. Gab. I thank your Ladyfhip,——not that I doubt your Word, Madam, or the bountiful Squire's in the leaft ;—but, but, but, an, an the Squire wou'd advance a Year's Sallery aforehand, it wou'd go a great Way with my Hufband ; for you muft know, that *Gregory Gabble* is an honeft Man, and won't vote againft his Confcience, if it were not for his Intereft ;——now Sir *John,* you know, Madam, promifes to renew his Leafe *Gratis,* if he votes for him, but an he votes againft him, he won't bate him a Groat fo he won't ; you know your Hufband's Temper, Madam.

Lady. Oh, prithee name him not, you'll give me the Vapours; there, there's Twenty Pound for you, let me hear his odious Name no more.

Tick. Take Notice *Goody Gabble,* thofe Twenty Pounds are to pay for nurfing of a Child that fhall be born,—— no Matter when.

G. Gab.

A GOTHAM Election. 163

G. Gab. No, no, no, no Matter whether ever or never, I'll take it when you fend it, fure fweet Squire.

Tick. It is not out of any finifter End to fuborn your Hufband; no, I fcorn it, I am an honeft Man, and a Lover of the Church, and will take Care the Roguifh Whigs don't pull down a Haffock in't.

Lady. Ay, Neighbours, Mr. *Tickup*'s a good Churchman, mark that! He is none of your occafional Cattle; none of your hellifh pantile Crew;——Oh, we fhall never thrive till all thefe canting Whigs are whipt out of the Kingdom;——Oh, that I had the Jerking of 'em, I'd teach 'em Paffive-Obedience, or make the Devil come out of 'em.

Good S. Well, your Ladyfhip is a very wife Woman, that's certain: Good lack, how fhe doth talk, Neighbour *Gabble?*——Oh, fhe's a great Woman.

Lady. Ay, and you fhall be a great Woman too, Goody *Shallow*, if Mr. *Tickup* carries the Day; well, I'll fay no more, but every Body don't know Mr. *Tickup*'s Power;— but there's a certain great Prince, that fhall be namelefs, that has a very great Kindnefs for him, and for ought I know, he may ftand as fair for a Garter as the beft of 'em, one Day.

Good. S. Pray, 'Squire, will you be fo kind as to recommend my *Tim*, to that fame great Prince, to be his Taylor?

Lady. He fhall do it: your Hufband fhall be his Taylor, and you fhall be Dreffer to his Queen.

Good. S. And will your Honour's Worfhip do this?

Tick. I'll do any Thing to ferve you, *Goody Shallow.*

Good. S. Will you, truly! Well, *Timothy Shallow*, thou art a made Man;——and am I born to be a Courtier? Good lack, good lack——

Good. G. Blefs me! Who wou'd have thought that you, with your Broomftick, wou'd have come to fuch Honour, *Goody Shallow?*

Good. S. Ay, who indeed;——but I ha no vine Cloaths to go to Court in tho'; what mun I do for that now?

Tick. Why, to fhow you that I have a Kindnefs for you and your Hufband, there is Ten Guineas to rig you, for the Honours I defign to prefer you to. [*Gives her Money.*

Good. S. Ah, Heaven blefs your good Worfhip, me and

and mine will be oblig'd to pray for you, as long as we live.

Lady. Look you there now, when wou'd a Whig have done as much?——Blefs me, I'm in a Sweat when I but name a Whig.—— [*Fans herfelf, and walks about.*

Tick. I take a Pleafure to ferve my Country Folks, and am proud of an Opportunity to do good Offices;——for my Part, I fhould not be concern'd if I loft the Election, otherways than not being in a Capacity to ferve my poor Country at this Juncture.

Lady. There's a Man for ye, Neighbours! Now cou'd you find in your Heart, *Goody Shallow,* to deny this Gentleman any Thing, any Thing, any Thing, I fay?

Good. S. No, by my truly, I think I cou'd not; why fhou'd I belie my Confcience? Madam, come, here's the 'Squire's Health. [*drinks.*

Tick. I am oblig'd to you, *Goody Shallow.* [*kiffes her.*

Good. S. Good Gentleman, he's not proud;——odd, he kiffes main fweetly, Madam.

Lady. Ay, does he not?——Well, you'll bring your Hufband over.

Good. S. Over! ay, Madam, or he fhall never come over——my Threfhold more, I can tell him but that.

Enter Drawer.

Draw. Sir, here's *Goodman Mallet,* the Carpenter, enquires for you; he fays you fent for him.

Lady. No,——I fent for him in your Name; he is a filly Fellow, but no Matter for that; he can do you great Service; humour him in all he fays,——bring him up. [*Exit Drawer,* Give him Money, if you can handfomely top it upon him; ——there's a hundred Guineas, when they are gone, you fhall have more!——if you can get *Mallet's* Vote, he'll bring you twenty at leaft.

Tick. My charming Woman,——you oblige me to be for ever your's. [*Kiffes her.*

Lady. Come, Neighbour, let's retire, it may not be proper for us to hear *Goodman Mallet's* Bufinefs, you know. [*Exit.*

Good. G. No, no, no, no; come, come, come, we'll go,

A GOTHAM *Election*.

go, we'll go. Good Sir, your moſt humble Servant, I'll bring you *Gregory Gabble*, I warrant you. [*Exit*.
Good S. And ſo will I, my *Timothy Shallow*, ſweet 'Squire. [*Exit*.

Enter Mallet.

Tick. Mr. *Mallet*, your Servant. [*Takes out* 20 *Guineas, and plays with them on the Table as he talks*.
Mall. Your humble Servant, Sir, pray what is your Buſineſs with me?
Tick. Come, ſit down, Sir;——here, the Houſe.

Enter Drawer.

Draw. Did you call, Sir?
Tick. Ay, what Wine do you drink, Mr. *Mallet*?
Mall. 'Tis all one to me, Sir.
Tick. Then bring up a Bottle of *French* Red.
Draw. You ſhall have it, Sir. [*Exit*.
Tick. Mr. *Mallet*, there is a very honeſt Gentleman gives his Service to you, charg'd me to ſee you, and gave me a Token to drink with you.
Mall. Pray, who may that be?
Tick. One Mr. *Double*.
Mall. Ha! Maſter *Double*.
Drawer within] A Bottle of *French* Red in the *Flower-de-Luce. Score.*

Enter with Bottle and Glaſs.

Tick. Come, Mr. *Mallet*, Mr. *Double's* Heath to you.
Mall. With all my Heart; I have earn'd many a fair Pound of him;——ſome ſays he's an ill Pay-maſter, but I won't ſay ſo; for he paid me very honeſtly, tho' I muſt needs ſay he's a little long winded.——Sir, an you pleaſe, my Service to you, remembring Maſter *Double*.
Tick. Thank you, Mr. *Mallet*; well, how do you like the Wine? I think 'tis pretty good. [*Drinks*.
Mal. I think ſo too, Sir;——but ſecond Thoughts is beſt.
Tick. Right;——Come, here's to your Fireſide, Mr. *Mallet*, I ſuppoſe you are a marry'd Man.
Mal. Ay, Maſter, I have been marry'd theſe Five and Twenty Years; I have a Son's Wife lies in now.
Tick.

166   *A* GOTHAM *Election.*

Tick. I'll ſtand Godfather, if he be not better provided, Mr. *Mallet.*

Tick. Sir, your humble Servant ; I dare ſay he'll accept your kind Offer, and thank you too.

Tick. Is he all the Children you have, Mr. *Mallet* ?

Mal. No Sir, I have four Sons and three Daughters in all, fine young Men and Women as any in the Pariſh, no Diſpraiſe to the beſt. My eldeſt Son is a Lawyer, juſt out of his Time, a ſmart young Fellow, I promiſe you, Sir ; My ſecond I brought up to my own Trade, and he is a very great Maſter of his Buſineſs, tho' I ſay't, as any is in all *Gotham.* My third Son is a Bookſeller, a notable Fellow, he lives in *London* ; he is a kind of a Wit too, they ſay, and makes Verſes : Then he has an admirable Knack at quacking Titles. Perhaps you may know what that is, Sir ; but for my Part, I do not, I confeſs, underſtand it ; but they tell me, when he gets an old good for nothing Book, he claps a new Title to it, and ſells off the whole Impreſſion in a Week.

Tick. 'Tis a good Way of impoſing on the Publick, why he'll be a rich Fellow in a ſhort Time ?

Mal. Ay, ſo they ſay ; but my youngeſt Lad troubles me moſt of all.

Tick. How ſo, pray ?

Mal. Why you muſt know, Sir, he is a main weakly Boy ; he had the Rickets till he was ſeven Years old, which took away his Strength, and hugely dull'd his Memory, ſo that he's dull, very dull, Sir ; I can't think what to breed him up to, that don't require much Strength of Body, nor Application of Mind : His Mother is for making him a Parſon, but the Rogue won't hear on't.

Tick. Oh, Mr. *Mallet !* by your Deſcription, he is very unfit for a Parſon.

Mal. Why ſo I tell her, Sir ; and, in my Opinion, we had better get him a Place at Court.

Tick. Ay, there indeed you are in the right ; I don't know but I may be able to ſerve you there, if you'd endeavour to put it in my Power.

Mal. As how, pray ?

Tick. Why, Sir, you muſt know, I ſtand one of the Candidates for this Borough of *Gotham* ; and if you'll be ſo kind to give me your own Vote, and engage your

Friends

A GOTHAM *Election*.

Friends to do the fame, I'll take care of your Son, I promife you.

Mal. Pray what may your Name be, Sir?

Tick. My Name is *Tickup*, Sir.

Mal. Tickup! Ah, Sir, you lofe it for a Wager with you.

Tick. Why do you think fo?

Mal. Why, Sir, our Town has an Averfion for the Family of the *Tickups*; it is a Name very much hated, I afsure you, an I might advife you, I'd change it into *Ready Cafh*, ha, ha.

Tick. You are witty upon my Name, Mr. *Mallet*, but no Matter for that : what will you lay I don't carry it? I'll hold you twenty Guineas to one I do, and you fhall hold Stakes.

Mal. By Mefs, I'll take this Wager, if I never hold another, done, Sir.

Tick. Done ; there, there's twenty Guineas. [*Pufhes 'em to him.*

Mal. Well, if I fhould lofe my Guinea, Mr. *Tickup*, you'll remember a Place for my Son.

Tick. That I will indeed, Mr. *Mallet*; but then you muft not vote againft me.

Mal. No, no, that I won't, I promife you ; but an I engage my Friends, you muft promife to do a Kindnefs or two more for me.

Tick Name 'em, and command me.

Mal. Why cou'd not you now get my Son, the Lawyer, made Lord Chancellor, think you?

Tick. Can't! Yes, and will too.

Mal. Will ye? Ay, pray you do—an, an, hold, hold, I have the Names of all the great Places in a Bit o'Paper fomewhere, if I find 'em, but——I took 'em out of the prefent State of *Gotham*,——ho ! here, here it is——Ay, let me fee,——yes, yes,—Lord Steward, ay, Lord Steward ! ay, that's a very pretty Poft ; that, d'you mark me, I wou'd have for my Son Ned—the Carpenter, he underftands how to keep the Houfe in good Repair—and that's a main Matter you know ; his Majefty need give himfelf no Manner of Trouble.

Tick. Oh, that will be a very great Advantage ; well, I'll take care about that too.

Mal.

Mal. And the Bookſeller, I'd have him——de ze—— ho! I'd have him Groom of the Stole.

Tick. There you are perfectly right, becauſe he will have an Opportunity to make Uſe of his Verſes.

Mal. Then for my youngeſt Son! What mun he be? Why, what an you ſhould make him Treaſurer now! for the Rogue always lov'd Money. And for my Daughters —I fancy they would do rarely well for the Queen's Maids of Honour.

Tick. Oh, excellently well——all this I promiſe you.

Mal. Do you truly?——Well, you are a huge civil Gentleman, and ſo my humble Service to yo—Well, I'll ſay no more——but an I do not bring you twenty Votes, my Name's not *Mallet*, d'ye ſee, that's all, that's all—and ſo, Sir, your Servant, with all my Heart. (*going.*) Hold! one Thing more I muſt deſire of you—I have an own Couſin, that is a Sailor——ſuppoſe now you ſhould make him ſomewhat—an Admiral—or a Boatſwain, or ſo d'ye ſee?

Tick. He ſhall be one of them, I promiſe you.

Mal. Shall he in troth?—well, good bye to you, and thank you kindly. [*going.*

Tick. Mr. *Mallet*, your humble Servant,——oh, the Devil!

Mal. Methinks I love to do Good in my Generation; tho' to ſay Truth, the gracelefs Dog does not deſerve it; but no matter—as long as you can have it for ſpeaking for, you know?

Tick. What is it? Death, this Fellow would tire a Porter.

Mal. I have a Nephew ſomewhere or other, his Name is *Sam Slaſh*, a Soldier; pray enquire him out, wol you, and make him—ay, make a Corporal, or a Colonel, or ſomewhat of that, now.

Tick. Well, well, this I promiſe you. Have you any Thing eleſe?

Mal. No, no, I won't trouble you any more, not I— your Servant. [*going.*

Tick. Give me leave to wait of you down.

Mal. Odſo! I had forgot my Wife *Joan*, well thought on I'faith—ſhe would never have forgiven me, if I had not remember'd her——*Joan* muſt have ſomewhat, Mr. *Tickup*,

Tickup, what can *Joan* have now, think; pray think a little for her.

Tick. Let me fee—why, fuppofe fhe were made Oyfter-Cracker to the Court now.

Mal. Oyfter-Cracker! I don't remember any fuch Poft in my Lift.

Tick. Oh! never trouble your Head about that, there is, or fhall be fuch a Poft.

Mal. Shall there! well, well, that will do then—but, but, but, I doubt *Joan* will never be content to live at Court without me——Can't you contrive fome fmall Place for me too——Any thing will ferve me—I'll be fatisfy'd with being Lord-Mayor; I am very modeft in my Requefts, you fee?

Tick. Modeft, quotha! ha, ha, well, well, you fhall be Lord-Mayor.

Mal. Well, well, that's enough—will you believe me, Mr. *Tickup?* I really love my Friends as well as myfelf—why here's an honeft Pot-Companion of mine, *Barnaby Bran*, the Baker; methinks I would fain make his Fortune too; can you think of nothing for him?

Tick. Honeft *Barnaby Bran*, the Baker! I have a rare Place for him.

Mal. Have you really now! What is it, pray?

Tick. Why, he fhall be——Mafter of the Rolls.

Mal. He will be main thankful. What, is it a Patent Place?

Tick. Yes, yes; a Patent Place.

Mal. And have you any Thing for his Wife?

Tick. His Wife, ay, fhe fhall have Pattins too.

Mal. Od, that will pleafe her Hufband mainly.

Tick. Ay, fhe has been a Clogg to him a great while, no Doubt on't. [*Afide.*

Mal. Well, honeft 'Squire, your humble Servant.

[*Exit.*

Tick. I'm glad I'm rid of him; blefs me, if it were in my Power now to keep my Word, what a prodigious Company this Fellow has provided for!——but thanks to Policy, a Man is not always oblig'd to keep his Word:

The Courtier, Politician, and the Beau,
Whate'er you afk, will never anfwer, No:

But

But *closely prest, you'll find their whole Proceeding,*
To be no more nor less, than pure good Breeding. [Exit.

SCENE *changes to the* Mayor's *House.*

Enter Mayor *with a Letter in his Hand.*

Friendly *dress'd like a* Frenchman.

May. Well, and how does all our Friends on t'other Side the Water, ha? Well, I hope.

Friend. Oh *fort bien*, Monsieur *Mayor*, and Monsieur *le Chevalier*, be varey much your Humble Serviteur, Begar.

May. I am very much his, I am sure—Come, Monsieur, to the Fatherless and Widow. [*Drinks.*

Friend. Vid all mine Heart, dat every Man may have his own, Begar. [*Drinks.*

May. Amen, I say——but I must desire you, Monsieur, to explain the Letter to me? My Daughter tells me it is not *English*.

Friend. No, dis be *French*, Sir.

May. French! what has my Son learn'd *French* already? ——But what makes him write *French* to me, when he knows that I can neither write nor read it——and that no Body understands a Word of *French* in the Parish.

Friend. Oh, for dat very Reason he did write in *French*, becaufe it be one great Secret, and he knows me to be de very fedelle Personne, in whom de grand Monarchs in dis Vorld put a der Confidance: You understand a me, Monsieur?

May. Yes, yes; Oh Blessings on my Boy, he will certainly raise his Family?——a Secret! pray read it softly.

Friend. Oh softly, by all Means.——First, den, he tell you here, dat de Knight of de Dragon give his most humble Service to you, and prays you to take a de care to make de good Members for him.

May. Ay, ay, I will do all that in me lies.

Friend. And for dat Purpose, you shall receive one, two, three hundred Pistoles, in one, two, three Days ma foy.

May. Very well, very well;——pray let him know, that the last Money, that was remitted, has been prudently employ'd for the Chevalier's Service: Our Parson Blow-Coal is right stanch; he distributed it, with a strict

Charge

A GOTHAM *Election.*

Charge to have Regard to the Church ; the Noife of the Church, you know, does much, Monfieur?——My Brother, Alderman *Credulous*, had two hundred Pounds.

Friend. Humph ; well faid Parfon ; this News fhall to Sir *Roger Trufly.* (*Afide.*) Ha, ha, ha, Begar, dat will do de Bufinefs ; de Cry of de Church will bring in de King *par blue* ; but one ting more, Monfieur *Mayor*, he fay here in dis Letter, dat de Knight of de Dragon charge you right or wrong, to return de vat do you call 'em——de High-Church.

May. Ay, ay, that he may depend on ; oh, my dear Boy ! And what is my Boy a Favourite abroad, ha ?

Friend. Oh, a great Favourite, I affure you—Den here be one ting more ;——he prays you to fend by me his Sifter for de Education,——becaufe it be whifper'd, dat if defe plaguey Low-Church get de Day,—dey vill make it Treafon for any one to fend der Children to *France*, Begar ; no, dey vill fend dem for Education to *Scotland*, and bring all de young Ladies to the Stool of Repentance, ma foy.

May. Zounds, I'd fend mine to *Lapland* fooner, tho' I am a Proteftant myfelf, becaufe I was born fo d'ye fee ; yet I had rather breed my Children at *Rome*, than *Geneva* ; Zounds I hate thefe Whiggifh Dogs.

Friend. Begar de Pope no love to them neither ; dey be dam Fellows for de Liberty and Property ; but your Daughter, your Daughter, Monfieur Mayor——

May. She fhall along with you, Monfieur——her Aunt left her five thoufand Pounds ; ——I wifh you could perfuade her to turn Nun ; one Thoufand would provide for her in the Nunnery--and the other four would make my Son a Lord.

Friend. Oh let de Prieft get her once, and begar he vill make her——fomething, I warrant you.

May. But which Way fhall I get her over, fhe'll never confent to leave *England* ; for you muft know fhe is plaguey low in her Principles ?

Friend. Me tell you one Politick——'tis vine Veder ! Afk her to go vid you and me to fee de Ship dat bring me hither, and ven fhe be in de Ship vid me, fome Body muft ftop your going up de Ship, and tell you dat Day came an Exprefs for you upon de grand Bufinefs of

H 2   de de Nation, ma Foy; fo you leave us, vid de Promife to return prefently;——fo as foon as you be gon, me make a de Mafter hoift a Sail, and away for *Calais*, Begar.

May. Excellent Contrivance!—we'll about it this Moment.——I can but laugh to think how I fhall choufe the young Jade into her Happinefs.

Friend. And I can but laugh to think how you'll be chous'd out of your Daughter, if Luck favours me.

[*Afide.*

May. And pray tell my Son, I'll obferve his Direction,——my Clerk fhall fit up all this Night to write Conveyances;——I'll make twenty Freeholders before Morning yet.

Friend. As how, pray, Monfieur Mayor?

May. Oh, we have Ways and Means :——Why, I'll undertake, d'ye fee, to make four Votes out of a Goofeberry-Bufh, and fix out of a Hog's-Sty——

Friend. Begar dofe be de very fweet Votes. [*Exit.*

SCENE *changes to the Street.*

A Cobler at work in his Stall under an Ale-houfe. Enter Mr. Tickup.

Tick. Speed your Work, Friend, your Trade depends upon good Hufbandry.

Cob. Ay, Mafter, zo't does, as you zay; but I make new Shoes fometimes, as well as mend old ones.——

Tick. Say you fo! why you fhall be my Shoe-maker—if you'll do me a fmall Kindnefs.

Cob. (*Getting up, with Cap in Hand.*) What is it Mafter? to put a Stitch in your Shoe, I warrant you?

Tick. No, only to give me your Vote, that's all.

Cob. (*Sits down to work again.*) All, quotha! why that's all many a Man has to live on; at this Time, a fmall Kindnefs! Ha, ha, ha, it is a fmall Kindnefs, truly.

Tick. What fay you, Friend, will you?

Cob. I don't know, I believe not.

Tick. Why, fo, pray you?

Cob. I can't tell,——mehap I may;——mehap I may not, d'ye fee.

Tick. Have you promis'd any body elfe?

Cob. Suppofe I have,——fuppofe I have not, what then?

A GOTHAM *Election*.

then? Look ye, my Vote's as good as the beſt Man's i'th' Pariſh, or next Pariſh to't, that's a proud Word d'ye zee; ——and I will take care who I gin to, zo I wol.

Tick. Nay, you are in the Right of that; but no Man ſhall do more for the Corporation than myſelf.

Cob. Ay, ay, you all talk it well affore you get in;—— but you are no ſooner choſe in, but whip you are as proud as the Devil, zo you are, and a Man can't ſpeak Truth, but you come with your *Candelum Natum* zous upon us.

Tick. Pride is the leaſt Sign of a Gentleman, and I don't know if I ſhould not rather be call'd Rogue, than a proud Man.

Cob. And mehap he would not lie that call'd you both, ha, ha.

Tick. I am ſorry you ſhould have ſo ill an Opinion of me.

Cob. Why are you not proud, now?

Tick. I think I may ſafely ſay I am not.

Cob. Why then——come and kiſs me.

Tick. With all my Heart. [*kiſſes him.* Well, what think you now? will you give me your Vote yet.

Cob. Look ye, vare and zoftly,—I am not throwly zatisfy'd, whether I ſhall give you my Vote or not.

Tick. I am ſorry for that——but if you'll go to the Tavern, I'll give you a Pint of Wine, whether you'll give me your Vote or not, for I like you for your Bluntneſs.

Cob. I dan't value your Wine of this Hog's Briſtle, d'ye zee;——I am an honeſt Man, d'ye zee——and am vor a vree Government; I'm none of thoſe that are to be brib'd——now an you are not proud, d'ye zee——why come into my Stall, here, and I'll give you a ₁Flaggon of Ale.

Tick. Oh, the Devil, that will dirty all my Cloaths; (*Aſide.*) Had not we better go into the Ale-Houſe?

Cob. Look ye there now, did I not zay you was proud? No, Sir, I wont leave my Stall; thoſe that are aſham'd of me—why I am aſham'd of them, d'ye zee, that's all.
[*Sings and marks.*

Tick. A Pox of the unpoliſh'd Blockhead, I muſt humour him. [*Gathers up his Cloaths, and goes in.*

Nay,

174   *A* GOTHAM *Election.*

Nay, nay, don't be angry——I only faid it, to fave you the Trouble of going for the Ale, that's all.

Cob. Oh, I have a Conveniency for that.   [*Whiſtles, and the Boy enters.*

Look you there, Sir ; Sirrah, bring me a Pot of humming Ale, de you hear——what are you afraid of your Cloaths ? Zblead, fit down, mun, tho' I'm a poor Fellow, I've zitten by as good as you affore now, mun.

[*Pulls him down rudely.*

Enter Boy with Drink on one Side, and Tolefree, *the Miller, on t'other.*

Tick. Ay, ay, Friend, who doubts it.

Tole. Hark ye, Neighbour *Laſt*, will you never have done cobling my Shoes ?

Cob. Oh, Neighbour *Tolefree*, you come in the Nick ; why here's Neighbour *Tolefree* has a Vote too, and he'll give it ye.——

Tick. I fhall be much oblig'd to him, if he will, pray drink to him.

Cob. By and by, let his Betters be ferv'd before him, my Service to you, Sir——come in, Neighbour *Tolefree* —come, we'll make you Room.   [*Drinks.*

Tole. With all my Heart. [*Gets on the other Side* Tickup.

Tick. I wifh the Devil had them both——what a fine Pickle I fhall be in, pray have a Care of my Cloaths.

Cob. Cloaths, nay, I hope I am a better Commonwealths-Man than to mind Cloaths ; fit clofe, Neighbour *Tolefree*, or you'll thruft me off the Form. [*The Miller hitches upon* Tickup, *and makes his Cloaths all white.*

Tick. Thefe Dogs have a Defign upon me, I wifh I was fairly out ; Death, what a Coat is here ?   [*Aſide.*

Tole. Come, come put about the Pot.

Tick. My Service to you, Sir, (*drinks*) the King's Health——

Cob. I love the King—and fo kifs me agen. [*Claps his Hands on his Cheeks, and pulls him to kifs him, and leaves them all black.*

Tick. Confound the Rafcal ! how his Breath ftinks— Well, what fay you now, Gentlemen, will you both give me your Votes ?

Tole.

Tole. Give you my Vote! that will bring no Grift to my Mill, d'ye fee.

Cob. Get out and walk before my Door, now, two or three Turns, and I'll tell you more of my Mind.

Tick. Death, he'll make me jump over a ftick by and by. [*Gets out and walks.*
Well, what fay you now?

Tole. You have a plaguy Hitch in your Pace, you learnt to dance of some *Frenchman*, I'm certain.

Cob. Ha, ha, ha, ha, I think that you'd think me a Fool, if I fhould give you my Vote, now.

Tick. How fo, pray?

Cob. How fo! ha, ha, ha, you that are a fine bred Gentleman, here d'ye fee——yet can ftoop fo low, as to kifs, and humour fuch a dirty Fellow as I am, purely to buy my Vote——I dan't know, d'ye zee, but for a good round Sum you might be prevail'd upon to zell my Country, ha, ha, ha, ha : Look ye, I da't like you comming Sparks——you fhou'd be a little more coy, ha, ha, ha.

Tick. You are merry, Friend.

Cob. Not fo merry as you think for, mehaps——but Vriend me no Vriend, go troop, Nouns, he looks like a Jefuit, does he not, Neighbour *Tolefree?*

Tole. Pull off his Whore's Hair, and ze an he has not a bald Crown.

Tick. The Devil! they'll ftrip me by and by, I had as good walk off, for thefe are both damn'd *Whigs*, I find that.

Cob. Ha, ha, he's gone! an he be not a plaguey High Boy, I'm miftaken. Come Neighbour *Tolefree*, you and I will take a Pot of Ale together, to Sir *John Worthy's* Health, you'll vote for him, wol you not?

Tole. Yes, that I wol——for all my Lady has been tampering with my Wife *Margery*, and has given her a vine Silk Gown, and a huge high Head——but I drefs'd my Dame's Jacket for her, and made her carry 'em agen; odsflesh, we fhould have rare Times, an we were to be rul'd by our Wives, you know, ha, ha. [*Exit.*

Enter Alderman Credulous.

Alderman. Ha, ha, ha, I can but laugh to think how

my Wife's Brother, the Mayor, has over-reach'd his Daughter.'

Enter Sir Roger Trufty.

Sir Roger. Mr. Alderman *Credulous!* your moſt humble Servant, Sir, I'm glad to fee you fo merry ; pray what may be the Occaſion ?

Ald. Family Affairs, Sir *Roger*; my Brother has diſ-pos'd of his Daughter——that's all.

Sir Rog. Humph ! not as he expected ; tho' I believe, for her Advantage, I hope. [*Aſide.*

Ald. Ay, ay, Sir *Roger*, we Fathers know what's good for our Children, better than they do themſelves ; they have nought to do but to fubmit to our Pleaſures ; paſſive Obedience is as abſolutely neceſſary in our Wives and Children, as in Subjects to the Monarch ; is not your Opinion the fame, Sir *Roger* ?

Sir Rog. Yes, whilſt Huſbands, Fathers and Monarchs exact nothing from us, contrary to our Religion and Laws : But pray, Mr. *Alderman*, how came you fo paſſive ? I re-member you wore other Principles in Eighty Eight—this is not natural, *Alderman*.

Ald. Eighty Eight ! that's a long Time ago ; I know ſome Men that have worn out twenty Sets of Principles ſince Eighty Eight, both Men of the Robe, and Men of the Gown.

Sir Rog. More the Pity, *Alderman*, I am forry Nature did not diſtinguiſh Men of ſuch Principles from the reſt of her Handywork, that we might enjoy her Gifts more amply, and be more thankful for the Bleſſing. When I reflect that I am of the same Species with the Betrayers of my Country (for fure that Crime is the greateſt of all others) I could almoſt wiſh to wear any other Form of the Creation. Life is a Bleſſing, or a Curſe, according to the Fame we purchaſe, and he that redeems twenty of his Fellow Creatures from the ſlaviſh Yoke of Tyrrany, does an Action worthy of a Man that bears the Image of his Creator, whilſt he who feeks by Treachery to inſlave his Kind, to feed Ambition, Avarice, or Revenge, is only the Peſt of human Society, and ought to have a Mark ſet upon him, that we might ſhun him as we would the Plague.

Ald.

Ald. Ay, ay, fo it ought to be, Sir *Roger*; but I have read fomewhere,
*Nature to Man's Breaſt has made no Window
To ſhow us what they aƈt within Doors*,
For my Part, I am for the Church, and my Country.

Sir Rog. So am I; their Intereſts are infeparable; who gives up one, betrays the other: For my Part, I intend to ſtand or fall by both; therefore I hope you'll do me the Honour of your Vote, Mr. *Alderman*.

Ald. Why truly, Sir *Roger*, I am pre-engag'd, I won't tell a Lie for the Matter.

Sir Rog. To who pray?

Ald. Why to Squire *Tickup*.

Sir Rog. Tickup! Why he's a Fellow not worth a Groat, and a known *Jacobite*.

Ald. Nay, look ye as to that, his Means and his Religion is nothing to me; let his Creditors take care of one, and our Parſon o'th' t'other; for my Part, I'm for the Church, as I faid before, and would rather be a Papiſt than a Preſbyterian.

Sir Rog. Why where's the Neceſſity of your being either? Come, come, there's a more convincing Argument than what you have nam'd—Mr. *Tickup* is recommended by fome great Man on whom you have Dependance.

Ald. Great Man! Why yes, truly, he is a pretty large Man; and I have, I truſt Heaven, very great Dependance on what he fays: The Parſon of the Pariſh, you know, ought to be regarded, Sir *Roger*, and he told me that Mr. *Tickup* was a good Churchman, and pray'd me to vote for him, and to get all my Friends to do the fame, if I would promote the Intereſt of the Church.

Sir Rog. Ay, the Intereſt of the Church of *Rome*, not that of *England*; why I'll undertake to prove this Fellow deep in the Intereſt of young *Perkin*, and that he and his Friend at *Villa Coumbe*, has bought up, and fent for his Service, more than two thouſand Horſes within theſe laſt four Years; and can ſuch a Man be a proper Perſon to reprefent you in that auguſt Aſſembly, where the People of *Gotham* expeƈt to have theſe pernicious Meaſures redreſt?

Ald. Why I am confounded at what you tell me.

Sir Rog. I am amaz'd to find you in the Intereſt of the High-Boys, you that are a Clothier! What, can you be for giving up Trade to *France*, and ſtarving poor Weavers?

Ald. Trade, piſh, piſh, our Parſon ſays that's only the Whig's Cant, and that if the Bill of Commerce had paſs'd, it wou'd have been of ſignal Service to us.

Sir Rog. Which Way, I pray, Alderman?

Ald. Nay, I never aſk'd him that; tho' not doubt but he can tell you, for he is a learn'd Man, and underſtands Matters better than I do.

Sir Rog. It is much to be wiſh'd for the Honour of our Religion, and the Safety of our State, that thoſe learned Men were more induſtrious in the Cure of Souls, and leſs buſy in Politicks——But come, come, Mr. *Alderman*, there is yet a Secret behind the Curtain; pray what cou'd Mr. *Tickup*, or any of his Friends oblige you with, that is not in my Power to have done?—You and I have been good Friends, and if a Brace of Hundreds had been wanting—why, we could have ſerv'd you as well as they.

Ald. So, ſo, I find whereabouts you are already. Well, there is nothing kept a Secret in this damn'd Town. However, I had not thoſe two hundred Pounds by Way of Bribe, I aſſure you, Sir *Roger*.

Sir Rog. Ha, ha, why then you had two hundred Pounds?

Ald. Yes, I confeſs, Mr. *Blowcoal* our Parſon did give me Bills for two hundred Pounds, part of a Sum, he ſaid, that was given him for charitable Uſes, and bade me diſpoſe of it to proper Objects, as I thought fit, but not to bribe Votes, I aſſure you.

Sir Rog. No, no, no, no, 'twas to build Churches, I ſuppoſe, and reward ſecret Merit, ha, ha, ha, ha; but I am ſorry, for your Sake, that they made their Payment in Paper:———Pray let me ſee thoſe Bills———who are they upon?

Ald. See them! Ay———there they are, Sir *Roger*.
[*Gives him Bills.*

Sir Rog. (*Looks on 'em.*) Upon Sir *Charles Wealthy!* As I ſuſpected:——Why he is a Bankrupt, not worth a Groat, ha, ha, ha; why you are bit, Alderman, *Blowcoal* has bit you, ha, ha, ha; Charity, quotha! Yes, this is Charity with a Vengeance.

Ald.

Ald. How! Am I trick'd? But you are not in Earneſt, Sir *Roger*, are you?

Sir Rog. As certainly as that I myſelf loſt five hundred Pounds by the ſame Banker: I tell you, Sir *Charles Wealthy* has been gone off this Month.

Ald. The Devil he has? Odſheart, I am finely ſerv'd; why, I'm out of Pocket the Lord knows what: Death! I ſhall loſe all Patience!

Sir Rog. Look ye, Mr. *Alderman*, if you'll yet hear Reaſon, I'll make up all this Matter; ſee here, (*pulls out a Purſe*) here's two hundred Guineas in this Purſe; all ready Caſh, hang Paper; here's the best Proviſion for charitable Uſes.—Mr. *Alderman*! hark how religiouſly they chink; what ſay you? Come, for once, ſerve yourſelf and your Country, old Boy.

Ald. But you are ſure thoſe Bills are not worth a Farthing, Sir *Roger*? [*Sir* Roger *claps the Bills into his Pockets, and takes out ſome Papers, and tears 'em in ſmall Pieces.*

Sir Rog. Sure on't, aye, as ſure as I am that my Name is *Roger Truſty*:——and thus I ſacrifice them to your Reſentment, Mr. *Alderman*, and now———

Ald. Death, Hell, and the Devil, I'm undone——— but if I'm not reveng'd.———

Sir Rog. (*Plays with the Purſe.*) It was a curſed Trick indeed to affront an Alderman of a Corporation at this Rate.

Ald. Give me the Purſe; (*Sir Roger ſlaps it into his Hand*) and now, Sir *Roger*, I am yours; if I do not fit Parſon *Blowcoal*, ſay I am the Son of a dead Cinder.—— I'll bring ſixteen Votes, Sir *Roger*; egad I'll over-reach the Rogues, I warrant em: This Purſe is a Pledge for my Performance. [*Exit.*

Sir Rog. And theſe Bills a Pledge for that Purſe. Ha, ha, ha, (*takes out the Bills*) I'll ſend my Servant to receive the Money immediately; I think I have paid them in their own Coin.

In this at laſt we have the Advantage got,
We give the Treat, but they ſhall pay the Shot.

SCENE Mallet's *Son's Houſe.*

Mallet, *his Son,* Lady *Worthy,* Goody *Gabble,* Goody *Shallow,*

low, Sly *and his Wife, and Midwife with the Child; feveral Men and Women drinking, as at a Chrift'ning, a Quaker filling Wine, and a Fidler playing.*

Enter Tickup.

Mallet. We began to defpair of your Company, Sir, we have Chriftened the Child——but we got one to ftand in your Place, 'Squire.

Tick. Very well, I'll take the Charge upon me.

Midwife. (*Prefenting the Child.*) Here's your Godfon, Sir, a fine thumping Boy, he is almoft big enough to afk your Bleffing.

Tick. A fine Child, indeed——(*He takes the Child and kiffes it, and gives it a Silver Cup.*) Here, Sirrah, here's a Cup for you, and be fure you drink my Health out of it as foon as you can fpeak, do you hear———Which is the Father?

Mal. This is my Son, 'Squire.

Son. Sir, you do me much Honour.

Tick. Sir, I wifh you much Joy of my Godfon,—and may your good Lady bring you every Year fuch another. Well, which are the Godmothers? that I may difcharge my Duty.

Goody Sly. Why, I am one, for want of a better, Sir.

Tick. Say you fo! Have at you then.   [*Kiffes her.*

G. Gab. And I'm t'other, fweet 'Squire.

Tick. Goody Gabble; (*kiffes her*) nay, I'm to go round, ——and you too, Mrs. Midnight; kifs me, you old Jade you——

Mid. Well, well, you Gentlemen are very happy at Midnight, fometimes——Old Jade! Not fo old neither, but I can have a Civility done me by as fine a Gentleman as your 'Squire's Worfhip, I'd have you to know.

Tick. P'fhaw, who difputes that?—Old Jade is my favourite Name; you muft know, egad, I love an old Woman——I would not give a Fig for your green Girls, not I.

G. Sly. Ah, you are a merry Gentlemon——He has a Breath as fweet as a Cow——he kiffes rarely well——*Roger*, you fhall give this Gentleman your Vote, *Roger*.
[*Afide to her Hufband.*

Roger. So, he has tickled her Fancy already,
G. Sly.

G. Sly. I fancy you are a rare Dancer, 'Squire; pray will you give us a Jigg?

Tick. A Jigg! Ay, with all my Heart, if you'll dance with me, Dame.

G. Sly. A lack, 'Squire, I can't dance, 'Squire.

Tick. I warrant thee, Dame:——Come, ſtrike up, Fidler. [*He kiſſes her.*

G. Sly. Nay, ſure I ſhall not be able to do it with ſuch a vine Gentleman as you. [*They dance.*

Roger. (*Goes up to his Wife*). Get home, you Beaſt, you, wol ye? A Plague o' your jigging, will you ne'er ha jigging enough?

Tick. I hope you are not angry! Rather than diſoblige you, I'll kiſs your Wife no more.

G. Sly. Look ye there now, *Roger?*——you are always doing Miſchief, ſo you are.

Lady. An't you aſham'd of yourſelf, *Roger?*

Roger. Aſham'd of myſelf; vor what, I tro?

Lady. Methinks you ſhou'd take it as an Honour.

Roger. What, vor him to lie with my Wife! Look ye, Madam, you may keep that Honour for Sir *John*, an you woll.

Lady. You ſaucy impudent Raſcal! Who do you talk to, Sirrah?

G. Gab. Fye, Neighbour *Sly*, you uſe my Lady like a common Woman, ſo you do.

Roger. If ſhe's as common as thoſe that take her Part, I'm ſure ſhe's common enough.

G. Gab. Meaning me, Sirrah——I'll make you prove your Words, you Rogue you:——Why *Gregory, Gregory Gabble*, I ſay—do you hear what this Rogue *Sly* ſays?

[*Gregory is kiſſing a Woman.*

See, ſee, the Villian is minding his Pleaſures, when he ſhould be vindicating his Wife;—but I'll ſwinge you,—I'll cool your Courage when I get you at home, I will ſo——— [*Clapping her Hands.*

Lady. This Raſcal, *Sly*, was againſt the Peace, I remember it well——and I'll have you hang'd for't, I will, you Pantile Monſter.

Roger. Nay, when ſuch as you talk of Peace, we know the Devil is beating up for Volunteers, ha, ha.

Tick. Prithee, my dear Life, don't put thyſelf into a
Paſſion.

Paffion.——Mr. *Sly*, I afk your Pardon, if I have given you any Offence.

Roger. I am no Pope, Sir;——but I ha done.

Mal. Why that's well faid——my Neighbour *Sly's* an honeſt Man, he takes nothing ill, I'll fay that for him. Pray, Mr. *Tickup*, drink to my Neighbour *Sly*.

Tick. I fill'd the Glafs for the fame Purpofe. Mr. *Sly*, my hearty Service to you. [*Drinks.*

Roger. Don't Mafter me, Sir,——I'm but a poor Man; my Name is *Roger Sly*, d'ye fee, that's all.

Mal. (*To the Quaker.*) Neighbour *Scruple*, will you do me the Favour to give this honeſt Gentleman your Vote!

Scruple. Verily, Neighbour *Mallet*,——I do think I fhall not do it.

Mal. Why fo?

Scru. Am I oblig'd to give thee my Reafons?

Mal. No, not oblig'd, but I would be glad to know them.

Scru. Why then thou fhalt know them. Between thee and me, Neighbour *Mallet*, I do not take him for an hɔneſt Man.

Lady. Not an honeſt Man! Why what can you fay againſt his Honefty——He's none of your canting Congregation, that's all.

Scru. I did not direct my Difcourfe to thee; and I wou'd advife thee not to put thyfelf into a Paffion, it will much diforder thy outward Woman——and make thy Lovers lefs defiring.

Lady. My Lovers! Goodman *Goofe-crown*, who told you that I had Lovers, ha? Goodman *Mallet*, why do you let your Son take Wine of this old canting Villian, when there is ten times better, either at the Pope's Head, —or the Devil?

Scru. Yea, verily, I do perceive that thou art much in the Intereſt of thofe two that thou haſt nam'd, by thy Language and thy Actions.

Lady. And what are you in the Intereſt of, Sirrah?— Not of your Country,—you, you, you—Spawn of old *Noll*, you——Here, Fidler, play me the tune of, *The King fhall enjoy his own again.*

Sly. Ay, Ay, let 'en, let en an he dares; 'zbud I ha' no Papiſts Tunes play'd where I am; play Lillibullera, you Rogue. [*Lady.*

Lady. You won't have no Papifts Tunes! Sirrah, play what I bad you.

Sly. Wounds, play what I bad ye, ye Dog, or I'll break your Fiddle about your Ears. [*He plays Lillibullera.*

Lady. You Prefbyterian Son of a Conventicle, how dare you contradict me, Sirrah? [*Strikes him on the Face, and makes his Nofe bleed.*

G. Sly. Murder, Murder, my Hufband's all of a gore Blood; ah, you are a good one to ftrike a Man, I warrant ye.

Lady. I'll murder you, you dirty, draggle-tail'd Slut; take that Hufwife. [*Strikes Goody Sly, and makes her Nofe bleed; fhe blows it into her Hand, and fhows it, crying.*

G. Sly. See, fee here, fee here, how they begin to fpill Proteftant Blood already; oh you Papift Devil, you;—— ay, this is what you wou'd be at.

Sly. Zounds, if fhe carries this off,—I'll be hang'd alive; I'll drefs her down, I warrant her, an fhe be for fighting.
[*Offers to ftrip; they hold him.*

Mal. O fie, is fhe not a Woman?

Sly. Nay, afk her Spark there, he knows beft, or he's foully bely'd on—A Woman! a fhameless Beaft is fhe!

Tick. Let me perfuade your Ladyfhip to leave the Room. [*Afide to the Lady.*

Lady. No, I'll have the Blood, the Blood, the Blood of thefe confounded Whigifh Dogs. [*Stamps and tears.*

Tick. Indeed you'll ruin the Defign by thefe Paffions; did not I intend to crufh them a more effectual Way? You fhou'd fee how we wou'd ufe them now; but we muft bear with their Saucinefs no, if we expect to gain our Ends;——you will by thefe Meafures fright 'em all into your Hufband's Intereft.

Lady. Oh, oh, oh, well, well, that Thought has cool'd me, and I'll retire to your Lodgings, make what Hafte you can after me, where we will meditate on Revenge to come. [*Exit.*

Enter Servant.

Ser. The Mayor is gone to the Hall, Sir, and the Election is begun.

Tick. Well, Gentlemen, I hope you'l give me your Votes;

Votes; none ſhall do more for your Town than I will, I promiſe you. [*Exit.*

Ser. Here's a Letter for you, Mr. *Scruple,* from your Wine Merchaut, Monſieur *Traffick,* the Man ſays.

[*Gives* Scruple *a Letter.*

Scru. (Reads.) *I ſhould take it as a particular Favour, if you wou'd give Mr.* Tickup *your Vote, who is now with you in* Gotham ; *he is an honeſt Gentleman, I aſſure you.*—Yes, it would be a very particular Favour, truly.

Mal. What wou'd, Mr. *Scruple?*

Scru. Why thou muſt know, that this Letter comes from a *Frenchman,* to direct my Vote for a Member in an *Engliſh* Senate, ha, ha.

Mal. Perhaps there may be no harm in it, the Gentleman might mean it well.

Scru. Yea, he doth mean it well for himſelf, no doubt on't ; but he doth not mean it well for me——But come, let us to the Hall. Neighbours.

Mal. Ay, ay, to the Hall, and act as Conſcience, or our Intereſt leads. [*Exeunt.*

SCENE *changes to the Street.*

Enter Friendly *and* Lucy.

Friend. I hope you are convinc'd, Madam, of your Father's Principle. and what you muſt have ſuffer'd from it, if I had been really what I am repreſented.

Lucy. I do believe the Deſign you ſpeak of ; a Nunnery ! Heaven ! I ſhudder at the Thought.

Friend. Ay ; where ſwarms of Nuns and Prieſts daily curſe your Country, by *Bell, Book,* and *Candle,* where you muſt have been taught to pray for its Deſtruction too.

Lucy. No! Had I been trapan'd to that curſed Place, tho' but a poor defencelefs Maid alone ; yet I'd have ſhown 'em a true *Britiſh* Soul, and dy'd before I wou'd have chang'd my Faith.

Friend. Well ſaid, Madam ; but to the Point—you will not ſure return to your Father, and put it in his Power to betray you a ſecond Time ?

Lucy. No, that I wont.

Friend. May I not hope ſome Share in your Eſteem ?

Lucy. No, whining, Love, I'm not to be caught that
Way ;

Way;—this Day I am of Age, and I chufe you for my Guardian,——and if you can bring me unqueftionable Ptoofs of your being an honeft Man;—that you have always been a Lover of your Country;—a true Affertor of her Laws and Privileges; and that you'd fpend every Shilling of my Portion, in Defence of Liberty and Property,· againft *Perkin* and the Pope, I'll fign, feal, and deliver myfelf into your Hands the next Hour.

Friend. If I do not this, may I meet the Fate which every Traytor to his Land deferves, my charming Heroine! [*A Noife of a Mob without, crying,* A Tickup, *a* Tickup; *A* Worthy, *a* Worthy; *A* Trufty, *a* Trufty.

Lucy. The Election is begun; where fhall I ftay conceal'd!

Friend. At my Lodgings, Madam, where you fhall quickly have the Proof that you demand, to make my Happinefs compleat.

Enter Mob with their Candidates at the Head of each Party one bearing a Pope, and wooden Shoes, with Wool in their Hats; the other a Tub, with a Woman Preacher in it, and Laurel in their Hats; crying on one Side, A Tickup, *a* Tickup; *on the other,* A Worthy, *a* Worthy, *huzza.*

Ben Blunt. No *Pope,* no *Perkin*; a *Worthy,* a *Worthy.*

Tim. Shal. No Tub-preaching; no Liberty and Property Men.

Gr. Gab. A *Tickup,* a *Tickup,* a *Tickup.*

Ben Blunt. No Fire and Faggot;—no wooden Shoes; no Trade-Sellers; a Low Bow, a Low Bow.

Tim. Shal. Z'blead! who made you a Politician in the Devil's Name? [*Knocks 'em down;* Blunt *gets up and collars him, and pulls him down, and gets on him, and boxes him: Half a Score more fall together by the Ears.*

Gr. Gab. Down with 'em, down with 'em.

Rog. Sly. Nay, an you're for that Sport, have at ye: No *Pope*; no *Perkin*; knock 'em down; down with the Dogs; down with their Champion——down with that frenchify'd Dog, *Tickup*: No High Boy; no High Boy.

Shal. No *Worthy,* no *Worthy*; a High Boy, a High Boy. [*Exeunt fighting.*
Enter

Enter Mr. Scoredouble, Friendly, *and* Lucy.

Score. I wifh you much Joy with all my Heart, Madam, you are the nineteenth Bride I have been Father to, and I never gave one to an honefter Man in my Life, I'll zay that for him.

Friend. I thank you, Landlord——And it fhall be my conftant Study to make you happy, Madam, and by my future Actions convince you, that you have not chofe amifs.   [*To* Lucy.

Lucy. I cannot be unhappy, if your Conduct anfwers your Character; a moderate Man, from a true innate Principle of Virtue, fcorns to betray even his Enemies, much lefs his County or Faith.   [*A great Shout within.*

Enter Mob, bearing the chofen Member on Poles, in a Chair, huzzaing crofs the Stage.

The Mayor following.

Mayor. I fay it is an unfair Election, and I'll return Mr. *Tickup.*——Ha! What do I fee?

Friend. Your Son and Daughter, Sir, if you pleafe to give us your Bleffing.   [*Kneels.*

Mayor. The Devil! Down-right *Englifh*, Sirrah; I'll have you laid by the Heels, for a Cheat.

Lucy. Then he'll recriminate, my dear Father, and, ten to one, tell how powerfully the Promife of *French* Piftoles fway'd your Confcience, ha, ha.

Mayor. There's a Jade, now; Zounds, that ever I begot her. Hufwife, if you are married to that rafcally, cheating, canting Low Boy—may—Hell confound you both.   [*Exit.*

Friend. Ha, ha, ha, mind not his Curfes, my dear *Lucy*, I'll be both a Father and a Hufband to thee.

Lucy. I do believe you, and thank you for this Deliverance; for if I had efcap'd a Nunnery, ten to one but I had been thrown into the Arms of fome of my Father's Principle, and that wou'd have been as bad.

This is my Maxim, in a marry'd Life,
Who hates his Country, ne'er can love his Wife.

A

A WIFE WELL MANAG'D.

A FARCE.

Dramatis Perſonæ.

MEN.

DON Piſalto, *deſigned to have been repreſented by* — —	} *Mr.* Norris.
Father Bernardo — — —	*Mr.* Shepherd.
Teague — — — —	*Mr.* Miller.

WOMEN.

Lady Piſalto — — — —	*Mrs.* Baker.
Inis — — — — —	*Miſs* Younger.

SCENE, *Lisbon.*

A WIFE WELL MANAG'D.

ACT I. SCENE I.

Lady Pisalto *and* Inis.

Lady. AH, *Inis*! My Indispofition is not to be cur'd.

Inis. Not without applying the proper Medicine, I grant ye.—Well, had I such a Confessor as Father *Bernardo*—I say no more—but I fancy nothing wou'd trouble my Conscience long.

Lady. What do you mean?

Inis. My Meaning depends upon yours, Madam; pray what do you mean by painting Father *Bernardo*'s Picture in every Room in the House, at your Bed's-head, your Toilet, at the Bottom of your Crucifix, at every Corner of your Handkerchief, nay, upon your very Fan too, as if the good Father, like the Traveller in the Fable, cou'd heat and cool at once?

Lady. Is there any harm in wearing a good Man's Picture? Is he not one of the Pillars of our Church? Eminent for declaiming againft Herefy and Schifm, and fain wou'd reconcile the World to *Rome*'s pure Religion? Oh, they are bleft that he converts; happy the Pair, who e'er they be, that are in Wedlock join'd by him. Wou'd I had been one of thofe.

Inis. If the good Father has this healing Art, why are you uneafy? A little of his comfortable Confolation wou'd revive the Colour in thofe Cheeks, and give great Satif-
faction

faction to your Mind, or I have loft my Judgment, and I don't ufe to be out in my Guefs, where Love's the Riddle.

Lady. Well, fince thou haft hit my Diftemper fo exactly, Girl, I'll confefs ingenuoufly to thee, I do love Father *Bernardo* to Diftraction ; but how to difcover my Paffion, or what Reception it may meet with when difcover'd, is that which racks me.

Inis. A kind one I warrant you, Madam : For tho' Priefts are forbid to marry, as a mortal Sin, Fornication was never reckon'd more than Venial ; and for a Difcovery, whilft there's Pen, Ink, and Paper in the World, a Woman can never be at a Lofs to tell her Mind. Write to him, Madam, write to him.

Lady. But who fhall carry it?

Inis. Your *Irifh* Footman ; he's a fimple, honeft Fellow, and may eafily be manag'd ; do you write your Letter, Madam, and I'll give him Inftructions in the mean Time.

Lady. I'll do it this Minute. [*Exit* Lady.
[Inis *goes to the Door and calls* Teague.

Enter Teague.

Teague. Well, Mrs. *Inis* ; what Commands have you for Teague now ?

Inis. Do you think you can do a Meffage cunningly, Teague?

Teague. Cunningly ! Yes, Faith, we are all fo cunning now—What for a Meffage is it ?

Inis. It is a Letter for Father *Bernardo* at the Convent of St. *Francis* ! if you do it handfomely, a Moidore is your Reward ; do you hear, but if you make any Miftake———

Teague. Hub, bub, bub, bu, Miftake ! No Faith won't I, Arra ! An will you be after giving me the Moidore indeed, and by my Shoul now ?

Inis. Upon Honour,———

Teague. Arra, fay no more now——I will be here agen in a Quarter of an Hour. [*Going*.

Inis. But you muft ftay for the Letter, *Teague.*

Teague. No, no, 'tis no Matter ; I have a very clean
Letter

Letter in my Pocket which will do very well, upon my Shoul, (*going*) and fave Time, yes Faith will it.

Inis. Ha, ha ; no, no, *Teague*, that won't do ; come along with me, and I'll give you the Letter ; but if you fhou'd meet my Mafter, *Don Pifalto*, not a Word of the Letter for your Life—And I charge you to give it into no Hands but the Prieft's, and bring me an Anfwer, and then the Moidore is your own.

Teague. Faith will I.—— [*Exeunt.*

Re-enter Teague *with the Letter*.

Teague. Arra, 'pon my Shoul, I have forgot this plaguy Prieft's Name——Yes, Faith have I.—Father *Bom, Bom, Bom*——By St. *Patrick* I don't know who to afk for now —Arra, What fhall I do ?——Who the Devil fhall I get to read the Outfide of this Letter now ?

Enter Don Pifalto *behind him, and looks over his Shoulder on the Letter.*

Don Pif. For Father *Bernardo.*

Teague. Oh, 'pon my Shoulvation dat is de Name now.
 [*Turns quick upon* Don Pifalto.
Ha, my Maiftre ! What fhall I fay now ? [*Afide.*

Don Pif. Whither are you going with that Letter, Sirrah ? It is my Wife's Hand ? [*Afide.*

Teague. Ha, ha, 'pon my Shoul, a very good Jeft ; firft reads the Direction, and then afks me whither it goes.

Don Pif. It may not prove fo good a Jeft as you think, Sirrah——Who gave you that Letter ?

Teague. Arra, Maiftre, you are very uncivil now to enquire into other Folks Bufinefs, fo you are ; yes Faith are you.

Don Pif. I fhall be fo very uncivil to break your Head, Rafcal, if you don't anfwer me to the Purpofe ; give me the Letter, you Dog you.

Teague. Faith won't I——That's the Way to lofe the Moidore, which I am to have for carrying it.

Don Pif. A Moidore for carrying it ! Sure the Bufinefs muft be very urgent, when the Poftage is fo dear. Give it me, I fay, or or, [*Lays his Hand to his Sword.*

Teague. No, 'pon my Shoul won't I.

Don Pif. Won't you, Sirrah ? [*Draws and beats him.*

Teague.

Teague. Arra, take the Letter. (*Throws it down.*) Pox upon me, if I don't wifh the Devil had you both, yes Faith do I ; for poor *Teague* lofes his Moidore now, and Mrs. *Inis* will never fend me of no more Arrands, no Faith won't fhe.

Don Pif. Inis, ho ! Did fhe give it you ?— [*Opens it.*

Teague. Yes, indeed now ; and I believe there is fome very great Sin in the Letter now, that the good Father was to fend his Pardon for, fo I do.

Don Pif. Monftrous ! What do I fee ? Yes, here is a Sin with a Witnefs—(*Reads*) " Dear Father, you'll for-
" give me when I tell you, that the more I fee you, the
" more I hate my Hufband ; (*very fine*) and the more I
" pray againft Temptation, the more powerfully my In-
" clinations plead in your Behalf (*Furies and Diſtraction*)
" ——I implore your charitable Affiftance to conquer
" this unruly Sin—(*Yes, I'll help you with a Vengeance*
" *to you*)——Nothing but your Company can prolong the
" Life of *Flora.*" (*Say you ſo, Miſtreſs ?*) Very well. *Inis* gave you this Letter, you fay ?

Teague. Yes, Faith did fhe—Arra dear honny Maiftre; an you have done with the Letter give it me now, that I may carry it to the good Father, what do you call him, or I fhall lofe the Moidore, yes Faith fhall I.

Don Pif. Ha ! A lucky Thought comes into my Head, and this Fellow's Simplicity is of Ufe : Hark ye, *Teague*, come you along with me, I am acquainted with Father *Bernardo,* I'll procure you an Anfwer to this Letter—It is as you fay, a Letter of Confeffion, and I believe *Inis* might not perform Articles with you, if fhe knew I had feen it ; but take you no Notice of that, do you hear— And there is two Moidores for you, Sirrah. [*Exit.*

Teague. Oh, by my Shoul *Teague* is dum——Now I fhall have three Moidores ; Faith, this is a lucky Beating for poor *Teague* ; now will I drink St. *Patrick*'s Health till I am as red as a Potato, yes Faith will I. [*Exit.*

Enter Father Bernardo.

Bern. I have had very odd Dreams to Night; me- thought I was in Bed with Lady *Piſalto*——Ah, wou'd it was true, for fhe is a charming Woman : by St. *Anthony* I never heard her Confeffion, but my Virtue is much ftag- ger'd ;

A WIFE *well Manag'd.*

ger'd ; the Flefh and Spirit hold ftrong Contention ; oh, fhe's a delicious Morfel.

Enter Don Pifalto.

Ha! Her Hufband, I hope did not overhear me.
Don Pif. So, I have difpatch'd the *Irifhman.* Ha! Father *Bernardo,* well met ; I was going to your Convent ; I have a Favour to afk of you.
Bern. You command me, Senior *Pifalto,* pray what is it?
Don Pif. Why, I muft defire you to procure me a Habit of your Order for an Hour or two.
Bern. I hope you have no Enterprize in View, that may fcandalize the Priefthood.
Don Pif. Fie, fie, does a Man of my Years give you Room for Sufpicion? Befides, I am a married Man you know.
Bern. And to the moft beautiful Lady in *Madrid*—— A religious, virtuous Lady : Ah, you are a happy Man, Senior.
Don Pif. A Curfe on the Happinefs—Her Virtue, and your Sanctity, Father, might have begot a Monfter, call'd a Cuckold, if Fortune had not flung me in the Way to prevent it.
Bern. What fay you, Senior?
Don Pif. I fay I am contented, Father.
Bern. Contented ! Why another Man wou'd be tranfported, ravifh'd, nay almoft guilty of Idolatry.
Don Pif. Humph ! There would have been fine Work if they had come together; oh, thefe Priefts are full of Abftinence, and Piety ! (*Afide*) If you'll oblige me with a Habit, let it be immediately, and I fhou'd be proud if you'd give me your Company this Evening to fup with my Wife and I ; I'll affure you, Father, fhe has a profound Refpect for you.
Bern. I am much oblig'd to her, Senior ; I'll not fail to accept your kind Invitation : Come along with me, and I'll give you the Habit——A profound Refpect for me— Oh, that it were Love. [*Afide.*
Don Pif. I'll fend for them this Minute, Father ; but

194   *A* WIFE *well Manag'd.*

now I muſt pay a Viſit to my virtuous Wife, and ſee how ſhe bears her Expectation.

'Mongſt all the Ills which clog this mortal Life,
The moſt accurſt, and verieſt Plague is Wife. [*Exit.*

SCENE *Changes.*

Enter Lady *reading a Letter;* Inis *following.*

Lady. He has anſwer'd me as I could wiſh——Dear, dear *Inis,* how ſhall I reward thee? Take that in Earneſt of my future Kindneſs: He ſays he will come in the Twilight, which will ſoon be here, though not ſo ſoon as I cou'd wiſh it:——He deſires, for Reaſons which he will give me, he ſays, to be admitted in the Dark, which Caution does not diſpleaſe me, ſince it will prevent the Confuſion I ſhou'd be in after ſuch a Declaration.—

Inis. He did that on purpoſe, Madam; he is a true Cavalier, and underſtands his Buſineſs to a Hair; he knows Darkneſs is neceſſary upon theſe Occaſions; it prevents a Lady's Bluſhes.—Ods heart, Madam, here's my Lord, I hear him cough.

Lady. Oh miſchievous Minute!——Here, here, run down the back Stairs, and burn that Letter immediately.
  [*Exit* Inis.
I'll to my Book.   [*Sits down, and takes up a Book.*

Enter Don Piſalto.

Don Piſ. There ſhe ſits—as if ſhe knew nothing of the Matter,—a Cockatrice;—What always at thy Devotion, Figgup?

Lady. How can I paſs my Time better in your Abſence, Pudſey? Were it not for theſe good Books, I ſhou'd be very melancholy, when you are from me, Pudſey.

Don Piſ. He'll confound her for a diſſembling Witch.
  [*Aſide.*

Lady. What ails my Pudſey? You look out of Humour with your nown Figgup: What have I done, ha?

Don. Piſ. Nothing yet, I hope;—but that's no Fault of her's.

Lady. Nay, what are you ſtudying for, Pud, ha!

Don. Piſ. Why if you muſt know, little Figgey,—then I'll tell thee; *Don Cammary* lays claim to Part of that Eſtate

A WIFE well Manag'd.

tate I bought laſt Year, and I muſt be obliged to leave my dear Figgup for two or three Hours this Evening, in Order to conſult my Lawyers about that Matter, that's all, Figgey :——And I was afraid thou ſhould'ſt take it ill of thy nown Pud.

Lady. Lucky beyond Expreſſion. (*Aſide.*) No, no, Pud, I am not ſo unreaſonable neither ;——I can divert myſelf with my Books till thy Return——But do Puddey—— make all the Haſte you can to your nown Figgup.—

Don Piſ. Ay, ay, more haſte than you wiſh I dare ſwear. (*Aſide.*) That I will my Precious.—— [*Going.*

Lady. What never a parting Kiſs, Pudſey ? Oh, you don't love your Figgup! Go, go, you are a naughty Hubby ;——I, I, I, I, wiſh I cou'd love you leſs than I do, ſo I do. [*Sobbing, taking out her Handkerchief.*

Don Piſ. Did ever Woman make a Cuckold with a better Grace ? Ounds, ſhe outdoes an *Engliſh* Wife——Nay don't weep, Figgup ; I'll ſtay with thee, let the Eſtate go how it will, rather than diſpleaſe my little Figgey.——

Lady. Heaven forbid ; that would be carrying the Jeſt too far. (*Aſide.*) No, no, I don't deſire that Pud.

Don Piſ. No, I dare ſwear it. [*Aſide.*

Lady. Go ; but give me a kind Kiſs firſt, Pudſey.

Don Piſ. Ah, you are a coaxing Baggage. (*Kiſſes her.*) Well, good-by, Figgey. [*Exit.*

Lady. Good-by, Pudſey——with all my Heart.

Enter Inis.

He is gone, Girl, moſt fortunately.

Inis. I overheard all, and wiſh you Joy of this lucky Opportunity———Come, come, Madam, away to your Chamber, 'tis near the Time——and there contemplate on your coming Joy ; whilſt I, your Harbinger of Bliſs, wait to conduct the Man that is to crown your Happineſs

Lady. I fly, I fly, Girl. [*Exeunt ſeverally.*

SCENE *changes, and diſcovers Lady* Piſalto *leaning on a Couch.*

Lady. Bleſs me, what Noiſe was that !——My Heart akes horribly, leſt this old Cuff ſhou'd return and prevent my charming Prieſt.

196 *A* WIFE *well Manag'd.*

Enter Inis, *leading in* Don Pifalto *in a Prieſt's Habit.*
Inis. Fear nothing, Father, ſtrait forward is your Way to Happineſs.
Don Piſ. A Happineſs, I fear, will bode ſomebody no Good. Hiſt, hiſt, Daughter ! Where are you ? [*Ex.* Inis.
Lady. Ha ! He's come ;—here, here, my too charming Father ; can you forgive a Woman's Weakneſs.——
[*groping about.*
Don Piſ. Common Frailties of Fleſh and Blood (*groping about* (if thou haſt pray'd againſt it, thou haſt done thy Part, and we are bound to comfort thoſe that faint.
Lady. Oh, I have often pray'd, Father, but to no Purpoſe ; you are the only Object of my Wiſhes ; I bluſh, tho' in the Dark, to own how much I love you——
Don Piſ. Come to my Arms, and hide thoſe Bluſhes in my Boſom. (*They meet and embrace.*) Is your Huſband ſafe ?
Lady. Safe enough, tho' long he will not ſtay ; Fortune ſmil'd upon my Wiſhes, and call'd him luckily abroad.
Don Piſ. Then let us improve the little Time we have ; thus let me cool the raging Fever in your Blood.
[*Catches hold of her Arms, and pulls out a Rope's End, and beats her ſoundly, ſhe roars out all the while.*
Lady. Oh ! What do you mean, to murder me ? Inhuman Monſter ! Oh ! Murder, Murder, Murder,—oh, oh, oh. [*Falls on the Couch.*
Enter Inis.

Inis. Bleſs me ! What's the Matter, Madam ?
[*Don* Pifalto *turns and beats her.*
Don Piſ. Only adminiſtring a little Penance, Miſtreſs ; it won't be amiſs to beſtow a little Charity upon you too.
Inis. The Devil take you, and your Penance too, you old ſanctify'd Dog you : Thieves, Thieves ; I'll have you equip'd for the Opera, Sirrah, I will ſo : A Light there, a Light, here's Thieves in the Houſe——Oh, oh, Murder, Thieves——my Lady's murder'd——
Don Piſ. I muſt not ſtay for a Light, leaſt they diſcover who I am :—One farewel Stroke——And now remember your Benefactor, Miſtreſs Bawd. [*Exit.*
Inis.

A WIFE *well Manag'd.*

Inis. Yes; I shall remember with a Vengeance.

Enter Teague *with a Candle.*

Teague. Arra, by my Shoul what is de Matter now? Is de Houfe haunted? Has de great Devil and de little Devil put de Fright upon you both together now?
Lady. Begone, impertinent Fool.
Teague. Fool! Pon my Shoul *Irifhmen* are no Fools: —By St. *Patrick*, we make Fools of de very great many *Englifh*; yes, Faith, and of de *Spaniards* too.
Inis. Get out, Sirrah, or I'll fling the Candle at your Head.
Teague. Arra, Pox take yoor ugly Face, and him that would put a Kifs upon't, for *Teague.* [*Exit.*
Lady. Oh, I am kill'd *Inis!* This curfed Prieft has kill'd me.
Inis. Was there ever fuch a Monfter? I dare fwear I am black from Head to Foot, he laid on moft unmercifully:——Well, my Mind mifgives me, this Prieft is no Man, this feels like an occafional Correction.
Lady. Occafional, do you call it? I'm fure he has given me Occafion to remember it this Twelve-month.

[*Don Pifalto within.*

Don Pif. Figgup, why Figgup——where are you Child?
Lady. Ah Heaven, my Hufband's Voice—Return'd fo foon! What fhall I fay for my Indifpofition?
Inis. Oh Invention? Where art thou? [*Paufes.*

Enter Don Pifalto.

Don Pif. What afleep little Figgy?
Inis. Afleep, Senior, no, no; alas, my poor Lady had like to have been kill'd fince you went.
Don Pif. Kill'd! As how? You make me tremble.
Inis. Going down Stairs, her Foot flipt, and down fhe tumbled from Top to Bottom, and bruis'd herfelf fo fadly, that fhe is not able to ftir a Finger; it is a Mercy fhe was not kill'd out-right.
Lady. Excellent Wench. [*Afide.*
Don Pif. Here's a pure Jade at Invention——They fay the Devil's a Lyar, but I'll be hang'd if this Wench won't out-lye the Devil—I'm heartily forry for this Misfortune, poor

poor dear Figgey ;——but I hope thou haſt not broke any Bones, my dear Figgup.

Lady. But I'm much hurt, Pudfey.

Don Pif. I'm forry for't ; for I have invited Father *Bernardo* to fup with us ; I met him hardly here, and brought him back with me—becaufe I know he is a Favourite with my Figgey.

Inis. Not fo great a Favourite as he was, if you knew all. [*Afide.*

Lady. I beg you wou'd excufe me, Pudfey, I cannot come down ; befides, I have no Stomach.

Inis. No ! The Prieſt has given her and me Supper enough, more than we can digeſt this Twelve-month. [*Afide.*

Don Pif. Well, if thou can'ſt not eat, there's no more to be faid. Take Care of your Lady, *Inis.*—We'll drink thy Health, little Figgup. [*Exit.*

Lady. My Heart rifes at the Villain ; if I ſhou'd fee him, I think in my Soul I ſhould tear his Eyes out. Oh that I cou'd be reveng'd

Inis. Reveng'd ! What Revenge could you take bad enough, Madam ? 'Tis impoſſible to find Revenge equal to the Affront ; a Rope's End to a Lady that expected— I cou'd flea him alive, fo I cou'd. [*In a Paſſion.*

Lady. My Head akes grievoufly.

Inis. Let me cover you up upon the Bed, Madam ; a little Sleep will fettle your Head agen. [*Exit.*

S C E N E *changes.*

Enter Don Pifalto *and Prieſt.*

Bern. Your Lady poſſeſt, fay you ?

Don Pif. 'Tis even fo, Father ; I left her well, and found in her Senfes, I thought, about two Hours ago ; but now ſhe raves, calls Names, fights, and talks of being beat by every Body that comes near her.

Bern. Poor Lady, I am exceeding forry ; I'll take care ſhe ſhall be pray'd for by the whole Convent.

Don Pif. I wiſh you wou'd fee her, Father, perhaps your ghoſtly Admonition might do her good. Men of your holy Function have Power over unclean Spirits ; pray, try what you can do for her.

Bern.

A WIFE well Manag'd. 199

Bern. With all my Heart, but I have no holy Water about me;—nothing frights the Devil like holy Water,—thence comes the Proverb, you know.

Don Pif. I can help you to fome, pleafe to walk this Way, Father. [*Exeunt.*

SCENE *changes, and difcovers Lady* Pifalto, *on a Couch afleep.*

Enter Prieft, fets a Bafon of Water on the Table.—— Don Pifalto *lift'ning.*

Bern. Peace be here——Ha! She fleeps:—How invitingly fhe lies! Why what a delicious Morfel has this old faplefs Log every Night to fnoar over.

Don Pif. Well faid, Prieft;——Oh, this is a holy Man; no Wonder he's the Women's Favourite.——

Bern. I feel a ftrange Diforder on the fudden,——my Pulfe beats quick, and every Senfe feems ravifh'd at this Object.——Ha! We are alone,——What hinders me to make Ufe of this Opportunity?——

Don Pif. Zounds, I fhall be cuckolded before my Face.

Bern. Befides, none dare to prefs upon our Privacy,—we have that Advantage above the Laity; I'll try; if fhe fhould prove virtuous, and refift, the Noife will pafs upon her Hufband, as the Effect of her Poffeffion; for I fhrewdly fufpect, fhe is not mad indeed, and only puts it on to avoid the Embraces of that Skeleton, unfit for a Woman of her Youth and Fire.

Don Pif. Well, for a thorough-pac'd Whore-mafter, commend me to a Prieft, I fay.

Bern. I'll try I'm refolv'd. [*Steals foftly to the Couch and kiffes her.*

Don Pif. Very well.——Zounds, I fhan't contain myfelf——

Bern. Rapture! Her very Lips gives Extafy!——She fleeps very found——once more. [*Goes to kiss her again, and fhe lifts up her Eyes and fees him.*

Lady. I dreamt! Ha! Blefs me, the Monfter's here! Oh, that I could look him dead.—— [*Going to rife,* Bernardo *ftops her, and kneels.*

Bern. Oh, do not rife, my charming Angel, let me feaft
I 4 my

my Eyes upon that lovely Face, the perfect Image of the Bleſt above.

Lady. Do not inſult me, thou ungrateful Traytor! Do not.

Bern. What means my Charmer? Oh, forgive my raſh Proceeding, and blame your Eyes, thoſe dear bewitching Eyes, for all that I have done. [*Kiſſes her in Extaſy.*

Lady. Off Monſter, Devil, worſe, if worſe can be, than Devil, thou very Prieſt.———

Don Piſ. Excellent, it works now as I wou'd have it.—

Lady. You thought you had kill'd me, I ſuppoſe,—but you ſhall find, I live to tear your Eyes out, Monſter.

[*Flies up and pulls his Hood off, and beats him.*

Bern. Help, Help, Help, bleſs me! She is really poſſeſt.

Enter Inis *with a Stick.*

Inis. Ha! You are here again, old Belzebub! but I'll be even with you now, I will ſo. [*Lays on upon the Prieſt.*

Don Piſ. Ha, ha, I ſhall dye with Laughing.

Bern. What do you mean, Madam, pray be calm, I would comfort you.

Inis. As how, pray, Father? I am much miſtaken if you have any Thing that can comfort a Lady.

Bern. Oh Wickedneſs! Have I nothing that can Comfort a Lady?

Lady. Yes, Villain, I can ſhow your Marks of Comfort, I can ſo, but I'll be reveng'd on thee, I will.

[*beats him.*

Inis. Yes, and I can ſhow 'em too; this for my Lady, this for myſelf. [*beats him.*

Don Piſ. Ha, ha, O rare Figgup, O rare *Inis.*

Bern. Bleſs me! By St. *Anthony* they are both poſſeſt; the Maid has caught her Frenzy, too, *in Nomine Domine*—

[*Runs to the Table, and catches up the holy Water, and flings, firſt on one, then on the other.*

Don Piſ. Ha, ha, O rare Prieſt, ha, ha.

Lady. I'll *Nomine Domine* you. You had better have hang'd yourſelf in your Rope's End, than have uſed it about me, I'll make it a dear Beating to you, Sirrah.

Bern. Oh *Maria Mater ora pro nobis.* [*Flings Water ſtill.*

Lady. Ah! He'll drown me.

Bern.

A WIFE *well Manag'd,* 201

Bern. Avant Satan, I conjure thee, by St. *Anthony,* St. *Bridget,* and our Lady of *Loretto.* [*Flings Water.*
Inis. (strikes down the Bafon and breaks it.)—What ho, a Rape, a Rape, I'll cant you, I'll have you hang'd;—I'll fhew the World the Jewel they doat on: I faw you when you wou'd have ravifh'd my Lady,——thou Monſter of Iniquity.

Bern. Mercy on me, the Devil is very ſtrong in them both.

Enter Don Pifalto.

Don Pif. Ha, ha, I muſt releaſe the Prieſt, or they'll murder him between them.——Oh, the Rage of a difappointed Woman.——What's the Matter here? Pray, Father, withdraw, I am heartily forry for your ill Treatment, it is their Height of Frenzy you fee, Father; I'll wait upon you in the next Room immediately, you can do them no Good, I fee, Father.

Bern. Alas, Senior, they are fo ſtrongly poſſeſt, that no one Man can deal with them both. [*Exit.*

Inis. Will you let him go, Senior? Why he would have ravifh'd my Lady, if I had not cry'd out.

Don Pif. No, Miſtrefs, you cry'd out becaufe he had not ravifh'd your Lady.——Go troop, Miſtrefs, I'll reckon with you within. [*Exit* Inis.

And now, Madam, for you.—Do you know this Letter?

Lady. Ha! My Letter to Father *Bernardo*! the Villain has betray'd me!——and I'm undone! [*Afide.*

Don Pif. Why don't you anfwer me? What, are you dumb? Then I muſt fetch you to your Speech with this.

[*Pulls out a Dagger*

Lady. Ah! defend me Heaven. (*falls on her Knees.*) But why name I Heaven;—I have offended that in wronging you, tho' but in Thought;——Oh, forgive me, have Pity on my Youth, and let me live: Punifh me as feverely as you pleafe; let even him who has betray'd me, name my Penance, and then I'm fure it will be harfh enough; whate'er it be, I will perform it moſt religiouſly.

Don Pif. I melt;——the cunning Baggage knows her Power.——

Lady. Oh! Do, Pudfey, do; won't you forgive you nown Figgup? Can you pierce this Bofom you have kifs'r fo often, and fee your Figgey's Blood run trickling downd

I 5 *Don*

Don Pif. I am conquer'd; I can hold no longer.—— Rife, Figgup, for this Time I will forgive thee; but on Condition you ne'er fee your ghoftly Father more; no more Harangues in Praife of his Sanctity, and Holinefs of Life; do you hear, Figgey?

Lady. No, never, indeed, Pudfey.

Don Pif. Take heed; for if again I catch you faulty, look to it, expect no Pardon.

Lady. *No, when I am, may I your Pardon mifs,*
Since you fo generoufly forgive me this.

Don Pif. *When Wives, like mine, gives Inclination Scope,*
No Cure for Cuckoldom like Oyl of Rope.

A Bold

A

Bold Stroke for a WIFE.

A

COMEDY.

PROLOGUE.

Spoken by Mrs. THURMOND.

TO Night we come upon a bold Design,
To try to please without one borrow'd Line:
Our Plot is new, and regularly clear,
And not one single Tittle from Moliere.
O'er buried Poets we with Caution tread,
And Parish Sextons leave to rob the Dead.
For you, bright British *Fair, in Hopes to charm ye,*
We bring To-night, a Lover *from the Army:*
You know the Soldiers *have the strangest Arts,*
Such a Proportion *of prevailing Parts,*
You'd think that they rid Post to Womens Hearts.
I wonder whence they draw their bold Pretence;
We do not chuse them sure for our Defence:
That Plea is both impolitick and wrong,
And only suit such Dames as want a Tongue.
Is it their Eloquence and fine Address?
The Softness of their Language?—Nothing less.
Is it their Courage that they bravely dare
To storm the Sex at once?——Egad! 'tis there.
They act by us as in the rough Campaign,
Unmindful of Repulses, charge again:
They mine, *and* countermine, *resolv'd to win,*
And, if a Breach *is made,——they will come in.*
You'll think, by what we have of Soldiers *said,*
Our Female Wit was in the Service bred:
But she is to the hardy Toil a Stranger,
She loves the Cloth indeed, but hates the Danger:
Yet to this Circle of the Brave and Gay,
She bid me for her good Intentions, say,
She hopes you'll not reduce her to Half Pay.
As for our Play, 'tis English *Humour all:*
Then will you let our Manufacture fall?
Would you the Honour of our Nation raise,
Keep English Credit *up, and* English Plays.

EPI-

EPILOGUE.

Written by Mr. *SEWELL*:

Spoken by Mrs. *BULLOCK*.

WHAT new ſtrange Ways our modern Beaus deviſe!
What Trials of Love-Skill, to gain the Prize!
The Heathen Gods, who never matter'd Rapes,
Scarce wore ſuch ſtrange Variety of Shapes:
The Devil take their odious barren Skulls,
To court in Form of Snakes *and filthy* Bulls:
Old Jove *once nick'd it too, as I am told,*
In a whole Lapfull of true ſtandard Gold:
How muſt his Godſhip then fair Danae *warm!*
In trucking Ware *for* Ware *there is no Harm.*
Well after all that Money *has a Charm.*
But now indeed that ſtale Invention's paſt;
Beſides you know that Guineas fall ſo faſt,
Poor Nymph muſt come to Pockpet-piece at laſt,
Old Harry's *Face, or good Queen* Beſs's *Ruff,*
Not that I'd take 'em——*may do well enough;*
No——*my ambitious Spirit's far above*
These little Tricks of mercenary Love.
That Man be mine, who, like the Col'nel here,
Can top his Character in ev'ry Sphere;
Who can a thouſand Ways employ his Wit,
Out promiſe Stateſmen, and out cheat a Cit:
Beyond the Colours of a Trav'ller paint,
And cant, and ogle too——*beyond a Saint.*
The laſt Diſguiſe moſt pleas'd me, I confeſs,
There's ſomething tempting in the preaching *Dreſs:*
And pleas'd me more than once a Dame *of Note,*
Who lov'd her Huſband *in his* Footman's *Coat.*
To ſee one Eye in wanton Motions play'd,
The other to the Heav'nly Regions ſtray'd,
As if for its Fellow's Frailties pray'd:
But yet I hope, for all that I have ſaid,
To find my Spouſe a Man of War *in Bed.*

Dramatis Perſonæ.

MEN.

Sir *Philip Modelove*, an old Beau. — Mr. *Knap*.
Periwinkle, a Kind of ſilly Virtuoſo. — Mr. *Spiller*.
Tradelove, a Change Broker. — Mr. *Bullock*, ſen.
Obadiah Prim, a Quaker, Hoſier.
All Four choſe Guardians to Mrs. *Lovely*. — Mr. *Puck*.

Colonel *Fainwell*, in Love with Mrs. *Lovely*. — Mr. *Charles Bullock*.
Freeman, his Friend, a Merchant. — Mr. *Ogden*.
Simon Pure, a Quaking Preacher. — Mr. *Griffin*.
Mr. *Sackbut*, a Vintner. — Mr. *Hall*.

WOMEN.

Mrs. *Lovely*, a Fortune of Thirty Thouſand Pounds. — Mrs. *Bullock*.
Mrs. *Prim*, Wife to *Prim* the Hoſier. — Mrs. *Kent*.
Betty, Servant to Mrs. *Lovely*. — Mrs. *Robins*.

SCENE *London ;* Footmen, Drawers, &c.

A Bold Stroke for a WIFE.

Act. I. Scene. I.

SCENE a Tavern.

Colonel Fainwell *and* Freeman *over a Bottle.*

Freeman.  OME, Colonel, his Majefty's Health.—You are as melancholy as if you were in Love : I wifh some of the Beauties of *Bath* han't fnapt your heart.

Col. Why, Faith, *Freeman*, there is fomething in't : I have feen a Lady at *Bath*, who has kindled fuch a Flame in me that all the Waters there can't quench.

Free. Women, like fome poifonous Animals, carry their Antidote about 'em---Is fhe not to be had, Colonel?

Col. That's a difficult Queftion to anfwer ; however, I refolve to try : Perhaps you may be able to ferve me ; you Merchants know one another.—The Lady told me herfelf, fhe was under the Charge of four Perfons.

Free. Odfo ! 'tis Mrs. *Ann Lovely.*

Col. The fame.——Do you know her?

Free. Know her ! Ay.—Faith, Colonel, your Condition is more defperate than you imagine : Why, fhe is the Talk and Pity of the whole Town ; and it is the Opinion of the Learned, that fhe muft die a Maid.

Col. Say you fo ? That's fomewhat odd, in this charitable City.—She's a Woman, I hope.

Free, For aught I know,——but it had been as well for her, had Nature made her any other Part of the Creation. The Man who keeps this Houfe, ferved her Father ; he is a very honeft Fellow, and may be of Ufe to you ; we'll fend for him to take a Glafs with us ; he'll give you her whole Hiftory, and 'tis worth your hearing.

Col. But may one truft him?

Free.

Free. With your Life : I have Obligations enough upon him to make him do any thing : I ferve him with Wine.
[*Knocks.*
Col. Nay, I know him pretty well myfelf. I once ufed to frequent a Club that was kept here.

Enter Drawer.

Draw. Gentlemen, d'ye call?
Free. Ay ; fend up your Mafter.
Draw. Yes, Sir. [*Exit.*
Col. Do you know any of this Lady's Guardians, *Freeman?*
Free. Yes, I know two of them very well.

Enter Sackbut.

Free. Here comes one will give you an Account of them all——Mr. *Sackbut*, we fent for you to take a Glafs with us. 'Tis a Maxim among the Friends of the Bottle, that as long as the Mafter is in Company, one may be fure of good Wine.
Sack. Sir, you fhall be fure to have as good Wine as you fend in——Colonel, your moft humble Servant ; you are welcome to Town.
Col. I thank you, Mr. *Sackbut.*
Sack. I am as glad to fee you, as I fhould a hundred Tun of *French* Claret Cuftom-free——My Service to you, Sir, (*drinks*) You don't look fo merry as you ufed to do ; ar'n't you well, Colonel?
Free. He has got a Woman in his Head, Landlord, can you help him?
Sack. If 'tis in my Power, I fhan't fcruple to ferve my Friend.
Col. 'Tis one Perquifite of your Calling.
Sack. Ay, at 'tother End of the Town, where you Officers ufe, Women are good Forcers of Trade: A well-accuftom'd Houfe, a handfome Bar-keeper, with clean obliging Drawers, foon get the Mafter an Eftate ; but our Citizens do feldom anything but cheat within the Walls. —But as to the Lady, Colonel, point you at Particulars, or have you a good *Champagne* Stomach ? Are you in full Pay, or reduc'd, Colonel?
Col. Reduc'd, reduc'd, Landlord.

Free.

A Bold Stroke for a WIFE.

Free. To the miferable Condition of a Lover!

Sack. Pifh! that's preferable to Half-pay; a Woman's Refolution may break before the Peace; pufh her home, Colonel, there's no parlying with the fair Sex.

Col. Were the Lady her own Miftrefs, I have fome Reafons to believe I fhould command in Chief.

Free. You know Mrs. *Lovely*, Mr. *Sackbut*?

Sack. Know her! Ay, poor *Nancy*; I have carried her to School many a frofty Morning. Alas! if fhe's the Woman, I pity you, Colonel: Her Father, my old Mafter, was the moft whimfical, out-of-the-Way temper'd Man I ever heard of, as you will guefs by his laft Will and Teftament——This was his only Child; I have heard him wifh her dead a thoufand Times.

Col. Why fo?

Sack. He hated Pofterity, you muft know, and wifh'd the World were to expire with himfelf——He ufed to fwear, if fhe had been a Boy, he would have qualified him for the Opera.

Free. 'Tis a very unnatural Refolution in a Father.

Sack. He died worth thirty thoufand Pounds, which he left to his Daughter, provided fhe married with the Confent of her Guardians: But that fhe might be fure never to do fo, he left her in the Care of four Men, as oppofite to each other as the four Elements; each has his quarterly Rule, and three Months in a Year fhe is obliged to be fubject to each of their Humours, and they are pretty different, I affure you——She is juft come from *Bath*.

Col. 'Twas there I faw her.

Sack. Ay, Sir, the laft Quarter was her Beau Guardian's— She appears in all publick Places during his Reign.

Col. She vifited a Lady who boarded in the fame Houfe with me: I lik'd her Perfon, and found an Opportunity to tell her fo. She reply'd, fhe had no Objection to mine; but if I could not reconcile Contradictions I muft not think of her, for that fhe was condemned to the Caprice of four Perfons, who never yet agreed in any one Thing, and fhe was obliged to pleafe them all.

Sack. 'Tis moft true, Sir; I'll give you a fhort Defcription of the Men, and leave you to judge of the poor Lady's Condition. One is a kind of Virtuofo, a filly halfwitted Fellow, but pofitive and furly, fond of every thing antique and foreign, and wears his Cloaths of the Fafhion of the laſt Century ; doats upon Travellers, and believes more of Sir *John Mandeville* than he does of the Bible.

Col. That muſt be a rare odd Fellow !

Sack. Another is a Change Broker ; a Fellow that will out-lie the Devil for the Advantage of Stock, and cheat his Father that got him, in a Bargain ; He is a great Stickler for Trade, and hates every Man that wears a Sword.

Free. He is a great Admirer of the *Dutch* Management, and ſwears they underſtand Trade better than any Nation under the Sun.

Sack. The Third is an old Beau, that has *May* in his Fancy and Dreſs, but *December* in his Face and his Heels; He admires all the new Faſhions, and thoſe muſt be *French* ; loves Operas, Balls, Maſquerades, and is always the moſt tawdry of the whole Company on a Birth-Day.

Col. Theſe are pretty oppoſite to one another, truly ! and the Fourth, What is he, Landlord ?

Sack. A very rigid Quaker, whoſe Quarter begun this Day.——I ſaw Mrs. *Lovely* go in, not above two Hours ago,——Sir *Philip* ſet her down. What think you now, Colonel, is not the poor Lady to be pitied ?

Col. Ay, and reſcu'd too, Landlord.

Free. In my Opinion, that's impoſſible.

Col. There is nothing impoſſible to a Lover. What would not a Man attempt for a fine Woman and thirty thouſand Pounds ? Beſides, my Honour is at Stake ; I promiſed to deliver her,—and ſhe bid me win her and wear her.

Sack. That's fair, Faith.

Free. If it depended upon Knight-errantry, I ſhould not doubt your ſetting free the Damſel ; but to have Avarice, Impertinence, Hypocriſy, and Pride, at once to deal with, requires more Cunning than generally attends a Man of Honour.

Col. My Fancy tells me, I ſhall come off with Glory. I reſolve to try however.—Do you know all the Guardians, Mr. *Sackbut* ?

Sack. Very well, Sir, they all uſe my Houſe.

Col. And will you aſſiſt me, if Occaſion requires ?

Sack. In every thing I can, Colonel.

Free. I'll anſwer for him ; and whatever I can ſerve you in, you may depend on. I know Mr. *Periwinkle* and Mr.

A Bold Stroke for a WIFE. 211

Mr. *Tradelove* ; the latter has a very great Opinion of my Interest abroad——I happen'd to have a Letter from a Correfpondent two Hours before the News arrived of the *French* King's Death : I communicated it to him ; upon which he bought up all the Stock he could, and what with that, and fome Wagers he laid, he told me he had got to the Tune of five hundred Pounds ; fo that I am much in his good Graces.

Col. I don't know but you may be of Service to me, *Freeman.*

Free. If I can, command me, Colonel.

Col. Ifn't it poffible to find a Suit of Cloaths ready made at fome of thefe Sale-fhops fit to rig out a Beau, think you, Mr. *Sackbut* ?

Sack. O hang 'em——No, Colonel, they keep nothing ready made that a Gentleman would be feen in : But I can fit you with a Suit of Cloaths, if you'd make a Figure ——Velvet and Gold Brocade——They were pawn'd to me by a *French* Count, who had been ftript at Play, and wanted Money to carry him Home ; he promifed to fend for them, but I have not heard any Thing of him.

Free. He has not fed upon Frogs long enough yet to recover his Lofs ; ha, ha !

Col. Ha, ha ! Well, the Cloaths will do, Mr. *Sackbut,* ——tho' we muft have three or four Fellows in tawdry Liveries : They can be procur'd, I hope.

Free. Egad ! I have a Brother come from the *Weft Indies* that can match you ; and, for Expedition-fake, you fhall have his Servants ; There's a Black, a Tawnymoor, and a *Frenchman* ; they don't fpeak one Word of *Englifh*, fo can make no Miftake.

Col. Excellent !——Egad ! I fhall look like an *Indian* Prince. Firft I'll attack my Beau Guardian ; where lives he ?

Sack. Faith, fomewhere about St. *James*'s ; tho' to fay in what Street, I cannot ; but any Chairman will tell you where Sir *Philip Modelove* lives.

Free. Oh ! you'll find him in the Park at Eleven every Day ; at leaft, I never pafs'd thro' at that Hour without feeing him there—But what do you intend?

Col. To addrefs him in his own Way, and find what he defigns to do with the Lady.

Free.

Free. And what then?

Col. Nay, that I cannot tell; but I shall take my Measures accordingly.

Sack. Well, 'tis a mad Undertaking, in my Mind: But here's to your Success, Colonel. [*Drinks.*

Col. 'Tis something out of the Way, I confess; but Fortune may chance to smile, and I succeed. Come, Landlord, let me see those Coaths. *Freeman*, I shall expect you'll leave Word with Mr. *Sackbut*, where one may find you upon Occasion; and send me the *Indian* Equipage immediately, d'ye hear?

Free. Immediately. [*Exit.*

Col. *Bold was the Man who ventur'd first to Sea,
But the first vent'ring Lovers bolder were.
The Path of Love's a dark and dang'rous Way,
Without a Landmark, or one friendly Star,
And he that runs the Risque deserves the Fair.* [Exit.

SCENE II. *Prim's* House.

Enter Mrs. Lovely, *and her Maid* Betty.

Betty. Bless me, Madam! Why do you fret and teaze yourself so? This is giving them the Advantage with a Witness.

Mrs. Lov. Must I be condemn'd all my Life to the preposterous Humours of other People, and pointed at by every Boy in Town?—Oh! I could tear my Flesh, and curse the Hour I was born.—Isn't it monstrously ridiculous, that they should desire to impose their Quaking Dress upon me at these Years? When I was a Child, no Matter what they made me wear, but now———

Betty. I would resolve against it, Madam; I'd see 'em hang'd before I'd put on the pinch'd Cap again.

Mrs. Lov. Then I must never expect one Moment's Ease: She has rung such a Peal in my Ears already, that I shant have the right Use of them this Month,—What can I do?

Betty. What can you *not* do, if you will but give your Mind to it? *Marry*, Madam.

Mrs. Lov. What! and have my Fortune go to build Churches and Hospitals?

Betty. Why, let it go.—If the Colonel loves you, as he pretends,

pretends, he'll marry you. without a Fortune, Madam; and I affure you a Colonel's Lady is no defpicable Thing; a Colonel's Poft will maintain you like a Gentlewoman, Madam.

Mrs. Lov. So you would advife me to give up my own Fortune, and throw myfelf upon the Colonel's.

Betty. I would advife you to make yourfelf eafy, Madam.

Mrs. Lov. That's not the Way, I'm fure. No, no, Girl, there are certain Ingredients to be mingled with Matrimony, without which I may as well change for the worfe as the better. When the Woman has Fortune enough to make the Man happy, if he has either Honour or good Manners, he'll make her eafy. Love makes but a flovenly Figure in a Houfe where Poverty keeps the Door.

Betty. And fo you refolve to die a Maid, do you, Madam?

Mrs. Lov. Or have it in my Power to make the Man I love Mafter of my Fortune.

Betty. Then you don't like the Colonel fo well as I thought you did, Madam, or you would not take fuch a Refolution.

Mrs. Lov. It is becaufe I do like him, *Betty*, that I do take fuch a Refolution.

Betty. Why, do you expect, Madam, that the Colonel can work Miracles? Is it poffible for him to marry you with the Confent of all your Guardians?

Mrs. Lov. Or he muft not marry me at all: And fo I told him; and he did not feem difpleafed with the News. ——He promifed to fet me free; and I, on that Condition, promifed to make him Mafter of that Freedom.

Betty. Well! I have read of enchanted Caftles, Ladies delivered from the Chains of Magick, Giants kill'd, and Monfters overcome; fo that I fhould be the lefs furprized if the Colonel fhould conjure you out of the Power of your four Guardians; if he does, I am fure he deferves your Fortune.

Mrs. Lov. And fhall have it, Girl, if it were ten Times as much——For I'll ingenuoufly confefs to thee, that I do like the Colonel above all Men I ever faw:——There's fomething fo *Jantée* in a Soldier, a Kind of *Je ne fcai quoi*
Air,

214 *A Bold Stroke for a* WIFE.

Air, that makes 'em more agreeable than the reſt of Mankind.—They command Regard, as who ſhould ſay, We are your Defenders. We preſerve your Beauties from the Inſults of rude and unpoliſh'd Foes, and ought to be preferr'd before thoſe lazy indolent Mortals, who, by dropping into their Father's Eſtate, ſet up their Coaches, and think to rattle themſelves into our Affections.

Betty. Nay, Madam, I confeſs that the Army has engroſſed all the prettieſt Fellows.—A laced Coat and Feather have irreſiſtible Charms.

Mrs. Lov. But the Colonel has all the Beauties of the Mind as well as the Body.——O, all ye Powers that favour happy Lovers, grant that he may be mine! Thou God of Love, if thou be'ſt aught but Name, aſſiſt my *Fainwell.*

*Point all thy Darts to aid his juſt deſign,
And make his Plots as prevalent as thine.*   [*Exit.*

ACT II. SCENE I.

SCENE the Park.

Enter Colonel finely dreſt, three Footmen after him.

Col. SO now, if I can but meet this Beau!—Egad! methinks I cut a ſmart Figure, and have as much of the tawdry Air as any *Italian* Count, or *French* Marquée of them all—Sure I ſhall know this Knight again.—Ah! yonder he ſits making Love to a Maſk, i'faith, I'll walk up the *Mall*, and come down by him. [*Exit.*

Scene draws, and diſcovers Sir Philip *upon a Bench, with a Woman mask'd.*

Sir *Phil.* Well but, my Dear, are you really conſtant to your Keeper?

Wom. Yes, really, Sir,——Hey day! Who comes yonder? He cuts a mighty Figure.

Sir *Phil.* Ha! a Stranger, by his Equipage keeping ſo cloſe at his Heels.—He has the Appearance of a Man of Quality,—Poſitively *French*, by his dancing Air.

Wom. He croſſes, as if he meant to ſit down here.——

Sir

A Bold Stroke for a WIFE.

Sir *Phil.* He has a Mind to make love to thee, Child.

Enter Colonel, and seats himself upon the Bench by Sir Philip.

Wom. It will be to no Purpose if he does.
Sir *Phil.* Are you resolv'd to be cruel then?
Col. You must be very cruel indeed if you can deny any Thing to so fine a Gentleman, Madam.
[*Takes out his Watch*
Wom. I never mind the Outside of a Man.
Col. And I'm afraid thou art no judge of the Inside.
Sir *Phil.* I am positively of your Mind, Sir, for Creatures of her Function seldom penetrate beyond the Pocket.
Wom. Creatures of your Composition have, indeed, generally more in their Pockets than in their Heads. [*Aside.*
Sir *Phil.* Pray what says your Watch? mine is down.
[*Pulling out his Watch.*
Col. I want thirty-six Minutes of Twelve, Sir.—
[*Puts up his Watch, and takes out his Snuff box.*
Sir *Phil.* May I presume, Sir?
Col. Sir, you honour me.   [*presenting the Box.*
Sir *Phil.* He speaks good *English,*—tho' he must be a Foreigner—This Snuff is extremely good,—and the Box prodigious fine; the Work is *French*, I presume, Sir.
Col. I bought it in *Paris*, Sir.—I do think the Workmanship pretty neat.
Sir *Phil.* Neat! 'tis exquisitely fine, Sir. Pray, Sir, if I may take the Liberty of enquiring,—What Country is so happy to claim the Birth of the finest Gentleman in the Universe? *France*, I presume.
Col. Then you don't think me an *Englishman?*
Sir *Phil.* No, upon my Soul don't I.
Col. I am sorry for't.
Sir *Phil.* Impossible you should wish to be an *Englishman*! Pardon me, Sir, this Island could not produce a Person of such Alertness.
Col. As this Mirror shews you, Sir.
[*puts up a Pocket-Glass to Sir* Philip's *Face.*
Wom. Coxcombs! I'm sick to hear them praise one another. One seldom gets any Thing by such Animals. not even a Dinner, unless one can dine upon Soop and Celery.

Sir

Sir Phil. O Gad, Sir!—Will you leave us, Madam? Ha ha!

Col. She fears 'twill be only lofing Time to ftay here, ha, ha! I know not how to diftinguifh you, Sir, but your Mien and Addrefs fpeak you Right Honourable.

Sir Phil. Thus great Souls judge of others by themfelves,—I am only adorn'd with Knighthood, that's all, I do affure you, Sir; my Name is Sir *Philip Modelove.*

Col. Of *French* Extraction?

Sir Phil. My Father was *French.*

Col. One may plainly perceive it.—There is a certain Gaiety peculiar to my Nation (for I will own myfelf a *Frenchman*) which diftinguifhes us every where.—A Perfon of your Figure would be a vaft Addition to a Coronet.

Sir Phil. I muft own I had the Offer of a Barony about five Years ago, but I abhorr'd the Fatigue which muft have attended it.—I could never yet bring myfelf to join with either Party.

Col. You are perfectly in the Right, Sir *Philip,*—a fine Perfon fhould not embark himfelf in the flovenly Concern of Politicks: Drefs and Pleafure are Objects proper for the Soul of a fine Gentleman.

Sir Phil. And Love.——

Col. Oh! that's included under the Article of Pleafure.

Sir Phil. Parbleu il eſt un Homme d'Eſprits, I muft embrace you,—*(riſes and embraces)*—Your Sentiments are fo agreeable to mine, that we appear to have but one Soul, for our Ideas and Conceptions are the fame.

Col. I fhould be forry for that. *(aſide.)*—You do me too much Honour, Sir *Philip.*

Sir Phil. Your Vivacity and *jantée* Mien affured me at firft Sight there was nothing of this foggy Ifland in your Compofition. May I crave your Name, Sir;

Col. My Name is *La Fainwell,* Sir, at your Service.

Sir Phil. The *La Fainwells* are *French,* I know; tho' the Name is become very numerous in *Great-Britain* of late Years.——I was fure you was *French* the Moment I laid my Eyes upon you: I could not come into the Suppofition of your being an *Engliſhman*: This Ifland produces few fuch Ornaments.

Col. Pardon me, Sir *Philip,* this Ifland has two Things fuperior to all Nations under the Sun.

Sir

Sir Phil. Ah! what are they?

Col. The Ladies, and the Laws.

Sir Phil. The Laws, indeed, do claim a Preference of other Nations,—but, by my Soul, there are fine Women every where.—I muſt own I have felt their Power in all Countries.

Col. There are ſome finiſh'd Beauties I confeſs, in *France*, *Italy*, *Germany*, nay even in *Holland*, *mais ſont bien rare*: But *les Belles Angloiſes*! -Oh, Sir *Philip*, where find we ſuch Women! ſuch a Symmetry of Shape! ſuch Elegancy of Dreſs! ſuch Regularity of Features! ſuch Sweetneſs of Temper! ſuch commanding Eyes! and ſuch bewitching Smiles.

Sir Phil. Ah! *parbleau vous eſtez attraper.*

Col. Non, je vous aſſure, Chevalier. But I declare there is no Amuſement ſo agreeable to my *Gout*, as the Converſation of a fine Woman,—I could never be prevailed upon to enter into what the Vulgar calls the Pleaſure of the Bottle.

Sir Phil. My own Taſte, *poſitivement.*—A Ball, or a Maſquerade, is certainly preferable to all the Productions of the Vineyard.

Col. Infinitely! I hope the People of Quality in *England* will ſupport that Branch of Pleaſure, which was imported with their Peace, and ſince naturaliz'd by the ingenious Mr. *Heidegger.*

Sir Phil. The Ladies aſſure me it will become Part of the Conſtitution.—Upon which I ſubſcribed an hundred Guineas.—It will be of great Service to the Publick, at leaſt to the Company of Surgeons; and the City in general.

Col. Ha, ha! it may help to enoble the Blood of the City. Are you married, Sir *Philip?*

Sir Phil. No; nor do I believe I ever ſhall enter into that honourable State : I have an abſolute *Tendre* for the whole Sex.

Col. That's more than they have for you, I dare ſwear.
                                                                                    [*Aſide.*

Sir Phil. And I have the Honour to be very well with the Ladies, I can aſſure you, Sir; and I won't affront a Million of fine Women to make one happy.

Col. Nay, Marriage is reducing a Man's Taſte to a Kind

K   of of half Pleafure; but then it carries the Bleffing of Peace along with it; one goes to fleep without Fear, and wakes without Pain.

Sir *Phil.* There's fomething of that in't; a Wife is a very good Difh for an *Englifh* Stomach,—but grofs Feeding for nicer Palates, ha, ha, ha!

Col. I find I was very much miftaken,——I imagined, you had been married to that young Lady whom I faw in the Chariot with you this Morning in *Grace-church-Street.*

Sir *Phil.* Who, *Nancy Lovely?* I am a Piece of a Guardian to that Lady: You muft know, her Father, I thank him, joined me with three of the moft prepofterous old Fellows,——that, upon my Soul, I am in Pain for the poor Girl;—fhe muft certainly lead Apes, as the Saying is; ha, ha!

Col. That's Pity, Sir *Philip.* If the Lady would give me Leave, I would endeavour to avert that Curfe.

Sir *Phil.* As to the Lady, fhe'd gladly be rid of us at any Rate, I believe; but here's the Mifchief, he who marries Mifs *Lovely* muft have the Confent of all four,—or not a Penny of her Portion.—For my Part, I fhall never approve of any but a Man of Figure,——and the reft are not only averfe to Cleanlinefs, but have each peculiar Tafte to gratify.—For my Part, I declare I would prefer you to all Men I ever faw.

Col. And I her to all Women——

Sir *Phil.* I affure you, Mr. *Fainwell,* I am for marrying her, for I hate the Trouble of a Guardian, efpecially among fuch Wretches; but refolve never to agree to the Choice of any one of them,——and I fancy they'll be even with me, for they never came into any Propofal of mine yet.

Col. I wifh I had your Leave to try them, Sir *Philip.*

Sir *Phil.* With all my Soul, Sir, I can refufe a Perfon of your Appearance nothing.

Col. Sir, I am infinitely obliged to you.

Sir *Phil.* But do you really like Matrimony?

Col. I believe I could with Lady, Sir.

Sir *Phil.* The only Point in which we differ—But you are Mafter of fo many Qualifications, that I can excufe one Fault; for I muft think it a Fault in a fine Gentleman; and that you are fuch, I'll give it under my Hand.

Col.

A Bold Stroke for a WIFE.

Col. I wifh you'd give me your Confent to marry Mrs. *Lovely*, under your Hand, Sir *Philip*.

Sir *Phil.* I'll do't, if you'll ftep into St. *James's Coffee-houfe*, where we may have Pen and Ink ;——tho' I can't forfee what Advantage my Confent will be to you, without you could find a Way to get the reft of the Guardians. —But I'll introduce you, however; fhe is now at a Quaker's, where I carried her this Morning, when you faw us in *Gracechurch ftreet*,—I affure you fhe has an odd *Ragoût* of Guardians, as you will find when you hear the Characters, which I'll endeavour to give you as we go along.—Hey! *Pierre, Jacque, Renno?* —Where are you all, Scoundrels?—Order the Chariot to *St. James's Coffee-houfe*.

Col. Le Noir, la Brun, la Blanc.——*Marbleu, ou font ces Coquins la? Allons, Monfieur le Chevalier.*

Sir *Phil.* Ah! *Pardonnez moy, Monfieur.*

Col. Not one Step, upon my Soul, Sir *Philip*.

Sir *Phil.* The beft bred Man in *Europe*, pofitively. [*Ex.*

SCENE changes to *Obadiah Prim's* Houfe.

Enter Mrs. Lovely, *followed by Mrs.* Prim.

Mrs. *Prim.* Then thou wilt not obey me: And thou doft really think thofe Fallals become thee?

Mrs. *Love.* I do, indeed.

Mrs. *Prim.* Now will I be judged by all fober People, if I don't look more like a modeft Woman than thou doft, *Anne?*

Mrs. *Lov.* More like a Hypocrite you mean, Mrs. *Prim.*

Mrs. *Prim.* Ah! *Anne, Anne,* that wicked *Philip Modelove* will undo thee.——Satan fo fills thy Heart with Pride, during the three Months of his Guardianfhip, that thou becomeft a Stumbling-Block to the Upright.

Mrs. *Lov.* Pray, who are they? Are the pinch'd Cap and formal Hood the Emblems of Sanctity? Does your Virtue confift in your Drefs, Mrs. *Prim?*

Mrs. *Prim.* It doth not confift in cut Hair, fpotted Face and bare Necks.——Oh, the Wickednefs of the Generation! The primitive Women knew not the Abomination of hoop'd Petticoats.

Mrs. *Lov.* No, nor the Abomination of Cant neither.

Don't

220 *A Bold Stroke for a* WIFE.

Don't tell me, Mrs. *Prim*, don't.——I know you have as much Pride, Vanity, Self-conceit, and Ambition among you, couched under that formal Habit, and fanctified Countenance, as the proudest of us all ; but the World begins to see your Prudery.

Mrs. *Prim*. Prudery ! What ! do they invent new Words as well as new Fashions ? Ah ! poor fantastick Age, I pity thee.—Poor deluded *Anne*, which doft thou think moft refembleft the Saint, and which the Sinner, thy Drefs or mine ? Thy naked Bofom allureth the Eye of the Byftander,—encourageth the Frailty of human Nature,—— and corrupteth the Soul with evil Longings.

Mrs. *Lov*. And, pray, who corrupted your Son *Tobias* with evil Longings ? Your Maid *Tabitha* wore a Handkerchief, and yet he made the Saint a Sinner.

Mrs. *Prim*. Well, well, fpit thy Malice—I confefs Satan did buffet my Son *Tobias*, and my Servant *Tabitha* ; the evil Spirit was at that Time too ftrong, and they both became fubject to its Workings,——not from any outward Provocation,—but from an inward Call ;——he was not tainted with the Rottenefs of the Fafhions, nor did his Eyes take in the Drunkennefs of Beauty.

Mrs. *Lov*. No ! that's plainly to be feen.

Mrs. *Prim*. *Tabitha* is one of the Faithful ; he fell not with a Stranger.

Mrs. *Lov*. So ! Then you hold Wenching no Crime, provided it be within the Pale of your own Tribe.—— You are an excellent Cafuift truly.

Enter Obadiah Prim.

Ob. Prim. Not ftripp'd of thy Vanity, yet, *Anne* ! Why doft thou not make her put it off, *Sarah* ?

Mrs. *Prim*. She will not do it.

Ob. Prim. Verily, thy naked Breafts troubleth my outward Man ; I pray thee hide 'em *Anne* : Put on an Handkerchief, *Anne Lovely*.

Mrs. *Lov*. I hate Handkerchiefs when 'tis not cold Weather, Mr. *Prim*.

Mrs. *Prim*. I have feen thee wear an Handkerchief ; nay, and a Mafk to boot, in the Middle of *July*.

Mrs. *Lov*. Ay, to keep the Sun from fcorching me.

Ob. Pr. If thou couldft not bear the Sun-Beams, how doft

doſt thou think Man would fear thy Beams? Thoſe Breaſts inflame Deſire, let them be hid, I ſay.

Mrs. Lov. Let me be quiet, I ſay. Muſt I be tormented thus for ever? Sure no Woman's Condition ever equalled mine? Foppery, Folly, Avarice and Hypocriſy are, by Turns, my conſtant Companions,——and I muſt vary Shapes as often as a Player.—I cannot think my Father meant this Tyranny! No, you uſurp an Authority which he never intended you ſhould take.

Ob. Pr. Hark thee, do'ſt thou call good Counſel Tyranny? Do I, or my Wife, tyrannize, when we deſire thee in all Love to put off thy tempting Attire, and veil thy Provokers to Sin?

Mrs. Lov. Deliver me, good Heaven! or I ſhall go diſtracted. [*Walks about.*

Mrs. Pr. So! now thy Pinners are toſt, and thy Breaſts pulled up;——verily they were ſeen enough before.—— Fie upon the filthy Taylor who made the Stays.

Mrs. Lov. I wiſh I were in my Grave! Kill me rather than treat me thus.

Ob. Pr. Kill thee? ha, ha! thou thinkeſt thou art acting ſome lewd Play ſure :——Kill thee! Art thou prepared for Death, *Anne Lovely?* No, no, thou would'ſt rather have a Huſband, *Anne*:——Thou wanteſt a gilt Coach, with ſix lazy Fellows behind, to flant it in the Ring of Vanity, among the Princes and Rulers of the Land,——who pamper themſelves with the Fatneſs thereof; but I will take Care that none ſhall ſquander away thy Father's Eſtate. Thou ſhall marry none ſuch, *Anne.*

Mrs. Lov. Wou'd you marry me to one of your own canting Sect.

Ob. Pr. Yea, verily, no one elſe ſhall ever get my Conſent, I do aſſure thee, *Anne.*

Mrs. Lov. And I do aſſure thee, *Obadiah,* that I will as ſoon turn Papiſt, and die in a Convent.

Mrs. Pr. Oh Wickedneſs!

Mrs. Lov. Oh Stupidity!

Ob. Pr. Oh Blindneſs of Heart!

Mrs. Lov. Thou Blinder of the World, don't provoke me,—leſt I betray your Sanctity, and leave your Wife to judge of your Purity :—What were the Emotions of your Spirit—when you ſqueez'd *Mary* by the Hand laſt Night in the Pantry——when ſhe told you, you buff'd ſo filthily ? Ah ! you had no Averſion to naked Boſoms, when you begged her to ſhew you a little, little, little Bit of her delicious Bubby :——Don't you remember theſe Words, Mr. *Prim.*

Mrs. Prim. What does ſhe ſay, *Obadiah* ?

Ob. Pr. She talketh unintelligibly, *Sarah.* Which Way did ſhe hear this ? This ſhould not have reach'd the Ears of the wicked Ones :—Verily, it troubleth me.
[*Aſide.*

Enter Servant.

Serv. Philip *Modelove*, whom they call Sir *Philip*, is below, and ſuch another with him, ſhall I ſend them up ?

Ob. Pr. Yea.

Enter Sir Philip *and* Colonel.

Sir *Phil.* How doſt thou do, Friend *Prim* ? Odſo ! my She-Friend here too ! What you are documenting Miſs *Nancy*, reading her a Lecture upon the pinch'd Coif, I warrant ye.

Mrs. Pr. I am ſure thou did'ſt never read her any Lecture that was good——My Fleſh riſeth ſo at theſe wicked On:s, that Prudence adviſeth me to withdraw from their Sight. [*Exit.*

Col. Oh ! that I could find Means to ſpeak with her ! How charming ſhe appears ! I wiſh I could get this Letter into her Hand. [*Aſide.*

Sir *Phil.* Well, Miſs *Cockey*, I hope thou haſt got the better of them.

Mrs. Lov. The Difficulties of my Life are not to be ſurmounted, Sir *Philip.*——I hate the Impertinence of him, as much as the Stupidity of the other. [*Aſide.*

Ob. Pr. Verily, *Philip*, thou wilt ſpoil this Maiden.

Sir *Phil.* I find we ſtill differ in Opinion ; but that we may none of us ſpoil her, prithee *Prim*, let us conſent to marry her.——I have ſent for our Brother Guardians to meet me here about this very Thing——Madam, will you give me leave to recommend a Huſband to you ?——Here's a Gentleman, whom in my Mind, you can have no Objection to.

[*Preſents the* Colonel *to her, ſhe looks another Way.*

Mrs. Lov. Heaven deliver me from the formal, and the fantaſtick fool !

Col.

Col. A fine Woman,——a fine Horfe, and fine Equipage, are the fineft Things in the Univerfe : And if I am fo happy to poffefs you, Madam, I fhall become the Envy of Mankind, as much as you outfhine your whole Sex.
[*As he takes her Hand to kifs it, he endeavours to put a Letter into it ; fhe lets it drop——* Prim *takes it up.*

Mrs. *Lov.* I have no Ambition to appear confpicuoufly ridiculous, Sir. [*Turning from him.*
Col. So fall the Hopes of *Fainwell* !
Mrs. *Lov.* Ha ! *Fainwell !* 'tis he ! What have I done ? Prim has the Letter, and it will be difcover'd. [*Afide.*
Ob. Pr. Friend, I know not thy Name, fo I cannot call thee by it ; but thou feeft thy Letter is unwelcome to the Maiden, fhe will not read it.
Mrs. *Lov.* Nor fhall you ; (*fnatches the Letter*) I'll tear it in a thoufand Pieces, and fcatter it, as I will the Hopes of all thofe that any of you fhall recommend to me.
[*Tears the Letter.*
Sir *Phil.* Ha ! Right Woman, Faith ?
Col. Excellent Woman. [*Afide.*
Ob. Pr. Friend, thy Garb favoureth too much of the Vanity of the Age for my Approbation ; nothing that refembleth *Philip Modelove* fhall I love, mark that ;—— therefore, Friend *Philip*, bring no more of thy own Apes under my Roof.
Sir *Phil.* I am fo entirely a Stranger to the Monfters of thy Breed, that I fhall bring none of them I am fure,
Col. I am likely to have a pretty Tafk by that Time I have gone thro' them all ; but fhe's a City worth taking, and 'egad I'll carry on the Siege : If I can but blow up the Out-works, I fancy I am pretty fecure of the Town.
[*Afide.*
Enter Servant.
Serv. Toby Periwinkle and *Thomas Tradelove* demandeth to fee thee. [*To Sir* Philip.
Sir *Phil.* Bid them come up.
Mrs. *Lov.* Deliver me from fuch an Inundation of Noife and Nonfenfe. Oh *Fainwell* ! whatever thy Contrivance be, profper it Heaven ;——but oh ! I fear thou never canft redeem me. [*Exit.*
Sir *Phil. Sic tranfit Gloria Mundi* !

Enter

224 *A Bold Stroke for a* WIFE.

Enter Mr. Periwinkle *and* Tradelove.

Thefe are my Brother Guardians, Mr. *Fainwell,* prithee obferve the Creatures. [*Afide to* Col.

Trad. Well, Sir *Philip,* I obey your Summons.

Per. Pray, what have you to offer for the Good of Mrs. *Lovely,* Sir *Philip* ?

Sir *Phil.* Firft I defire to know what you intend to do with that Lady ? Muft fhe be fent to the *Indies* for a Venture,—or live to be an old Maid, and then enter'd amongft your Curiofities, and fhewn for a Monfter, Mr. *Periwinkle* ?

Col. Humph, Curiofities, that muft be the Virtuofo. [*Afide.*

Per. Why what wou'd you do with her ?

Sir *Phil.* I would recommend this Gentleman to her for a Hufband. Sir,——a Perfon whom I have pick'd out from the whole Race of Mankind.

Ob. Pr. I would advife thee to fhuffle him again with the reft of Mankind, for I like him not.

Col. Pray, Sir, without Offence to your Formality, what may be your Objections ?

Ob. Pr. Thy Perfon ; thy Manners ; thy Drefs ; thy Acquaintance ;——thy every Thing, Friend.

Sir *Phil.* You are moft particularly obliging, Friend, ha, ha !

Trade. What Bufinefs do you follow, pray Sir ?

Col. Humph, by that Queftion he muft be the Broker. (*Afide*)—Bufinefs, Sir ! the Bufinefs of a Gentleman.

Trade. That is as much as to fay, you drefs fine, feed high, lie with every Woman you like, and pay your Surgeon's Bills better than your Taylor's or your Butcher's.

Col. The Court is much oblig'd to you, Sir, for your Character of a Gentleman.

Trade. The Court, Sir ! What wou'd the Court do without us Citizens ?

Sir *Phil.* Without your Wives and Daughters, you mean, Mr. *Tradelove.*

Per. Have you ever travell'd, Sir ?

Col. That Queftion muft not be anfwer'd now——In Books I have, Sir.

Per. In Books ! That's fine travelling indeed !——Sir *Philip,* when you prefent a Perfon I like, he fhall have my Confent

A Bold Stroke for a WIFE.

Confent to marry Mrs. *Lovely*, 'till when your Servant. [*Exit.*

Col. I'll make you like me before I have done with you, or I'm miftaken. [*Afide.*

Trad. And when you can convince me that a Beau is more ufeful to my Couutry than a Merchant, you fhall have mine; 'till then you muft excufe me. [*Exit.*

Col. So much for Trade——I'll fit you too. [*Afide.*

Sir *Phil.* In my Opinion, this is very inhuman Treatment, as to the Lady, Mr. *Prim.*

Ob. Pr. Thy Opinion and mine happens to differ as much as our Occupations, Friend; Bufinefs requireth my Prefence, and Folly thine; and fo I muft bid thee farewel.

Sir *Phil.* Here's Breeding for you, Mr. *Fainwell!*—— Gad take me.

Half my Eftate I'd give to fee 'em bit.
Col. I hope to bite ye all, if my Plot hit. [Exit.

ACT III. SCENE I.

SCENE *the Tavern*; Sackbut *and the* Colonel *in an* Egyptian *Drefs.*

Sack. A Lucky Beginning, Colonel——you have got the old Beau's Confent.

Col. Ay, he's a reafonable Creature; but the other three will require fome Pains.—Shall I pafs upon him, think you? Egad, in my Mind, I look as antique as if I had been preferv'd in the Ark.

Sack. Pafs upon him! ay, ay, as roundly as White-wine dafh'd with Sack does for Mountain aud Sherry, if you have Affurance enough.——

Col. I have no Apprehenfion from that Quarter; Affurance is the Cockade of a Soldier.

Sack. Ay, but the Affurance of a Soldier differs much from that of a Traveller.——Can you lye with a good Grace?

Col. As heartily, when my Miftrefs is the Prize, as I would meet the Foe when my Country call'd, and King com-

commanded ; fo don't you fear that Part ; if he don't know me again, I'm fafe— -1 hope he'll come.

Sack. I wifh all my Debts would come as fure ; I told him you had been a great Traveller, had many valuable Curiofities, and was a Perfon of a moft fingular Tafte ; he seem'd tranfported, and begg'd me to keep you till he came.

Col. Ay, ay, he need not fear my running away—Let's have a Bottle of Sack, Landlord, our Anceftors drank Sack.

Sack. You fhall have it.

Col. And where-abouts is the Trap-door you mentioned?

Sack. There's the Conveyance, Sir. [*Exit.*

Col. Now if I fhould cheat all thefe roguifh Guardians, and carry off my Miftrefs in Triumph, it would be what the *French* call a *Grand Coup d'Eclat*—Odfo! here comes *Periwinkle*——Ah! duce take this Beaid ; pray *Jupiter* it does not give me the Slip, and fpoil all.

Enter Sackbut *with Wine, and* Periwinkle *following.*

Sack. Sir, this Gentleman hearing you have been a great Traveller, and a Perfon of fine Speculation, begs Leave to take a Glafs with you ; he is a Man of a curious Tafte himfelf.

Col. The Gentleman has it in his Face and Garb; Sir, you are welcome.

Per. Sir, I honour a Traveller, and Men of your enquiring Difpofition ; the Oddnefs of your Habit pleafes me extreamly ; 'tis very antique, and for that I like it.

Col. 'Tis very antique, Sir :—This Habit once belong'd to the famous *Claudius Ptolemeus*, who liv'd in the Year a Hundred and Thirty-five.

Sack. If he keeps up with the Sample, he fhall lye with the Devil for a Bean-ftack, and win it every Straw. [*Afide.*

Per. A Hundred and Thirty-five! why, that's prodigious now! — Well, certainly 'tis the fineft Thing in the World to be a Traveller.

Col. For my Part I value none of the modern Fafhions of a Fig-Leaf.

Per. No more don't I, Sir ; I had rather be the Jeft of a Fool, than his Favourite,—I am laugh'd at here for my Singularity——This Coat, you muft know, Sir, was formerly

A Bold Stroke for a WIFE.

merly worn by that ingenious and very learned Perfon, Mr *John Tradefcant* of *Lambeth*.

Col. John Tradefcant! Let me embrace you, Sir,—*John Tradefcant* was my Uncle, by Mother-fide; and I thank you for the Honour you do his Memory; he was a very curious Man indeed.

Per. Your Uncle, Sir,—nay then, 'tis no Wonder that your Tafte is fo refined; why you have it in your Blood. ——My humble Service to you, Sir, to the immortal Memory of *John Tradefcant*, your never-to-be-forgotten Uncle. [*Drinks.*

Col. Give me a Glafs, Landlord.

Per. I find you are primitive, even in your Wine; *Canary* was the Drink of our wife Forefathers, 'tis Balfamick, and faves the Charge of 'Pothecaries Cordials—Oh! that I had liv'd in your Uncle's Days! or rather, that he were now alive;—Oh! how proud he'd be of fuch a Nephew!

Sack. Oh Pox! that would have fpoil'd the Jeft. [*Afide.*

Per. A Perfon of your Curiofity muft have collected many Rarities.

Col. I have fome, Sir, which are not yet come afhore, as an *Egyptian* Idol.

Per. Pray, what might that be?

Col. It is, Sir, a Kind of an Ape, which they formerly worfhipp'd in that Country, I took it from the Breaft of a female Mummy.

Per. Ha, ha, our Women retain Part of their Idolatry to this Day, for many an Ape lies on a Lady's Breaft, ha, ha.——

Sack. A fmart old Thief. [*Afide.*

Col. Two Tufks of an *Hippopotamus*, two Pair of *Chinefe Nut-crackers*, and one *Egyptian Mummy*.

Per. Pray, Sir, have you never a Crocodile?

Col. Humph! the Boatfwain brought one with Defign to fhew it, but touching at *Rotterdam*, and hearing it was no Rarity in *England*, he fold it to a *Dutch* Poet.

Sack. The Devil's in that Nation, it rivals us in every Thing.

Per. I fhould have been very glad to have feen a living Crocodile.

Col. My Genius led me to Things more worthy of Regard.—Sir, I have feen the utmoft Limits of this globular World:

World; I have feen the Sun rife and fet; know in what Degree of Heat he is at Noon, to the Breadth of a Hair, and what Quantity of Cumbuftibles he burns in a Day, how much it turns to Afhes, and how much to Cinders.

Per. To Cinders! You amaze me, Sir; I never heard that the Sun confum'd any Thing.—*Defcartes* tells us——

Col. Defcartes, with the reft of his Brethren, both Ancient and Modern, knew nothing of the Matter.——I tell you, Sir, that Nature admits an annual Decay, tho' imperceptible to vulgar Eyes.——Sometimes his Rays deftroy below, fometimes above——You have heard of blazing Comets, I fuppofe?

Per. Yes, yes, I remember to have feen one, and our Aftrologers tell us of another which fhall happen very quickly.

Col. Thofe Comets are little Iflands bordering on the Sun, which at certain Times are fet on fire by that luminous Body's moving over them perpendicular, which will one Day occafion a general Conflagration.

Sack. One need not fcruple the Colonel's Capacity, faith. [*Afide.*

Per. This is marvellous ftrange! Thefe Cinders are what I never read of in any of our learned Differtations.

Col. I don't know how the Devil you fhould. [*Afide.*

Sack. He has it at his Fingers Ends; one would fwear he had learn'd to lye at School, he dces it fo cleverly.
[*Afide.*

Per. Well! you Travellers fee ftrange Thngis! Pray. Sir. have you any of those Cinders?

Col. I have, among my other Curiofities.

Per. Oh, what have I loft for want of Travelling! Pray, what have you elfe?

Col. Several Things worth your Attention——I have a Muff made of the Feathers of thofe Geefe that fav'd the *Roman* Capitol.

Per. Is it poffible?

Sack. Yes, if you are fuch a Gander as to believe him.
[*Afide.*

Col. I have an *Indian* Leaf, which open, will cover an Acre of Land, yet folds up in fo little a Compafs, you may put it into your Snuff-box.

Sack. Humph! That's a Thunderer. [*Afide.*
Per.

A Bold Stroke for a WIFE.

Per. Amazing!

Col. Ah! mine is but a little one; I have feen fome of them that would cover one of the *Carribbee* Iflands.

Per. Well, if I don't travel before I die, I fhan't reft in my Grave.——Pray, what do the *Indians* with them?

Col. Sir, they ufe them in their Wars for Tents, the old Women for Riding-hoods, the Young for Fans and Umbrellas.

Sack. He has a fruitful Invention. [*Afide.*

Per. I admire our *Eaft-India* Company imports none of them; they would certainly find their Account in them.

Col. Right, if they could find the Leaves.——*Afide.*—Look ye, Sir, do you fee this little Vial?

Per. Pray you what is it?

Col. This is call'd *Poluflofboio*.

Per. *Poluflojboio!*——It has a rumbling Sound.

Col. Right, Sir; it proceeds from a rumbling Nature.——This Water was part of thofe Waves which bore *Cleopatra*'s Veffel when fhe fail'd to meet *Anthony*.

Per. Well, of all that ever travell'd, none had a Tafte like you.

Col. But here's the Wonder of the World—This, Sir, is call'd *Zona*, or *Moros Mufphonon*, the Virtues of this are ineftimable.

Per. Moros Mufphonon! What in the Name of Wifdom can that be?——To me it feems a plain Belt.

Col. This Girdle has carried me all the World over.

Per. You have carried it, you mean.

Col. I mean as I fay, Sir:——Whenever I am girded with this, I am invifible; and by turning this little Screw, can be in the Court of the Great Mogul, the Grand Signior, and King *George*, in as little Time as your Cook can poach an Egg.

Per. You muft pardon me, Sir, I can't believe it.

Col. If my Landlord pleafes, he fhall try the Experiment immediately.

Sack. I thank you kindly, Sir, but I have no Inclination to ride Poft to the Devil.

Col. No, no, you fhan't ftir a Foot, I'll only make you invifible.

Sack. But if you could not make me vifible again.

Per.

Per. Come, try it upon me, Sir, I am not afraid of the Devil, nor all his Tricks——'Sbud, I'll ſtand 'em all.

Col. There, Sir, put it on——Come, Landlord, you and I muſt face the Eaſt. (*They turn about.*) Is it on, Sir?

Per. 'Tis on. [*They turn about again.*

Sack. Heaven protect me! Where is he?

Per. Why here, juſt where I was.

Sack. Where, where, in the Name of Virtue? Ah, poor Mr. *Periwinkle!*——Egad, look to't, you had beſt, Sir; and let him be ſeen again, or I ſhall have you burnt for a Wizard.

Col. Have Patience, good Landlord.

Per. But really don't you ſee me now?

Sack. No more than I ſee my Grandmother, that dy'd forty Years ago.

Per. Are you ſure you don't lye; methinks I ſtand juſt where I did, and ſee you as plain as I did before.

Sach. Ah! I wiſh I could ſee you once again.

Col. Take off the Girdle, Sir. [*He takes it off.*

Sack. Ah, Sir, I am glad to ſee you with all my Heart.
[*Embraces him.*

Per. This is very odd; certainly there muſt be ſome Trick in't——Pray, Sir, will you do me the Favour to put it on yourſelf.

Col. With all my Heart.

Per. But firſt I'll secure the Door.

Col. You know how to turn the Screw, Mr. *Sackbut?*

Sack. Yes, yes——Come, Mr. *Periwinkle*, we muſt turn full Eaſt. [*They turn, the Colonel ſinks down a Trap-door.*

Col. 'Tis done, now turn. [*They turn.*

Per. Ha! Mercy upon me; my Fleſh creeps upon my Bones——This muſt be a Conjurer, Mr. *Sackbut.*

Sack. He is the Devil, I think.

Per. Oh, Mr. *Sackbut*, why do you Name the Devil, when perhaps he may be at your Elbow?

Sack. At my Elbow; marry, Heaven forbid.

Col. (*Below.*) Are you ſatisfied, Sir?

Per. Yes, Sir, yes.——How hollow his Voice ſounds!

Sack. Yours ſeems juſt the ſame——Faith, I wiſh this Girdle were mine, I'd ſell Wine no more. Hark ye, Mr. *Periwinkle* (*takes him aſide, 'till the* Colonel *riſes*
(*again*

again) if he would fell this Girdle, you might travel with great Expedition.

Col. But it is not to be parted with for Money.

Per. I am forry for't, Sir, becaufe I think it is the greateft Curiofity I ever heard of.

Col. By the Advice of a learned Phyfiognomift in *Grand Cairo*, who confulted the Lines in my Face, I returned to *England*, where he told me I fhould find a Rarity in the Keeping of *four* Men, which I was born to poffefs for the Benefit of Mankind; and the *firft* of the *four* that gave me his Confent, I fhould prefent him with this Girdle— Till I have found this Jewel, I fhall not part with the Girdle.

Per. What can that Rarity be? Didn't he name it to you?

Col. Yes, Sir: he called it a chafte, beautiful unaffected Woman.

Per. Pifh! Women are no Rarities——I never had any great Tafte that Way; I married, indeed, to pleafe a Father, and I got a Girl to pleafe my Wife; but fhe and the Child (thank Heav'n) died together——Women are the very Geugaws of the Creation; Playthings for Boys, who, when they write Man, they ought to throw afide.

Sack. A fine Lecture to be read to a Circle of Ladies! [*Afide.*

Per. What Woman is there, dreft in all the Pride and Foppery of the Times, can boaft of fuch a Foretop as the *Cockatoo?*

Col. I muft humour him—(*Afide*)—Such a Skin as the *Lizzard?*

Per. Such a fhining Breaft as the *Humming-Bird?*

Col. Such a Shape as the *Antelope?*

Per. Or in all the artful Mixture of their various Dreffes, have they half the Beauty of one Box of Butterflies?

Col. No, that muft be allow'd—For my Part, if it were not for the Benefit of Mankind, I'd have nothing to do with them, for they are as indifferent to me as a Sparrow, or a Flefh Fly.

Per. Pray, Sir, what Benefit is the World to reap from this Lady?

Col. Why, Sir, fhe is to bear me a Son, who fhall revive the Art of embalming, and the old *Roman* Manner of burying

burying the Dead ; and for the Benefit of Pofterity he is to difcover the Longitude fo long fought for in vain.

Per. Od ! thefe are valuable Things, Mr. *Sackbut*.

Sack. He hits it off admirably, and t'other fwallows it like Sack and Sugar—*Afide*—Certainly this Lady muft be your Ward. Mr. *Periwinkle,* by her being under the Care of *four* Perfons.

Per. By the Defcription it fhould— —Egad, if I could get that Girdle, I'd ride with the Sun, and make the *Tour* of the World in *four and twenty* Hours. (*Afide*) And are you to give that Girdle to the *firft* of the *Four* Guardians that fhall give his Confent to marry that Lady, fay you, Sir ?

Col. I am fo order'd, when I can find him.

Per. I fancy I know the very Woman—her Name is *Anne Lovely*.

Col. Excellent !——He faid, indeed, that the firft Letter of her Name was *L*.

Per. Did he, really?———Well, that's prodigioufly a-mazing, that a Perfon in *Grand Cairo* fhould know any Thing of my Ward.

Col. Your Ward !

Per. To be plain with you, Sir; I am one of thofe *four* Guardians.

Col. Are you indeed, Sir ? I am tranfported to find the Man who is to poffefs this *Moros Mufphonon* is a Perfon of fo curious a Tafte.—Here is a Writing drawn up by that famous *Egyptian*, which if you will pleafe to fign, you muft turn your Face full North, and the Girdle is your's.

Per. If I live till this Boy is born, I'll be embalm'd, and fent to the Royal Society when I die.

Col. That you fhall moft certainly.

Enter Drawer.

Draw. Here's Mr. *Staytape* the Taylor enquires for you, Colonel.

Col. Who do you fpeak to, you Son of a Whore.

Per. Ha ! Colonel ! [*Afide*.
Col. Confound the blundering Dog ! [*Afide*.
Draw. Why, to Colonel——
Sack. Get you out, you Rafcal.

[*Kicks him out, and goes after him.*
Draw.

A Bold Stroke for a WIFE. 233

Draw. What the Devil is the Matter?

Col. This Dog has ruin'd all my Schemes, I fee by *Periwinkle's* Looks. [*Afide.*

Per. How finely I fhould have been chous'd—Colonel, you'll pardon me that I did not give you your Title before —it was pure Ignorance, faith it was—— Pray — hem, hem! Pray, Colonel, what Poſt had this learned *Egyptian* in your Regiment?

Col. A Pox of your Sneer. (*Afide.*) I don't underſtand you, Sir.

Per. No, that's ſtrange! I underſtand you, Colonel— An *Egyptian* of *Grand Cairo!* ha, ha, ha—I am forry fuch a well invented Tale fhould do you no more Service—— We old Fellows can fee as far into a Milſtone as them that pick it——I am not to be trick'd out of my Truſt——mark that.

Col. The Devil! I muſt carry it off, I wiſh I were fairly out. (*Afide.*) Look ye, Sir, you may make what Jeſt you pleafe—but the Stars will be obey'd, Sir, and, depend upon't, I fhall have the Lady, and you none of the Girdle. —Now for *Freeman's* Part of the Plot. (*Afide.*) [*Exit.*

Per. The Stars! ha, ha—No Star has favour'd you, it feems—— The Girdle! ha, ha, ha, none of your *Legerdemain* Tricks can pafs upon me——Why, what a Pack of Trumpery has this Rogue pick'd up—His *Pagod, Polufloſboios,* his *Zonas, Moros Muſphonons,* andthe Devilknows what—But I'll take Care—Ha, gone——Ay, 'twas Time to fneak off—Soho! the Houfe! [*Enter* Sackbut.] Where is this Trickſter? Send for a Conſtable, I'll have this Rafcal before the Lord Mayor; I'll *Grand Cairo* him, with a Pox to him—I believe you had a Hand in putting this Impoſture upon me, *Sackbut.*

Sack. Who I, Mr. *Periwinkle?* I fcorn it; I perceiv'd he was a Cheat, and left the Room on purpofe to fend for a Conſtable to apprehend him, and endeavour'd to ſtop him when he went out—But the Rogue made but one Step from the Stairs to the Door, call'd a Coach, leap'd into it, and drove away like the Devil, as Mr. *Freeman* can wltnefs, who is at the Bar, and defires to fpeak with you; he is this Minute come to Town.

Per. Send him in. [*Exit* Sackbut.] What a Scheme this Rogue has laid! How I fhould have been laugh'd at, had

i

it ſucceeded! [*Enter* Freeman *booted and ſpur'd.*] Mr. *Freeman,* your Dreſs commands your Welcome to Town, what will you drink? I had like to have been impos'd upon here by the verieſt Raſcal———

Free. I am ſorry to hear it.—The Dog flew for't—he had not 'ſcap'd me, if I had been aware of him; *Sackbut* ſtruck at him, but miſs'd his Blow, or he had done his Buſineſs for him.

Per. I believe you never heard of ſuch a Contrivance, Mr. *Freeman,* as this Fellow had found out.

Free. Mr. *Sackbut* has told me the whole Story, Mr. *Periwinkle*; but now I have ſomething to tell you of much more Importance to yourſelf.—I happen'd to lie one Night at *Coventry,* and knowing your Uncle, Sir *Toby Periwinkle,* I paid him a Viſit, and, to my great Surprize, found him dying.

Per. Dying!

Free. Dying, in all Appearance; the Servants weeping, the Room in Darkneſs; the 'Pothecary ſhaking his Head, told me, the Doctors had given him over; and then there is ſmall Hopes, you know.

Per. I hope he has made his Will—he always told me, he would make me his Heir.

Free. I have heard you ſay as much, and therefore reſolv'd to give you Notice. I ſhould think, it would not be amiſs if you went down to-morrow Morning.

Per. It is a long Journey, and the Roads very bad.

Free. But he has a great Eſtate, and the Land very good —Think upon that.

Per. Why that's true, as you ſay; I'll think upon it: In the mean Time, I give you many Thanks for your Civility, Mr. *Freeman,* and ſhould be glad of your Company to dine with me.

Free. I am oblig'd to be at *Jonathan's* Coffee-Houſe by Two, and now it is half an Hour after One; if I diſpatch my Buſineſs, I'll wait on you; I know your Hour.

Per. You ſhall be very welcome, Mr. *Freeman,* and ſo your humble Servant. [*Exit.*

Re-enter Colonel *and* Sackbut.

Free. Ha, ha, ha—I have done your Buſineſs, Colonel, he has ſwallow'd the Bait.

Col.

Col. I overheard all, though I am a little in the Dark; I am to perſonate a Highwayman, I ſuppoſe—That's a Project I am not fond of; for though I may fright him out of his Conſent, he might fright me out of my Life, when he diſcovers me, which he certainly muſt do in the End.

Free. No, no, I have a Plot for you without Danger, but firſt we muſt manage *Tradelove*——Has the Taylor brought your Clothes?

Sack. Yes, Pox take the Thief.

Col. Well, well, no Matter, I warrant we have him yet —But now you muſt put on the *Dutch* Merchant.

Col. The Duce of this trading Plot——I wiſh he had been an old Soldier, that I might have attack'd him in my own Way, heard him fight over all the Battles of the civil War—But for Trade, by *Jupiter* I ſhall never do it.

Sack. Never fear, Colonel, Mr. *Freeman* will inſtruct you.

Free. You'll ſee what others do, the Coffee-houſe will inſtruct you.

Col. I muſt venture, however——But I have a farther Plot in my Head upon *Tradelove*, which you muſt aſſiſt me in, *Freeman*; you are in Credit with him, I heard you ſay.

Free. I am, and will ſcruple nothing to ſerve you, Colonel.

Col. Come along, then—Now for the *Dutchman*— Honeſt *Ptolemy*. By your Leave.

Now muſt Bag Wig and Buſ'neſs come in Play,
A Thirty-Thouſand-Pound Girl leads the Way.

ACT IV. SCENE I.

SCENE Jonathan's *Coffee-Houſe in* Change-Alley. *A Crowd of People with Rolls of Paper and Parchment in their Hands; a Bar, and Coffee-Boys waiting.*

Enter Tradelove *and* Stock-Jobbers, *with Rolls of Paper and Parchment.*

1ſt Stock. South-Sea at ſeven Eighths; who buys?

2d Stock. South-Sea Bonds due at *Michaelmas*, 1718. Claſs Lottery-Tickets.

236 A Bold Stroke for a WIFE.

3d Stock. *Eaſt-India* Bonds?
4th Stock. What, all Sellers and no Buyers? Gentlemen, I'll buy a thouſand Pound for *Tueſday* next, at *three Fourths.*
Coff. Boy. Freſh Coffee, Gentlemen, freſh Coffee?
Trade. Hark ye, *Gabriel,* you'll pay the Difference of that Stock we tranſaƈted for t'other Day.
Gabr. Ay, Mr. *Tradelove,* here's a Note for the Money upon the *Sword-Blade* Company. [*Gives him a Note.*
Coff. Boy. Bohea-Tea, Gentlemen?

Enter a Man.

Man. Is Mr. *Smuggle* here?
1ſt Coff. Boy. Mr. *Smuggle's* not here, Sir, you'll find him at the Books.
2nd Stock. Ho! here come two Sparks from t'other End of the Town; what News bring they?

Enter two Gentlemen.

Trade. I would fain bite that Spark in the Brown Coat; he comes very often into the Alley, but never employs a Broker.

Enter Colonel *and* Freeman.

2d Stock. Who does anything in the Civil-Liſt Lottery? or *Caco?* Zounds, where are all the *Jews* this Afternoon? Are you a Bull or a Bear To-day, *Abraham?*
3d Stock. A Bull, Faith,——But I have a good Putt for next Week.
Trade. Mr. *Freeman,* your Servant! Who is that Gentleman?
Free. A *Dutch* Merchant, juſt come to *England*; but hark ye, Mr. *Tradelove,*—I have a Piece of News will get you as much as the *French King's* Death, if you are expeditious.
Trade. Say you ſo, Sir! Pray, what is it?
Free. (*Shewing him a Letter.*) Read there, I receiv'd it juſt now from one that belongs to the Emperor's Miniſter.
Trade. (Reads.) *Sir, As I have many Obligations to you, I cannot miſs any Opportunity to ſhew my Gratitude; this Moment my Lord has received a private Expreſs, that the* Spaniards *have rais'd their Siege from before* Cagliari; *if this*

proves

A Bold Stroke for a WIFE.

proves any *Advantage to you, it will anfwer both the Ends and Wifhes of, Sir, Your moft obliged humble Servant,*
Henricus Duffeldorp.

Poftfcript.

In two or three Hours the News will be publick.
May one depend upon this, Mr. *Freeman?*
[*Afide to* Freeman.
Free. You may.——I never knew this Perfon fend mc a falfe Piece of News in my Life.
Trade. Sir, I am much oblig'd to you, 'Egad, 'tis rare News.——Who fells *South-Sea* for next Week.
Stock Job. (*All together.*) I fell; I, I, I, I, I fell.
1ft Stock. I'll fell 5000*l.* for next Week, at *five Eighths.*
2d Stock.——I'll fell ten thoufand, at *five Eighths*, for the iame Time.
Trade. Nay, nay, hold, hold, not altogether, Gentlemen, I'll be no Bull, I'll buy no more than I can take: Will you fell ten thoufand Pounds at a Half, for any Day next Week, except *Saturday?*
1ft Stock. I'll fell it to you, Mr. *Tradelove.*
Free. (*Whifpers to one of the Gentlemen.*)
Gent. (*Afide.*) The *Spaniards* rais'd the Siege of *Cagliari!* I don't believe one Word of it.
2d Gent. Rais'd the Siege; as much as you have rais'd the Monument.
Free. 'Tis rais'd I affure you, Sir.
2d Gent. What will you lay on't.
Free. What you pleafe.
1ft Gent. Why, I have a Brother upon the Spot, in the Emperor's Service; I am certain if there were any fuch Thing, I fhould have had a Letter.
2d Stock. How's this? The Siege of *Cagliari* rais'd?——I wifh it may be true, 'twill make Bufinefs ftir, and Stocks rife.
1ft Stock. Tradelove's a cunning fat Bear; if this News proves true, I fhall repent I fold him the ten thoufand Pounds.——Pray, Sir, what Affurance have you that the Siege is rais'd?
Free. There is come an Exprefs to the Emperor's Minifter.
2d Stock. I'll know that prefently. [*Exit
1ft Gent.*

238   *A Bold Stroke for a* WIFE.

1st Gent. Let it come where it will, I'll hold you fifty Pounds 'tis falſe.
Free. 'Tis done.
2d Gent. I'll lay you a Brace of Hundreds upon the ſame.
Free. I'll take you.
4th Stock. 'Egad, I'll hold twenty Pieces 'tis not rais'd, Sir.
Free. Done with you too.
Trade. I'll lay any Man a Brace of Thouſands the Siege is rais'd.
Free. The *Dutch* Merchant is your Man to take in.
                                       [*Aſide to* Tradelove.
Trade. Does not he know the News?
Free. Not a Syllable; if he did, he wou'd bet a Hundred thouſand Pound as ſoon as one Penny;—he's plaguy rich, and a mighty Man at Wagers.   [*To* Tradelove.
Trade. Say you ſo,—'Egad, I'll bite him, if poſſible; ——Are you from *Holland*, Sir?
Col. Ya, Mynheer.
Trade. Had you the News before you came away?
Col. Wat believe you, Mynheer?
Trade. What do I believe? Why, I believe that the *Spaniards* have aƈtually rais'd the Siege of *Cagliari.*
Col. What Duyvel's News is dat? 'Tis niet waer, Mynheer,——'tis no true, Sir.
Trade. 'Tis ſo true, Mynheer, that I'll lay you two thouſand Pounds upon it.——You are ſure the Letter may be depended upon, Mr. *Freeman?*
Free. Do you think I would venture my Money, if I were not ſure of the Truth of it?   [*Aſide* to Tradelove.
Col. Two duyſend Pound, Mynheer, 'tis gadaen—dis Gentleman ſal hold de Gelt.   [*Gives* Freeman *Money.*
Trade. With all my Heart—this binds the Wager.
Free. You have certainly loſt, Mynheer, the Siege is rais'd indeed.
Col. Ik gelov't niet, Mynheer *Freeman,* ik ſal ye dubbled houden, if you pleaſe.
Free. I am let into the Secret, therefore won't win your Money.
Trade. Ha, ha, ha! I have ſnapt the *Dutchman,* Faith,
                        I   ha,

ha, ha! this is no ill Day's Work,——pray, may I crave your Name Mynheer?

Col. Myn Naem, Mynheer! myn Name is *Jan van Timtamtirelereletta Heer Fainwell.*

Trade. Zounds, 'tis a damn'd long Name, I ſhall never remember it.—*Myn Heer van, Tim, Tim, Tim,*——What the Devil is it?

Free. Oh! never heed, I know the Gentleman, and will paſs my Word for twice the Sum.

Trade. That's enough.

Col. You'll hear of me ſooner than you'll wiſh, old Gentleman, I fancy. (*Aſide.*) You'll come to *Sackbut*'s, *Freeman.* [*Exit.*

Free. Immediately. [*Aſide to the* Colonel.

1ſt Man. *Humphry Hump* here?

2d Boy. Mr. *Humphry Hump* is not here; you'll find him upon the *Dutch* Walk.

Trade. Mr. *Freeman* I give you many Thanks for your Kindneſs.———

Free. I fear you'll repent when you know all. [*Aſide.*

Trade. Will you dine with me?

Free. I'm engag'd at *Sackbut*'s; adieu. [*Exit.*

Trade. Sir, your humble Servant. Now I'll ſee what I can do upon *'Change* with my News. [*Exit.*

SCENE *the Tavern.*

Enter Freeman *and* Colonel.

Free. Ha, ha, ha! The old Fellow ſwallowed the Bait as greedily as a Gudgeon.

Col. I have him, Faith, ha, ha, ha!—His two thouſand Pounds ſecure.——If he would keep his Money, he muſt part with the Lady, ha, ha.——What came of your two Friends? They perform'd their Part very well; you ſhould have brought 'em to take a Glaſs with us.

Free. No matter, we'll drink a Bottle together another Time.—I did not care to bring them hither; there's no Neceſſity to truſt them with the main Secret, you know, *Colonel.*

Col. Nay, that's right. *Freeman.*

Enter Sackbut.

Sack. Joy, Joy, *Colonel!* The luckieſt Accident in the World! *Col.*

Col. What say'st thou?

Sack. This Letter does your Business.

Col. (*Reads.*) To *Obadiah Prim*, Hosier, near the Building call'd the *Monument*, in *London*.

Free. A Letter to *Prim!* How came you by it?

Sack. Looking over the Letters our Post-Woman brought as I always do, to see what Letters are directed to my House, (for she can't read, you must know) I spy'd this to *Prim*, so paid for it among the Rest; I have given the old Jade a Pint of Wine on purpose to delay Time, till you see if the Letter be of any Service; then I'll seal it up again, and tell her I took it by Mistake;—I have read it, and fancy you'll like the Project—Read, read *Colonel*.

Col. (Reads) *Friend* Prim, *there is arriv'd from* Pensilvania *one* Simon Pure, *a Leader of the Faithful, who hath sojourn'd with us eleven Days, and hath been of great Comfort to the Brethren.—He intendeth for the Quarterly Meetings in* London; *I have recommended him to thy House. I pray thee treat him kindly, and let thy Wife cherish him, for he's of weakly Constitution*——*he will depart from us the third Day; which is all from thy Friend in the Faith.* Aminadab Holdfast.

Ha, ha, excellent! I understand you, Landlord, I am to personate this *Simon Pure*, am I not?

Sack. Don't you like the Hint?

Col. Admirably well!

Free. 'Tis the best Contrivance in the World, if the right *Simon* get not there before you.——

Col. No, no, the Quakers never ride Post; he can't be here before To-morrow at soonest: Do you send and buy me a Quaker's Dress, Mr. *Sackbut*; and suppose *Freeman*, you should wait at the *Bristol* Coach, that if you see any such Person, you might contrive to give me Notice.——

Free I will--the Country Dress and Boots, are they ready?

Sack. Yes, yes, every Thing——Sir.

Free. Bring 'em in then.—[*Exit* Sack.] Thou must dispatch *Periwinkle* first—remember his Uncle Sir *Toby Periwinkle* is an old Batchelor of Seventy-five,—that he has Seven hundred a Year, most in Abbey Land, that he was once in Love with your Mother, and shrewdly suspected by some to be your Father,——that you have been thirty Years his Steward,—and ten Years his Gentleman,——remember to improve these Hints. *Col.*

A Bold Stroke for a WIFE.

Col. Never fear, let me alone for that—but what's the Steward's Name?

Free. His Name is *Pillage*.

Col. Enough.—[*Enter* Sackbut *with Clothes.*] Now for the Country Put——— [*Dreſſes.*

Free. 'Egad, Landlord, thou deferveſt to have the firſt Night's Lodging with the Lady for thy Fidelity; — what fay you, *Colonel*, ſhall we fettle a Club here, you'll mak one?

Col. Make one; I'll bring a Set of honeſt Officers, ti at will ſpend their Money as freely to the King's Health, as they would their Blood in his Service.

Sack. I thank you, *Colonel*; here, here! [*Bell rings.*
[*Exit* Sackbut.

Col. So, now for my Boots. [*Puts on Boots.*] Shall I find you here, *Freeman*, when I come back?

Free. Yes, —— or I'll leave Word with *Sackbut*, where he may fend for me—Have you the Writings, the Will, ——and every Thing?

Col. All, all!—— [*Enter* Sackbut.

Sack. Zounds! Mr. *Freeman!* yonder is *Tradelove* in the damned'ſt Paſſion in the World——He ſwears you are in the Houſe—he ſays you told him you was to dine here.

Free. I did ſo, ha, ha, ha! he has found himſelf bit already.——

Col. The Devil! he muſt not fee me in this Dreſs.

Sack. I told him I expeĉted you here, but you were not come yet———

Free. Very well,——make you haſte out, *Colonel*, and let me alone to deal with him: Where is he?

Sack. In the *King's-Head*.

Col. You remember what I told you?

Free. Ay, ay, very well. Landlord, let him know I am come in,—and now, Mr. *Pillage*, Succeſs attend you.
[*Exit* Sack.

Col. Mr. *Proteus* rather.———
From changing Shape, and imitating Jove,
I draw the happy Omens of my Love,
I'm not the firſt young Brother of the Blade;
Who made his Fortune in a Maſquerade. [*Exit* Col.
Enter Tradelove.

Free. Zounds! Mr. *Tradelove*, we're bit it feems.

Trade.

Trade. Bit do you call it, Mr. *Freeman?* I am ruin'd. ——Pox on your News.

Free. Pox on the Rafcal that fent it me.——

Trade. Sent it you! Why *Gabriel Skinflint* has been at the Minifter's, and fpoke with him, and he has affur'd him 'tis every Syllable falfe; he receiv'd no fuch Exprefs.

Free. I know it: I this Minute parted with my Friend, who protefted he never fent me any fuch Letter.—Some roguifh Stockjobber has done it on purpofe to make me lofe my Money, that's certain; I wifh I knew who he was, I'd make him repent it.—I have loft 300*l*. by it.

Trade. What fignifies your three hundred Pounds to what I have loft? There's two thoufand Pounds to that *Dutchman* with a curfed long Name, befides the Stock I bought; the Devil! I could tear my Flefh——I muft never fhew my Face upon 'Change more;——for, by my Soul, I can't pay it.

Free. I am heartily forry for it! What can I ferve you in? Shall I fpeak to the *Dutch* Merchant, and try to get you Time for the Payment?

Trade. Time! Ads'heart; I fhall never be able to look up again.

Free. I am very much concern'd that I was the Occafion, and wifh I could be an Inftrument of retrieving your Misfortune; for my own, I value it not. Adfo! a Thought comes into my Head, that, well improv'd, may be of Service.

Trade. Ah! there's no Thought can be of any Service to me, without paying the Money, or running away.

Free. How do you know? What do you think of my proposing Mrs. *Lovely* to him? He is a fingle Man—and I heard him fay he had a Mind to marry an *Englifh* Woman——nay, more than that, he faid fomebody told him, you had a pretty Ward——he wifh'd you had betted her inftead of your Money.

Trade. Ay, but he'd be hang'd before he'd take her inftead of the Money; the *Dutch* are too covetous for that; befides, he did not know that there were three more of us, I fuppofe.

Free. So much the better; you may venture to give him your Confent, if he'll forgive you the Wager; it is

not

not your Bufinefs to tell him, that your Confent will fignify nothing.

Trade. That's right as you fay; but will he do it, think you?

Free. I can't tell that; but I'll try what I can do with him——He has promis'd me to meet me here an Hour hence; I'll feel his Pulfe, and let you know: If I find it feafible, I'll fend for you; if not, you are at Liberty to take what Meafures you pleafe.

Trade. You muft extol her Beauty, double her Portion, and tell him I have the intire Difpofal of her, and that fhe can't marry without my Confent;——and that I am a covetous Rogue, and will never part with her without a valuable Confideration.

Free. Ay, ay, let me alone for a Lye at a Pinch.

Trade. 'Egad, if you can bring this to bear, Mr. *Freeman*, I'll make you whole again; I'll pay the three hundred Pounds you loft, with all my Soul.

Free. Well, I'll ufe my beft Endeavours——Where will you be?

Trade. At Home; pray Heaven you profper—If I were but the fole Truftee now, I fhould not fear it. Who the Devil would be a Guardian,

*If, when Cafh runs low, our Coffers t'enlarge,
We can't, like other Stocks, transfer our Charge?* [*Exit.*

Free. Ha, ha, ha——he has it. [*Exit.*

SCENE *changes to* Periwinkle's *Houfe.*

Enter Periwinkle *on one Side, and* Footman *on t'other.*

Foot. A Gentleman from *Coventry* enquires for you, Sir.

Per. From my Uncle, I warrant you; bring him up—This will fave me the Trouble, as well as the Expence of a Journey.

Enter Colonel.

Col. Is your Name *Periwinkle*, Sir?

Per. It is, Sir.

Col. I am forry for the Meffage I bring—My old Mafter, whom I ferv'd thefe forty Years, claims the Sorrow due from a faithful Servant to an indulgent Mafter.

[*Weeps.*
Per.

Per. By this I underſtand, Sir, my Uncle Sir *Toby Periwinkle* is dead.

Col. He is, Sir, and he has left you Heir to ſeven Hundred a Year, in as good Abbey-Land as ever paid *Peter-Pence* to *Rome*.——I wiſh you long to enjoy it, but my Tears will flow when I think of my Benefactor—(*Weeps.*) Ah! he was a good Man——he has not left many of his Fellows——the Poor lament him ſorely.

Per. I pray, Sir, what Office bore you?

Col. I was his Steward, Sir.

Per. I have heard him mention you with much Refpect; your Name is———

Col. Pillage, Sir.

Per. Ay, *Pillage*, I do remember he called you *Pillage* ——Pray, Mr. *Pillage*, when did my Uncle die?

Col. Monday laſt, at Four in the Morning. About Two he ſign'd his Will, and gave it into my Hands, and ſtrictly charged me to leave *Coventry* the Moment he expir'd, and deliver it to you with what Speed I could? I have obey'd him, Sir, and there is the Will. [*Gives it to* Per.

Per. 'Tis very well, I'll lodge it in the Commons.

Col. There are Two Things which he forgot to inſert, but charg'd me to tell you, that he deſir'd you'd perform them as readily as if you had found them written in the Will, which is to remove his Corpſe, and bury him by his Father at St. *Paul*'s, *Covent-Garden*, and to give all his Servants Mourning.

Per. That will be a conſiderable Charge; a Pox of all modern Faſhions. (*Aſide.*) Well! it ſhall be done. Mr. *Pillage:* I will agree with one of Death's Faſhion-Mongers, call'd an Undertaker, to go down, and bring up the Body.

Col. I hope, Sir, I ſhall have the Honour to ſerve you in the ſame Station I did your worthy Uncle; I have not many Years to ſtay behind him, and would gladly ſpend them in the Family, where I was brought up—(*Weeps.*) He was a kind and tender Maſter to me.

Per. Pray don't grieve, Mr. *Pillage*, you ſhall hold your Place, and every Thing elſe which you held under my Uncle——You make me weep to ſee you ſo concern'd. (*Weeps.*) He liv'd to a good old Age, and we are all mortal.

Col.

Col. We are fo, Sir, and therefore I muft beg you to fign this Leafe ; You'll find Sir *Toby* has taken particular Notice of it in his Will—I could nòt get it Time enough from the Lawyer, or he had fign'd it before he dy'd.
                                    [*Gives him a Paper.*
Per. A Leafe ! for what ?
Col. I rented an hundred a Year of Sir *Toby* upon Leafe, which Lèafe expires at *Lady Day* next. I defire to renew it for Twenty Years——that's all Sir.
Per. Let me fee.   [*Looks over the Leafe.*
Col. Matters go fwimmingly, if nothing intervene.
                                    [*Afide.*
Per. Very well——Let's fee what he fays in his Will about it.   [*Lays the Leafe upon the Table, and looks on the Will.*
Col. He's very wary, yet I fancy I fhall be too cunning for him.   [*Afide.*
Per. Ho, here it is——*The Farm lying*——*now in Poffeffion of* Samuel Pillage, *fuffer him to renew his Leafe—at the fame Rent.*—Very well, Mr. *Pillage*, I fee my Uncle does mention it, and I'll perform his Will. Give me the Leafe—Col. *gives it him, he looks upon it, and lays it upon the Table.*) Pray you ftep to the Door, and call for a Pen and Ink, Mr. *Pillage*.
Col. I have Pen and Ink in my Pocket, Sir, (*Pulls out an Inkhorn.*) I never go without that.
Per. I think it belongs to your Profeffion——(*He looks upon the Pen, while the* Col. *changes the Leafe, and lays down the Contract.*) I doubt this is but a forry Pen, tho' it may ferve to write my Name.   [*Writes.*
Col. Little does he think what he figns.   [*Afide.*
Per. There is your Leafe, Mr. *Pillage.* (*Gives him the Paper.*) Now I muft defire you to make what Hafte you can down to *Coventry*, and take Care of every Thing, and I'll fend down the Undertaker for the Body ; do you attend it up, and whatever Charge you are at, I will repay you.
Col. You have paid me already, I thank you Sir. [*Afide.*
Per. Will you dine with me ?
Col. I would rather not, there are fome of my Neighbours which I met as I came along, who leave the Town
                  this

this Afternoon, they told me, and I fhould be glad of their Company down.

Per. Well, well, I won't detain you.

Col. I don't care how foon I am out. [*Afide.*

Per. I will give Orders about Mourning.

Col. You will have Caufe to mourn, when you know your Eftate imaginary only.

You'll find your Hopes and Cares are vain,
In Spite of all the Caution you have ta'en,
Fortune rewards the faithful Lover's Pain. [Exit.

Per. Seven Hundred a Year! I wifh he had died feventeen Years ago;——What a valuable Collection of Rarities might I have had by this Time!—I might have travell'd over all the known Parts of the Globe, and made my own Clofet rival the Vatican at *Rome.*—Odfo, I have a good Mind to begin my Travels now;——let me fee. ——I am but Sixty! my Father, Grandfather, and Great Grandfather reach'd Ninety odd;——I have almoft forty Years good:——Let me confider! what will feven hundred a Year amount to in——ay! in thirty Years, I'll fay but Thirty——Thirty times Seven, is feven times Thirty ——that is——juft twenty-one thoufand Pounds,——'tis a great deal of Money.——I may very well referve fixteen Hundred of it for a Collection of fuch Rarities, as will make my Name famous to Pofterity;——I would not die like other Mortals, forgotten in a Year or two, as my Uncle will be——No,

With Nature's curious Works I'll raife my Fame,
That Men,'till Doom's-Day, may repeat my Name. [*Exit.*

S C E N E *changes to a Tavern; Freeman and* Tradelove *over a Bottle.*

Trade. Come, Mr. *Freeman,* here's Mynheer *Jan, Van, Tim, Tam, Tam* ;——I fhall never think of that *Dutchman's* name——

Free. Mynheer *Jan Van Timtamtireliretta Heer Van Fainwell.*

Trade. Ay, *Heer Van Fainwell,* I never heard fuch a confounded Name in my Life—here's his Health, I fay.

Free. With all my Heart.

Trade. Faith, I never expected to have found fo generous a Thing in a *Dutchman.*

Free.

A Bold Stroke for a WIFE.

Free. Oh, he has nothing of the *Hollander* in his Temper——except an Antipathy to Monarchy——As foon as I told him your Circumftances, he reply'd, he would not be the Ruin of any Man for the World—and immediately made this Propofal himfelf—Let him take what Time he will for the Payment, faid he; or if he'll give me his Ward, I'll forgive him the Debt.

Trade. Well, Mr. *Freeman*, I can but thank you.—'Egad, you have made a Man of me again; and if ever I lay a Wager more, may I rot in a Gaol.

Free. I affure you, Mr. *Tradelove*, I was very much concern'd, becaufe I was the Occafion,——tho' very innocently, I proteft.

Trade. I dare fwear you was, Mr. *Freeman*.

Enter a Fidler.

Fid. Pleafe to have a Leffon of Mufick, or a Song, Gentlemen?

Free. A Song; fay, with all our Hearts; have you ever a merry one?

Fid. Yes, Sir, my Wife and I can give you a merry Dialogue. [*Here is the Song.*

Trade. 'Tis very pretty, Faith.

Free. There's fomething for you to drink, Friend; go, lofe no Time.

Fid. I thank you, Sir. [*Exit.*

Enter Drawer, *and* Colonel *dreft for the* Dutch *Merchant.*

Col. Ha, Mynheer *Tradelove*, Ik been forry voor your Troubles—maer Ik fal you eafie macken, Ik will de gelt nie hebben——

Trade. I fhall for ever acknowledge the Obligation, Sir.

Free. But you underftand upon what Condition, Mr. *Tradelove*; Mrs. *Lovely.*

Col. Ya, de Frow al fal te regt fetten, Mynheer.

Trade. With all my Heart, Mynheer; you fhall have my Confent to marry her freely.——

Free. Well then, as I am a Party concern'd between you, *Mynheer Jan Van Timtamtirelireletta Heer Van Fainwell* fhall give you a Difcharge of your Wager under his own Hand,——and you fhall give him your Confent to marry

marry Mrs. *Lovely* under yours—that is the Way to avoid all Manner of Difputes hereafter.

Col. Ya, Weeragtig.

Trade. Ay, ay, fo it is, Mr. *Freeman,* I'll give it under mine this Minute. [*Sits down to write.*

Col. And fo Ik fal. [*Sits down to write.*

Free. So ho, the Houfe. (*Enter Drawer.*) Bid your Mafter come up——I'll fee there be Witneffes enough to the Bargain. [*Afide.*

Enter Sackbut.

Sack. Do you call, Gentlemen?

Free. Ay, Mr. *Sackbut,* we fhall want your Hand here—

Trade. There Mynheer, there's my Confent as amply as you can defire; but you muft infert your own Name, for I know not how to fpell it; I have left a Blank for it.
[*Gives the* Colonel *a Paper.*

Col. Ya Ik fal dat well doen.——

Free. Now, Mr. *Sackbut,* you and I will witnefs it.
[*They write.*

Col. Daer, Mynheer *Tradelove,* is your Difcharge.
[*Gives him a Paper.*

Trade. Be pleafed to witnefs this Receipt too, Gentlemen. [*Freeman and* Sackbut *put their Hands.*

Free. Ay, ay, that we will.

Col. Well Mynheer, ye moft meer doen, ye moft Myn voorrfprach to de Frow Syn.

Free. He means you muft recommend him to the Lady—

Trade. That I will, and to the reft of my Brother Guardians.

Col. Wat voor, de Duyvel heb you meer Guardians?

Trade. Only *Three,* Mynheer.

Col. Wat donder heb ye Myn betrocken Mynheer?— Had Ik dat gewoeten, Ik foude eaven met you geweeft Syn.

Sack. But Mr. *Tradelove* is the Principal, and he can do a great deal with the reft, Sir.

Free. And he fhall ufe his Intereft I promife you, Mynheer.

Tade. I will fay all that ever I can think on to recommend you, Mynheer; and if you pleafe, I'll introduce you to the Lady.

Col. Well, dat is waer.—Maer ye muft firft fpreken of Myn to de Frow, and to de oudere Gentlemen.

Free.

A Bold Stroke for a WIFE.

Free. Ay, that's the beſt Way,—and then I and the *Heer van Fainwell* will meet you there.

Trade. I will go this Moment, upon Honour.——Your moſt obedient humble Servant.——My ſpeaking will do you little Good, Mynheer, ha, ha; we have bit you, faith, ha, ha.
   Well,—my Debt's diſcharged, and for the Man,
   He 'as my Conſent—to get her, if he can.   [*Exit.*

Col. Ha, ha, ha? this was a Maſter-Piece of Contrivance, *Freeman.*

Free. He hugs himſelf with his ſuppoſed good Fortune, and little thinks the Luck's on our Side;——but come, purſue the fickle Goddeſs while ſhe's in the Mood.—Now for the Quaker.

Col. That's the hardeſt Taſk,
   Of all the Counterfeits perform'd by Man,
   A Soldier makes the ſimpleſt Puritan.   [*Exit.*

ACT V. SCENE I.

SCENE Prim's *Houſe.*

Enter Mrs. Prim *and Mrs.* Lovely *in Quaker's Dreſſes, meeting.*

Mrs. *Pr.* SO, now I like thee, *Anne*; art thou not better without thy monſtrous Hoop-Coat and Patches?—If Heaven ſhould make thee ſo many black Spots upon thy Face, wou'd it not fright thee, *Anne?*

Mrs. *Lov.* If it ſhould turn your Inſide outward, and ſhew all the Spots of your Hypocriſy, 'twould fright me worſe!

Mrs. *Pr.* My Hypocriſy! I ſcorn thy Words, *Anne,* I lay no Baits.

Mrs. *Lov.* If you did you'd catch no Fiſh.

Mrs. *Pr.* Well, well, make thy Jeſts——but I'd have thee to know, *Anne,* that I cou'd have catch'd as many Fiſh (as thou call'ſt them) in my Time, as ever thou did'ſt with all thy Fool-Traps about thee—If Admirers be thy Aim, thou wilt have more of them in this Dreſs than the other.—The Men, take my Word for't, are more deſirous to ſee what we are moſt careful to conceal.

Mrs. Lov. Is that the Reaſon of your Formality, Mrs. *Prim?* Truth will out : I ever thought, indeed, there was more Deſign than Godlineſs in the pinch'd Cap.

Mrs. Pr. Go, thou art corrupted with reading lewd Plays, and filthy Romances,—good for nothing but to lead Youth into the high Road of Fornication.—Ah ! I wiſh thou art not already too familiar with the wicked Ones.

Mrs. Lov. Too familiar with the wicked Ones ! Pray no more of thoſe Freedoms, Madam,—I am familiar with none ſo wicked as yourſelf ;—How dare you thus talk to me ! you, you, you, unworthy Woman you.

[*Burſts into Tears.*

Enter Tradelove.

Trade. What in Tears, *Nancy ?* What have you done to her, Mrs. *Prim,* to make her weep ? .

Mrs. Lov. Done to me ! I admire I keep my Senſes among you ;—but I will rid myſelf of your Tyranny, if there be either Law or Juſtice to be had ;—I'll force you to give me up my Liberty.

Mrs. Pr. Thou haſt more need to weep for thy Sins, *Anne*——Yea, for thy manifold Sins.

Mrs. Lov. Don't think that I'll be ſtill the Fool which you have made me—No, I'll wear what I pleaſe— go when and where I pleaſe—and keep what Company I think fit, and not what you ſhall direct—I will.

Trade. For my Part, I do think all this very reaſonable, Mrs. *Lovely.*—'Tis fit you ſhould have your Liberty, and for that very Purpoſe I am come.

Enter Mr. Periwinkle, *and* Obadiah Prim, *with a Letter in his Hand.*

Per. I have bought ſome black Stockings of your Huſ- band, Mrs. *Prim,* but he tells me the Glover's Trade be- longs to you ; therefore I pray you look me out five or ſix Dozen of mourning Gloves, ſuch as are given at Funerals, and ſend them to my Houſe.

Ob. Pr. My Friend *Periwinkle* has got a good Wind- fall to Day—ſeven hundred a Year.

Mrs. Pr. I wiſh thee Joy of it, Neighbour.

Trade. What, is Sir *Toby* dead, then ?

Per. He is ! You'll take care, Mrs. *Prim.*

Mrs.

A Bold Stroke for a WIFE. 251

Mrs. Pr. Yea, I will, Neighbour.

Ob. Pr. This Letter recommendeth a Speaker; 'tis from *Aminadab Holdfaſt* of *Briſtol*; peradventure he will be here this Night; therefore, *Sarab*, do thou take Care for his Reception.――― [*Gives her the Letter.*

Mrs. Pr. I will obey thee. [*Exit.*

Ob. Pr. What art thou in the Dumps for, *Anne?*

Trade. We muſt marry her, Mr. *Prim.*

Ob. Pr. Why truly, if we could find a Huſband worth having, I ſhould be as glad to ſee her married as thou would'ſt, Neighbour.

Per. Well ſaid; there are but few worth having.

Trade. I can recommend you a Man now, that I think you can none of you have an Objection to!

Enter Sir Philip Modelove.

Per. You recommend? Nay, whenever ſhe marries, I'll recommend the Huſband.―――

Sir *Phil.* What muſt it be, a Whale or a Rhinoceros, Mr. *Periwinkle*, ha, ha, ha? Mr. *Tradelove*, I have a Bill upon you (*gives him a Paper*) and have been ſeeking for you all over the Town.

Trade. I'll accept it, Sir *Philip*, and pay it when due―

Per. He ſhall be none of the Fops at your End of the Town, with full Perukes and empty Skulls,—nore yet none of your trading Gentry, who puzzle the Heralds to find Arms for their Coaches.―――No, he ſhall be a Man famous for Travels, Solidity, and Curioſity—one who has ſearch'd into the Profoundity of Nature! When Heaven ſhall direct ſuch a One, he ſhall have my Conſent, becauſe it may turn to the benefit of Mankind.

Mrs. Lov. The Benefit of Mankind! What, would you anatomize me?

Sir *Phil.* Ay. ay, Madam, he would diſſect you.

Trade. Or, pore over you through a Microſcope, to ſee how your Blood circulates from the Crown of your Head to the Sole of your Foot—ha, ha! But I have a Huſband for you, a Man that knows how to improve your Fortune; one that trades to the four Corners of the Globe.

Mrs. Lov. And would ſend me for a Venture perhaps.

Trade. One that will dreſs you in all the Pride of *Europe, Aſia, Africa*, and *America*――a *Dutch* Merchant, my Girl. L 6 Sir

Sir Phil. A *Dutchman!* ha, ha, there's a Hufband for a fine Lady.——Ya Frow, will you meet myn Slagen—ha, ha ; he'll learn you to talk the Language of the Hogs, Madam, ha, ha !

Trade. He'll learn you that one Merchant is of more Service to a Nation than fifty Coxcombs.—The *Dutch* know the trading Intereft to be of more Benefit to the State, than the landed.

Sir Phil. But what is either Intereft to a Lady?

Trade. 'Tis the Merchant makes the *Belle*—How would the Ladies fparkle in the Box without the Merchant ! The *Indian* Diamond ! The *French* Brocade ! The *Italian* Fan ! The *Flanders* Lace ! The fine *Dutch* Holland ! How would they vent their Scandal over their Tea-Tables? And where would their Beaus have *Champagne* to toaft your Miftreffes, were it not for the Merchant?

Ob. Pr. Verily, Neighbour *Tradelove,* thou doft wafte thy Breath about nothing—All that thou haft faid tendeth to debauch Youth, and fill their Heads with the Pride and Luxury of this World—the Merchant is a very great Friend to Satan, and fendeth as many to his Dominions as the Pope.

Per. Right ; I fay Knowledge makes the Man.

Ob. Pr. Yea, but not thy Kind of Knowledge—it is the Knowledge of Truth—Search thou for the Light within, and not for Bawbles, Friend.

Mrs. Lov. Ay, ftudy your Country's Good, Mr. *Periwinkle,* and not her Infects—Rid you of your homebred Monfters, before you fetch any from abroad—I dare fwear you have Maggots enough in your own Brain to ftock all the *Virtuofo's* in *Europe* with Butterflies.

Sir Phil. By my Soul, Mifs *Nancy's* a Wit.

Ob. Pr. That is more than fhe can fay by thee, Friend ——Look ye, it is in vain to talk, when I meet a Man worthy of her, fhe fhall have my Leave to marry him.

Mrs. Lov. Provided he be of the Faithful——Was there ever fuch a Swarm of Caterpillars to blaft the Hopes of a Woman ! (*Afide.*) Know this, that you contend in vain : I'll have no Hufband of your chufing, nor fhall you lord it over me long.——I'll try the Power of an *Englifh* Senate——Orphans have been redrefs'd, and Wills fet afide —And none did ever deferve their Pity more—Oh *Fainwell !*

A Bold Stroke for a WIFE.

well! where are thy Promiſes to free me from theſe Vermin? Alas! the Taſk was more difficult than he imagin'd!
*A harder Taſk than what the Poets tell
Of Yore, the fair Andromeda befel;
She but one Monſter fear'd, I've four to fear,
And ſee no Perſeus, no Deliv'rer near.*   [Exit.

Enter Servant, and whiſpers to Prim.

Serv. One *Simon Pure* enquireth for thee.
Per. The Woman is mad.   [*Exit.*
Sir *Phil.* So you are all in my Opinion.   [*Exit.*
Ob. Pr. Friend *Tradelove*, Buſineſs requireth my Preſence.
Trade. Oh, I ſhan't trouble you—Pox take him for an unmannerly Dog—However, I have kept my Word with my *Dutchman*, and will introduce him too for all you.
            [*Exit.*

Enter Colonel in a Quaker's Habit.

Ob. Pr. Friend *Pure*, thou art welcome; how is it with Friend *Holdfaſt*, and all Friends in *Briſtol?* *Timothy Littleworth*, *John Slenderbrain*, and *Chriſtopher Keepfaith?*
Col. A goodly Company! (*Aſide.*) They are all in Health, I thank thee for them.
Ob. Pr. Friend *Holdfaſt* writes me Word, that thou cameſt lately from *Penſilvania*, how do all Friends there?—
Col. What the Devil ſhall I ſay? I know juſt as much of *Penſilvania* as I do of *Briſtol*.   [*Aſide.*
Ob. Pr. Do they thrive?
Col. Yea, Friend, the Bleſſing of their good Works fall upon them.

Enter Mrs. Prim *and Mrs.* Lovely.

Ob. Pr. Sarah, know our Friend *Pure?*
Mrs. Pr. Thou art welcome.   [*He ſalutes her.*
Col. Here comes the Sum of all my Wiſhes——How charming ſhe appears, even in that Diſguiſe!   [*Aſide.*
Ob. Pr. Why doſt thou conſider the Maiden ſo intentively, Friend?
Col. I will tell thee: About four Days ago I ſaw a Viſion. This very Maiden, but in vain Attire, ſtanding on a Precipice, and heard a Voice, which called me by my Name—and bid me put forth my Hand and ſave her from the Pit—I did ſo, and methought the Damſel grew to my Side.   Mrs.

Mrs. Pr. What can that portend?

Ob. Pr. The Damfel's Converfion—I am perfuaded.

Mrs. Lov. That's falfe, I'm fure—— [*Afide.*

Ob. Pr. Wilt thou ufe the Means, Friend *Pure?*

Col. Means! what Means? Is fhe not thy Daughter, already one of the Faithful?

Mrs. Pr. No, alas! fhe's one of the Ungodly.

Ob. Pr. Pray thee mind what this good Man will fay unto thee; he will teach thee the way that thou fhouldeft walk, *Anne.*

Mrs. Lov. I know my Way without his Inftruƈtions: I hop'd to have been quiet, when once I had put on your odious Formality here.

Col. Then thou weareft it out of Compulfion, not Choice, Friend?

Mrs. Lov. Thou art in the Right of it, Friend.——

Mrs. Pr. Art thou not afhamed to mimick the good Man? Ah! thou art a ftubborn Girl.

Col. Mind her not; fhe hurteth not me—If thou wilt leave her alone with me, I will difcufs a few Points with her, that may perchance foften her Stubbornefs, and melt her into Compliance.

Ob. Pr. Content: I pray thee *put it home to her*—Come, *Sarah*, let us leave the good Man with her.

Mrs. Lov. (*Catching hold of* Prim, *he breaks loofe, and* Exit.) What do you mean—to leave me with this old Enthufiaftical Canter? Don't think, becaufe I comply'd with your Formality, to impofe your ridiculous Doƈtrine upon me.

Col. I pray thee, young Woman, moderate thy Paffion.

Mrs. Lov. I pray thee walk after thy Leader, you will but lofe your Labour upon me——Thefe Wretches will certainly make me mad.

Col. I am of another Opinion; the Spirit telleth me I fhall convert thee, *Anne.*

Mrs. Lov. 'Tis a lying Spirit, don't believe it.

Col. Say'ft thou fo? Why then thou fhalt convert me, my Angel. [*Catching her in his Arms.*

Mrs. Lov. (*Shrieks.*) Ah! Monfter hold off, or I'll tear thy Eyes out.

Col. Hufh! for Heaven's sake——doft thou not know me? I am *Fainwell.*

Mrs.

A Bold Stroke for a WIFE.

Mrs. *Lov.* *Fainwell!* [*Enter old* Prim.] Oh, I'm undone! *Prim* here——I wifh with all my Soul I had been dumb.

Ob. Pr. What is the Matter? Why didft thou fhriek out, *Anne*?

Mrs. *Lov.* Shriek out! I'll fhriek and fhriek again, cry Murder, Thieves, or any Thing, to drown the Noife of that eternal Babbler, if you leave me with him any longer.

Ob. Pr. Was that all? Fie, fie, *Anne.*

Col. No Matter, I'll bring down her Stomach, I'll warrant thee.——Leave us, I pray thee.

Ob. Pr. Fare thee well. [*Exit.*

Col. My charming lovely Woman! [*Embraces her.*

Mrs. *Lov.* What mean't thou by this Difguife, *Fainwell*?

Col. To fet thee free, if thou wilt perform thy Promife.

Mrs. *Lov.* Make me Miftrefs of my Fortune, and make thy own Conditions.

Col. This Night fhall anfwer all my Wifhes—See here, I have the Confent of *three* of thy Guardians already, and doubt not but *Prim* will make the *fourth.* [Prim *liftening.*

Ob. Pr. I would gladly hear what Arguments the good Man ufeth to bend her. [*Afide.*

Mrs. *Lov.* Thy Words give me new Life, methinks.

Ob. Pr. What do I hear?

Mrs. *Lov.* Thou beft of Men, Heaven meant to blefs me fure, when firft I faw thee.

Ob. Pr. He hath mollified her.——Oh wonderful Converfion!

Col. Ha! *Prim* liftening.—No more, my Love, we are obferv'd; feem to be edified, and give 'em Hopes that thou wilt turn Quaker, and leave the reft to me. (*Aloud.*) I am glad to find that thou art touch't with what I faid unto thee, *Anne*; another Time I will explain the other Article unto thee; in the mean-while, be thou dutiful to our Friend *Prim.*

Mrs. *Lov.* I fhall obey thee in every Thing.

Enter Obadiah Prim.

Ob. Pr. O what a prodigious Change is here! Thou haft wrought a Miracle, Friend! *Anne,* how doft thou like the Doctrine he hath preached? Mrs.

Mrs. *Lov.* So well, that I could talk to him for ever, methinks—I am aſhamed of my former Folly, and aſk your Pardon, Mr. *Prim.*
Col. Enough, enough, that thou art ſorry ; he is no Pope, *Anne.*
Ob. Pr. Verily, thou doſt rejoice me exceedingly, Friend ; will it pleaſe thee to walk into the next Room, and refreſh thyſelf——Come, take the Maiden by the Hand.
Col. We will follow thee.

Enter Servant.

Serv. There is another *Simon Pure* enquireth for thee, Maſter.
Col. The Devil there is. [*Aſide.*
Ob. Pr. Another *Simon Pure !* I do not know him, is he any Relation of thine?
Col. No Friend, I know him not—Pox take him, I wiſh he were in *Penſilvania* again, with all my Blood. [*Aſide.*
Mrs. *Lov.* What ſhall I do? [*Aſide.*
Ob. Pr. Bring him up.
Col. Humph ! then one of us muſt go down, that's certain.—Now Impudence aſſiſt me.

Enter Simon Pure.

Ob. Pr. What is thy Will with me, Friend?
S. Pu. Didſt thou not receive a Letter from *Aminadab Holdfaſt* of *Briſtol,* concerning one *Simon Pure?*
Ob. Pr. Yea, and *Simon Pure* is already here, Friend.
Col. And *Simon Pure* will ſtay here, Friend, if poſſible.
[*Aſide.*
S. Pu. That's an Untruth, for I am he.
Col. Take thou heed, Friend, what thou doſt ſay ; I do affirm that I am *Simon Pure.*
S. Pu. Thy Name may be *Pure,* Friend, but not that *Pure.*
Col. Yea, that *Pure,* which my good Friend *Aminadab Holdfaſt* wrote to my Friend *Prim* about, the ſame *Simon Pure* that came from *Penſilvania,* and ſojourned in *Briſtol* eleven Days ; thou would'ſt not take my Name from me, would'ſt thou?—'till I have done with it. [*Aſide.*
S. Pu. Thy Name ! I am aſtoniſh'd !
Col. At what ? at thy own Aſſurance?
[*Going up to him,* S. Pure *ſtarts back.*
S. Pu. Avant, *Satan,* approach me not ; I defy thee and all thy Works.

Mrs.

Mr. Lov. Oh, he'll out-cant him—Undone, undone for ever. [*Aside.*

Col. Hark thee, Friend, thy Sham will not take—Don't exert thy Voice, thou art too well acquainted with *Satan* to ſtart at him, thou wicked Reprobate—What can thy Deſign be here?

Enter a Servant and gives Prim *a Letter.*

Ob. Pr. One of theſe muſt be a Counterfeit, but which I cannot ſay.

Col. What can that letter be? [*Aside.*

S. Pu. Thou muſt be the Devil, Friend, that's certain, for no human Power can ſtock ſo great a Falſhood.

Ob. Pr. This Letter ſayeth that thou art better acquainted with that Prince of Darkneſs, than any here—Read that I pray thee, *Simon.* [*Gives it the* Col.

Col. 'Tis *Freeman*'s Hand. (*Reads*) *There is a Deſign formed to rob your Houſe this Night, and cut your Throat; and for that Purpoſe there is a Man diſguiſed like a Quaker, who is to paſs for one* Simon Pure; *the Gang, whereof I am one, though now reſolved to rob no more, has been at* Briſtol, *one of them came in the Coach with the Quaker, whoſe Name he hath taken; and from what he hath gathered from him, formed that Deſign, and did not doubt but he ſhould impoſe ſo far upon you, as to make you turn out the real* Simon Pure; *and keep him with you. Make the right Uſe of this, Adieu*——Excellent well! [*Aside.*

Ob. Pr. Doſt thou hear this? [*To* S. Pure.

S. Pu. Yea, but it moveth me not; that, doubtleſs, is the Impoſtor. [*Pointing to the* Col.

Col. Ah! thou wicked One—now I conſider thy Face, I remember thou didſt come up in the Leathern Conveniency with me—thou hadſt a black Bob-wig on, and a brown Camblet Coat with Braſs Buttons—Can'ſt thou deny it, ha?

S. Pu. Yea, I can, and with a ſafe Conſcience too, Friend.

Ob. Pr. Verily, Friend, thou art the moſt impudent Villain I ever ſaw.

Mrs. *Lov.* Nay, then I'll have a Fling at him. [*Aside.* I remember the Face of this Fellow at *Bath*—Ay this is he that pick'd my Lady *Raffle*'s Pocket in the Grove—Don't you remember that the Mob pump'd you Friend?—This is the moſt notorious Rogue.

S. Pu. What doſt provoke thee to ſeek my Life? Thou wilt not hang me, wilt thou, wrongfully? *Ob.*

Ob. Pr. She will do thee no Hurt, nor thou ſhalt do me none; therefore get thee about thy Buſineſs, Friend, and leave thy wicked Courſe of Life, or thou may'ſt not come off ſo favourably every where.

Col. Go, Friend, I would adviſe thee, and tempt thy Fate no more.

S. Pu. Yea, I will go, but it ſhall be to thy Confuſion; for I ſhall clear myſelf: I will return with ſome Proofs that ſhall convince thee, *Obadiah*, that thou art highly impoſed upon. *Exit.*

Col. Then there will be no ſtaying for me, that's certain ——What the Devil ſhall I do? [*Aſide.*

Ob. Pr. What monſtrous Works of Iniquity are there in this world, *Simon!*

Col. Yea, the Age is full of Vice——Z'death, I am ſo confounded, I know not what to ſay. [*Aſide.*

Ob. Pr. Thou art diſorder'd, Friend—art thou not well?

Col. My Spirit is greatly troubled, and ſomething telleth me, that 'tho I have wrought a good Work in converting this Maiden, this tender Maiden, yet my Labour will be in vain; for the evil Spirit fighteth againſt her; and I ſee, yea, I ſee with the Eye of my inward Man, that *Satan* will re-buffet her again, whenever I withdraw myſelf from her; and ſhe will, yea, this very Damſel will, return again to that Abomination from whence I have retriev'd her, as if it were, yea, as if it were out of the Jaws of the Fiend.——

Ob. Pr. Good lack, thinkeſt thou ſo?

Mrs. *Lov.* I muſt ſecond him. (*Aſide.*) What meaneth this ſtruggling within me? I feel the Spirit reſiſteth the Vanities of this World, but the Fleſh is rebellious, yea the Fleſh——I greatly fear the Fleſh and the Weakneſs there-of——hum———

Ob. Pr. The Maid is inſpired. [*Aſide.*

Col. Behold, her Light begins to ſhine forth——Excellent Woman!

Mrs. *Lov.* This good Man hath ſpoken Comfort unto me, yea Comfort, I ſay; becauſe the Words which he hath breathed into my outward Ears, are gone thro' and fix'd in mine Heart, yea verily in mine Heart, I ſay;——and I feel the Spirit doth love him exceedingly, hum.———

Col. She acts it to the Life. [*Aſide.*

Ob. Pr. Prodigious! The Damſel is filled with the Spirit, *Sarah.* *Enter*

Enter Mrs. Prim.

Mrs. Pr. I am greatly rejoiced to fee fuch a Change in our beloved *Anne*.

Col. I am not difpofed for thy Food, my Spirit longeth for more delicious Meat ;—fain would I redeem this Maiden from the Tribe of Sinners, and break thofe Cords afunder wherewith fhe is bound,—hum.——

Mrs. Lov. Something whifpers in my Ears, methinks—that I muft be fubject to the Will of this good Man, and from him only muft hope for Confolation,——hum.—— It alfo telleth me, that I am a chofen Veffel to raife up Seed to the Faithful, and that thou muft confent that we *two* be *one* Flefh according to the Word,——hum.——

Ob. Pr. What a Revelation is here ! This is certainly Part of thy Vifion, Friend, this is the Maiden's *growing to thy Side* ; Ah ! with what Willingnefs fhould I give thee my Confent, could I give thee her Fortune too,—but thou wilt never get the Confent of the wicked Ones.

Col. I wifh I was fure of yours. [*Afide.*

Ob. Pr. My Soul rejoiceth ; yea, rejoiceth, I fay, to find the Spirit within thee ; for lo, it moveth thee with *natural* Agitation,—yea, with *natural* Agitation, towards this good Man—yea, it *ftirreth*, as one may fay,—yea, verily I fay it *ftirreth* up thy Inclination,——yea, as one would *ftir* a Pudding.

Mrs. Lov. I fee, I fee ! the Spirit guiding of thy Hand, good *Obadiah Prim*, and now benold thou art figning thy Confent ;—and now I fee myfelf within thy Arms, my Friend and Brother, yea, I am become *Bone* of thy *Bone* and *Flefh* of thy *Flefh*. (*Embracing him.*)——hum.——

Col. Admirably perform'd. (*Afide*)——And I will take thee in all Spiritual Love for an Helpmate, yea, for the Wife of my Bofom,——and now methinks——I feel a *Longing*,——yea, a *Longing*, I fay, for the Confummation of thy Love,——yea, I do *long* exceedingly.

Mrs. Lov. And, verily, verily, my Spirit feeleth the fame *Longing*.

Mrs. Prim. The Spirit hath greatly moved them both, ——Friend *Prim*, thou muft confent, there's no refifting of the Spirit !

Ob. Pr. Yea, the Light within fheweth me, that I fhall fight a good Fight,——and wreftle thro' thofe reprobate Friends;

Friends, thy other Guardians;——yea, I perceive the Spirit will hedge thee into the Flock of the Righteous.— Thou art a chofen Lamb,——yea, a chofen Lamb, and I will not pufh thee back.—No, I will not I fay;——no, thou fhalt leap-a, and frifk-a, and fkip-a and *bound*, and *bound* I fay,——yea, *bound* within the *Fold* of the Righteous, yea, even within thy *Fold*, my Brother.—Fetch me the Pen and Ink, *Sarah*——and my Hand fhall confefs its Obedience to the Spirit.

Col. I wifh it were over.

Enter Mrs. Prim *with Pen and Ink.*

Mrs. Lov. I tremble left this quaking Rogue fhould return and fpoil all. [*Afide*

Ob. Pr. Here, Friend, do thou write what the Spirit prompteth, and I will fign it. [*Col. fits down.*

Mrs. Pr. Verily, *Anne*, it greatly rejoiceth me, to fee thee reformed from that original Wickednefs wherein I found thee.

Mrs. Lov. I do believe thou art, and I thank thee.

Col. (Reads) *This is to certify all whom it may concern, that I do freely give all my Right and Title in* Anne Lovely, *to* Simon Pure, *and my full Confent that fhe fhall become his Wife, according to the Form of Marriage. Witnefs my Hand.*

Ob. Pr. That's enough, give me the Pen. [*Signs it.*

Enter Betty *running to Mrs.* Lovely.

Betty. Oh! Madam, Madam, here's the quaking Man again, he has brought a Coachman and two or three more.

Mrs. Lov. Ruin'd paft Redemption! [*Afide to* Col.

Col. No, no, one Minute fooner had fpoil'd all, but now—here's Company coming, Friend, give me the Paper. [*Going up to* Prim *haftily.*

Ob. Pr. Here it is, *Simon*; and I wifh thee happy with the Maiden.

Mrs. Lov. 'Tis done, and *now* Devil *do thy worft.*

'*Enter* Simon Pure, *and Coachman,* &c.

S. Pu. Look, thee, Friend, I have brought thefe People to fatisfy thee that I am not that Impoftor which thou did'ft take me for, this is the Man that did drive the Leathern Conveniency, and brought me from *Briftol*,——and this is—— *Col.*

Col. Look ye, Friend, to fave the Court the Trouble of examining Witneffes—I plead guilty,——ha, ha !
Ob. Pr. How's this ! Is not thy Name *Pure*, then?
Col. No really, Sir, I only made bold with this Gentleman's Name——but I here give it up fafe and found ; it has done the Bufinefs which I had Occafion for, and now I intend to wear my own, which fhall be at his Service upon the fame Occafion at any Time.—Ha, ha, ha !
S. Pu. Oh ! the Wickednefs of the Age !
Coachman. Then you have no further Need of us. [*Exit.*
Col. No, honeft Man, you may go about your Bufinefs.
Ob. Pr. I am ftruck dumb with thy Impudence, *Anne*, thou haft deceiv'd me,——and perchance undone thyfelf.
Mrs. Pr. Thou art a diffembling Baggage, and Shame will overtake thee. [*Exit.*
S. Pu. I am grieved to fee thy Wife fo much troubled : I will follow and confole her. [*Exit.*

Enter Servant.

Serv. Thy Brother Guardians enquire for thee ; here is another Man with them.
Mrs. Lov. Who can that other Man be ? [*To the* Col.
Col. 'Tis one *Freeman*, a Friend of mine, whom I ordered to bring the reft of the Guardians here.

Enter Sir Philip, Tradelove, Periwinkle, *and* Freeman.

Free. (*To the Col.*) Is all fafe? did the Letter do you Service ?
Col. All, all's fafe ! ample Service. [*Afide.*
Sir *Phil.* Mifs *Nancy*, how do'ft do, Child ?
Mrs. Lov. Don't call me Mifs, Friend *Philip*, my Name is *Anne*, thou knoweft.——
Sir *Phil.* What, is the Girl metamorphos'd ?
Mrs. Lov. I wifh thou wert fo metamorphos'd ? Ah ! *Philip*, throw off that gaudy Attire, and wear the Cloaths becoming thy Age.
Ob. Pr. I am afhamed to fee thefe Men. [*Afide.*
Sir *Phil.* My Age ! the Woman is poffefs'd.
Col. No, thou art poffefs'd rather, Friend.
Trade. Hark ye, Mrs. *Lovely*, one Word with you.
[*Takes hold of her Hand.*
Col. This Maiden is my Wife, Thanks to Friend *Prim*, and thou haft no Bufinefs with her. [*Takes her from him.*
Trade.

262 *A Bold Stroke for a* WIFE.

Trade. His Wife! hark ye, Mr. *Freeman.*

Per. Why, you have made a very fine Piece of Work of it, Mr. *Prim.*

Sir *Phil.* Married to a Quaker! thou art a fine Fellow to be left Guardian to an Orphan, truly—there's a Huſband for a young Lady!

Col. When I have put on my Beau Cloaths, Sir *Philip,* you'll like me better.———

Sir *Phil.* Thou wilt make a very ſcurvy Beau—Friend—

Col. I believe I can prove it under your Hand that you thought me a very fine Gentleman in the Park t'other Day, about thirty-ſix Minutes after Eleven; will you take a Pinch, Sir *Philip*——One of the fineſt Snuff-boxes you ever ſaw. [*Offers him Snuff.*

Sir *Phil.* Ha, ha, ha! I am overjoy'd, Faith I am, if thou be'ſt the Gentleman.——I own I did give my Conſent to the Gentleman I brought here To-day; but whether this is he, I can't be poſitive.

Ob. Pr. Can'ſt thou not?——Now I think thou art a fine Fellow to be left Guardian to an Orphan.—Thou ſhallow-brain'd Shuttlecock, he may be a Pick-pocket for ought thou do'ſt know.

Per. You would have been two rare Fellows to have been truſted with the ſole Management of her Fortune, would ye not, think ye? But Mr. *Tradelove* and myſelf ſhall take care of her Portion.———

Trade. Ay, ay, ſo we will—Didn't you tell me the *Dutch* Merchant defired me to meet him here, Mr. *Freeman?*

Free. I did ſo, and I am ſure he will be here, if you'll have a little Patience.

Col. What, is Mr. *Tradelove* impatient? Nay then, ik been gereet voor you, heb be, *Jan van Timtamtirelireletta Heer van Fainwell,* vergeeten?

Trade. Oh! pox of the Name! what have you trick'd me too, Mr. *Freeman?*

Col. Trick'd, Mr. *Tradelove!* did not I give you two Thouſand Pounds for your Conſent fairly? And now do you tell a Gentleman he has tricked you?

Per. So, ſo, you are a pretty Guardian, Faith, to ſell your Charge; what, did you look upon her as a Part of your Stock?

Ob. Pr. Ha, ha, ha! I am glad thy Knavery is found out,

out, however——I confefs this Maiden over-reached me, and no finifter End at all.

Per. Ay, ay, one Thing or other over-reach'd you all, —but I'll take care he fhall never finger a Penny of her Money, I warrant you,——over-reach'd quoth'a ! Why I might have been over-reach'd too, if I had had no more Wit : I don't know but this very Fellow may be him that was directed to me from *Grand Cairo* t'other Day. Ha, ha, ha !

Col. The very fame.

Per. Are you fo, Sir? but your Trick would not pafs upon me.———

Col. No, as you fay, at that Time it did not, that was not my lucky Hour ;——but hark ye, Sir, I muft let you into one Secret——you may keep honeft *John Tradefcant's* Coat on, for your Uncle Sir *Toby Periwinkle* is not dead, —fo the Charge of Mourning will be faved, ha, ha, ha !— Don't you remember Mr. *Pillage*, your Uncle's Steward, Ha, ha, ha !

Per. Not dead, I begin to think I am trick'd too.

Col. Don't you remember the figning of a Leafe, Mr. *Periwinkle?*

Per. Well, and what fignifies that Leafe, if my Uncle is not dead ?——Ha ! I am fure it was a Leafe I figned.—

Pol. Ay, but it was a Leafe for Life, Sir, and of this beautiful Tenement, I thank you.   [*Taking hold of Mrs.* Lovely.

Omnes. Ha, ha, ha ! Neighbours Fare.

Free. So then, I find you are all trick'd, ha, ha !

Per. I am certain I read as plain a Leafe, as ever I read in my Life.

Col. You read a Leafe, I grant you, but you fign'd this Contract.   [*Shewing a Paper.*

Per. How durft you put this Trick upon me, Mr. *Freeman?* Didn't you tell me my Uncle was dying?

Free. And would tell you twice as much to ferve my Friend, ha, ha !

Sir *Phil.* What the learned and famous Mr. *Periwinkle* chous'd too !——Ha, ha, ha !—I fhall die with Laughing, ha, ha, ha !

Ob. Pr. It had been well if her Father had left her to wifer Heads than *thine* and *mine*, Friends, ha, ha, ha !

Trade.

Trade. Well, since you have outwitted us all, pray you what and who are you, Sir?

Sir *Phil.* Sir, the Gentleman is a fine Gentleman——I am glad you have got a Person, Madam, who understands Dress and good Breeding.——I was resolved she should have a Husband of my chusing.

Ob. Pr. I am sorry the Maiden is fallen into such Hands.

Trade. A Beau! nay, then she is finely help'd up.

Mrs. *Lov.* Why, Beaus are great Encouragers of Trade, Sir, ha, ha, ha!

Col. Look ye, Gentlemen——I am the Person who can give the best Account of myself, and I must beg Sir *Philip*'s Pardon, when I tell him, that I have as much Aversion to what he calls Dress and Breeding, as I have to the Enemies of my Religion. I have had the Honour to serve his Majesty, and headed a Regiment of the bravest Fellows that ever pushed Bayonet in the Throat of a *Frenchman*; and notwithstanding the Fortune this Lady brings me, whenever my Country wants my Aid, my Sword and Arm are at her Service.

Therefore, my Dear, if thou'lt but deign to smile,
I meet a Recompence for all my Toil:
Love and Religion ne'er admit Restraint,
And Force makes many *Sinners, not* one *Saint;*
Still free as Air the Active Mind does rove,
And searches proper Objects for its Love;
But that once fix'd, 'tis past the Pow'r of Art
To chase the dear Idea from the Heart:
'Tis Liberty of Choice that sweetens Life,
Makes the glad Husband *and the happy Wife.*

A BICKERSTAFF's BURYING;

OR,

Work for the UPHOLDERS.

A
F A R C E.

To the Magnificent Company of
UPHOLDERS, &c.

*C*Ustom *has made some Things absolutely necessary, and three Sheets without a Dedication, or a Preface, by Way of Excuse, would be an unpardonable Indecency: To avoid which, I was considering at whose Feet to lay these following Scenes. First I thought of offering it to all those young Wives who had sold themselves for Money, and been inter'd with Misery, from the first Day of their Marriage; but supposing their chief Pleasure to consist in Pride, and that they had rather gratify their Ambition in the Arms of a Fool, of Fourscore, then wed a Man of Sense of narrower Fortunes, I concluded 'em unworthy of my Notice.*

Then the Race of Old Men presented themselves in my Mind, who, despising Women of their own Years, marry Girls of fifteen, by which they keep open House for all the young Fellows in Town, in order to encrease their Families, vnd make their Tables flourish like the Vine: But my Aversion to Fools of all Kinds, made me decline them too.

At last, casting my Eyes upon the Title of the Farce, I found it could justly belong to none but the Magnificent Company of Upholders, *whom the judicious Censor of* Great Britain *has so often condescended to mention; to you then, worthy Sirs, whose solemn Train keeps up the pompous State of Beauty, beyond the Limits of a Gasp of Breath, and draws the gazing World to admire, even after Death; to you this Piece I dedicate; 'tis but Reason that you should receive some Tribute from us living, who so truly mourn us dead. What does not Mankind owe to you? All Ranks and Conditions are obliged to you; the Aged and the Young, the Generous and the Miser, the well descended and the baser born. The Escutcheons garnish out the Hearse, the Streamers and Wax Lights, let us into the Name of a Man, which, all his Life had been hid in Obscurity; and many a Right Honourable would fall unlamented, were it not for your decent Cloaks, and dismal Faces,*
that

DEDICATION.

that look as sorrowfully as the Creditors they leave unpaid. What an immense Sum might be rais'd from your Art to carry on the War, would you, like true Britons, *exert your Power? The People being fond of Sights, what might not be gather'd at a Funeral, when the Rooms are clad in Sable, the Body dress'd out with all your skilful Care, the Tapers burning in their Silver-Sockets, the weeping Virgins fixt like Statues round, and aromatic Gums perfume the Chambers, I think it preferable to the Puppet-show, and a Penny a Head for all the Curious, would, I dare be positive, amount to more than the Candle-Tax; and so make Death subservient to the Living.*

But this, Gentlemen, I leave to your superior Judgment in Politick Principles; and only beg leave to remind you, that in this crouded Town, there are a prodigious Number of Mr. Bickerstaff's *dead Men, that swarm about Streets; therefore, for the Sakes of the most ingenious Part of Mankind, you ought to take Care to inter them out of the Way, since he that does no Good in his Generation, should not be reckon'd among the Living.*

And now to conclude, Gentlemen, I hope you'll pardon this Liberty I have taken, and accept this as a Token of the Respect I bear your noble Society: I honour you tho' I have no Desire of falling into your Hands, but I think we Poets are in no Danger of that, since our real Estate lies in the Brain, and our Personal consists in two or three loose Scenes, a few Couplets for the Tag of an Act, and a slight Sketch for a Song, and as I take it, you are not over-fond of Paper-Credit, where there is no Probability of recovering the Debt: So wishing you better Customers, I except no Return, but am proud of subscribing myself,

GENTLEMEN,

Your most obedient humble Servant.

Dramatis Perſonæ.

MEN.

Mezro, — — — — Mr. *Norris*.
Captain, — — — — — Mr. *Bickerſtaff*.
Boatſwain, — — — — Mr. *Spiller*.
Firſt Sailor, — — —— Mr. *Pack*.
Second Sailor, —— — — Mr. *Miller*.

WOMEN.

Lady *Mezro*, — — —— Mrs. *Knight*.
Iſabinda, her Niece, — —— Mrs. *Cox*.
A *Lady* — — — — Mrs. *Kent*.

Officer, —— —— —— Mr. *Carnaby*.
Servants, —— —— —— Mr. *Cole*.
Lucy, —— — —— — Mrs. *Spiller*.

A BICKERSTAFF's BURYING;
OR,
Work for the UPHOLDERS.

SCENE I.

A working Sea seen at a Distance, with the Appearance of a Head of a Ship bulging against a Rock: Mermaids rise and sing: Thunder and Lightning: Then the Scene shuts.

Enter Lady Mezro, *and her Niece* Isabinda, *veil'd.*

Isab. HY don't you tell me whither you are going, Aunt, this Morning? I can scarce keep Pace with you. What is it that transports you so? you do not use to be so gay.

Lady *M.* Oh, my Girl, just now, from my Chamber-Window, I beheld a Ship, by Stress of Weather, driven on our Coast; which, since the last unhappy one that brought me here, I have never seen; pray Heav'n it be *English!*

Isab. So say I, then I shall see the fine Men you have so often talk'd of, Aunt.

Lady *M.* Ay, and the Country that breeds those Men, Child, if we can handsomly get off.

Isab. With all my Heart; for I hate this Isle of *Casgar*, and all its barbarous Laws, since you have inform'd me of those of *Great Britain.*

Lady *M.* Hush, here's some of the Ship's Crew; let's step a-side and observe them. [*Exeunt.*

Enter Captain, Boatswain, *and* Sailors.

Capt. Well, how fares the Ship, has she any Damage?
M 3   *Boat.*

270 A BICKERSTAFF's *Burying*; or,

Boat. Only the Leak, which the Carpenter has ſtop'd, Captain.

Capt. That's well: I can't imagine what this Iſland produces!

Boat. Monſters, I think; for they ſtare as if they never had any Commerce with Mankind, or ever ſaw a Ship in their Lives.

Capt. I queſtion if ever they did, and wiſh it had not been our Fortune to have improv'd their Knowledge.

1ſt Sail. I wiſh ſo too; I hate making ſtrange Land: Who the Devil knows where to find a Wench now?

Boat. Here's a Dog, that two Hours ago, drown'd his neceſſary Orders with his Prayers, and now is roaring as loud for a Whore.

1ſt Sail. 'Tis our Cuſtom, you know; out of Danger the Sailor muſt be merry, i'Faith; ha, ha.

2nd Sail. Nell, at the Ship at *Chatham*, ſhall know this.

1ſt Sail. I care not a Rope's-End if ſhe does: Why, what the Devil do you think I'll come into a ſtrange Land, and not examine what Commodity it produces? No, no, Faith; *Nick* muſt know if the Females here be Fiſh or Fleſh, before he puts off again.

Capt. Ha, ha; Well, well, take Care you han't your Brains beat out; Go, diſperſe yourſelves, and ſee what Proviſions you can get. I juſt now met a Native of the Country; who tells me, that the Prince is coming this Way: He underſtands a little of the *Arabian* Tongue, and has promis'd to introduce me to him; that I may endeavour, by ſome Preſents, to gain his Leave to refit our Ship, and ſupply our Wants.

Boat. Where ſhall we find you, Maſter?

Exeunt Boatſwain *and* Sailors.

Capt. Here, or hereabouts. Now for this *Cabbacuca*. Adſheart, what a Name's there! If the Prince be as barbarous as his Name, we had as good periſh'd in the Storm: But I wonder the Fellow comes not, that is to conduct me to Court; that is, I ſuppoſe, to a King ſitting under a Palm-tree: What would I give for a Friend there?

Enter Lady Mezro *and* Iſabinda.

Lady *M.* (*Clapping him on the Shoulder.*) What would you give, Captain?

Capt.

Work for the UPHOLDERS.

Capt. Ha! *Englifh!* Nay, then I am not fo far out of Knowledge as I imagin'd.

Lady M. You are a great Way from the Rofe in *Covent-Garden*, I promife you.

Capt. The Rofe in *Covent-Garden!* Let me fee thy Face, thou dear Angel, or I die. [*Embraces her.*

Lady M. Die! Nay, then you have chang'd your Inclination with the Clime; you never us'd to die for an old Acquaintance.

Capt. Ah! an old Acquaintance, here, Child, is welcomer than old Wine, and the Accident will give it a new Relifh.

Lady M. Say you fo? well, whether you fpeak Truth or not, I proteft this Sight of you pleafes me better than the firft; and now, Sir, I am your humble Servant.

[*Turns up her Veil.*

Capt. Ha! Mrs. *Take-it!* Why, what Wind blew you hither?

Lady M. Juft fuch another as brought you, I fancy; our Ship was bound to *Madrafs.*

Capt. So was mine.

Lady M. After three Days tempeftuous Weather, having loft our Main-maft, and all our Tackle, expecting nothing but Death, when by a fudden Guft our Veffel was driven upon yon dreadful Rock, which fplit her into a thoufand Pieces, and only I by Providence was fav'd.

Capt. Thank Heav'n, I've not loft one Man; I pity your Misfortune, and yet, by your Appearance, 'tis a Fault to pity you, for it has turn'd to your Advantage. Prithee what Bufinefs had you in the *Indies*?

Lady M. To get a Hufband; you know few Women go there but to make their Fortunes.

Capt. Which I fuppofe you have done here, Madam?

Lady M. An Emir, which is a Lord, you muft underftand, walking by the Sea-fide, fpied me on the Rock, and kindly help'd me down, fell in Love, and married me; and I am now one of the greateft Women upon the Place.

Capt. I am glad on't, with all my Soul. Who is this Lady? another of my old Acquaintance too?

Lady M. No, I promife you; there's a Face never faw *Covent-Garden.* She's my Hufband's Niece, the beft humour'd Woman in the World; and for her Beauty, let

that

that fpeak for itfelf, (*turns up her Veil*) fo, I fee by your Eyes you like her.

Ifab. Grant, Great Prophet, that he may! for I like him, I'm fure. [*Afide.*

Capt. Like her! I'Gad, if your Ifland's peopled with fuch Angels, 'tis certainly the Land of Promife, and every Ship will put in here for Provifion.

Lady M. She's the only handfome one in it, I promife you; her Mother was *Englifh*, and caft hither by fuch another Accident as myfelf.

Ifab. And do you think this Face will do in *Covent-Garden*, Captain?

Capt. In *Covent-Garden*, Madam! Where would it not do? Ha! your Skin's as fmooth as the Sea in a Calm, and your Eyes outfhine the Sun after a Storm; your Voice as fweet as Syrens Songs; and 'tis greater Pleafure to behold you, than Land after a dangerous Voyage. I'll fettle here, I'm refolv'd.

Lady M. Ah, the right *London* ftrain. [*Afide.*
Ifab. And I'de rather go with him. [*Afide.*
Capt. Where the Devil is my Ship's Crew? I'll have the Bottom of my Veffel beat out immediately, that I may never put to Sea again.

Ifab. I'm afraid, young Gentleman, you'll change your Note if you knew the Cuftom of this Country.

Lady M. Indeed, my *quondam* Spark, you'd be glad to get off in a Cock-Boat if you do, by that Time you have been married half fo long as I have been——I'm fure I would.

Capt. Ay! why fo? you fhine in Jewels.

Lady M. I once thought Riches the greateft, but now find them the leaft Part of Happinefs.

Capt. Oh, you want to fee dear *England* again, and dazle the Eyes of your old Acquaintance.

Lady M. That's not the Caufe.
Capt. Your Hufband is old, I fuppofe.
Lady M. True.
Capt. What is that to my Repentance? This Lady is young.

Lady M. Then he is as ugly as a Baboon.
Capt. Yet wide; this Lady's as handfome as a Cherubim.
Lady M. He's as jealous as a *Spaniard*, as barbarous as
a *Turk*,

Work for the UPHOLDERS.

a *Turk*, and as ill-natur'd as an old Woman; and I hate him as heartily as one Beauty does another; yet fear him as much as you Merchant-Men do a *French* Privateer.

Capt. Why there's nothing fuper-natural in all this; Women hate their Hufbands all the World over.

Ifab. I'm fure I fhould never hate you, if I had you once. (*Afide.*) And are not you even with us, Captain?

Capt. I won't anfwer for the whole Sex; but I'll engage for myfelf, if thou'lt but try me, Child.

Ifab. Firft hear the Conditions annext to Matrimony; then, if you'll venture——

Capt. Venture! What the Devil doft think I that have fac'd fo many Dangers, fhould be afraid of frefh Water?

Lady M. Have a care what you fay, Captain; for fix to four but you'll wifh yourfelf unmarried again, as heartily as I do.

Enter Lucy.

Lucy. Oh Madam! undone! undone! my Lord's juft dying.

Lady M. Ah!

Capt. Undone! Pifh, Pox, 'tis the beft News thou ever brought'ft in thy Life, Wench.

Lady M. Ruin'd! paft Redemption! Oh, that ever I was born!

Capt. Ha! what's the Meaning of this?

Ifab. Oh unhappy Woman!

Capt. Unhappy! Adfheart, I fhou'd have guefs'd her the happieft Woman in the World, now.

Lady M. Fly, call Phyficians ftrait, here, bribe 'em with Jewels, *(tears off the Jewels)* give 'em a King's Ranfom, if they can but fave his Life, load 'em with Wealth 'till they fink beneath the Weight. Oh! my lateft Hour is come!

Capt. What the Devil can be the Matter? why all this Noife? Here's none but Friends; I don't apprehend that any body can over-hear you; this is fomething like the *Irifh* Cry; I fuppofe it is the Cuftom of the Country.

[*Afide.*

Lady M. Oh no! Neither Heaven nor Earth will hear me now! I'm loft, for ever loft! Oh, oh, oh!

Capt. Humph! now I have found it; all the Eftate goes with him, I warrant.

Lady *M.* Eſtate! ſink the Eſtate! my Life goes with him?

Iſab. Oh cruel, oh inhuman Law!

Capt. What a-pox, ſhe wont die for the Man ſhe hates, will ſhe? Did you not wiſh to be unmarried juſt now? and are you ſorry that your Huſband's a-dying? The Woman's diſtracted ſure!

Lady *M.* Oh, I muſt be buried with him alive! O dreadful Thought. [*Runs off.*

Capt. Ha! how's that? Buried alive! I'm Thunder-ſtruck! Say, I conjure you, Madam, (*To Iſabinda*) and explain to me this Riddle.

Iſab. It is, Sir, the barbarous Cuſtom of our Country; firſt ordain'd from frequent Poiſoning here, that which ſo-ever of the married Pair died firſt, the Survivor is buried with alive, dreſt, and adorn'd, for a ſecond Nuptial.

Capt. E'gad, it has turn'd my Stomach againſt the firſt. (*Aſide.*) Unheard of Barbarity! Is none exempt the Pain of the Country?

Iſab. None; all let down a deep hollow Mountain, with ſome Loaves of Bread, and ſome Bottles of Water on which they may feed for ſome time, and then expire with-in the loathſome Dungeon. My Mother in her Bloom was with my Father buried: I was but thrice three Moons old; yet I remember even then it rais'd a Horror in me, and as I grew up, fixt a Reſolution in me, never to wed in this curſt Place.

Capt. Faith, you had Reaſon, Madam, and I admire that any body does.

Iſab. Cuſtom has made it eaſy to the true *Coſgarian* Race, but I have a *Britiſh* Soul.

Capt. You muſt be reſcued from this Impoſition; your Aunt too muſt be ſav'd.

Iſab. But how? If he dies, the Officers of Juſtice ſeize her; nay, 'tis Death for all the Houſhold if Information be not given ſtrait. Upon the Wedding-day, two Coffins are always brought into the Bride-Chamber, as part of the Ceremony.

Capt. E'gad, I ſhould have ſmall Appetite to finiſh the Ceremony at the Sight of 'em.

Iſab. This is the deplorable State of Matrimony in our Country.

Capt.

Work for the UPHOLDERS.

Capt. If it were the Cuſtom all over the World, we young Fellows ſhould live deliciouſly; Women would be as plenty as Blackberries; we might put forth our Hands and take them without Jointures, Settlements, Pin-money, Parſon, and ſo forth.   [*Noiſe.*]

Iſab. Hark! I hear a Noiſe! Oh, my poor Aunt! I muſt in, and ſee the Event.

Capt. Firſt promiſe me that if I contrive a Way to bear you hence, you'll conſent to go with me?

Iſab. With all my Heart, there's my Hand upon it; we have no Time for Courtſhip; I'll meet you here again in an Hour.   [*Exit.*

Capt. Now if I can but handſomly carry off theſe Women, their Jewels will turn to better Account than an *Eaſt-India* Voyage.

Enter Boatſwain *and* Sailors.

Well, what Cheer, my Lads? I have ſeen the Prince, and obtain'd his Leave for every Thing I aſk'd.

1ſt Sail. Cheer! why Faith, Captain, we ſail directly before the Wind; and I want but your Conſent to make the richeſt Port in the Univerſe.

Capt. What do you mean?

1ſt Sail. What! why I can have a fine Lady here, with as many Jewels about her as will ballaſt a Ship, if you'll but give me my Diſcharge; nay, I won't be ungrateful for it neither, you ſhall have all my Pay: What ſay you, Maſter, will you lend me your Hand to heave me into good Fortune?

2d Sail. Will you be falſe-hearted then, *Nick?* *Nell* will hang herſelf in her Garters when ſhe hears it.

1ſt Sail. Let her, let her, what care I: Odsfiſh! do you think I'd leave a firſt Rate for a Frigate; forſake a fine Lady for *Nell?* That's quitting a Bowl of Punch for a Draught of Sea-water.   [*Spitting.*

Boat. I wonder what ſhe ſaw in that ugly Phiz of thine, that's always as dirty as the Hammock you ſwing in; and as ſeldom waſh'd as your Shirt, which is not once a Quarter.

2d Sail. Ha, ha! Oh, ſhe fell in Love with his Noſe or his Legs.

1ſt Sail. Why, what Fault can you find with my Noſe?

Bob. Ha! 'tis found, and perhaps that's more than yours is.   *Boat.*

Boat. Nay, nay, don't find Fault with his Nofe, it is like the Bowfprit, and his Legs would ferve for a Mainmaft ; I warrant the Jade underftands Sailing, and fo wifely provides againft Strefs of Weather, ha, ha.

1ft Sail. I'faith, fhe's a tite Veffel, and I'll man her as titely, I warrant ye, my Lads.

Capt. Ha, ha ; hark ye, Sirrah ; there's fuch Conditions entail'd upon this Woman, you are fo fond of, that will make you as Wife-fick, as the Sea did in your firft Voyage.

1ft Sail. Aye, it's no Matter for that, Captain ; you muft not think to ferve me as you do a Whale, fling out an empty Cafk till the Subftance gets by. Look ye, Mafter, to fetch up half her Wealth, I'd dive to the Bottom of the Sea, and venture being fwallow'd by a Shark, *Nick* would, I'faith, Mafter.

2d Sail. Well faid, *Nick*; E'gad I warrant you think to be an Ambral now.

1ft Sail. Why, why not, if I have Money enough to buy it ? And I will be an Ambral too, for all you, and my Mafter here, fhall be my Rear-Ambral.

Capt. Oh, your very humble Servant, Mr. Admiral—— but fuppofe your Wife fhould die, *Nick*?

1ft Sail. Better and better ftill ! her Gold, and precious Stones, won't die too ; and E'gad, I'll drink to her good Voyage in a Bowl of Punch, clap my Riches abroad, and hoift Sail for merry *England*.

Capt. Ha, ha, Do you know that the Law of this Ifland buries the living Hufband with the dead Wife.

1ft Sail. Ha ! The Devil it does !

Capt. 'Tis even fo.

Boat. Ambral, I wifh you much Joy.

1ft Sail. Alive !

2d Sail. What, is the Wind chop'd full in your Teeth, *Nick* ? Ha, ha, ha !

1ft Sail. Ay, Faith, and blows fo hard, that it fhall blow my Head off e're I make the Port of Matrimony in this Ifland. Buried with her ? quotha ! E'gad, I always thought the Wedding-fheet the Winding-fheet of Pleafure, after a Month ; but to have no Hopes beyond her ; Zounds ! I had rather fit in the Bilboes all Days of my Life. I'll aboard this Minute. *Boatfwain*, you grumbl'd at my good Fortune juft now, take her yourfelf if you will. *Boat.*

Work for the UPHOLDERS.

Boat. The Devil take me if I do.

Capt. I told you I ſhould take off the Edge of your Appetite : Go, go, try and get the Ship off : I'll be aboard immediately. Have you got any Proviſions?

Boat. That we have, good Store.

Capt. Well, well, be gone then.

1ſt. Sail. Ay, with all my Heart ; if I get once aboard, I'll ſtick as cloſe to the Ship as Pitch to a Rope ; and ſink with her rather than come aſhore again. Buried with a Wife ! the Devil ! *Exeunt* Sailors.

Capt. Let me conſider ; what Stratagem ſhall I uſe to carry off the Women.

Enter Iſabinda.

Iſab. There's a ſad Houſe within ; but hang me if I don't fancy my Uncle counterfeits ; for in my Mind his Pulſe beats as regular as mine.

Capt. Ha ! Say you ſo ? Then I have it. Convey me into the Houſe, where I'll tell you the Plot, to free you from theſe Apprehenſions.

Iſab. If you effect it you are a Deity. Come along with me ; in this Confuſion I can preſerve you undiſcover'd.

Capt. Along then. [*Exeunt.*

SCENE II.

The Emir *on a Couch, with his Wife weeping by him, and Attendants round about. Table, Couch, 2 Chairs, Gallypots,* &c.

Lady. Oh Diſtraction ! Look up my Lord, my Love, my Huſband ! Oh, you will break my Heart, and I ſhall go before you ! Oh, oh, oh !

Emir. The Stars forbid ! Oh, oh ! [*Groans.*

Lady. Ah ! Help ye Slaves——Gently bear him up— Rub his Temples——Apply the Hartſhorn to his Noſe— Oh ſpeak and tell me how you do, my Dear !——Oh, oh, oh ! [*Roars out.*

Emir. Very bad——Oh, oh !

Lady. Are you very bad, my Love ? What will become of me ? [*Aſide.*

Em. Very bad indeed, Wife——Oh, I ſhall not live this Day, I doubt.

Lady. Ah ! What do I hear !——Oh, ye cruel Powers, —Why was I caſt upon this Shoar ? Curſe on theſe glittering

ing Bawbles, whofe bewitching Luftre cheats us of true Happinefs. (*Tears off her Jewels.*) A Thirft of Riches drew me from that Land where Widow-hood is happy—to die within a loathfome Dungeon, unpitied and forlorn.

Em. What does fhe fay now?——Prithee, my Dear, don't afflict yourfelf fo much——You'll be fick my Love—

Lady. But you'll die, my Love——Sick, quotha! Good Heaven! Can I be well when you are dying?

Em. Oh, you think of the Cuftom of our Country, Wife; you fear to be buried with me, that's all.

Lady. All does he call it—— [*Afide.*

Em. Now, if it had pleas'd Great *Mahomet*, that thou fhouldft have gone firft, I fhould have accompanied thee with Pleafure——

Lady. That's more than I fhall do you, I'm fure. [*Afide.* So fhall I you, my Dear, as to any Bufinefs I have with Life, when thou'rt gone : but the Pain to fee thee die, to part with thee for ever, is the Shock that Nature feels— but 'tis unkindly urg'd to think I fear the Cuftom of the Ifland—for what Joy could I have when thou art gone?

Em. I doubt fhe lies—But this is the only Way I could ever find to keep her in Subjection; for as foon as I am well, whip! fhe's fcamper'd, and I have no more Comfort of a Wife than I fhould have in her Grave : If all *Englifh* Wives are fuch Gadders, Heaven help their Hufbands, I fay——

Lady. How doft thou do, Jewel?

Em. I think I am a little better ; I believe I could eat a Leg of that Chicken within——

Lady. Fly ye Slaves, and fetch it inftantly. Oh, all ye Powers, that protect our Lives, I thank ye; I feel the Springs of Joy recruit ; thy Words run thro' my Soul with fuch exulting Pleafure, that 'tis all one Rapture——Oh, let me hold thee ever in my Arms——Oh! that fingle Word, Better——has more Harmony in it than the Mufic of the Spheres——Thus let me kifs it from thy Lips, 'tis the richeft Cordial Nature could produce to raife my finking Hopes. (*Embraces and kiffes him in an Extafy.*) Where are you, Slaves, why do you ftay so long.

Enter Servants.

Em. Ah, this Wife of mine does but countefeit this Love

Work for the UPHOLDERS.

Love to me, I fear——If our Law did not bury the Living with the Dead, here would be no Joy for my Recovery.
Lady. Come, my Dear, fhall I cut it for thee?
Em. No, I'll not trouble thee. [*He cuts and eats greedily.* 'Tis very good : Won't you eat a Bit of it, Deary?
Lady. No, thou fhalt eat it all——He feeds heartily: Ah, if I had him in Old *England*, I fhould wifh it were his laft——Oh, the vaft Difference between a Widow's Weed and a Winding-Sheet, between the civil Ceremonies of fhedding Tears at the Grave, and the barbarous Cuftom of making one's Bed there.
Em. How pleas'd fhe is? Ah, wou'd fhe be in this good Humour always——
Lady. Much good may do you, my Dear. [*Kiffes him.*
Em. I thank you, my Love——Ah, you little Rogue, how warm your Buffes are——(*Rifes from the Table*) Od, they infufe new Life into me ; and methinks I feel Health pop into my Heart, like a Pop-gun——Another Kifs, my Deareft——(*Kiffes her.*) So, fo, thou haft done it, thou haft done it, thou dear Rogue——Go, what do you ftare at? be gone and leave your Lady and I alone——
[*To the Servants.*
Lady. Say you fo——alone! alas, are you fit to be left alone——leave a dying Man alone—— Let them ftir if they dare——I fhall take better Care of you than that comes to, my Dear.
Em. Pifh, Pifh, I tell thee I am out of Danger.
Lady. I wifh thou wert——
Em. Indeed I am, and thou fhalt find it fo; therefore, prithee let them go—— [*Winking at her.*
Lady. Alas, I fear you are light-headed, my Dear; Aye, your Pulfe is upon the Galop; you are in a raging Fever, ——Oh, woe is me! Oh, oh, oh! Away, fome of ye, and fetch a Doctor.
Em. Pfha, pfha ; I tell thee thou art miftaken ; I am in no Fever but what proceeds from thy pretty pouting Lips, and thou art the beft Phyfician, let me kifs them again; ye, ye, ye, ye, dear foft Charmer, ye, ye.
Lady. Are you fure you are well?
Em. Very fure on't, my Dear——Come, let us take a Nap together.
Lady. You know I can't fleep in the Day-time : befides, you

you ought to return your Prophet Thanks for your Recovery——

Em. Oh, that I'll do To morrow.

Lady. To-morrow! A Man of your Years ought to be afham'd of deferring Things of that Kind till To-morrow.

Em. Why, Child, upon Occafion one may——

Lady. Occafion! What Occafions have People of your Age for Life, but to pray———

Em. Have Women in your Country no other Bufinefs for their Hufbands, my Dear?

Lady. No——

Em. Humpth! That was the Reafon you left it, I doubt——

Lady. Ah! would I had never left it——

Em. But come, come, you jeft but with me. *Lucy,* fetch your Lady's Night gown——I love to fee her in her Night-gown——Ah, thofe roguifh Eyes! Another Kifs and then——

Lady. You love to fee me in my Night-gown, I think I fhan't confult your Fancy much——Prithee no more Sleeping; your Breath's ready to ftrike one down, and your Beard's as rough as a Hedge-hog. *Lucy,* fetch me my Veil, I have a Vifit to make.

Lucy. Yes, Madam. [*Exit.*

Em. So, fhe's no Changeling, I find; never Man had fuch a Wife, certainly——I muft always be fick, or fhe'll always be out of Humour. (*Afide.*) Sure you'll not leave me, Wife.

Lady. Indeed but I fhall, Hufband. [*Enter* Lucy.

Lucy. Here's the Veil, Madam. [*She puts it on.*

Em. Well, go then, I won't hinder you——*Shadock,* give me my Cloak; I'll go fee the Grand Emir, and pafs away the Time a little till your Lady's Return,

Lady. Well, now I like your Humour. You fhou'd always let your Wife go, when and where fhe pleafes.

Em. That I refolve for the future——Ha! what ails me——Blefs me, I'm very fick o'th' Sudden; oh, oh! pray lead me to my Bed, or I fhall die this Moment.——

Lady. Ha! what's that, die fay you? [*throws off her Veil.* Oh wretched me! here, here, here, here, take a little of this, my Lord. Judgment is pronounc'd againft my Life,

and

Work for the UPHOLDERS.

and I muſt die at laſt. (*Aſide*.)——Away, and call the Phyſicians : Haſte, fly, oh, oh, oh !

Em. No, no, 'twill off again ; 'tis only a Fit——thy Kindneſs is my beſt Cordial. I'll try to reſt a little.

Lady. Withdraw all of you, and ſeparate into Silence. I'll watch by thee. Heaven ſend my Love a comfortable Nap——What Diſtractions tear my Breaſt—Now Hope, then Deſpair, with alternate Sway, exerciſe their Power, and no kind Glimpſe of Safety offers me Relief.

Enter Iſabinda.

Iſa. Oh Aunt, the Captain is without, and has a Secret to deliver us from this Place if you'll but help the Deſign.

Lady. Bring him in : If your Uncle wakes I'll tell him it is a Doctor.

Enter Captain *and whiſpers the* Lady.

Iſab. Here he is.

Capt. Do ye this, and I'll be ready to finiſh it. [*Exit.*

Lady. I'll venture. Oh Fortune, be this once propitious, and I'll ſubmit my future Life, without the leaſt Complaint. Ah ! my Head turns round ! Oh, I faint, I die ! [*Swoons.*

Iſab. Ah Help ! Help ! Where are you ? My Aunt's dead. Help ! Help ! [*The* Emir *riſes, runs, and catches hold of his Wife.*

Em. I'm Thunder-ſtruck——Oh, oh, oh, oh !

Serv. Ha ! Dead ! Nay, then, where are the Coffins ? [*Exeunt* Servants.

Emir. Oh, woe is me ! Speak to me, my Dear ; ſpeak to me ; ſpeak to me.

Iſab. As I ſuſpected : See how nimble he is at the Apprehenſion of being buried with her. What ſhall I do ? ſhe's breathleſs quite———

Emir. Oh, oh, oh ! (*Roars out.*) Undone, undone, for ever———

Iſab. Ay, it is you who have been the Cauſe, oh, wretched Man ! Prophet, thou art not juſt.

Emir. Wretched indeed. I confeſs I did but counterfeit——Oh Alla, (*kneels*) pardon my Deceit, and give me back her Life, and let her cuckold me with every Thing ſhe meets ; let her be the verieſt Wife that ever *England* bred,

bred, I never will be jealous more! oh, oh! (*Gets up and runs to her, and feels her Pulfe, then rubs her Temples, and prays again——*) Is there any Hopes, Niece?

Ifab. No, none. Oh diftracting Thought! This comes of your frightening her fo.

Emir. Oh forgive me, Niece, for I truly repent: Alas! I did it only to keep her in Subjection. Oh fetch the Cordial which I, like a falfe Wretch, had no Occafion for! Oh! I do believe fhe lov'd me now! Oh Niece, try, try, to pour fome down her Throat; for I tremble fo, I cannot guide it to her Lips.

Ifab. Alas! her Teeth are fet: She's gone! for ever gone!

Emir. Then I'm gone too! [*Burfts out again into Tears.* Oh, oh, oh!

Enter Servants *with two Coffins.*

Ifab. Oh killing Sight! (*kneels*) Thou glorious Sun affift us now and we are happy. [*Afide.*

Emir. Ay do, do pray for thy Uncle, Child: Oh, oh, oh!

Ifab. I have Occafion for my Prayers myfelf, at this Time, I thank ye, for I am afraid we are in the greater Danger at prefent. [*Afide.*

Emir. (*Turns and fees the Coffins.*) Oh, oh, oh, that ever I married! Where fhall I hide myfelf? Oh, oh, oh!

[*Runs off.*

Serv. Stop him, ftop him. [*Exeunt* Servants.

Ifab. Call the Officers of Juftice ftrait; I muft be cruel here. So he's gone, Captain, come forth.

Enter Captain.

Lady. I'm almoft choak'd with holding my Breath fo long; what's to be done now? Pray Heaven we profper!

Capt. I warrant you, Madam, come, come, be quick, you muft aboard this Minute. Have you any Thing you would take with you?

Ifab. I have pack'd up all your Jewels, and every Thing of Value here, Madam: Mercy on me, how I tremble!

Lady. And I'm ready to fink with Fear: If we are taken we are undone, and you lofe your Lives.

Capt. Nothing like a good Courage: Come, let's not ftand difputing, and lofe the lucky Minute.

Lady.

Lady. From thefe curft Laws, oh let me 'fcape with Life.
Ifab. And make me any Creature but a Wife.
Capt. Your Wealth at any Time decides the Strife.
[*Exeunt.*

SCENE III.

A Cofgarian *Lady, dragging in the firft Sailor.*

Lady. Nay, don't think to leave me, Sir, did you not promife to ftay here?

1ft Sail. But will you promife not to die before me then? Anfwer me that: Adfbud, who do you think to choufe? ha!

Lady. What are you afraid to die with her you love?

1ft Sail. Love! Zounds! does any body love a Woman well enough to die with her?

Lady. Yes, certainly, with their Wives.

1ft Sail. That's a Miftake, d'ye fee; for of all the Women in the World we care the leaft for our Wives, in my Country.

Lady. That's ftrange. Why, I fhould rejoice to die with you, pretty *Englifhman.*

1ft Sail. Aye, one Way, perhaps, pretty Devil! But to be plain with you, I defire to die no Way with you at all; and fo I fhear off. [*Going.*

Lady. Stay. Cannot Gold and Jewels tempt you?
[*Shews Gold and Jewels.*

1ft Sail. No.

Lady. What are you *Englifhmen* made on?

1ft Sail. Flefh and Blood, Child: If I can find one of Iron and Stcel, I'll recommend him to you.

Lady. Iron and Steel! What kind of Men are they?

1ft Sail. Oh, Things that are fo well acquainted with the Earth, that they'll lie twenty Years in it and take no Hurt: Now for my Part, I have as much Antipathy to frefh Mould as frefh Water; and had rather eat Sea-Bifket than a green Sod; and the Wind will as foon blow North and by South, as I be prevail'd upon to turn in with you.

Lady. Faint-hearted Wretch! Take me with you, then, to your World.

1ft Sail. Look ye, I'll have nothing to do with you at all; and there's your Anfwer; and if you offer to ftop me, I fhall make ufe of my Cat of Nine Tails, in troth I fhall.
Zounds!

Zounds! I never had fuch an Averfion for a Woman in my Life. [*Exit* Sailor.

Lady. Sure this is fome Sea-Monfter, it cannot be a Man, and Proof againft Gold and Jewels.
The *European*'s God is Gold, we *Indians* fay,
Then dare they fly from that to which they pray?
When next ———
To th' fhining Ore thou doft for Mercy fue,
As you've been deaf to me, may that be deaf to you.
[*Exit.*

Enter fecond Sailor.

2d Sail. Ha! the Woman here that *Nick* fhould have had; a faint-hearted Dog! Now have I a Mind to knock her Brains out, and carry off her Jewels.

Lady. What's here——another of the puny Knaves?
[*A Whiftle within.*

2d Sail. Ha! the Bofon's Whiftle! nay then I muft be fpeedy; and yet I can't find in my Heart to kill her.
[*Whiftle again.*
Adfheart, I fhall be left afhoar; I muft away.

Lady. You look diforder'd, Sir; are you in Love?

2d Sail. With your rare glift'ning Stones I am; and if your damn'd Fafhion did not heave the living Hufband o're board with the dead Wife, I did not care if I faid I was in love with you.

Lady. Then take me where we may live for ever; for indeed I don't like this Cuftom amongft us, but muft obey it. Come, bear me hence, and I will load thee with Wealth enough to buy thy Country.
[*Whiftle and hollow within.*

2d Sail. Ha! I have no Time to think; come along then; I'll venture to fwing in a Hammock with you for once.

Blow gently, *Boreas*, *Neptune*'s Rage confound,
And fet us fafely upon *Britifh* Ground,
Where we will drink and fing till the whole World goes round. [*Exeunt.*

SCENE IV.

The Emir *dragg'd in by* Officers, *with Servants bringing in Loaves of Bread and Bottles of Water.*

Off. What, a Native of *Cofgar*, and tremble at its Laws!

Work for the UPHOLDERS.

Laws! when even our Kings are subject to 'em. For Shame, *Emir*, bear yourself like a Man——Come, open the Coffin, and put in the Loaves and Water.

Emir. Ah, I shall have but small Stomach to eat. [*aside.* Confound our Laws; I'm inform'd that no Part of the World is curst with such, but only us, the rest live as long as they can: To be buried alive——Oh curs'd Custom! Oh, oh, oh! In perfect Health too! Oh, oh, oh!

Off. In Health! nay my Lord, that you are not; every body expected your Death this Morning; the Fright of which, I suppose, has caus'd your Lady's: I'm sure every body thought you very ill.

Emir. Aye, and may be every body thought me willing to die, but every body was mistaken.

Off. My Lord, we have no Time for Talking; it is not in our Powers to prevent your Fate. Here, lift him into the Coffin. Where are your Cords to let the Coffins down the Mountain? [*They seize him.*

Emir. I will not go down the Mountain: Unconscionable Rogues! (*struggles with them.*) I hope your Wives will die To-morrow——Hold, hold, let me see my Wife first; she died suddenly, and may come to Life again.

Off. Pish! Pish! This is Trifling, in with him, I say.

Emir. I tell you my Wife was an *English* Wife, and troubled with Vapours, as all that Country Wives are; she us'd to die and come to Life again ten Times in an Hour, therefore I will see her.

[*Struggling to reach at her Coffin.*

2d Off. Shall he see her, Brother?

1st Off. No, no.

Emir. Ye Dogs, I will. (*Gets hold on't, and pulls off the Lid.*) By Alla, Sun, Moon and Stars, here's no body! Huzza, here's no body, she's alive. [*Jumps and dances about.*

Off. Alive! bring her out then.

Emir. Nay, do you bring her out, if you will, for you shall never bring me in.

Off. My Lord, I shall make you bring her out; you have buried her in your Garden, I suppose; but that shan't serve: Produce her living, or I'll instantly proceed to the Ceremony of Burial with you: Where is she?

Emir. Sir, I told you before she was an *English* Wife, and I believe few Husbands know where to find them.

Off.

Off. This fhan't ferve : Where's Mrs. *Ifabinda,* your Niece?

Emir. With her Aunt, for ought I know.

Enter a Servant.

Serv. Oh, my Lord, the Ship that was caſt here, yeſterday, is gone off, and with it your Lady, Niece and Maid, with all your Jewels.

Emir. With all my Soul ; and there's fomething for thy News ; a boon Voyage, and a merry Gale to them, fay I ; it is the moſt comfortable Lofs that ever Man had.

Off. Why, what a Misfortune's this? Here's our Fees loſt. [*Afide.*

Emir. And if ever you catch me marrying again, I'll give you leave to ufe thy Cords. Dogs ! get out of my Houfe, go ; troop, Vermin, no going down the Mountain now—Here, kick the Coffins after them, with their Loaves and Water ; for there ſhall never be more Occafion for 'em in this Houfe, I promife you——Come, where are my Servants? Here, let me have Mufick and Dancing, to cheer my Spirits.

The Laws of Wedlock all Men think fevere ;
But 'tis Damnation fure to marry here.

THE

THE

ARTIFICE.

A

COMEDY.

As it is ACTED

At the THEATRE-ROYAL in *Drury-Lane*.

PROLOGUE. Written by Mr. BOND.

Spoken by Mr. MILLS.

OUR Wits of late, grown wond'rous Weather-wife,
Change, like the various Seafons of the Skies.
They, each dull Winter, fullen and fevere
And cloudy, as its gloomieft Days appear:
Yawn o'er their Defks, figh forth fome Tragic-Scene,
Then treat the Town with Products of their Spleen.
Our Author takes a different Way to pleafe;
Heals injur'd Love, *and cures its* Jealoufies.
You tender Virgins, *and neglected* Wives,
For You, She all her ARTIFICE *contrives.*
You can't deny her———Your Protection furely,
She hides your Slips, and brings you off—fo purely!
Bold in her Sex's *Caufe, She always rouzes*
'Gainft their worft *Foes, falfe Lovers, and* dull Spoufes.
But, O! ye Critics! Comic-Bards *are few,*
And we've no Wit *beneath the Sun, that's* New:
Afk not, in fuch a General Dearth, *much Wit,*
If fhe your Tafte in Plot, *and* Humor *hit:*
Plot, Humor, Bufinefs, *form the* Comic *Feaft,*
Wit's *but a* higher-relifh'd Sauce, *at beft;*
And where too much, *like* Spice, *deftroys the Tafte.*
You Sparks in Red, *fhe knows, will all befriend her;*
Nay, Faith, you're bound in Honour to defend her.
You, in her Plays, her choiceft Favours fhare;
She never fails to raife her Men of War.
'Tis feldom known, you Brothers of the Blade,
Let Women *make Advances un-repaid.*
You Chiefs in War, who Monarchs can fubdue,
Yet own———The Ladies Victors *over* You.
A fingle Helen, *once divinely Fair,*
Summon'd a Croud of Heroes to the War:
And brighter Helens *raife your Courage*—There.
You, while our Author pleads in Beauty's Caufe,
Join on her Side, and Arm in her Applaufe:
Be Heroes in a WOMAN's *Caufe to Day,*
And as you Love *the* Sex, Defend *the* PLAY.

EPI-

EPILOGUE.

Written by Dr. SEWELL, 1723.

Spoken by Mrs. OLDFIELD.

SINCE Plotting *is the* Bufinefs *of the* Age,
   Our Bard has paid it off *upon the Stage.*
And *ſtrongly labour'd in theſe Scenes, to ſhew Ye,*
How WOMAN *can in* ARTIFICE *out-do Ye.*
You bungle ſadly, and are always caught
'Ere half your Work is to Perfection brought.
Did our Town-Wives their Schemes no better lay,
What monſtrous Plots *wou'd break out ev'ry Day?*
Ladies, I hope, I've acted to your Mind,
And ſerv'd my Jealous Monſter *in his Kind.*
To play the Prieſt, *and ſteal a Wives Confeſſion* ;
What Man can make amends for ſuch Tranſgreſſion?
Show'd all our Engliſh *Huſbands ſhrive their Wives,*
Women wou'd lead moſt comfortable Lives.
For of all Slavery, 'tis the worſt Condition,
To live beneath a Marriage Inquiſition.
   What think you of our Hogan-Mogan Belle?
Didn't ſhe trick the Trickſter nicely well?
The Whipſter thought, forſooth, 'twas ſmart and clever,
To ſwell the young Vrow *up, and then to leave her.*
But on the Younker a Dutch *Trick ſhe palms* ;
Poiſon *for* Poiſon *gives, and* Qualms *for* Qualms.
What Rake among you, but, in his Condition,
Wou'd even think a Wife *a good* Phyſician?
Did this Dutch *Law our roving Gentry bind,*
How charming wou'd it be for Woman-kind!
Then ev'ry Nymph who has vouchſaf'd the Favour,
Might tye her Lover up to good Behaviour :
And after ſhe has put him to the Teſt,
Might take, *or* leave *him,*——*as ſhe* lik'd it beſt.
   You, who are noos'd, let me adviſe ; *beware,*
Give o'er your Jealous *Freaks, and truſt the* Fair :
For, look ye, you may rant, and play the Devil ;
There's nought but Patience *cures the* Marriage-Evil.
The Thing is plain, *and Inſtances are* common ;
No MAN *is half a Match for any* WOMAN.

Dramatis Personæ.

MEN.

Sir *Philip Moneylove*, Father to *Olivia*, a Man whose Morals are only subservient to his Interest. — Mr. *Miller*.

Sir *John Freeman*, Heir to 4000*l. per annum*, but disinherited. In Love with *Olivia*. — Mr. *Wilks*.

Ned Freeman, his Younger Brother; possess'd of the Estate. — Mr. *Mills*.

Fainwell, an Ensign under the Name of *Jeffery*; in Disguise, Footman to the Widow *Heedless*. — Mr. *W. Wilks*.

Mr. *Watchit*, A Country-Gentleman, very jealous of his Wife. — Mr. *Griffin*.

Tally, One belonging to a *Pharoah-Bank*; an humble Servant to Widow *Heedless*, under the Character of Lord *Pharoah-Bank*. — Mr. *Harper*.

Demur, a Doctor of the Civil law.

WOMEN.

Olivia, Daughter of Sir *Philip Moneylove*. In love with Sir *John Freeman*. — Mrs. *Horton*.

Louisa, a *Dutch* Lady, formerly contracted to *Ned Freeman*. — Mrs. *Younger*.

Mrs. *Watchit*, Wife to Mr. *Watchit*. — Mrs. *Oldfield*.

Widow *Heedless*, worth 20,000*l*. affected, vain, and an Admirer of Quality, and resolv'd never to marry beneath a Lord. — Mrs. *Thurmond*.

Lucy, Servant to Mrs. *Watchit*.
Flora, Servant to *Louisa*.
Judith, Servant to Mrs. *Heedless*.

Constable, Watch, and other Attendants.

THE

THE
ARTIFICE.

ACT I.　　SCENE I.
St. James's PARK.

Enter Fainwell *in a Livery, meeting Sir* John Freeman *in Mourning.*

Fain.  A! *Freeman* in *Black?* Dear *Jack* how muſt I diſtinguiſh thee?
　　Sir *John.* Dear *Jack!*——How came you and I ſo well acquainted Fellow!
　Fain. O!——that's too long a Story at preſent.
　Sir *John.* What the Devil is this *Metamorphoſis* for, *Fainwell.*
　Fain. Love! Almighty Love! Copying of the *Gods,* you know.
　Sir *John.* What Game are you in purſuit of?
　Fain. The old ſtanding Diſh, a W I F E! There's no Hopes of War, no Riſing in View! and *Subaltern*'s Pay will make a Man rub but ſlowly thro' the World. I have got Leave of my Colonel to be abſent from my Poſt for Two Months, in which Time, I intend to make my Fortune.——You know the Widow *Heedleſs!*
　Sir *John.* Very well! Ha!——is not that her Livery?
　Fain. Yes, Faith, I march in the Number of her Retinue.
　Sir *John.* To what End?
　Fain. That's uncertain. If you know the Widow, you are no Stranger to her Taſte in Servants.
　Sir *John.* I know ſhe keeps none but awkward *Country Louts.*
　Fain. Ay! and is a perfect Jockey in her Family, and
　　　　　　　　　　　　　　　　　　　　　　　　take

takes as much Pains to polifh her Train, as they do to break their young Colts. Now, you muft know I pafs with her for as arrant a *Ruftick*, as ever wielded Cudgel at a Country Wake, or tumbled Girl upon a Hay mow.

Sir John. But wherein can this advance your Defign?

Fain. Why, you muft know, I make Love to her.

Sir John. Make Love to her! what under the Character of a Footman?

Fain. No, no, under the Character of a Gentleman of Fifteen hundred Pounds a year in *Gloucefterfhire*, of which Country I pretend to be; for having quarter'd heretofore in that Shire, I counterfeit the Dialect very well.

Sir John. But what Service can this be to you?

Fain. Why, I write to her as from Mr. *Worthy*; my Man brings the Letters; and I deliver them as *Jeffrey*, her Footman; and when I find her in Humour, I intend to give her my Picture, in fo fimple a manner, that fhe fhall take it all for Gofpel.

Sir John. But what fignifies the Copy? How will you introduce the Original?

Fain. That has been done already. I have made her feveral Vifits. My Man is now gone to her with a Letter.

Sir John. But fuppofe fhe fhould inquire after this Mr. *Worthy?* It is an eafy Matter to know all the Gentlemen in *Gloucefterfhire*, and what Eftates they are poffefs'd of too.

Fain. She can't trap me there, if fhe does: For, between you and I, there is fuch a Perfon as Mr. *Worthy*, Mafter of the very Eftate I mention, who has given me Leave to take his Name.——But I have discover'd fince I have been in her Houfe, that an *Irifh* Baron is my Rival.

Sir John. Then you are undone; for I am told, fhe declares againft Matrimony without a Title. But who is he?

Fain. My Lord *Pharoah-Bank*, I think they call him, of the County of *Tipperary*.

Sir John. I don't remember ever to have heard of any fuch Nobleman.

Fain. Recommended, they fay, by Sir *Philip Moneylove*.

Sir John. For which he is to have a valuable confideration; for I am fure, he does nothing out of Honour or Honefty. I wifh thee fuccefs with all my Heart.

Fain. I thank you, *Freeman*; but prithee who are you

in

in Mourning for? Is the old Knight at Reſt Six Foot deep, ha, *Jack?*

Sir John. He has been dead to me theſe Seven Years; but is now ſo to all the World, *Fainwell.*

Fain. Sir *John!* I give thee Joy of Four thouſand Pounds *per annum.* [*Embracing him.*

Sir John. I hope you'll give me the Eſtate too, *Fainwell*; for, I aſſure you, I have not one Foot of Land by the Death of my Father.

Enter Sam.

Fain. He did not diſinherit thee, ſure.

Sir John. Neither better nor worſe.

Sam, I ever thought my old Maſter would dye hard, and take the Left-hand Road.

Sir John. Ha! what is *Sam* with you ſtill?

Sam. You know, Sir, I always ſtick as cloſe to my Maſters, as their Breeches.

Sir John. Ay! whilſt there is any Money in them; but, I remember, you left me for fear of ſtarving.

Sam. Starving, Oh, no, no!—Not ſtarving, Sir; tho' I muſt confeſs, my Waiſt-band was Three inches too wide for me.

Fain. You ſaucy Raſcal! ha, ha? Well, did you deliver my Letter.

Sam. Yes, I did, Sir; and into the Widow's own Hands; and, truly, by what I can find Sir, you have nothing to hope for, if I have any Judgment.

Fain. Why! What have you diſcover'd?

Sam. Why, I obſerv'd when ſhe read your Epiſtle, ſhe ſmil'd ſcornfully, thus——toſs'd your Letter upon her Toylet; turn'd upon her heel; tipp'd her Maid a Box o' the Ear for grinning, and bid me tell you, it required no Anſwer.

Sir John. Cold Comfort!

Fain. Not a Jot the leſs for giving herſelf that Air. But is it poſſible, that pure Party-Rage could make thy Father ſo unkind, Sir *John?*

Sir John. Add to that ſome little Wildneſſes. But the main thing that did my Buſineſs, was this; When I found nothing wou'd open his Purſe-ſtrings, I pretended to embrace his Principles.

Sam.

The ARTIFICE.

Sam. I remember that Time, Sir: We lived in Clover then! Many a delicious Morſel of Fleſh have I ſerv'd up and ſupp'd luxuriouſly out of your Leavings, Sir.

Sir John. But, as the Devil wou'd have it, one Day, in my Cups, I chanced to ſtumble into a Non-juring-Meeting, with half a Dozen honeſt Officers at my Back, drove out the Congregation, ty'd the Parſon Neck and Heels, lock'd the Door, and took the Key in my Pocket.

Fain. Good! And what became of Old Sedition?

Sir John. Some of his Flock returning to Evening Prayer, broke open the Door, and freed him from Durance; amongſt which Number was my natural Father.

Fain. Rather Unnatural! That was very unlucky, Sir John.

Sir John. Ay; for that Aċtion not only loſt me a paternal Bleſſing, but a paternal Eſtate.

Fain. Which would have afforded thee many Bleſſings, Wine and Women, Sir *John*, the only Bleſſings in this World! So your younger Brother *Ned* has the Eſtate, I ſuppoſe.

Sir John. Every Acre! My Fortune is cramm'd into ſuch a narrow Circumference, I can cover it with my Thumb. Only——a ſingle Shilling.

Fain. Damn'd Barbarity! 'S'Death! were he my Brother, I'd cut his Throat.

Sam. There's the Inſide of a Soldier for you! [*Aſide.*

Sir John. So ſay Paſſion and Neceſſity; but Conſcience and Humanity offer to my cooler Thoughts a brown Muſquet rather. I confeſs, I long to exert the elder Brother, and beat him a little; in order to which, I have done all I could to provoke him to give me Occaſion; but he avoids me as carefully as if he durſt not fight, though I know he's no Coward.

Fain. Well! Heaven be prais'd, I am not afraid of being diſinherited. I wear my fortune with my Red-Coat; and whilſt there is one Miſchief making Prieſt in the World, Soldiers will never want Bread.

Sam. Ay, the Prieſts have ever been faſt Friends to the Soldiers. Nothing like a Pulpit Drum.——But it ruins the Surgeons Buſineſs quite.

Sir John. Ay! how ſo?

Sam. Why, where's the Occaſion for their retailing Lancet,

Lancet, when the other lets the Nation Blood by Wholefale?

Fain. My Rafcal has a Kind of fmattering after Wit, ha, ha, No more of your Impertinence.

Sam. Impertinence! thefe Gentlemen will allow no body to fay a good Thing but themfelves. [*Afide.*

Sir *John.* Ha! yonder's my Brother coming this Way. How ftately the Rogue walks, with three Footmen at his Heels.

Fain. Whilft thou haft not fo much as one Scoundrel to pick up a Wench for thee.

Sam. Oh, for that, Sir! with your Leave, he may always command his humble Servant.

Fain. He ftruts like an elder Brother. He wants nothing but your Title, Sir *John.*

Sir *John.* I wifh I could transfer it; for it is of no Ufe to me. Honour's a Commodity not vendable among the Merchants; there is no Draw-back upon't.

Fain. That's a Miftake, Sir *John*; I have known a Statefman pawn his Honour as often as Merchants enter the fame Commodity for Exportation; and like them, draw it back fo cleverly, that thofe who give him Credit upon't, never perceiv'd it 'till the Great Man was out of Poft.

Sir *John.* Honour's a ftale Cheat.

Fain. It may pafs at Court, or the Groom-Porter's; but no Citizen will lend a Shilling upon it.

Enter Ned Freeman.

Ned. Brother! Your Servant. If this young Fellow had not been in a Livery, I fhould have fworn it had been Enfign *Fainwell!*

Fain. The very Numerical Perfon you mention, is as you fee, at your Service, Mr. *Freeman.* I believe you are furpriz'd at the Figure I make; but there are Reafons, which another Time fhall be yours. In the mean while, I muft intreat, that wherever you fee me, you know me for nothing above my prefent Appearance.

Ned. Whatever Defign you may have in View, it fhall never mifcarry through any Fault of mine.—Well! how go Matters in the North, Captain?

Sir *John.* Your Party perform'd no Wonders there.

Ned.

Ned. Nay, if you are entring upon Party Matters, good by-t'ye ; You know I always decline Politics in your Company.

Sir John. 'Tis the sign of an ill Cause.

Ned. Then Disputes won't mend it. Here——which Colour would you advise me for a Wedding Suit?

Fain. What ; just upon the Brink of Matrimony? 'Is it with the *Dutch* Lady you wrote such Panegyrics on, when you was in *Holland?*

Ned. What, the old Burgo master's Daughter of *Haerlem?* No, no ! that Affair's ended long since. She was a good-natured fond Fool, and, to say Truth, I did love her ; but the old Carl her Father, did not like a younger Brother for a Son-in-Law then, and I'm a better Friend to my Country, than to take a *Dutch* Wife now, I did him one Piece of Service ; I left some *English* Blood in his Family. I met a Gentleman at *Paris*, who told me, she was brought to Bed of a fine Boy.

Sir John. If I mistake not, you made that Lady a Promise of Marriage, Brother.

Ned. Cou'd I do less for a Maidenhead?

Fain. It is the custom in *Holland*, after such a Promise, the Girl never scruples to go to Bed, and thinks herself as much your Wife, as if the Parson had said Grace ; and if ever you are found in that Country, their Laws will oblige you to perform Articles.

Ned. Ay, if they catch me in the Corn, let 'em put me in the Pound.

Sir John. Whatever you think of such Proceedings, I assure you, I should have very little Confidence in that Man who forfeited his Faith and Honour to a Woman.

Ned. Preserve your Opinion, Brother ; the Ladies will like you never the better for't. Every Female has Vanity enough to believe her Charms sufficient to secure what another lost.

Fain. But who is the Object of your present Passion?

Sir John. Pray Heaven, it proves not where I guess ! [*aside.*

Fain. Who is the Beauty that inslaves you now?

Ned. Nay, I'm not so prodigiously inslav'd as you imagine.

Sir John. What ! and just a going to be married.

Sam. Mr. *Freeman* speaks like an experienc'd Traveller ;

ler; he is entring upon a Journey for Life; the Whip and Spur are for the fhort Stages of Love. It would kill the Devil to ride full Speed down a Lane that has neither End nor Turning.

Ned. Ha, ha, ha! *Sam* has a right Notion of Matrimony.

Sir *John.* A Lady muft be extremely happy with fuch a Hufband. But may we not know the Lady?

Ned. Yes, yes, Brother, I'm not afham'd of the Lady; fhe has Beauty enough for a Wife, and one Charm, as defirable, as a new Miftrefs.

Fain. Videlicet.

Ned. Twenty thoufand Pounds.

Sir *John.* Ha! that one Article ftrikes thro' me. [*Afide.*

Ned. 'Tis Sir *Philip Moneylove*'s Daughter.

Sir *John.* As I imagin'd!——This Blow wounds deeper than my being difinherited. Have you that Lady's Confent, Brother?

Ned. I have her Father's; and he has the Difpofal of her Fortune, though left by her Grandfather. She commands not a Penny, if fhe marries without his Confent.

Sir *John.* A moft pernicious Claufe!——Yet, if *Louifa*, his *Dutch* Miftrefs, who I have fent for, comes Time enough, I may chance to fpoil your Market. [*Afide.*

Ned. I think I ftand very fair; I have had his Promife thefe ten Days.

Sir *John.* Juft the Time that *Sir Philip* forbid me his Houfe! fince when, I have often watch'd him in, and, fearing the Confequence, I fent for his Miftrefs! and if there is the leaft Grain of Virtue left in that Heap of Muck and Immorality, Sir *Philip*, I may yet prevent this hateful Match. [*Afide.*

Fain. I wifh you Joy, Mr. *Freeman.*——

Sir *John.* Wifh him Hell! where he may tafte in part the Pains he gives me now.—*Olivia!*—Oh! my *Olivia.* [*Afide.*

Ned. My Brother has no Relifh for my good Fortune. ——I perceive you affect Gravity in my Company, Sir *John*, and feem to have no Tafte for any Joy of mine.—Prithee, how have I offended? You may have Reafon to blame our Father, perhaps; but how is that my Fault? I have really as much Love for you, as if you had been born a Year after me, and will treat you as well. *Fain*

Fain. That is to ſay, he ſhall live like your Brother.—
Ned. He ſhall live as he thinks fit, Sir ; I ſhan't pretend to direct him.
Fain. But you muſt put it in his Power !——Come, ſhall I make a Propoſal ?
Ned. Out with it.
Fain. Buy him a Colonel's Poſt in the Guards.
Ned. I don't think to part with any Money that way.—
Sir *John.* Not without it were to ſerve a certain Perſon, you know where. Oh ! that vile reſtleſs Principle of yours !———
Ned. Shall never diſturb you with a Commiſſion any where. Look ye, Brother, you ſhan't want for what is Neceſſary.
Sir *John.* Neceſſary ! I ſuppoſe you reſerve to your own Judgment how far that Word may extend.
Ned. It ſhall extend ſo far, Sir, as becomes a Brother who has the Eſtate, to him that has none.
Sam. Humph ! That is as much as to ſay, in plain *Engliſh*, you may ſtarve or ſteal, and be hang'd, for him.
[*Aſide.*
Sir *John.* As far as becomes your elder Brother.
Ned. I can't ſay that, for perhaps you may fancy my Eſtate may become you better than it does me.
Sir *John.* Your Eſtate ! [*Going up to him.*
Sam. (*Stepping between.*) Sir, Sir, With your Leave ! Where-abouts do you think the Soul of my old Maſter may be now ?
Ned. That Thought never enter'd my Head, Sirrah. I know where his material Soul, the Eſtate is, and how to ſpend it too. So, Brother, if you will be chearful.—
Sir *John.* Chearful ! Bid the Directors, when there's a Run upon the Bank, be chearful ; the Merchant who hears the Shipwreck of his freighted Veſſel ; or bid the Mother, weeping over the Corps of her departed Son, be chearful. ——Bid them be mad rather, to avoid Reflection.—— Chearful, quotha !
Sam. That's breaking a Man's Legs, and then bidding him cut Capers. [*Aſide.*
Fain. Philoſophy is a noble Study, Sir *John* ; but few of us poor Rogues can purſue it.
Sir *John.* With what Elegance might my Brother there, diſplay the Beauty of Patience and Poverty ! *Ned.*

Ned. No, Faith, *Jack*, I am no Orator.
[*Keeps looking upon the Paper.*
Sir *John.* Oh! What Serenity of Mind attends Four Thousand Pounds a Year? whilst Passion, Pride, and all the deadly Sins, fill up the Train of a poor Dog like me.

Sam. That's true to a Tittle, I know it by myself. [*aside.*

Sir *John.* Poor *Olivia!* now I understand thy Letter, wherein thou said'st, That we must part for ever; but I will see thee now, tho' certain Death attend it; though robb'd of Birthright by his younger Brother, let him not hope to take my Mistress from me.
Such an Attempt will far more dang'rous prove:
He robs me of my Life, that robs me of my Love. [Exit.

Ned. That is the Colour for my Money.

Fain. Ay, White is the Bridegroom's Colour.

Ned. Ha! What is my Brother gone?

Fain. So it seems——Poor Sir *John.*

Ned. Pox of this Livery, I should have been glad we cou'd have din'd together to Day.

Sam. Now you talk of dining——your Uncle call'd at your Lodging this Morning, Sir, and bad me tell you, he wonders how you bestow your Time, that you don't come and dine with him as usual.——

Ned. Who's that?

Fain. An Uncle of mine, to whom I had once some hopes of being Heir.

Ned. And what has stifled them?

Fain. Why, the Devil put Matrimony in his Head, and spoil'd my Fortune.——

Ned. Then he has Children, has he?

Fain. One, which happening to be Red-hair'd, and the Parson of the Parish being Sandy, my Uncle, not content with forbidding him his House, bid adieu to the Country, and brought my Aunt to Town.

Sam. An excellent Place to preserve Virtue in.

Ned. How came he to suspect the Doctor?

Fain. Why, my Aunt is a *Roman Catholic*, you must know, and I suppose my Uncle had a mind to make a good Protestant of her, and brought the Doctor to convert her; but finding his Arguments more prevalent for Love, than Religion, thought fit to remove her.

Ned. Ha, ha, ha! Where has he lodg'd her?

The ARTIFICE.

Fain. He has taken a Houſe in the *Pall-Mall*, within a Door of my Colonel's.——

Sam. Who has as good a hand at converting, as the Parſon, if he can find a Way to come at her. [*Aſide.*

Ned. In the *Pall-Mall!* If this ſhou'd be my Miſtreſs now? (*Aſide.*) So, the old Fellow is very Jealous of her, you ſay?

Fain. So Jealous, that he locks her up, it ſeems, reſolving to father no Children for the future, but his own; He allows her the Sight of nothing that's Male.

Ned. It muſt be ſhe; this agrees exactly with her Story, (*Aſide.*) Such Reſtraint ſets all the Wheels of Invention at Work, and a Million to nothing, but ſhe'll find a Way to uſe him as he deſerves. And how does ſhe take it?

Sam. Oh! not at all, Sir——You hear my Maſter ſay; ſhe's lock'd up.

Ned. Her Confinement, I mean, Sirrah?

Sam. Oh! her Confinement.

Fain. Not ſeeing her the laſt Time I din'd there, I inquir'd after her Health, and was anſwer'd, ſhe was indiſpos'd; yet I obſerv'd he cut her a Plate of ev'ry Thing that came to Table, and ſent up to her Chamber, which, as the Maid told me afterwards, is his conſtant Cuſtom of late, when any body dines with him. He is a true *Spaniſh* Huſband.

Ned. And if ſhe proves but a true *Engliſh* Wife, his Children may be nothing a-kin to him, for all his Caution. Is ſhe handſome?

Fain. So handſome, that I could venture my Soul with her; and if I had her Conſent, my Uncle *Watchit*, ſhould be advanc'd in Honours.——You underſtand me.

Ned. Watchit! Mum! that's the Name. *Fainwell* muſt not know where I live. (*Aſide.*)—You would not cuckold your Uncle, would ye?

Fain. Why not? I think a well-bred Gentleman ought to have as much Regard to the Breed of his Family, as a Fox hunter has to thoſe of his Dogs and Horſes. Where do you lodge, Mr. *Freeman?* I muſt bring a School-Fellow of mine to wait on you, one who has a Play upon the Stocks: You muſt give him leave to dedicate to you. It is young *Diſtich.*

Ned. Ha! Little *Diſtich!* I ſhall be glad to ſee him.

When

The ARTIFICE.

When I have finiſh'd an Affair which I have upon my Hands at preſent, I ſhall come ſomewhere to this End of the Town ; but I am *Incog.* for a little while.

Fain. What, are you upon an Intrigue ?

Ned. Yes, Faith, and with one of the prettieſt Women in Town ; a Citizen's Wife, whoſe Huſband is tinctur'd with thy Uncle's Diſtemper : He permits her neither to pay, or receive Viſits ; but in Spight of his *Blockade*, I have found means to open a Communication between myſelf and his Female, and hope I ſhall be able to ſpring a Mine, and blow up the Fort of her Chaſtity, maugre all his Iron Guards.

Fain. You talk like an Engineer, Mr. *Freeman* ; but if ſhe is ſo cloſely confin'd how got you acquainted with her ?

Ned. Very accidentally. You muſt know, her Houſe, and that which I lodge in, were formerly one, ſo that there are Doors remaining, tho' faſten'd up.—Sitting one Evening in my Chamber reading, I heard the Voice of Women, and found by their Diſcourſe 'twas a Lady complaining to her Maid of her Huſband's ill Uſage. If I were in your Place, ſays the Maid, I'd be reveng'd of the old Brute : Ay, quoth the Lady, but ſhew me the Means.— Upon which, having bor'd a Hole in the Door, I put my Mouth to it, and cry'd, the Means is ready, Madam, if you'll conſent to it. She was a little ſurpriz'd at firſt, but we ſoon came to a right Underſtanding.

Fain. Ha, ha ! ſo ſhe open'd the door !

Ned. Not that door : But the Chamber-Maid, who knew her Buſineſs perfectly well, after inquiring who lodg'd at next Houſe, in the Morning, knock'd gently at this private Door, and calling me by my Name, gave me to underſtand that there was a Door, between her Room, and a Garret in our Houſe, which if I cou'd find the Way to open, I might have an Opportunity of playing a Game at Picquet with her Lady ſometimes, in her Maſter's Abſence : I took the Hint, agreed with my Landlord for that Garret, and fell to work immediately. The Paſſage was ſoon open'd, and we came to an Interview, lik'd one another's Propoſals, call'd for the Cards, and ſat down to play, where I had the Game all to nothing, having *Point*, *Quint*, and *Quatorze*, the firſt Deal, had not the old Fellow come in, and forc'd us throw up our Cards.

Fain.

Fain. For which you both curs'd him, I fuppofe; but you have found a Time, 'tis to be hop'd, to finifh your Game.

Ned. I fhall do, this Day, I believe. Wifh me Succefs, *Fainwell.*

Fain. I do with all my Heart : I know you us'd to be generous, you'll not expofe her. When you have corrupted her, you may help your Friends, before fhe falls into the Hands of the Public.

Ned. With all my Heart ! Now for the finifhing Stroke : I'll Home, and watch the old Fellow out, and then *L'Affair il fera fait*, as the *French* fay—Which Way are you going, *Fainwell?*

Fain. Every Way ! I have fome Twenty How-d'ye's to deliver; the conftant Bufinefs of Men of my Cloth, you know.

Ned. Ha ! yonder comes my Father-in-Law that is to be. I muft avoid him.

Fain. And the Widow's Lord with him. (*Afide.*) Pray who is the Gentleman with him, Mr. *Freeman?*

Ned. His Name is *Bite*, to the beft of my Memory. He belongs to a *Pharoah-Table*, I us'd to fee him tally fometimes, that's all I know of him. Adieu. [*Exit.*

Fain. I'm glad you know fo much of him. *Bite*, quotha! Egad, I'll take care he fhan't bite me of the Widow.—— Is this her Man of Quality?—*Sam*, go you Home, and don't you be out of the Way, if I fhould want you. Do you hear?

Sam. Yes, yes, Sir. [*Exit* Sam.

Fain. Egad, this Woman fatigues me more than a long March. But the Hopes of her Gold, like the Hopes of Plunder, gives me frefh Courage for continuing the Siege.

For, to befiege, *and* ftorm *the Soldier's* Trade *is,*
In War, *to conquer* Towns ;——*In* Peace, *the* Ladies.

ACT II.

SCENE *Sir* Philip Moneylove's *Houſe.*

Enter Olivia *and* Louiſa *weeping.*

Oli. YOUR Story, I confeſs, Madam, is moving; but I am more ſurpriz'd at *Freeman*'s Infenſibility than at his Perjury. It is no Wonder to find a Man falſe; but that he ſhould be blind to ſo much Beauty, is an Argument of Stupidity.

Lou. Not when he changes for ſuperior Merit;
But if you love not the Diſſembler,
Oh, give him back to my deſiring Arms!
For we are fit Companions for each other.

Oli. All I can, beſure I'll do to ſerve thee.
Dear haſt thou bought, the faithleſs, worthleſs Man!

Lou. Too late, I blame my credulous Nature.
Our Sex, like Roſes blooming on the Tree,
Admir'd by ev'ry gazing Paſſenger:
The Flow'r once cropt, a while 'tis worn in Triumph;
Then thrown aſide to wither in Diſgrace.

Oli. Be pleas'd to give this Letter to Sir *John*, and purſue whatever he directs you. Depend upon any Thing in my Power to ſerve you, Madam; my Soul abhors this Treachery, and had he been as dear to me, as his poor injur'd Brother is I would renounce him now, tho' Life went with him.

Enter Sir Philip.

Oli. My Father! that's unlucky. [*Aſide.*

Sir *Phil.* Pray, Daughter, what is this pretty Reſolution of yours? Who wou'd you renounce?

Oli. One whom you wou'd have me, Sir, if you but wiſh me Happineſs; 'tis that Deceiver *Freeman.*

Sir *Phil.* How! Why, what has Sir *John* recover'd the Eſtate then? If ſo, Egad I ſhall renounce him too, Girl.— Ho'now, who have we here? Some Letter-Carrier, ha! Pray, who let you in, Miſtreſs?

Oli. Juſtice.
Look on this Lady, Sir, with Eyes more human,
On her whom *Freeman* baſely has betray'd,
Juſt in her riſing Bloom and Pride of Youth.

I   Sir

The ARTIFICE.

Sir Phil. Why, you'd make an excellent Actrefs ; you Rant and Strut it well ; but who is this Lady you are fo tender of, pray?

Oli. She's *Freeman*'s Wife, by all the Ties of Love.

Sir Phil. Ties of Love——Hark ye ! Has the Parfon ty'd em? Love makes none but running Knots, and a Man may flip thofe at Pleafure ; but the Parfon's Noofe is as fure as the Hangman's ; nothing but the Grave unties it.——Now if you have him in that String, Madam, you are on the right Side of the Hedge, and I muft look out for another Son-in-law—Otherwife, you muft look fharp for another Hufband—that's all.

Lou. By my Country's Cuftom 'tis I claim him. I can have no other Hufband ; For all our Vows are regifter'd in Heaven.

Sir Phil. Humph ! that's a long Way off, and very few Lawyers go that Circuit. I doubt you'll lofe your Caufe for want of Evidence too.

Oli. No, Sir, fhe has a living Witnefs of his Guilt. A Boy, the very Picture of the Villain.

Lou. A Pledge of Love and everlafting Faith.

Oli. Can you defend his Treachery, Sir?

Sir Phil. Can you defend her Folly ? Treachery quotha ! He's a Traytor who weakens his King, not he who adds to the Number of his Subjects.——You fay, you claim him by your Country's Cuftom, pray what Country is that, Madam ?

Lou. Holland, Sir.

Sir Phil. Odfo ! *Holland* ; why their High Mightineffes ought to fettle a Penfion upon you. I wifh you much Joy of your Son, Madam. I warrant him a Hero, or a Politician. Every *Englifhman*'s Son, merrily begot, proves a great Man. Fools and Cowards are the Product of our wedding Sheets. I wifh he had laid fuch a Foundation in my Family, before the Lawfulnefs of the Pleafure fpoils the Breed.

Oli. Are thefe fit Speeches for a Daughter's Ear ? And this the Language of a virtuous Parent !

Sir Phil. The Virtue of a Parent confifts in Intereft and Cunning now-a-Days, as your Sex's Modefty does in Pride and Affectation.

Oli. Monftrous . Precepts !

The ARTIFICE.

Sir Phil. I suppose, Madam, you had nothing but Mr. *Freeman's* bare Word?

Lou. Words of the most sacred Form! Vows of eternal Faith! Eternal Constancy!

Sir Phil. But how the Devil could you expect Performance? Can any Man promise for Futurity? You should have got him into Bonds. Hereafter let me advise you: Do nothing till you have 'em under Black and White.— Then, if they fly the Parson, catch 'em with the Proctor.

Lou. Unmannerly Advice; but I was told before I came, what small Regard you paid to Justice——It is in you, Madam, that all my Hopes are center'd.

Oli. Depend on me, in all I can.

Sir Phil. No whispering in my House; no caballing; no underhand Dealing.——Look ye, Madam, the Man's dispos'd of; but if you will let me know whereabouts your Fortune may be, I'll do my Endeavour to get you a Husband—I will, Faith.

Lou. Since injur'd Virtue is become your Sport,
And you, instead of pitying, mock my Sorrow,
I'll try all Arts that may his Soul subdue;
But if I fail his Passion to renew,
The Traytor dies, to be revenged on you. [*Exit.*]

Oli. Why will you raise her Indignation thus?
Do you not dread the Consequence?
Base as he is, will you not guard his Life?
O! call her back, and calm her Passion;
If you prevent not, you encourage Murder.

Sir Phil. No, no, the Threats of your Sex, like Courtiers Promises, vanish into nothing. Passion has left the weeping Corner, and now it blusters like the North Wind, that's all. I wonder who let this Woman in. I shall examine that Point with my Servants. [*Aside.*

Oli. Are you a Man yet void of all Humanity?

Sir Phil. If your Mother were alive, she'd tell you: How dare you call me Father, and question my Manhood? What would you make your Mother, hussey? ha!

Oli. Oh do not name my Mother! Were she alive, you would not treat me thus. Remember your Promise to Sir *John*

Sir Phil. But when I made that Promise, he was Heir Apparent to four thousand Pounds a Year. and nobody dreamt

The ARTIFICE.

dreamt of his being difinherited.—Zounds, do you think I'll throw away my Money upon your Inclination, Miftrefs? No, mark me, Were thy Mother here all in her Bloom of Beauty; here, here, upon her Knees before me, I would not break my Word to *Freeman*; that is to fay, whilft he is Mafter of his Father's Eftate; therefore urge me no more, but prepare to be his Wife to morrow. D'ye hear? [*Exit.*

Oli. To morrow! fhort Warning! yet fhort as 'tis, I fhall have Time for Refolution; and you fhall find it, Father, as unalterable as your own.

If where I've fix'd my Love, *I muft not wed,*
I'll chufe a Coffin *for my* bridal Bed. · [*Exit.*

SCENE Watchit's *Houfe.*
Mrs. Watchit *fola.*

Since my Hufband refolves to immure me, I'm glad my Jayl is fo luckily fituated. Here I may hope for fome Confolation: The agreeable Addrefs of *Freeman* charms me; my Hufband's Jealoufy provokes me, and the Conveniency of that dear Door is fo irrefiftable, that if I fhould not be able to withftand Temptation, my Hufband may take it for his Pains: Befides, as the Poet fays,

One had as good commit the Fault,
As always to be guilty thought.

There's fome Pleafure in reflecting upon paft Delights: and Confinement will fit more eafy, when one knows one deferves it; but to be fhut up for nothing, is not to be borne.

· *Enter* Lucy.

Well, *Lucy* have you given the Signal?

Lucy There was no need of the Signal, Madam: I found Mr. *Freeman* in my Chamber, waiting the happy Minute. Oh! where thefe Men but half fo eager after Poffeffion!—But then, the Park, the Play, the Bottle, nay an Afternoon's Nap, fhall have important Bufinefs in it. ——But here he is, Madam.

Enter Ned Freeman, *running into her Arms.*

Ned. My Charmer! I have ftood Centinel at my Window thefe two Hours, to watch your old Jaylor out; and the Moment I faw him hobble over the Channel, I flew to the kind Door, impatient to be let into Paradife. Mrs.

The ARTIFICE.

Mrs. *Wat.* The impatient Lover, at the Beginning of an Amour, commonly proves the moſt indolent after Poſſeſſion, they ſay.

Ned. That, Madam, in a great meaſure, depends upon the Wit and Temper of the Lady ; after Enjoyment, Love grows nice ; Beauty kindles up the Flame : Yet there is more required to keep that Flame alive : But you may boaſt your Sex's whole Perfection : He who puts on your Chains, muſt be your Slave for ever. Where Souls ſympathize, the Bodies fear no Separation. When I but kiſs thee (*embracing her*) my Heart flutters at my Lips, as if 'twould tell you every Thought within.

Mrs. *Wat.* Bleſs me, what do you mean ? I doubt you have naughty Thoughts !—Give me the Cards—Come, I muſt have my Revenge.

Ned. That you ſhall, with all my Soul, inſtantly.

Mrs. *Wat.* Be quiet then, and take the Cards.

Ned. The Cards ! No, no, my Angel, I ſhall beat you at Cards ; there is a ſweeter Game for your Revenge.

Mrs. *Wat.* Pith ! what Game?—Lud !— you ſmother one. Suppoſe any of the Servants ſhould be upon the Stairs ?——*Lucy !*

Lucy. (*Aſide.*) Humph ! I underſtand her. I'll take Care of that, Madam. [*Exit.*

Ned. You ſee, my Life, Mrs. *Lucy* knows her Buſineſs : Why ſhould we neglect *ours ?*

Mrs. *Wat.* Buſineſs ! what Buſineſs ? Oh Lud ! what would you have me do ? [*Struggling a little.*

Ned. Make me the happieſt of Mankind. A thouſand Loves are dancing in your Eyes. Your balmy Lips and heaving Breaſts invite me to the Banquet.

Mrs. *Wat.* Don't talk to me thus, you inſinuating Devil, you !—Let me go !—Oh gad ! I a'nt able to ſtruggle any longer?——

Ned. Why will you ſtruggle at all ! Why deſtroy that Pleaſure which your Conſent ſo infinitely would raiſe ? Come, lead me to my Bliſs, where, folded in each other's cloſe Embraces, we'll bid Defiance to a Huſband's Frown, and kiſs, and laugh at all his jealous Folly.

Mrs. *Wat.* O Gad !—O, O Lud !—I have not Breath to anſwer————O, O ! I muſt not—dare not—will not — O Lud !—I have ſuch a Swimming in my Head !—

Let

The ARTIFICE.

Let me go! —Tho' if you do, I am fure I fhall fall down.
[*Sinks into his Arms.*
Ned. O my yielding Dear!—Where the Duce fhall I find the Bed-Chamber?
Mrs. *Wat.* 'Tis the next Room——Ha! What have I faid? Did you name the Bed-Chamber? Oh Gad! I won't go into the Bed-Chamber.
Ned. No, no, no, my Dear, I would not offer to injure your Modefty with fuch a Thought for the World. Go into the Bed-Chamber! No, no, I'll carry thee thither. [*Takes her in his Arms.*
Mrs. *Wat.* Nay, how can you be fo rude? Lord, whither are you a going? I fwear I have a good Mind to cry out. [Lucy *fhrieks without.*
Ned. Ha! What Shriek is that?
Mrs. *Wat.* 'Tis *Lucy's* Voice! Set me down! my Hufband is moft certainly return'd. What fhall I do? O Invention! O Invention! [*Paufes.*
Ned. Pox take him for an unmannerly Churl, to make a Gentleman rife from Table before he has tafted the firft Difh; and with fuch an Appetite too!
Mrs. *Wat.* Oh gad! don't loiter here; but fly, fly, Sir!
Ned. But whither, Madam, whither? Which way can I get up Stairs, without meeting him full in the Teeth? Except you have any back-way.
Mrs. *Wat.* I'll venture; (for it is impoffible for him to get out.) Here, here, Sir, ftep behind this Screen, and ftir not for your Life, 'til I give you Notice.
[Ned *goes behind the Screen.*
Enter Watchit *and* Lucy.
Wat. What the Devil did you fhriek out for? To give Warning, Mrs. *Screech-Owl?*
Lucy. Warning! of what, I wonder? Who could you expect to catch, that you came creeping up in this Manner, to fright a-body out of one's Wits? You fuffer nothing to come near my Lady but Flies, that I know of.
Mrs. *Wat.* (*Throwing herfelf upon the Floor.*) Oh, Mifery!——Oh, oh, oh!——
Wat. Nothing but Flies! why Flies breed Maggots, Huffey.
Mrs. *Wat.* Oh undone! Undone for ever!
Lucy. Oh my poor Lady on the Floor! Help, Sir, help.

The ARTIFICE.

help.——Where have you put the Gentleman, Madam? [*Aside to Mrs.* Wat.

Mrs. Wat. Behind the Screen, (*Aside.*) Oh, oh!

Wat. Pud, What is the Matter, *Pud?*

Mrs. Wat. I fear I have broke my Leg, *Mumps.*

Wat. Heaven forbid!——Though if she has, there will be one Advantage in't; she won't teize me to go abroad these two Months. (*Aside.*)—Let me see; where abouts hast thou hurt thy pretty Leg?

Mrs. Wat. Just in my Instep, *Mumps!*—Oh, oh!

Wat. Lucy! Where are you, Huffey! help me to set your Mistress in a Chair. How cameft thou to fall, *Pudsey*. [*They lift her into a Chair.*

Mrs. Wat. Why, hearing her shriek, I ran hastily to see what was the Matter; and my Heel happening to catch in my Hoop, down I came, with my Foot double under me.——Oh dear *Mumps!* you hurt me terribly! Pray lead me to my Bed, that I may lie down 'till a Surgeon can be sent for.

Ned. (*Peeping.*) Well propos'd.

Wat. No, no, let me rub it a little; I don't find it is broke: One must not make Surgeon's Work of every little Accident. It is not broke, *Pudsey*, that's certain.

Lucy. I wish your Neck had been broke, when you came Home. [*Aside.*

Wat. It may be sprain'd, perhaps. I have some camphorated Spirits of Wine in the Corner-Cupboard, behind that Screen. I'll fetch it, and bathe it with some of that. It is exceeding good for a Sprain.

Ned. (*Peeping*) So! I find a Law-suit commenced already.

Mrs. Wat. If he comes near the Screen, I'm undone. [*Aside*

Lucy. What, in the Name of *Jupiter*, will become of the Gentleman?

Mrs. Wat. Oh dear, dear, *Mumps!* do not leave me. Give *Lucy* the Key; let her fetch it. [*Catches hold of him.*

Lucy. Ay, ay, Sir, give me the Key; and do you keep rubbing, that the Blood may circulate.

Ned. (*Peeping.*) Well said, Mrs. *Abigail.*

Mrs. Wat. Ay, do, dear *Mumpsy!* Methinks there's a kind of Ease whilst you are rubbing it, Oh, oh!

Wat. (*Rising.*) No, no, she can't find it; she'll fling down some of the Bottles; that's all the Good she'll do.

Mrs.

Mrs. *Wat.* Oh, I shall swoon, if you stir, *Mumps!*—— I shall, I shall! [*Catches hold of him.*

Wat. Well, well! I won't go!—You Women are so impatient! Here, *Lucy*, take the Key. It is in a chrystal Bottle. Don't you do Mischief now, amongst the rest of the Spirits.

Ned. (*Peeping.*) I wish I were a Spirit, to go out unseen.—— *Mrs.* Watchit *beckons* Ned *to go off, whilst old* Watchit *is rubbing her Foot.*

Lucy. She beckons you to go out, Sir.

Ned. I understand her. But if the old Fellow should look up?

Lucy. No, no, never fear; I'll help to screen you from his Sight. (*Runs, and flaps herself down by* Watchit.) Here, here, Sir, here's the Bottle. I'm sure 'tis the right.

Wat. What is the Devil in the Wench! have you a Mind to lame me, Huffey? Why don't you pull out the Cork? [Ned *advances, but as* Watchit *looks up, retires.*

Mrs. *Wat.* Hang the Cork—Rub, rub, rub, dear *Mumps.*

Lucy. (*Beckons* Ned.) Now, now, now.

Wat. What's now, now! Ha!

Lucy. Why, now the Cork's out! Lord, you don't mind my Mistress's Foot?

Mrs. *Wat.* (*Aside.*) Ah! he will catch him, that's certain.——I have such a Terror upon me, that I'm disarm'd of all Excuses.

Wat. Where lies thy Pain, *Pud?*

Mrs. *Wat.* Just where you are.

Lucy. That I dare swear. (*Aside.*)—Bless me, Sir, how my Lady's Ancle swells?

Wat. Your Nose swells, don't it? What do you fright your Mistress for, Huffey? I see no Swelling.

Lucy. I don't know how he should. [*Aside.*

Ned. (*Aside.*) She might have laid a Foundation for a Swelling, if you had been civil enough to have stay'd away half an Hour longer.

[*Advancing to the Middle of the Stage.*

Wat. Come, try to stand upon't, *Pudsey.*

Mrs. *Wat.* (*Shrieking.*) Ah! my dear, dear Life and Soul! I cannot bear it! [*As* Watchit *is raising her up, she throws her Arms about his Neck, to prevent his seeing* Ned.

Wat. (*Struggling.*) What, will you smother me? How now! Who have we here? *Ned.*

The ARTIFICE.

Ned. So! he has me!—I admire you leave your Doors open, Sir, and not a Servant in the Way to take a Meſſage.

Wat. Had you any to ſend up, Sir? I don't like a Man that comes up to my Noſe; then tells me, *I admire you leave your Doors open.*—Zounds, was there not a Knocker to the Door?

Ned. I did knock, Sir; but my Buſineſs would not give me Leave to wait.

Wat. Buſineſs! What, to rob my Houſe? or lie with my Wife, I warrant, had I been out of the Way. (*Aſide.*) I pray you, ſweet Sir, what may your haſty Buſineſs be?

Ned. What, in the Name of *Jupiter*, ſhall I pretend? [*Aſide.*

Mrs. *Wat.* (*Aſide to* Lucy.) Oh Lud! What Tale can he invent? I tremble every Joint of me.

Lucy. (*Aſide to Mrs.* Wat.) If he proves of the *Iriſh* Breed, all may go well yet.

Wat. I am afraid, Sir, you have forgot your Buſineſs— A clean-limb'd young Raſcal, this;——and has a damn'd Cuckold-making Air: Zounds, how my Wife eyes him! [*Aſide.*

Ned. I have it; Impudence protect me. (*Aſide.*) The Affair I come upon, Sir, requires your private Ear.

Wat. Sir, I keep my private Ears, for my publick Friends. I have ſurvey'd you round, and round; and, to be plain, I don't like your Phiz, and, may be, I ſhall like your Buſineſs worſe. Therefore, will hear, whether it be worth going out of the Room for, or not.

Ned. I can eaſily pardon your Diſlike to my Face; but I muſt inſiſt upon ſpeaking with you alone.

Wat. I inſiſt upon your ſpeaking here, Sir—The Dog will cut my Throat, perhaps. [*Aſide.*

Mrs. *Wat.* I'm in Pain for the Event. [*Aſide to* Lucy.

Lucy. The Gentleman promiſes well; have Courage, Madam. [*Aſide to Mrs.* Wat.

Ned. But your Reputation is concern'd, Sir.

Wat. My Reputation does not depend upon your Tongue, Sir; and I'll not ſtir a Foot.

Ned. But have you no Regard to your Lady, Sir? for I perceive this is your Wife.

Wat. And what of that, Sir? What have you to ſay againſt my Wife? Out with it. *Ned*

Ned. I have nothing to fay, Sir, againſt your Wife.
Wat. 'S'death, Sir! What is your Buſineſs? What have you to fay? Speak, Sir;——Or, or——
Ned. Nay! if I muſt ſpeak here! Then know, Sir, I am employ'd by Sir *Andrew Gudgeon.*
Wat. Gudgeon! I doubt, Friend, you have Miſtaken your Fiſh; for I know no man of that Name.
Ned. Hark ye, Sir, a Word. (*Speaks in his Ear.*) You know his Wife, I ſuppoſe, if you don't know him.
Wat. Wife! what Wife? Ad's Heart! ſpeak out, and keep farther off——This Dog is a Pick-pocket, for aught I know. [*Aſide.*
Ned. Why then, I muſt tell you, Sir, that Sir *Andrew* will have Satisfaction, before he and you have done.
Wat. Satisfaction! for what, Sir?
Ned. For lying with his Wife, Sir, ſince you will have it out.
Mrs. *Wat.* Adultery! Very fine, truly!
Lucy. Bleſs me! who could have thought that my Lady had not been ſufficient for you, Sir?
Wat. Zounds! what do you mean, Sir? Do you think to make a *Gudgeon* of me?
Ned. Nor you muſt not think to make a Cuckold of Sir *Andrew*, without making him Satisfaction, Sir. I don't value your high Words, nor your big Looks. I am not to be frightened out of my Buſineſs, Sir. I am a Proctor in the Biſhop's Court, and employed by Sir *Andrew*, to exhibit a Libel againſt you for Incontinency.
Wat. Oh Lord! Oh Lord! I incontinent! I'll be judg'd by my own Wife.—*Pud!*—come hither, *Pud*—ſpeak the Truth, and no more but the Truth——Didſt thou ever find me a Man given that Way?
Mrs. *Wat.* I wonder you have the Aſſurance to look me in the Face! I find your Suſpicions of my Virtue, proceeded from the Weakneſs of your own——Ungrateful Man! Have I kifs'd and hugg'd you in my Arms for this?
[*Burſts ſeemingly into Tears.*
Lucy. Ah! Did ever I think this of you, Sir? You, who have ſuch a tender, fond, loving, lovely Wife of your own! I can't help weeping to ſee my poor Lady ſo ill treated.
Wat. Was ever innocent man thus baited?
Mrs.

The ARTIFICE.

Mrs. *Wat.* Ah, *Mumps!* I never thought you were such a Hypocrite———How often have you told me, what a crying fin Adultery is! And———

Wat. This muft be a Trick to abufe me !———Get out of my Houfe, Sir. Zounds, get out of my Houfe !

Ned. Get out of your Houfe ! Get ready your Bail, Sir. The Allegations againft you are fo plain, and pofitive, you'll fcarce have an evafive Anfwer, or to crofs-examine Witneffes upon new Interrogatories, Sir,———Mind that.

Wat. You and your Interrogatories had beft March off, Sir, without any more to do, or———

Mrs. *Wat.* If I might advife you, make up this Matter, and don't expofe yourfelf.

Wat. Why *Pud!* do you think I'm guilty, *Pud?* Oh Lud ! oh Lud ! oh Lud !

Mrs. *Wat.* Why, can you have the Affurance to deny it, after what the Gentleman has faid.

Ned. His denying it, Madam, will fignify nothing ; we have unqueftionable Proofs ; Caufes of this Nature never come into our Court, without Demonftration———He muft undergo the Sentence ufual in thefe Cafes—Which is, to ftand in a white Sheet, and humbly confefs his Faults before the Congregation. Befides which (*turning to him*) you will be compelled to pay Cofts and Damages.—And if you are found guilty of Contumacy, as your prefent Behaviour feems to promife, we fhall get you excommunicated.

Mrs. *Wat.* Excellent Fellow !   [*Afide.*

Ned. Upon which comes out the Writ *Excommunicato Capiendi :* That, whips you up in an inftant ; carries you to the next Jail, and delivers you into *Salvo Cuftodio* without Bail, or Mainprize.

Wat. What hoa ! within there ? Where are all my Rafcals ? Huffey, go look 'em, (*pufhes* Lucy) and bid 'em call a Conftable. I'll Bail and Mainprize you, I warrant you, Sirrah : Why don't you go ?   [*To* Lucy.

Lucy. I'll not ftir a ftep : You wicked Man, you !—

Ned. A Conftable !—that may not be fo well. (*Afide.*) I'm not afraid of a Conftable, Sir. Send for him, and welcome ; but the leaft Noife you make in this Affair, the better, Sir *Nicholas!*

Mrs. *Wat.* Sir *Nicholas!* here muft be fome Miftake in this ; my Hufband's Name is not *Nicholas,* Sir !

Ned.

The ARTIFICE.

Ned. What fay you, Madam? Is not this Sir *Nicholas Widgeon*?

Wat. No, nor *Woodcock* neither, as you fhall find, Sir!

Ned. Blefs me! What have I been faying all this while? I afk your Pardon, Sir, with all my Heart. How the Vengeance could I make fuch a Blunder? I was directed next Door to the *Sun*.

Lucy. If I miftake not, Sir *Nicholas* lives at the next Houfe but one. I am glad to find it a Miftake, Sir, and that you are not guilty of wronging fo good a Woman, as my Lady is.

Wat. It is a very pretty Miftake tho', to come into a Man's Houfe, and abufe, and threaten him with white Sheets, Penance, and the Devil; and then, *I afk your Pardon, Sir*. A Pox on you, and your Pardon too, Sir.

Ned. Nay, you have Reafon to be angry, I own, Sir— and I wifh I knew how to make you fome Satisfaction.— Madam, can you forgive me? Upon Honour, I'm in fuch Confufion!

Mrs. *Wat.* I believe him. (*Afide.*) The Pleafure of finding my Hufband innocent, inclines me the more eafily to pardon your Miftake, Sir.

Ned. I proteft, Sir, I am very much out of Countenance!

Wat. I wifh you were out of my Houfe, Sir——

Ned. If you fhould ever have any Bufinefs in *Doctors Commons*, Sir, I affure you, no Body fhall be——

Wat. I affure you, Sir, that nothing can oblige me more, than to fee your Backfide; and fo, fweet Mr. *Proctor*, with your *Excommunicato Capiendi*, I am your very humble Servant.

Ned. Sir, I am yours entirely. [*Exit.*

Mrs. *Wat.* Charming Fellow! [*Afide.*

Wat. Pox take him, he has given me the Palpitation of the Heart, which I fhan't get rid of thefe two Hours—— Why, what a Multitude of Troubles will this poor Sir *Nicholas* be in now? His *fweet Meat will have four Sauce*. Odd, there's a pretty Penny to be made of thefe Cuckold-making Dogs, if one could but catch 'em napping. [*Afide.*

Mrs. *Wat.* (*Afide.*) Well, this is a Jewel of a Man, *Lucy*.

Lucy. Ay, Madam, this Man has a Genius, and deferves a Woman. [*Afide to her.*

Wat.

Wat. I can't get this Fellow's Miſtake out of my Head; it is a curſed odd one, methinks. [*Aſide.*

Lucy. How does your Foot do, Madam?

Mrs. *Wat.* Pretty well, I think, *Lucy:* Your Hand has done me exceeding Service, *Mumps*——

Wat. Ay, ay, Chick, ev'ry one don't know the Virtue of a warm Hand——I don't like this ſudden Cure.--To roar out, but now when I touch'd it; and now to walk about, as if nothing ail'd her. [*Aſide.*

Lucy. If you were a Surgeon, Sir, and could effect Cures ſo ſoon, you'd grow rich apace.

Wat. (*Aſide.*) I wiſh you and your Miſtreſs have not all your——I might not always be ſo lucky.

Lucy. To prevent your being made a Cuckold, I grant you. [*Aſide.*

Wat. I took this, juſt in the Nick.

Lucy. Or ſhe had nick'd you. [*Aſide.*

Wat. That is to ſay, juſt as 'twas done.

Lucy. Nay, before it was done; to my Lady's Sorrow. [*Aſide.*

Mrs. *Wat.* Well, *Mumps*, I muſt remind you of your Promiſe: I muſt go out to Day.

Wat. Fy, fy, you would not walk upon your Foot ſo ſoon; would you?

Mrs. *Wat.* Pho! I tell you my Foot is well: Beſides, I can take a Chair.

Wat. Prithee, what Buſineſs haſt thou abroad, Wife?

Mrs. *Wat.* Why, I want to go to Chapel, in the firſt Place.

Wat. The Saints will hear you as well, from your Cloſet.

Mrs. *Wat.* I can't pray in my Cloſet.

Wat. Nor any where elſe, I believe. [*Aſide.*

Mrs. *Wat.* Beſides, here are Prieſts in *London*.

Wat. Ay! Enough to corrupt the whole Nation——

Mrs. *Wat.* And it is a mortal Sin not to confeſs, when 'tis in one's Power to do it.

Wat. Pray, what Sins have you committed that you are in ſuch haſte to unburthen?

Mrs. *Wat.* You are not qualify'd to know.

Wat. Well, ſince your Conſcience accuſes you, you ſhall have a Prieſt. I'll ſend to the What-d'ye-call 'em Ambaſſador's, for one of his; who ſhall take your Confeſſion in your Clofet; but I'll ſtand at the Door: For I would not truſt one of theſe Pardon felling Rogues: They have ſuch convincing Arguments for Cuckoldom.

Mrs. Wat. Why, do you think, Sir, that I'll be ſhut up thus, for ever?

Wat. Nay, if you begin to exalt your Voice, then I muſt tell you, it is my Pleaſure to have it ſo. Let that ſuffice.

Mrs. Wat. No, that will not ſuffice; for it's againſt my Inclination.

Wat. Which is not to be ſuffic'd; for you are never ſatisfy'd with gadding; if we Huſbands ſhould always follow our Wives Inclinations, we ſhould be in a fine Condition.

Lucy. I am ſure you have all Conditions, but good ones.
[*Aſide.*

Mrs. Wat. Is this your matrimonial Vow! to impriſon me; you that wou'd cheriſh, love, and worſhip me!

Wat. So I do, don't I, my dear Fleſh and Blood? Thou art my Goddeſs, and I adore thee; and cannot ſuffer thee out of my Sight.

Lucy. If you two are one Fleſh, how come you to have ſuch different Minds, pray, Sir?

Wat. Becauſe the Mind has nothing to do with the Fleſh.

Mrs. Wat. That's your Miſtake, Sir; the Body is govern'd by the Mind. So much Philoſophy I know.

Wat. Yes, yes; I believe you underſtand natural Philoſophy very well, Wife: I doubt the Fleſh has got the better of the Spirit in you.—Look ye, Madam! Every Man's Wife is his Vineyard; you are mine, therefore I wall you in. Ads-budikins, ne'er a Coxcomb in the Kingdom ſhall plant ſo much as a Primroſe in my Ground.

Mrs. Wat. I am ſure, your Management will produce nothing but Thorns.

Wat. Nay, ev'ry Wife is a Thorn in her Huſband's Side: Your whole Sex is a kind of Sweet-brier, and he who meddles with it, is ſure to prick his Fingers.

Lucy. That is, when you handle us too roughly.——

Mrs. Wat. You are a kind of Rue; neither good for Smell nor Taſte.

Wat. But very wholeſome, Wife.——

Mrs. Wat. Ay, ſo they ſay of all Bitters; yet I wou'd not be oblig'd to feed upon Gentian and Wormwood.

Wat.

The ARTIFICE.

Wat. No, you like Sweet-meats better.

Mrs. *Wat.* Confinement wou'd cloy me with them too.

Wat. Or you are no Woman.——

Mrs. *Wat.* But what do's this fignify to our Marriage-Articles? You know the Forfeiture, if you deny me ghoftly Aid.

Wat. A thoufand Pounds,——You bit me there.—— Have a care I don't bite you again. (*Afide.*)——Well, well, you fhall have this ghoftly Aid——But do you confider, you never had the Small-Pox, and it never was fo mortal as now; therefore it is not convenient you fhou'd go abroad; indeed it is not, *Pudfey*——'Tis out of pure Love to thee, Faith, my Dear; for the Small-Pox would fpoil that pretty Face: It wou'd truly, *Pudfey*. Prithee now, believe thine own *Mumps*.——

Mrs. *Wat.* Away!——I hate your wheedling. Thofe who languifh under the Plague, need not fear the Small-Pox. *Exit with* Lucy.

Wat. Humph! Say you fo? I fhall indeed be a Plague to you, if I catch you tardy, Gentlewoman. Odd, I can't put this Foot of hers out of my Head; it looks like an Excufe to conceal fome fecret Failing, and puts me in mind of a youthful Stratagem of my own. Having been a little familiar with one of my Mother's Maids, and like to have been caught, I cut my Finger, and pretended I came for a Rag to bind it up.——This Fellow with his *Excommunicato Capiendi* too, may have more in't than I can fee through: I refolve to examine my Servants, if ever they faw him before; but in perfonating this Prieft, I fhall know all.

Lucy *liftening.*

Lucy. Shall you fo?

Wat. I have befpoke a Difguife; and am refolv'd to take her Confeffion myfelf.

Lucy. Indeed!——My Lady fhall know your Contrivance; and if fhe does not fit you for your Curiofity, I am miftaken, old Gentleman. [*Exit.*

Wat. If fhe has Cuckolded me, tho' but in Thought, I will injoin her fuch a Penance!

Zoons! I'll fo fwinge, *fo* mortify *the Jade,*
That fhe fhall ne'er forget *my* ghoftly Aid.

ACT III.

SCENE *Widow* Heedlefs's *Houfe. She wiping down the Duft with her Handkerchief.*

Enter Judith.

Wid. JUDITH! What haft thou been doing all this Morning, that my Dreffing-Room is in this pickle?

Jud. Pickle!

Wid. Ay, pickle, Sauce-box; why doft thou eccho me?

Jud. Eccho you!

Wid. Again!——Indeed I fhall flap your Chaps if you don't learn to leave off repeating my Words after me.

Jud. After you!——Marry, I——

Wid. (*Gives her a Box o' the Ear.*) You will do it then.

Jud. Will do what? Chem zhour, chem can do nothing to pleafe you! Chem clean'd it as it had bin vor mine Life; zo I dud.

Wid. Life! what is thy Life, Muck-worm, to a clean Room? Doft thou imagine Rooms lie thus at Court? Ha, Slattern?

Jud. They can't lie better, I think.

Wid. Think! why doft thou think, Animal? What haft thou to do with Thought? Mind thy own Bufinefs, and never puzzle thy Noddle with Thought.

Enter Sir Philip *and* Tally.

Blefs me! my Lord, and Sir *Philip!*—I am afham'd to be caught in this Diforder!

Sir *Phil.* My Lord and I have been fetching a Walk, and I could not perfuade his Lordfhip to pafs by your Door, Coufin, without calling. You are his North, and he is embark'd in the Cock-boat of Love, and is conftantly pointing this way.

Wid. You are very pleafant this Morning, Sir *Philip.* But-

Tally. I afk your Pardon, Madam; but finding your Door open, and no-body in the Way, the Knight undertook to be Mafter of the Ceremonies, as well as to anfwer the Reproaches I might reafonably expect from you, for this Liberty——

Wid. Oh, good my Lord, no Apology! That ought to be

be done by me for the Diforder your Lordfhip finds me in.——Go, Beefom, and look for your Fellow Puzzles, and afk 'em, Why they leave my Doors open? I fhall be robb'd one of thefe Days.——Sure, never any body was fatigu'd with Servants as I am. Did you ever vifit a Lady in a Stable before, my Lord? Oh gad, I fhall be ftuck, mir'd, and laid faft, and forc'd to be dug out like a Potatoe.

[*Holds up her Coats and walks cautioufly.*

Tally. A Stable, Madam! I proteft I think your Houfe is as much in Order, as any Lady's in *London*.

Sir *Phil.* Ay, my Lord, there are few of the Quality fuch Houfewives, as my Coufin. If it be your Lordfhip's good Fortune to marry her, fhe'll fet the Ladies at Court a Pattern.

Wid. Fy, Sir *Philip!* This to my Face! it looks like Flattery.

Tally. What would be Flattery to another, is but doing you Juftice, Madam.——

Wid. Women have no Defence againft the fine Things you well-bred Men fay. To raife our Vanity, and make us have a good Opinion of ourfelves, you are fure, is one way to be well in our Efteem.

Tally. I fhould think myfelf the happieft Man living, if I cou'd perceive I had the leaft fhare in yours, Madam.

Sir *Phil.* His Lordfhip complains, Coufin, that you are inexorable.——Hark ye, one Word with you.——Don't overftand your Market. A Man of Quality is not to be caught every Day.

Fain. (*Liftening.*) There's an old Rogue now. [*Afide.*

Wid. Wou'd you have me marry a Man as foon as he afks me the Queftion, Sir *Philip?* I think, to have an Amour with a Perfon of Rank known and talk'd of, is one of the greateft Inducements to Matrimony; efpecially if it gives the Reft of my Sex Pain.

Fain. (*Afide.*) Right Woman, on my Confcience!

Wid. My Lord! won't your Lordfhip pleafe to reft yourfelf?

Tally. My Reft depends upon your Ladyfhip.

Fain. (*Afide.*) Who fhall never be a Refting-Place for you to Tally on.

Wid. I'm certain, it is not in my Power to give your Lordfhip Pain.

Fain.

Fain. So—Another Trap! but I'll fpoil the Dialogue.
Enter Fainwell.
Tally. More than your whole Sex.
Wid. Your Lorſhip will make me vain.
Sir *Phil.* If there could be any Addition to the Vanity that thou haſt already.   *[Aſide.*
Wid. Oh, *Jeffery!*———Well, have ycu delivered all my Meſſages?
Fain. By Mefs, I think fo.
Wid. Ha!   *[Looking wiſtful at him.*
Fain. How many dud you gi' me, Forſooth?
Wid. Madam——Oh the Clodhopper!   *[Aſide.*
Fain. Mrs. What-ni-cull-um, at the *Hog's-Head*, was gone out, chu'd feem.
Wid. Madam! Blockhead. *[Gives him a Box on the Ear.*
Sir *Phil.* Ha, ha, ha! this is like to be a diverting Scene.
Wid. How often muſt I inſtruct you to behave yourſelf before Company? Will you never learn Manners, Booby?
Fain. No I ſhan't, an you go on at thik fame flip-flap Rate.——Nouns, an thick be *London* Breeding, fend me into the Country agen, I fay.
Tally. If I were thy Lady, Fellow, thou ſhould'ſt have thy Wiſh.
Fain. Say you fo? Ay! But *curſt Cows have ſhort Horns.* we fay in our Country,—I ſhall never be your Servant, I hope!
Wid. How now, Sauce-box! do you know who you talk to?
Fain. Yes, I do—better than you think for, mehap.
Tally. (*Aſide.*) How's that? S'death if this Bumkinly Dog ſhould know me, he'll fpoil all.
Wid. I have a good Mind, Sirrah, to daſh your Teeth down your Throat.
Fain. So yow ma' an you wol. What does he meddle with me for, then? I dud not meddle wi' him; dud I?
Sir *Phil.* You'll have your Bones broke in *London*, Sirrah. I admire my Lord does not cane you, Scoundrel.
Tally. His being this Lady's Servant protects him.
Fain No, it is that protects yow; for an I had yow in my Country——
Tally. This Fellow and I muſt have a little Confabulation. I muſt ſtop his Mouth.

Wid.

The ARTIFICE. 321

Wid. Sirrah, no more of your Impudence; but give me an Account of the Bufinefs I fent you about. How does Lady *Lucy*, Lady *Lock-up*, Lady *Love-it*, Lady *Set-up*, Lady *Comely*, Lady *Revel*, Lady *Ramble*, Mrs. *Prim*, Mrs. *Prude*, Mrs. *Coftly*, and Mrs. *Travel?*

Fain. Nowns! her Tongue runs like the Mill at Vather's Orchard-end, that fcares Crows fro' the Cherry-tree.

Wid. Does it fo, Sirrah?

[*Runs to beat him, but* Tally *fteps in between.*

Tally. Hold, hold, dear Madam, let me intercede for Mr. *Jeffery* this once.

Fain. How civil the Dog is! [*Afide.*

Wid. Your Lordfhip commands me. Well, Mrs. *Fifk-out*, at the *Boar's-Head*, which you call the *Hog's-Head*, Clumfy! was gone out, you fay?

Fain. So fhe was.

Wid. How's that?

Tally. (*Afide to* Fainwell.) Madam?——*Jeffery*——Madam——You forget.

Fain. Madam——

Wid. Hoa! you have fqueez'd out Madam at laft.

Fain. Squeez'd——Od! would I had the fqueezing of you.

Wid. How, Sirah! you fqueeze me? My Lord! Sir *Philip!* Did you ever hear fuch a Varlet?

Tally. You fee, Madam, your Beauty reaches all Degrees. He fpeaks from his Heart, I dare fwear.

Sir *Phil.* You have him as you breed him.

Wid. Oh, that's barbarous, Sir *Philip*. You don't know the Pains I take with my clodpated Family.——Well!

[*Looking at* Fainwell.

Fain. Yes, they are well, Madam——And hope yow are well, Madam—And they'll all,—or fome of them, will come to fee yow, Madam——So they gi' their Loves——Loves? No, no,——So they gi' their Service to yow, Madam——An, an, an, an——So that's all, Madam——There's Madam enough for yow now, I think, if yow know when yow have enough.

Tally. Now *Jeffery* has done it. Ha, ha, ha!

Wid. I have been teaching him the diftinguifhing Rap, thefe three Days! and yet, I warrant, he'll knock with the

the sneaking Air of a Taylor. Let's hear how you perform? [*He knocks awkwardly.*
Wid. Execrable!——Didn't I tell you so?——There, Blockhead.—— [*She thunders at the Door.*
Fain. By'r Lady! that's enough to fright all the Dogs in Town.
Wid. In the Opinion of such a Puppy as you are—— Go, bid the Cook set on the Tea-kettle, and cut some Bread and Butter.——But d'ye hear? don't you bring it dangling in your Fist, as you did Yesterday, Sloven—— If you do, I shall throw it at your Head, Sir. Remember to bring me nothing without a Plate : D'ye hear?—You han't breakfasted, I hope, Sir *Philip?*
Sir *Phil.* Yes, long since.
Tally. So have I, Madam.
Sir *Phil. Jeffery's* talking of Dogs, puts me in Mind of a Message from my Daughter. She bid me tell you, she expects a Puppy : Has your Bitch litter'd yet, Cousin?
Wid. Not yet, Sir *Philip.* You never saw a poor Creature so big in your Life. *Jeffery,* fetch *Misha* hither. (Fainwell *going.*)——Hark-ye! Hark-ye!—Come back, (*He runs up to her Nose.*) What!—will you run your Nose into my Mouth? Where are your Manners, when you leave the Room?——Still that Scrape? I thought I had shew'd you to bend your Body only, and keep your Feet upon the Ground.
Fain. By'r Lady, you'll make an ambling Nag o'me by-and-by. [*Exit.*
Tally. (*Aside.*) Nothing but the twenty thousand Pounds could make Amends for thy Impertinence.—I admire you give yourself the Trouble of Country Servants, Madam.
Wid. I would not keep a Town Servant, my Lord, if they would live with me for nothing. Their whole Attention is Drunkenness and Pride. The dirtiest Trollup in the Town must have her Top-knot and Tickin-shoes. This City spoils all Servants. I took a *Welsh* Runt last Spring, whose Generation scarce ever knew the Use of Stockings : And——will you believe me, my Lord? She had not liv'd with me three Weeks, before she sew'd three Penny Canes round the Bottom of her Shift, instead of a Hoop-Petticoat.
Sir *Phil.* That was something better tha n a Wench at my

my Houfe, who difrob'd a Barrel, and let all the Ale about the Cellar. One of the Ends of the Hoop working out, difcover'd the Trick, and at the fame time flung down a Side-Board of Glaffes.——Ha, ha, ha!

Tally. Ha, ha, ha!

Wid. Ay, they do more Mifchief than their Necks are worth. If the Parliament don't lay a Tax upon their Pride, there will be no living. I wifh your Lordfhip would take it into Confideration.

Enter Fainwell.

Wid. Well!——Where's *Mifha?*

Fain. By Mefs, I can't bring her; not I.

Wid. How fo? Is fhe fo heavy?

Fain. No, fhe's not fo heavy: But I can't make her lie upon a Plate, for the Blood o'me, fo I can't.

Sir *Phil.* Ha, ha, ha! Ridiculous enough!——Ha, ha!

Wid. A Plate, Blockhead! a Plate! did you ever fee a Dog brought on a Plate, Clod-hopper? Did you?

[*Following him about.*

Sir *Phil.* Pure Innocence, Faith!

Fain. Nay, how do I know your *London* Vafhions?— You bad me but now, I am zure, to bring you naught without a Plate; fo you dud.

Wid. What?—Living Things?—Ha, did I fay Living Things?

Fain. Living Things! S'Blead, the Devil would not live wi'you——The Cobler wants Six-pence for mending your Clogs, *Judith* bod.me tell yow.

Wid. Thefe Wretches will diftract me!——Is that a Meffage to be delivered to me in Publick? Ha, Thick-fcull!—But fince you have no more Wit, let me fee what he has done for the Money——My Lord, you'll excufe this Piece of Oeconomy. [*Exit Fainwell.*

Tally. O! Madam——

Fainwell *returns with the Clogs upon a Plate.*

Wid. Did you ever fee the Fellow of him, Sir *Philip?* I proteft he puts me into an Agony! Why, you Thick-fcull'd Rafcal!——You unthinking Dolt!——You fenfe-lefs Ideot!——Was ever a Pair of dirty Clogs brought upon a Plate, Sirrah?—Ha!—Was there?—Was there? Was there? Hedge Hog? [*Follows him about and beats him,* Sir Philip *interpofing.*

Fain.

Fain. What d'ye ſtrick me vor?——The Clogs ar'n't Living Things too, are they?——By the Meſs, I'll take the Law of you, ſo I will, an you thraſh me about at thick ſame Rate. S'Blead, an yow were a Man, I'd dreſs your Jacket for yow.

Sir *Phil.* Fy, fy, Couſin, this is not like a fine Lady.

Wid. That's your Miſtake, Sir *Philip* ; my Lady *Flippant* beats her whole Family, from her Huſband to her Coachman.

Tally. (*Aſide.*) I ſhall teach you better Manners, if once I get you.

Wid. Out of my Sight, Sirrah !

Fain. Who the Murrain, cares to ſtay in it, I wonder? Ah ! *Jeffery* ! *Jeffery* ! thou art right enough ſerv'd !—— Why didſt thou leave thy Sweetheart, *Cicely*, to pine away like a Gooſe in a Pen?

Sir *Phil.* Why, then you are falſe-hearted, *Jeffery?*

Fain. I have been, Sir ; with Shame I confeſs it, or I had never come under Miſtreſs's Clutches.——But

May all falſe-hearted Men my Fortune have,
And who ſlights Woman, *be a* Woman's *Slave.*

I've ſomewhat to ſay to you, my Lord, when Time ſhall ſerve. [*As he goes out.*

Tally. I'll meet you in *Covent-Garden Piazza*, in Half an Hour. [*Aſide to* Fainwell.

Re-enter Fainwell.

Fain. Here's the Knight in Black to ſpeak wi'yow.—— Sir *Freeman*, I think they call him.

Wid. Sir *John Freeman*, you mean——Shew him up.

Sir *Phil.* Hold, hold, let me be gone firſt. I have ſome Reaſons why I don't care to ſee him.——I had ſome Buſineſs with you, Couſin, but I ſhall ſend to you.——Will you walk, my Lord? Or ſhall I leave your Lordſhip?

Tall. I'll wait on you, Sir *Philip.*——I take an unwilling Leave, Madam : But it may not be convenient to preſs upon your Buſineſs——I long to know what this Fellow has to ſay to me. (*Aſide.*)——Your moſt obedient humble Servant. [*Exit* Tally *and Sir* Philip.

Wid. I am your Lordſhip's——

Enter Sir John.

Sir *John.* I aſk your Pardon, Madam ; I fear my Viſit has robb'd you of better Company.

Wid.

The ARTIFICE.

Wid. Not at all, Sir *John :* Your Father-in-Law, that was to have been, is juft gone out ; he feem'd unwilling to meet you.

Sir *John.* Well he might, after his perfidious Ufage.

Wid. But is your Brother really to marry my Coufin *Olivia ?*

Sir *John.* I have Reafon to fear it ; but hope he will be difappointed. I receiv'd Inftructions from *Olivia* to wait on you, Madam, to afk a Favour of you.

Wid. She may command every Thing in my Power, Sir *John.* What is it?

Sir *John.* That you would give a Lady Entertainment in that Apartment which opens into the Back-ftreet.

Wid. What, is that the *Dutch* Lady, Sir *John?*

Sir *John.* The fame, Madam.

Wid. She's welcome. May her coming prove propitious!

Enter Judith.

Jud. Here's one Mr. *Freeman* to wait on you, he fays.

Sir *John.* My Brother ; what can he want ? Does he ufe to vifit you, Madam?

Wid. He never was here in his Life ! I can't imagine his Bufinefs !——Would you fee him?

Sir *John.* Yes, yes ; but not a Word of the Bufinefs I came about.

Wid. You don't think me fo indifcreet, I hope : Shew him up, *Judith.*

Enter Ned Freeman.

Ned. Madam, your Servant. Ha ! Brother ! I'm glad to find you in fuch good Company. My Brother *Jack's* a pretty Fellow, Madam.

Wid. So he is, indeed, Sir. He wants nothing but a Wife, in my Opinion.

Ned. (Afide.) Brother, I hope you conceive a Widow, when fhe makes fuch Wifhes in your Favour.——She has Twenty Thoufand Pounds.

Sir *John.* And what then, Sir?

Ned. What then, Sir ? Why, then he who marries her, will be worth Twenty Thoufand Pounds——That's all !

Sir *John.* I would advife you to marry her yourfelf.

Ned. I thank you, Sir ; but I am provided.

Sir *John.* So am I.

Ned. Why then I wifh you Joy, Brother, if you are fo

fure

fure of it.——Madam, I have a Meffage to you from Sir *Philip Moneylove*, who intended to have delivered it to you himfelf; but Company coming in, and being to meet a Lawyer at the *Rummer*, where I now left him, he was obliged to leave your Ladyfhip without telling you, that he came to know your Refolution about a Piece of Land that he mentioned to you fome Time ago. He would gladly buy it, or exchange with you for another; becaufe that Ground is contiguous to fome Part of his Eftate, which he is about to fettle upon his Daughter.

Wid. Pray, Sir, let my Coufin know, that I gave my Lawyer Orders to treat with him about that Matter.

Ned. Where does your Lawyer live, Madam.

Wid. At Number 2 in the *King*'s-Bench Walks in the *Temple*. Sir *Philip* knows him.

Ned. Very well, Madam.——Brother, where fhall I fee you in the Evening?

Sir *John.* I am engaged this Evening.

Ned. You'll make one in a Country-Dance to Morrow I hope? for that is to be my Wedding-Day————

Sir *John.* I hope to baulk you yet. (*Afide.*)——I can promife nothing for Futurity, Sir.

Ned. Humph! you can't!——what you pleafe, Sir.— Madam, your moft humble Servant.

Wid. How he triumphs!——How can you bear the Airs he gives himfelf, Sir *John?*

Sir *John.* To do him Juftice, Madam, I believe he knows nothing of my Pretenfions to *Olivia*. He was travelling, when firft I made my Addreffes; and fince his Return, we have not been fo well with one another, to communicate Things of this Nature.

Wid. I afk your Pardon, Sir *John*, for keeping you ftanding. Won't you pleafe to fit, Sir?

Sir *John.* Excufe me, dear Madam; I intend to take this Opportunity to fee *Olivia*, whilft her Jaylor's abroad, let the Confequence be what it will; and let her know, how much we are oblig'd to you, Madam.

Wid. My good Wifhes attend you both, Sir *John.* [*Ex.*

SCENE *changes to* Covent-Garden *Piazzas.*

Enter Fainwell, *folus.*

Fain. Ha! not here! fure he don't fufpect me; and apprehend

prehend a Duel might enfue; all my Meafures are broke, if he fhould——Ho! here he comes.

Enter Tally.

Tally. What can this Fellow have to fay to me, I wonder? If he has difcovered me, he wants a Bribe. But I hope it is not fo: for I fhou'd be loth to have a Secret of this Nature lie in the Breaft of fuch a Blunderer. (*Afide.*) ——Mr. *Jeffery*! I proteft I did not fee you.——Well, what can I ferve you in?

Fain. In nought, that I know of, Zir; but me-haps, I may zerve you in zomewhat, Zir;——my Lord I wou'd zay. I beg your Pardon, Zir; we dan't zee zuch vine Voke in our Country every Day—zo that I hope yow won't be angry an I fhou'd not hit on your Worfhip's Name at every turn.

Tally. Angry! no, no, Mr. *Jeffery*, I hate Ceremony. ——I find he does not know me; all's fafe. (*Afide.*) If it were not neceffary that we People of Quality fhou'd be diftinguifh'd by the Titles and Degrees his Majefty has been pleas'd to exalt us to, I wou'd not care if I were call'd plain *Jack*.

Fain. If you were exalted according to your Merit, you'd take your Degree at *Tyburn*. (*Afide.*)——Ay, ay, nothing but right, Zir, nothing but right.

Tally. But which Way am I to be oblig'd to you, Mr. *Jeffery*? I fhan't prove ungrateful, I affure you.——

Fain. Nay, as for that, d'ye zee—that's not the Matter ——I dan't want a Bribe. An tho' I be but a poor Fellow, and wears a tawdry Coat here, and am thumpt, and beaten about as you zee, I have an honeft Heart in my Belly, and good Blood in me too, for aught I know: For yow mun underftand, Vather was my Lord *Firebrand's* Gardiner when I was got, chou'd zeem, and they fay Mother was a deadly pretty Woman.——

Tally. From whence you would infer, that his Lordfhip might be your Father.——Not unlikely; but go on.

Fain. I perceive your Lordfhip is a Suitor to my Miftrefs.

Tally. I confefs you are a Man of Penetration. I am indeed an Admirer of hers.——

Fain. The more's the pity.——I'm zorry for't.

Tally. Why fo?

Fain. Becaufe, I'm zure fhe'll ufe yow like a Dog: I han't liv'd a Month wi'her, and to my Knowledge, fhe

has

has made Fools of Three or Four ; main fightly Men, I promife yow.

Tally. The Devil.

Fain. (Starts.) Mercy o' me ! Where, Zir ? Dud yow zee any Thing, my Lord?

Tally. No, no, I was only furpriz'd.——Curfedly ignorant. [*Afide.*

Fain. Surpriz'd ! be Mefs, the Devil wou'd furprize ony Man, and tho' he were the Parfon o' the Parifh.

Tally. But has fhe had fo many Lovers, fay you ?

Fain. Oh, a mort, Zir, a mort : But I can tell yow one Thing ; fhe likes yow woundy well.

Tally. Ay ! How doft thou know that, my Boy ?

Fain. Why, our *Mary* knows all her Heart, mun, an fhe tells me ev'ry Thing. Odd, an yow knew as much as I cou'd tell yow, your Bufinefs might zoon be done, Sir ; my Lord, I wou'd zay.

Tally. Ay ! How, prithee?

Fain. But won't yow be falfe-hearted now, and tell?

Tally. What, againft myfelf ? No, no, there's no Danger of that. Befides, I hope you don't think I wou'd be fo ungenerous to you !

Fain. Nay, as for that,——I'm but a Servant ; an one Place won't do, another woll, for that Matter. Now what I am going to tell your Lordfhip, is none o' my Bufinefs, as one may zay ; but it would make a-body mad to zee a Woman flounze about the Houfe, like a Dog in a Ducking-Pond.——Now, Zir, an fhe had a Hufband—He, he, he, he ! why me-haps,——he, he !——me-haps, I zay, he might vind her fomewhat elfe to do, zometimes. Yow underftand me, Zir.

Tally. Yes, yes, very well, *Jeffery* : If I had her once, I'd make her turn over a new Leaf.

Fain. That I dare fwear. (*Afide.*) Why, that was my very Thought now.——I wifh yow had her, Zir ; but you'll find it a knotty Piece of Work, let me but tell you that ; fhe deals as fcurvily with her Sweet-hearts, one Way, as with her Servants another ; and, I Cod, I ha' found her Fingers flip-flap, this a-way, and that a-way, like a Flail upon a Wheat-fheaf. [*Flinging out his Arms, and hits* Tally *a Slap on the Face.*

Tally. A Pox of your Similies.—— [*Afide.*
Fain.

Fain. Odſave me! Dud I hit yow, Zir?
Tally. Oh, no Matter, *Jeffery*,——Go on——
Fain. I hope your Lordſhip's Worſhip will forgive me. Zir; I meant no Harm, not I, Zir.—But as I was zaying,——Miſtreſs will give you the Dog to hold, and yow do'no'give her ſomewhat.
Tally. Think'ſt thou ſo, *Jeffery?* Why, what woud'ſt thou have me do?
Fain. Don't yow know that without telling? There is ſomewhat to be done, Zir, beſide the Parſon, or yow muſt dangle after her till Doom's Day, to no more Purpoſe, than to winnow Corn without a Wind.—Her t'other Huſband dudn't get her with Compliments, my Lord.
Tally. No!
Fain. No, no! He had been in *Ireland*, and knew better Things, Mun.
Tally. Ha, ha, ha, ha! Are we thought to have a particular Method to gain the Women, *Jeffery?* For I am of that Country, you muſt know.———
Fain. Are you zo, my Lord: Nay, then, and all be true they zay o' yowr Country Men, one need not tell yow which End to begin your Work at.
Tally. Ha! Is ſhe to be won that Way? I thank you for the Hint.———I find thou art a Lad of Parts; and when I am thy Maſter, I'll have thee taught to ſhave, and make thee my *Valet de Chambre.*
Fain. I ſhall ſhave you, I believe, before I have done with you.—With what aſſurance the Rogue talks. [*Aſide.* I ſhall be main thankful to your Lordſhip, an yow do, Zir; when wol yow come to our Houſe agen?
Tally. This Evening——What is the beſt Time to find her alone?
Fain. Be meſs, I known't that; but an yow find her alone, I'll take Care, Nobody ſhall diſturb yow, an yow'll put it home to her.———
Tally. Wo't thou! Egad, there's a Guinea for thee to drink my Health, then.-——Never fear, I warrant thee, Boy, I'll have her. [*Exit.*
Fain. Ha, ha, ha! How generous the Rogue is: Well, I hope by this Stratagem to give her a Diſguſt to his pretended Lordſhip; at leaſt, I ſhall prove if ſhe has any Thing valuable, beſides her Money.

The ARTIFICE.

To talk *of* Virtue *is the* Womens Pride ;
But they give Proofs on't, *who* refift, *when try'd.* [*Exit.*
Enter Sir John, *folus.*
Sir *John.* This is the Houfe ! Oh ? for an Art to make myfelf invifible ! [*Knocks, the Porter opens the Door.*
Por. Who would you fpeak with, Sir?
Sir *John.* With your young Lady, Friend.
Por. I wonder you'll be fo troublefome, Sir, I told you before, I would not difobey my Orders. [*He offers Money.*
—I'll have none of your Money, Sir,—I'm not to be brib'd to betray my Truft, I'd have you to know that.
Sir *John.* Then you muft be kick'd out of it, Sir.
[*Pulls him out, gives him a Kick, enters, and fhuts the Door.*
Por. Murder ! Thieves ! Murder !—This is a terrible Fellow. For my Part I'll never hinder him going in again. —And now he is in, I wifh I had taken the Money.—— He has fhut the Door, and the Devil take them that open it, for *Dick.* [*Exit.*

The SCENE *changes to the Infide of the Houfe.*

Olivia *and Sir* John *meeting.*
Olivia. Dick ! Will ! *John* ! What Noife of Murder is that ?——Ah ; *Freeman* ! [*Half fainting* ; *he catches her.*
Sir *John.* My Life ! my Soul ! Am I become fo hateful to thee, that thou can'ft not bear my Sight ?
Oliv. How ill doft thou interpret my Surprize ?
The unexpected Joy of feeing thee,
When no one Means fupply'd me with a Hope,
To tell thee,——That to Morrow,——
Sir *John.* Thou art to be my Sifter.
Oliv. Blaft the Name !
Sir *John.* Perifh my Brother firft,—If thou art true. If thy Heart has not confented.——
Oliv. To him nor any, but thyfelf.
Sir *John.* Then not all the Brothers upon Earth fhall take thee from me. Mrs. *Heedlefs* readily comply'd with your Requeft, and I have fent *Louifa* thither.
Oliv. Alas ! I fear that Lady's come too late.
The Time's fo fhort, the Plot cannot fucceed !
Sir *John.* Doft thou think fo ? Yet wilt thou ftay, and
facrifice

sacrifice thyself and me? Consent to fly with me, now, whilst Sir *Philip* is abroad.

Oliv. But whither shall we fly?

Sir *John.* Where Love directs us.

Oliv. I could, methinks, run any Risque with thee; and thou perhaps, wouldst do the same with me. Now in the Summer of our Love, little Cares would not offend us; But when the Glowing of the Passion's over, and pinching Cold of Winter follows, will amorous Sighs supply the Want of Fire? Or kind Looks and Kisses keep off Hunger?

Sir *John.* I think they would. But Love ne'er reasons thus, *Olivia.* I fear my Brother's gawdy Train, has rais'd this Picture of Despair. He, he, has my Estate! Dare I, stript as I am, pretend to vye with him? I, who live upon his Bounty!—Bounty! damn the Word! Live on a younger Brother's Bounty, and see him wed the Woman I adore!—That Thought will hurry me to Madness!

Oliv. You wrong my Love, and I should chide you for it, were our Condition happier. But to shew you I am a Lover-errant, consider what Trade you can take up for a Livelihood. For my Part I can make Purses by Day, and sing Ballads by Night. Now, if you can grind Knives, or turn Tinker, I'm yours. [*Slapping her Hand into his.*

Sir *John.* Fortune can never cast us so low. She owes thy Vertues more; methinks this Dawn of Mirth, portends a joyful Day. Haste then my Fairest: Let us leave this Place, that we may gain Time, at least, to work *Louisa's* Purpose.

Oliv. I'll only fetch a few Jewels; a sure Relief in Time of Need. [*Goes to the Door, starts, and runs back.* Undone for ever! my Father is coming up!

Sir *John.* Mischievous Accident!—What shall we do? Humph: (*Pauses.*) I have it—Run you to your Chamber, my Angel, and when you hear a Noise, come forth, and wonder. [*Exit* Olivia, *Sir* John *lies down on a Couch, and pulls his Hat over his Eyes.*

Enter Sir Philip.

Sir *John.* Thus to be circled, thus to be embrac'd! Oh! that I could hold thee for ever!

Sir *Philip.* Ha! What's this of embracing and holding for ever?

Sir *John.* The Curtain's drawn, and see! She's here again!   Sir

The ARTIFICE.

Sir. *Phil.* She's here!—Who's here? What is the Meaning of this?
Sir *John. Jocaſta*! Ha! What fall'n aſleep ſo ſoon?
Sir *Philip. Jocaſta*! Who is *Jocaſta*? What in the Name of Vengeance have we here?
Sir *John.* How fares my Love?
Sir *Phil.* Nay, who the Devil knows?
Sir *John.* Ha! Lightening blaſt me! Thunder rivet me for ever to *Prometheus*' Rock, and *Vultures* gnaw out my inceſtuous Heart!
Sir *Phil.* With all my Soul.
Sir *John.* By all the Gods, it is my Mother *Merope*.
Sir *Phil. Merope*! Who, in the Devil's Name, is ſhe? Ouns! Where are all my Raſcals? Now will I be hang'd if here isn't a Pack of Strollers got into my Houſe. Why, Rogues! Villains! Where are you all? Who have you let in, Raſcals? [*Enter two or three Servants.*
1ſt. *Serv.* We let in Nobody, Sir, not we.
Sir *John.* My Sword.—A Dagger.—Ha! who waits there?
Sir *Phil.* Go look!
2d *Serv*, O Lord! No-body, no-body at all, Sir. Fly, Maſter, fly! It is a Madman, to be ſure!
1ſt. *Serv.* Come away, Sir, come away? He'll certainly kill us. [*Exeunt Servants.*
Sir *Phil.* The Devil go with you all.———
Sir *John.* (*Riſing.*) Moſt triumphant Miſchief!——
And now, whilſt thus I ſtalk about the Room,
I challenge Fate to find another Wretch
Like *Oedipus*!
Sir *Phil. Oedipus*! Juſt as I thought; Strollers! neither better nor worſe. But how the Devil they got into my Houſe, that's the Queſtion?
Sir *John.* Horror! Death! Confuſion! Hell! and Furies!
Where am I?
Sir *Phil.* Where you ſhan't belong, I promiſe you.--Ouns, 'tis that beggarly Badge of Quality, Sir *John Freeman*!
Sir *John.* Oh, my *Jocaſta*!
Let me hold thee thus, thus to my Boſom,
Ages let me hold thee? [*Runs and catches Sir* Philip *in his Arms.*
Sir

The ARTIFICE.   333

Sir *Phil.* Murder, Murder! S'Death! the Rogue will fqueeze my Guts out.

Enter Olivia.

Oliv. Blefs me! What is the Matter, Sir?—Ha! Sir *John!*

Sir *Phil.* How you ftare, Miftrefs!—You did not know that he was here!—No, not you.—You was not to have been an Actor in this Droll, I warrant.

Oliv. Not I, indeed, Sir. I heard you cry out, and came to know the Caufe.

Enter Footmen.

1ft Foot. What is the Matter, Sir?

Sir *Phil.* I'll tell you, Rafcals, by-and-by.

Sir *John.* Gentlemen, you are very welcome to ftay and fee the Play: but I muft beg it may be on the other fide the Houfe. You'll crowd the Scenes fo much, that the Actors can't enter.

Sir *Phil.* The Actors! What Actors, Sir?—Ouns, do you think I am to be droll'd out of my Daughter?——I thought I had forbid you my Houfe?

Sir *John.* Pifh, pifh; you are out, Sir; confoundedly out—Hark ye! did you ever rehearfe this Part, Sir?

Sir *Phil.* 'S'Death he'll make me mad!—I fhall make my Part good with you, I fancy. Fetch me a Conftable.

Sir *John*, Out again!—Conftable! Why, there is not fuch a Word in the whole Play. A Conftable! Why, they never heard of fuch a Thing in *Thebes*!

Oliv. Alas, Sir! don't you perceive his Brain is turn'd?

Sir *Phil.* His Brain! If he had had any Brains, he had not loft his Eftate.

Sir *John.* If I had had your Confcience, I fhould not.
[*Afide.*

Sir *Phil.* (*Pulling off his Hat.*) Sir, will you be pleas'd to walk out of my Houfe.

Sir *John.* Look-ye, Sir, if you ftudy your Part no better, I'll forfeit you, by *Jupiter.*—Hold, hold, hold! Ad's-Heart, Madam! You entered too foon.—Oh, think of fomething to defer this Marriage but for a Day.
[*Afide to* Olivia.

Sir *Phil.* What a Vengeance are you whifpering! ha?

Sir *John.* Why, was that your Cue now? If you don't mind your Cues, you can never make an Actor, Sir———
Here,

Here, Sir! here's a Woman for you, who never trod the Stage before, yet I'll be bold to ſay, that ſhe'll ſurprize you.—Come! hold up your Head, my Dear—Mind your Buſineſs.—Enter boldly, and when you *Exit*, *Exit*—nimbly—Thus——— [*Exit*.

Oliv. I wiſh I could *Exit* with thee. [*Aſide*.

Sir *Phil*. Stark Mad! This comes of ſticking to Principles! I have known Principle ſtarve Five hundred Fools; but never knew it feed one wiſe Man yet.

Oliv. It will never ſtarve you, I'm ſure. [*Aſide*.

Sir *Phil*. I'm glad he's gone.——Come, come, dry up your Tears, and think of him no more. A Coach with Six before, and Six behind, with a pretty Fellow in the middle, will make Amends for Beggary and Madneſs.

Enter Ned Freeman.

Here's Mr. *Freeman*! Leave your Snivelling, and mind your Obedience, I command you.

Oliv. Souls know no Command, tho' Bodies do.

Ned. I deny that Poſition! I'm all yours—in *all* and *ev'ry* Part.

Command me, Madam, now; and try your Pow'r.

Oli. *It ſhall be then, to ſee my Face no more.* [Exit.

Ned. A very extraordinary Wife, I'm like to have, truly!—Very ſingular in her Manners, Faith!———

Sir *Phil*. Oh, never mind what a Woman ſays or does before Marriage. She'll be gentler after.

Ned. That's doubtful; for I can't perceive her to have the leaſt Inclination for me.

Sir *Phil*. Piſh, piſh; when you have been married a Night or Two, you'll tell me another Story, Mr. *Freeman*. —Her Mother was thus before her.

Ned. I wiſh it may prove ſo, Sir *Philip*:
For who by Force *the Courted Bliſs receives,*
Ne'er taſtes that Joy the willing *Fair-One gives.*

ACT IV.
SCENE *Watchit's* Houſe.

Watchit, *ſolus*.

Wat. WAS ever Man ſo cheated, chous'd, and cuckolded, as I am? By a Prieſt too, a Pox of his Sanctity!

Sanctity ! Well, this was an admirable Contrivance. Little did fhe think who was her Ghoftly Father. Ah ! the Wickednefs of this Age ! Ah ! *Tim* ! *Tim*. *Watchit* ! all thy Care is vain. Zounds ! why did I grope for what I fear'd to find ? I was but a Cuckold in Conceit before ! now ev'ry Fool will hang his Hat upon my Horns ! Oh ; that I had her in *Spain* ! I'd Spitch-cock her, like an Eel. —But juft Revenge is counted Murder, in our Country ; and a Man muft be hang'd for doing himfelf Juftice.—— The Prieft muft be a Conjurer ! he muft have fome Charm to make me fleep found ; or, he never cou'd have come to Bed, and I not hear him. Nay, fhe fays ev'ry Door in the Houfe flies open as foon as he approaches.—— Thefe are fine holy Guides, truly ; no wonder there are fo many Female Profelytes, when the Priefts take fo much Pains to convert 'em.——Which way fhall I be reveng'd of this Cuckold-making Dog ? (*Paufes.*)—No, that won't do.—Ay, it muft be fo.— [*Goes to the Scene, and calls,* *Pud*, Why *Pud*, where are you, *Pudfey ?*
Enter Mrs. Watchit.

Mrs. *Wat.* Did you call. *Snub ?*

Wat. Snub ! How many Names muft I have, ha ? *Snub* ! Pray who taught you that Name, Wife ?

Mrs. *Wat.* Taught me ! Why do you think I don't know how to put three Letters together ?

Wat. Ay, the Prieft has taught her the Art of Coupling ! Pox take him for't. [*Afide.*

Mrs. *Wat.* But what did you call me for ?

Wat. To tell you that fome Affairs oblige me to go out of Town to Night ; and that you muft not take it ill, if I lock you into the Houfe, that Nobody may come in or out, till I come back.

Mrs. *Wat.* Ay, into my Chamber if you pleafe ; I begin to relifh my Confinement very well——But may it not be dangerous to travel fo late ?

Wat. For her Ghoftly Father, it may, if I catch him. (*Afide.*) No, no, not at all. Go, get you to your Chamber, *Pud*, I'll follow you ; perhaps I may take a Nap before I go.——

Mrs. *Wat.* I wifh it might be your laft.——*Lucy* fhall give Mr. *Freeman* Notice of this lucky Opportunity.[*Afide.* Well, as you pleafe, *Snub* : I'm all Obedience. [*Exit.*
Wat.

Wat. If you were, *Snub*, I fhould be too happy. Ah! She is a delicious Bit! a tempting Morfel. Ah! thefe Priefts! thefe pamper'd Priefts! What would become of good old *Englifh* Property, had they once Footing here again? S'death, what had I to do with Beauty? What Bufinefs had I for a Wife, a handfome Wife? Of all Men living I'm the moft unqualify'd for a Hufband! Hufbands fhou'd be kind, fociable, courteous, gentle, loving, blind Animals? if they are fo bewitch'd to pitch on Beauty.

For He whoever weds a handfome *Wife,*
Engroffes all the Plagues *of human Life.* [Exit.

SCENE *changes to Mrs.* Heedlefs's *Houfe.*
She *enters on one Side, and* Fainwell *on the other.*
Fain. Dud yow call, forfooth,——Madam?
Wid. Fy, fy, *Jeffery*, will you always be this ftupid Wretch, notwithftanding all the Pains I take with you? Is not Madam, as foon, and as eafily pronounc'd, as For-footh?

Fain. Ay, every whit, d'ye zee, an I could but hit on't; but my Memory is fhort, and yow hare a-body zo, that yow fright it out of one's Head——Madam.

Wid. Hare you, quotha! I'm fure you craze me. You behave yourfelf fo awkwardly before Strangers, they will believe, perhaps, that I don't underftand better. When I'm alone, I don't care: Nay, fometimes your Blunders conduce to my Pleafure.

Fain. I cou'd find a way more conducive to her Plea-fure, if fhe'd give me leave. [*Afide.*

Enter Judith *and* Sam.

Jud. There's Miftrefs; and yow mun gi't her yowrzelf; gi't her, an yow wol. [*Exit.*

Sam. My Mafter, Madam, gives his humble Service to you, and begs the Favour of an Anfwer. [*Gives her a Letter.*

Wid. I admire your Mafter will give himfelf and me this Trouble, when I have fo often affur'd him 'tis to no Purpofe. [*Opens the Letter, and looks over it.*

Sam. Sure, I have feen your Face before, Brother.

Fain. Ma-hap, yow may, Friend, and ma-hap, yow mayn't.

Sam. Ar'n't you *Gloucefterfhire*?

Fain. Yes, I am.——I won't deny my Country.——
Sam.

Sam. Is not your Name *Crumplin?*
Fain. Ay, marry, is it ; be mefs, I fhou'd know yow too!
Sam. Honeft *Jeffery Crumplin*! I'm glad to fee thee.
[*Kiffes him.*
Fain. P'fhaw ; I dan't like this fame flabbering Vafhion. ——But, pray, what may one call yow? I know you'r Face.——Ah.——
Sam. My Face ! Why I can't be alter'd in Six or Seven Years, fure ! my Name is *Sly !*
Fain. Odd fa' me ! *Sam Sly* ! gi' me thy Hond, (*Shakes him by the Hand.*) Well, an how ! an how have yow done, *Sam*, e'er fen we us'd to break one another's Heads at Cudgels, ha? They told me you was gon over Seas.——
Sam. I han't been in *England* above Six Weeks.
Fain. Say you zo ! good lack ! Well, an have yow bin in *Gloucefterfhire?*
Sam. Yes, I came from thence but t'other Day ; I live with Mr. *Worthy.*
Fain. What, Mafter *Worthy*, of *Worthy*-Hall?
Sam. The fame.
Fain. Odd, yow had rare Luck, hark-ye, to light on zo brave a Place. Well, and dud yow zee our Volk? how do Vather, and Mother, and Sifters? Ha?
Sam. All well, and brifk, *Jeffery.*
Fain. Odd, Mafter *Worthy* is a main honeft Mon.
Sam. As lives by Bread, and as well belov'd.
Wid. Ha ! thefe two Fellows are acquainted, I find.
[*Afide.*
Sam. They would have my Mafter fet up for Parliament-Man.
Fain. I wifh he were qualify'd for it. (*Afide.*) An he does I'm zure he'll carry't : An Mr. *Worthy* comes to rule the Roaft, we fhall zee better Times, I'm perfuaded.——Well, before I'm huge glad to zee yow, *Sam.*——Where may a Body zee yow fome Day to drink a Pot to all our Friends in *Gloucefterfhire?* ha? I have zome there, I believe ; ha?
Sam. I'll call on you fome Evening, an fhew you were I live.
Wid. Mr. *Worthy* writes me Word, that he is going to *Jamaica.* It is only a Pretence, I fuppofe. I'll hear what his Servant fays. (*Afide.*) Is your Mafter going to travel, young Man?

Sam. Not for his Pleasure, Madam——
Wid. I did not speak of Pleasure; I ask'd you, if he is going abroad?
Sam. It is in your Power to stop him, I believe, if he is, Madam.
Wid. Still foreign to my Question! Can't you answer directly, Friend?
Sam. That depends so intirely upon your Ladyship, that it is impossible to answer you directly.——I know he has an Uncle dead in *Jamaica*, that has left him Forty Thousand Pounds; but I also know, he is so much in love with your Ladyship, that he does not care Forty Shillings for't.
Wid. The Fellow's mad! Not care for Forty Thousand Pounds? Why, the fourth Part on't would purchase a Barony.
Fain. If I had the sixth Part of it, I'm sure thou shou'dst never purchase me. (*Aside.*) What! is that zame Uncle dead, that came over once with a huge sight o' Blackamoors at's Tail?
Sam. Ay, ay, *Jeffery*! he's dead.
Fain. Is he zo? He was mainly rich, chu'd zeem?
Wid. You are mainly impertinent, chu'd seem.——
Pray ask your Country-man here, if *he* puts in his Verdict, when his Master is talking?—Pray tell Mr. *Worthy*, that I shall be at home this Evening; and he may, if he pleases, give me the Opportunity of wishing him a good Voyage.· -
Fain. To the Island of Matrimony, or I shall make but a broken Voyage of it. [*Aside.*
·*Sam.* I shall inform him, Madam. [*Exit.*
Wid. How came you to know this Gentleman, *Jeffery?*
Fain. Who, Master *Worthy?*· Why, every Body knows him in *Gloucestershire*; Vather has work'd for him, and the old 'Squire, these twenty Year chu'd zeem. He's a fine Man, and has no more Pride in him, than I have. He keeps a topping House.——He has humming *March* Beer, and deadly strong Cyder; there's rare Doings at *Cursmas.*
Wid. What Doings?
Fain. Why, he keeps open House for all Comers.
Wid. He ought to be very rich; whose Oeconomy is so profuse.
Fain. Rich, Quotha! Nouns, he knows no End of his
                                                    Means;

Means; he has a mort of Land! I ha' feen a Hundred at Dinner in the great Hall, one *Plough-Monday*; all his own Tenants; and Mafter was fo familiar and fo merry wi' 'em, and made 'em fo drunk! Lord, what Work was there!—

Wid. It was a beaftly Pleafure; and no Sign of his Frugality, whatever it may be of his good Nature.

Fain. Ah! he is the fweeteft natur'd Man in the World. Nobody ever faw him out of Humour, that ever I could hear on: His Vather, indeed, wou'd bawl and make a Noife, chu'd zeem; but as for thick fame Gentleman, he's quite another Thing; he is fo good to the Poor, and fo loving to his Neighbours; that there's not a Man twenty Miles round him, but would run thro' Fire and Water for him.——He is counted a main wife Man too; he makes no more of a Lawyer, or a Juftice of the Peace, than, than, than yow do of me, Madam.——Nay, it's thought by zome Volk, that he is fo deep learned, than an he wou'd, he cou'd puzzle, even the Parfon o' the Parifh.

Wid. That may be; and be no Conjurer neither. He fhall know what a Favourite he is of yours.——

Fain. That he knows already. [*Afide.*

Wid. You feem to know him perfectly well.

Fain. I wifh you knew him as well— Madam!

Wid. It is a pity he is not a Man of Quality; thefe Qualifications, tho' I confefs they are very bright ones, fignify nothing without a Title, *Jeffery!*

Fain. I'm fure thy Vanity will never intitle thee to the Heart of any Man of Senfe. [*Afide.*

Wid. Go, get me fome Tea.

Fain. Did I not hope to command in my Turn; I fhou'd not obey fo readily. [*Exit.*

Enter Judith.

Jud. There's a Lady below, that wants yow, fhe fays, ——Madam.

Wid. Bring her up.——This muft be the Lady, Sir *John* mentioned.

Enter Louifa, *with a Letter.*

Lou. 'Tis from *Olivia*, Madam.

[*Gives her the Letter, fhe opens it, and reads.*

Wid. You are welcome, Madam——I'll wait on you to that Apartment my Coufin mentions. It is impoffible Mr. *Freeman* fhould know it to be any part of my Houfe, when

The ARTIFICE.

he is brought in by the Back-door; your own Servants muft attend; I'll give Orders that none of mine are feen on that Side of the Houfe.

Lou. I am extremely obliged to you, Madam. I have fent a Letter to Mr. *Freeman*, and expect his Return every Moment.——I'll wait on you, Madam.

Wid. Be pleas'd to walk this Way. [*Exeunt.*

SCENE *draws*, Louifa *coming forwards, meets* Flora.

Lou. Is *Frederick* come back, *Flora*?

Flor. Yaw, ye Vrow, an he heb dat Letter gi brought.
[*Gives her a Letter.* Exit *Flora.*

Lou. What Pleafure once thefe Letters gave me! And with what Eagernefs I broke the Seals! Then kifs'd and dwelt upon each poifon'd, pleafing Vow! And thought the Perjury all faithful Love.
——But now!——
I fear to read; fo much his Stile is alter'd!——
[*Opens the Letter, and reads.*

MADAM,

I AM not more furpriz'd to hear you are in England, *than that you fo earneftly defire to fee me before I am married. But fince you promife it fhall be the laft Trouble you'll give me of this Kind, I defign to oblige and wait on you immediately, to know your important Bufinefs. If it be to upbraid me with Paft Conduct, you muft expect but a fhort Vifit, from*
Your humble Servant, FREEMAN.

Lou. Perfidious Man; we'll may'ft thou not ftay,
To hear thofe folemn Vows repeated
Which thou didft make fo falfely.
Enter Flora.

Flora. Here bin Minheer *Freeman*, ye Vrow.

Lou. Shew him up. [*Exit* Flora.
Oh, my Heart!——Lie ftill, thou Flutterer!
And aid me all the cunning Courage of my Sex!
Enter Freeman. *Salutes her.*

Lou. That cold Salute, is not like my *Freeman*.
You was not wont to kifs me thus!

Ned. Faith, Madam, I keep no Journal of my Pleafures; fo can't recollect how I us'd to behave myfelf. [*walks about.*

Lou. With what Indifference he regards me!
Hold in Refentment. [*Afide.* *Ned.*

The ARTIFICE. 341

Ned. Pray, Madam, what brought you to *England?*
Lou. Do you aſk? Why I follow where you lead me. Where ſhould I be, but where my Huſband is?
Ned. Hold, hold——You'll ſpoil my Marriage—— Huſband! Ha, ha, ha! Don't you rave, Child!
Lou. Have you forgot the Promiſes you made me?
Ned. No, nor what you gave me in Return, neither, my Dear.
Lou. Did not you love me, *Freeman?*
Ned. Did I not give thee Proofs of it? How does my Boy do? Ha! I think you muſt lend him me for a Pattern. You have heard I am going to be married, I find.
Lou. Yes—I've heard ſuch a News, but cannot think it true.   [*Weeps.*
Ned. I can't help that. Nay, nay, nay, if you are at that Sport, good bye t'ye.—— [*Going, ſhe ſtops him.*
Lou. You ſhall not go.
Ned. Indeed but I ſhall, Madam——Piſh, prithee ſhew me none of your Tragedy-Airs. Let go my Coat. You know, I hate to ſee Women cry.——To what purpoſe are theſe Tears?——I thought I gave you a Caution of it in my Letter.   [*Struggles to get from her.*
Lou. O do not ſtruggle to be gone, but hear me; my Tears will fall, but I'll ſtrive to ſuppreſs 'em.
Ned. Do ſo; for if you have anything to ſay to me, you muſt deliver it in a more entertaining Manner, or I'm your Humble Servant. Again! Humph!——I imagin'd how 'twould be——S'Death! what a Fool was I to come; I hate Upbraidings of this Nature.
Lou. I ſent not for you to upbraid you.
I ſee too well I've loſt your Heart.
May ſhe be happy who enjoys it now.
Yet ſure your Pity's not extinguiſhed too.
Not for my Sake, but for your Child's, I hope it;
Who, if you relieve him not, muſt periſh,——
My Father, ſome three Weeks ago, expir'd,
And left me but a Shilling to ſupport me.
No Friend have we on Earth if you are not one.
Ned. Well! and could not you have told me this without whimpering?—Pox o' the old Dog! A Shilling!— What a Duce ſhall I do with this Heifer and her Calf now! She comes very unlucky too at this Time. If *Olivia* ſhould
P 3   hear

The ARTIFICE.

hear of her, my Bufinefs will be done there. (*Afide.*) Send out your Maid, *Louifa*.

Lou. Leave the Room ; but when I call, do as I directed. (*Afide.*) [*Exit* Flora.

Ned. (*Sitting down.*) What do you pay for thefe Lodgings?

Lou. The People are related to a Friend of mine in *Holland*, from whom I brought a Letter. I believe they let no Lodgings. I would not willingly trefpafs long upon them.

Ned. Well, my Servant fhall take Lodgings for you. (*Pulls her on his Knee, and kiffes her.*) You foolifh Girl you, to blubber and fpoil your Face at this Rate, when you have nothing elfe to truft to! (*He wipes her Eyes.*)—So, there! Kifs me again, you Chit, you.—I'll take Care of you. I have a Man in my Eye ; a Lord too, that is very fond too, of your Country-women.

Lou. What means my Deareft. [*Rifes.*

Ned. To get thee a good Settlement. A Lord's Miftrefs lives as great as his Wife, and is as much refpected in our Country.——And thou fhalt be initiated, according to Cuftom.

Lou. Monftrous, filthy Cuftom ! Indeed, my *Freeman*, I'll be only thine : For after thee, I ne'er can love another.

Ned. Pifh, pifh ; yes, yes, a Hundred, I warrant thee.—

Lou. Unkind, and cruel !——Can I love——

Ned. Well, well, as to Love, that's not effential to a Miftrefs : Provided the Gallant has your Perfon, you may difpofe as you think fit of your Inclination.

Lou. Sometimes to fee my *Freeman*'s all I wifh.

Ned. Well, well, you fhall fee me ; but we muft manage that Point with Prudence : There muft be a *Decorum* obferved at home. For if it fhould reach my Wife's Ear, it wou'd prevent me feeing you at all.—Ah, *Louifa!* I wifh the Lady I'm to marry, lov'd me as well as thou doft.

Lou. I hope fhe does.

Ned. No, faith, fhe fays fhe hates me ; fo that, for ought I know, thou'rt in as fair Way to be revenged of me.

Lou. I wifh it not, nor would I feek Revenge on thee, more than on my own Heart.—*Flora* ! (*Goes to the Scene, and calls.*)——You muft drink fomething with me.——

Enter Flora, *with two Glaffes of Wine on a Salver.*

Lou. Come, here's to your future Happinefs !

Ned.

The ARTIFICE.

Ned. I'll pledge that generous Toaſt, and kifs thee for't.——Why this is as it ſhould be now. (*Kiſſes her.*) If Women underſtood their own Intereſt, they'd find us lefs prepared to refiſt the Force of their good Humour, than all the Artillery of Tears and Ranting!——Egad! methinks thou art as handfome now, as when I firſt enjoyed thee: Lips as foft, and panting Breaſt as hard as ever!—Oh, you are a tempting Baggage; (*embracing her.*)—What if we ſhould try to get a Girl to our Girl, *Louiſa*?

Lou. What! Sin-a-new, e'er we have repented of the paſt?

Ned. Sin, you filly Jade! Come, come, we'll repent once for all, my Dear. [*Pulling her.*

Lou. It muſt be quickly then——Or Life will be too ſhort to do it!

Ned. What fay'ſt thou?

Lou. Forgive me, *Freeman*! thou art poifoned.

[*Falls on her Knees.*

Ned. Ha!——Dye thou then, from whofe Hand I took it! [*Draws and runs at* Flora.

Flora. (*Shrieking.*) Ha! ick hab nit dat gedan, Mynheer.

[Louiſa *riſes, and runs between the Maid and him.*

Lou. O ſpare the Maid, who acted by my Order, And turn the Point on me the fole Aggreſſor. I had no other Way to keep thee mine.

Ned. Am I then caught! poifon'd!—What! Die the Death of Rats!—Confuſion! Murdered by my Whore!

Lou. No, I'm thy Wife, thou vile Detractor! Thou wou'dſt have made me that deteſted Thing!——— Shame on thy Project to expofe thy Wife!

Ned Wife! Name that no more, I charge thee, Leſt I forget thy Sex, and ſpurn thee from me!

Lou. Not name it? Yes, I will, whilſt living, name it. Call Heaven to Mind, who witnefs'd to your Vows; By whom you fwore when firſt our Faiths were plighted. It was by yon All-feeing Power above, At whofe Tribunal we ſhall foon appear. Death fummons now our trembling Souls to Trial; Stript of Excufes, Cuſtom, and Evaſion, This guilty Deed of mine will fall to thee. There, there, our Marriage Contract is recorded! There is a Judge from whom you can't appeal:

Your

The ARTIFICE.

Your Jury can't be brib'd to fave you :
Your cafting Witnefs is your broken Vows !
  Ned. Methinks her Words pierce like a Dagger, thro' me,
And more than ever, now I wifh to live——
Repair thy Fault, and call Phyficians hither. [*To* Flora.
  Lou. Call the kind Phyfician of the Soul,
Thy Body can receive no help from Art.
The Poifon is too ftrong, t'admit of Antidotes.
  Ned. Then Heav'n have mercy on my Soul. [*Kneels.*
O my *Louifa* ! canft thou forgive me ?]*Rifes.*
O could Revenge, the blackeft Fiend in Hell,
Shroud itfelf beneath that Angel's Form ?
  Lou. Call't not Revenge, but Love.—— Be Witnefs,
     Heav'n.
I drank the healing Draught, with greater, ftronger
Guft of Pleafure, than other take rich Cordials,
To lengthen fleeting Life, which I defpife.
Since in fair Fame I could not live thy Wife,
My only Wifh was, we might dye together.
Oh ! my Heart.
  Ned. The Poifon works ! I feel it too in mine !
Oh ! might I live to make thee Satisfaction.——
  Lou. And wou'dft thou do it ? wou'dft thou marry me ?
  Ned. As willingly as I did ever promife thee.
  Lou. My Soul revives at thy returning Virtue,
Only to bear the Rack of deep Defpair——
Now, now, I do repent the defperate Deed,
And wifh my *Freeman*'s Life a longer Date.
I fhould have trod the Paths of Death alone !
But 'twill not be !——A few fhort Minutes hence
We both fhall be no more !
  Ned. Oh ! Shock of Nature ! Bitternefs of Thought !
O ! whither am I going ?———
Hafte ! Let the holy Man be call'd !
And 'tis moft fit a Lawyer too be fent for.
Something I muft adjuft before I go——
And then, oh ! World, farewell !
  Lou. Hafte *Flora,* and obey. *Exit* Flora.
  Ned. I feel a ftrange Diforder in my Brain !
My Heart beats faft too, and my Spirits flutter !
My boiling Blood runs fwiftly thro' my Veins,
In hafte to man the laft Retreat of Life !
Oh ! *Louifa* ! wou'd I had married thee—— *Lou.*

Lou. Do it now. 'Twill wipe off many Sins from thee. When we appear in t'other World together——— The virtuous Act may plead my Pardon too, If thou canſt but forgive the Raſhneſs of my Love. Again, upon my Knees I aſk it.
  Ned. As willingly as I would be forgiven. A ſudden Faintneſs ſeizes me all over : I will be thine, if Life will laſt ſo long.
  Lou. Bleſt Sound !——Come lean on me. I'll lead thee to my Bed. Where we will reſt, and wait the holy Man.
  The Bridal Bed, *from whence we both ſhall riſe, Diſrob'd of Scandal, to ſubſtantial Joys.* [Exeunt.
  S C E N E *changes to* Watchit's *Houſe.* Mrs. Watchit *in a Night-Dreſs on a Couch.*
  Mrs. *Wat.* I wonder what carries my Huſband out of Town ſo late ! But no Matter, it gives me an Opportunity to ſee *Freeman,* who I know will be here as ſoon as *Lucy* has given the Signal.--Ha ! ſure I heard the Door go.
          Enter Watchit.
  Wat. I have unluckily forgot my Powder-horn ; and how I ſhall find it in the Dark, I can't tell—I don't care to diſturb the Family for a Candle.
  Mrs. *Wat.* He is here already—Oh, the dear impatient Man !—Bleſs me, *Lucy,* why did you let him come ſo ſoon ? I don't think your Maſter is got out of the Street yet.
  Wat. How's this ? [*Aſide.*
  Mrs. *Wat.* And if he ſhould take it into his Head to come back, I ſhould be terrible frighted.
  Wat. Ounds ! I'm Thunder-ſtruck ! this Dog of a Fryar is here already ! and of *Lucy's* bringing. Oh ! the Jade ! Ad's-heart ! I might have waited without Doors 'till Dooms-day.
  Mrs. *Wat.* Diſtraction ! What have I ſaid ?--It is my Huſband's Voice ; what will become of me now ? [*Aſide.*
  Wat. Here needs no Conjuration. My Turtle ſeems willing enough to coo with him ; and is only afraid I ſhould return to ſpoil the Sport. Oh the Strumpet ! But let me hear what the Rogue anſwers. Which Way will ſhe get off now, I wonder ? [*Aſide.*
  Mrs. *Wat.* I have no Pretence to get off, but by going on.

on. (*Aside.*) Well, *Lucy* tells me you are the moſt dextrous Fellow at this Buſineſs.——

Wat. ,Buſineſs ! What are they come to Buſineſs, already ?

Mrs. *Wat.* I know not why; but methinks, I'm half afraid to venture on a Stranger.

Wat. A Stranger? What, then this is a new Rogue?— Ounds ! I ſhall be cuckolded by Church and State.

Mrs. *Wat.* How now ? What do you mean ? You won't come to Bed to me, ſure ?

Wat. You'll take it very ill if he don't——Ounds, I han't Patience to hear it out.

Mrs. *Wat.* O Gemini ! What do you do?——How dare you be ſo rude ?

Wat. There's a Queſtion to aſk a Man that ſhe has brought into her Bed-chamber.

Mrs. *Wat.* If my Huſband ſhould come.

Wat. As he really is——

Mrs. *Wat.* If he ſhould catch you——

Wat. As he moſt ſurely will——Thou Sorcereſs.

Mrs. *Wat.* Nay, nay ; indeed, and indeed, but I won't.

Wat. Indeed, and indeed, but you will.——This is a thorough-pac'd Cuckold-making Dog !——How ſoftly the Villain whiſpers !—I can't hear one Word he ſays.

Mrs. *Wat.* What gave you the Aſſurance to imagine I'd cuckold my Huſband, who is the beſt of Huſbands ?

Wat. That's a Lye.

Mrs. *Wat.* Let me go, will you ? I proteſt I'll cry out.

Wat. That's another Lye.

Mrs. *Wat.* Nay ; Lord ! Piſh ; don't—Fy !—What do you do ? [*Speaks as if ſhe was ſtruggling with ſomebody.*

Wat. 'S'Death ! I ſhall ſtand and hear myſelf cuckolded ! —A Light ! a light, there ! Thieves, Thieves ! A Light, a Light !—— [*She riſes haſtily. He pulls out a Piſtol.*

Mrs. *Wat.* Ah, Heavens ! What Noiſe is that ? Why, *Lucy, Lucy!* Thieves, Thieves ! A Light, a Light ! (*She gropes about, and lays hold on his Piſtol.*) Thieves !—Ah, a Piſtol ! Murder, Murder ! Oh ſave my Life, and I'll lead you to all the Money, Plate, and Jewels in the Houſe. Oh, oh, oh !

Enter Lucy *with a Light.*

Mrs. *Wat. Mumps* ! Oh, ſave me, ſave me !

[*Flies about his Neck.* *Wat.*

The ARTIFICE.

Wat. Off, thou foul Adultrefs! Don't think to fmuggle me, 'till your leud Paramour efcapes.
[*Snatches the Candle, and looks about.*
Lucy. Blefs me, Madam! Mafter looks as if he would eat a-body! What was all this Outcry for?
Mrs *Wat.* I'll tell you anon. [*Afide to* Lucy.
Wat. Where have you hid this Rogue of your providing, Huffey? Ha?
Lucy, Of my providing? what do you mean, Sir?
Mrs. *Wat.* Nay, nay, don't ftand prating; but call up the Servants to affift your Mafter.——Don't, dear *Mumps,* don't be too venturefome. The Thieves have Piftols, and may kill thee.

Wat. May they fo! A Pox o' your Sneer—Now does fhe look as if fhe knew one Word of the Matter.

Mrs. *Wat.* I hope to prevent your knowing one Word of the Matter, that's my Comfort. [*Afide.*
Lucy. Why, what fhould fhe know, Sir?
Wat. Go look, Mrs. *Pander.*
Mrs. *Wat.* I'm fure, I know nothing, but that I was wak'd with the Cry of Thieves, Thieves! If it was a falfe Alarm, fo much the better: It did me Service, however, for it wak'd me out of a Dream, that frighted me as bad as the Noife did.

Wat. A Dream! Why, what was you dreaming on, pray?

Mrs. *Wat.* Why, methought *Lucy* had brought me a Corn-cutter, a great, fat, clumfy, black Fellow; but the moft dextrous Fellow in the World, fhe told me, at that Bufinefs.

Wat. (*Afide.*) Ha! I remember dextrous was one of the Words fhe fpoke. Perhaps it might be nothing but a Dream.

Mrs. *Wat.* And the impudent ugly Villain, methought, would have come to bed to me. I was ftruggling with him in my Sleep, and vowed I'd cry out juft as the Noife wak'd me.

Wat. Say'ft thou fo, *Pud!* And was all this fplutter about a Corn-cutter?——Why then, to tell thee the Truth, thou didft cry out, and I thinking Thieves were got into the Houfe, cry'd out too; for I never dream't of thy talking in thy Sleep, Child.——I don't remember ever to have heard thee before. P 6 *Lucy.*

Lucy. So have I, an hundred Times; but you fnore fo loud, that nobody's Noife can be heard but your own.—— This Corn-cutter has put the Corn-maker out of his Head. I fmell the Plot already. [*Afide.*

Mrs. *Wat.* (*Afide.*) It takes, as I could wifh——But where was *Freeman, Lucy?*

Lucy. Gone out, Madam. [*Afide.*

Mrs. *Wat.* (*Afide.*) 'Twas lucky that he was——Ah! *Mumps!* I know what you thought.

Lucy. Ay, Madam, he thought you had got a Gallant through the Key-hole. Had I a Hufband of Mafter's Temper, I'd fit him, I warrant him. He fhould not be jealous of me for nothing.

Wat. That I dare fwear.

Lucy. As you are of my Lady. She has a comfortable Life, has fhe not? To have you vex and teaze, and break her Reft for nothing.

Wat. Take care I don't break your Head for fomething.

Lucy. I care not if you do. I will fpeak. You could not ufe my Lady worfe, if fhe had cuckolded you.—— You are like fome litigious Farmers, who pound their Neighbours Cattle for a Trefpafs, tho' they have more Ground than they can ftock themfelves.

Wat. Huffey! You have Stock for the whole Parifh! ——Get out of my Sight, or I'll break your Neck down Stairs.

Mrs. *Wat.* Excellent Wench! (*Afide.*) Fy, *Lucy,* how you talk to your Mafter? I affure you I fhall difcharge you my Service, if you don't behave yourfelf better.

Lucy. I fhall get another, I hope, if you do? Don't think I'll be fufpected of procuring Gallants for you! Did he not afk where the Rogue was of my procuring——I'll bring my Action againft you for Scandal. I have nothing but my Reputation to live by. Take that from me, and you take all. If he's your Hufband, Madam, he's not mine. [*Burfts into Tears.*

Wat. No, thank Heaven, I have enough of one of you.

Mrs. *Wat.* Leave the Room, I fay.

Lucy. It's for. for, your Sake—or, or—I'd tear his Eyes out! (*Sobs.*) Take away *my* Reputation! [*Exit.*

Wat. Oh! the wondrous Reputation of a Chambermaid!—This Slut has ftrangely provok'd me. I wifh I were rid of her. [*Afide.* Mrs

Mrs. Wat. (*Aside.*) I wish I knew what brought him back; and if he intends to go again.

Wat. (*Aside.*) Ah! that the Husband of that charming Woman should be cornuted by a Priest!——

Mrs. Wat. (*Aside.*) What would I give to be rid of his Company? Yet I dare not ask him, how he designs to dispose of himself, for my Soul.

Wat. What art thou thinking of, *Pudsey* ?

Mrs. Wat. Of your Unkindness, *Mumps !* To pretend Business out of Town, and leave me starving in Bed by myself. I'm sure if you lov'd me, you would not let Business take you from my Arms. Indeed, indeed, you would not, *Mumpsey.*   [*In a wheedling Tone.*

Wat. Ah! those pretty Pouters! I must kiss them, thou coaxing Pug thou: (*Kisses her.*) Dost thou really love thine own *Mumpy* ?

Mrs. Wat. Naughty *Mumps !* is that a Question now! Han't I given you all the Signs of it? Don't I lie close to your Back? and warm your Feet every Night in my Lap? And creep gently out o' Bed in the Morning, without waking you? Don't I? Can you deny all this, *Mumps* ?

Wat. No, nor I won't deny it, *Pudsey.* And I hope you'll allow me some Merit in my Turn, *Pudsey.*

Mrs. Wat. Nay, *Mumps*, I scorn to derogate from your Merit. I must confess, you never do any thing to break my Rest, but when you are so naughty to leave me—— For then I do so tumble, and toss—and dream—and am so terribly frightened—as I was now, you know——Well, I protest you shan't go out again to Night!—If you do, I won't love you again these three Days; so I won't.

[*Pats him on the Cheek.*

Wat. Thou handsome Creature! Oh! 'twas that bewitching Leer, that snapt my Heart.——What has she in her Head now?—I never knew her in this wheedling Humour, but she had some Design. (*Aside.*)—Well, *Pudsey*, what is this begging Face put on for?

Mrs. Wat. That's a secret past your finding out. [*Aside.*

Wat. What can I do to please my *Pudsey* ?

Mrs. Wat. E'en very little, truly. (*Aside.*)—I could tell you, *Mumpy* ; but may be, you won't do it.

Wat. But may be I will do it.   [*In a fond Tone.*

Mrs. Wat. Won't you go out no more to Night, then? But

But ſay your Prayers, and go to Bed, and ſnore like any little Pig in your *Punny's* Boſey?

Wat. (*Aſide.*) Humph! Now is ſhe afraid of her ghoſtly Father. She certainly ſmokes my Deſign—On my Conſcience, ſhe's in Love with him—I warrant, he's a ſtrapping young Dog——Ounds! if I can but light of him?

Mrs. *Wat.* What is he pondering on? Pray Heaven he does not take me at my Word, and ſtay at home in Complaiſance. (*Aſide.*)—What, won't you anſwer me, *Mumps?*

Wat. Why *Pudſey,* thy Kindneſs ſo confounds me, that I know not what to anſwer thee—I am loth to diſpleaſe thee, and yet I muſt leave thee inſtantly.

Mrs. *Wat.* (*Aſide.*) Little does he think, that 'tis the only Thing he can do to pleaſe me. I hope *Freeman* is come home by this Time.

Wat. I only come back for my Powder-horn; that's all, *Pud*; but I'll make all poſſible haſte back, I will indeed, *Pudſey,* to make thee eaſy.

Mrs. *Wat.* Or otherwiſe. (*Aſide.*) Well if it muſt be ſo (*ſighing*) I muſt be content, and make myſelf as happy as I can without you, *Mumps.* [*In a melancholy Tone.*

Wat. Ay, ay, I won't be long from thee; go, prithee, get me a Dram, I'll but take my Powder-horn, and follow thee—— [*Enter Mrs.* Watchit.

Watchit *ſolus.*

I know not what to think. Sometimes I think ſhe loves me—and ſometimes I think ſhe does not. And if Father *Domine* comes within the Reach of my Blunderbuſs, have at him: If not, ſhe ſhall produce him: I'll confront her by her own Confeſſion. If I once get him in my Power, I'll turn his own *Inquiſition* upon him. His *Church* ne'er tortur'd Heretick, as I will him.

I'll teach him to keep Handmaids *of his own,*
And let his honeſt Neighbours Wives *alone.* [Exit.

ACT V.

SCENE *Mrs.* Heedleſs's *Houſe.*

Heedleſs, *Sola.*

Wid. I AM ſtrangely divided between Inclination and Grandeur. I confeſs, I like Mr. *Worthy's* Perſon better

The ARTIFICE.

better than my Lord's; but marry him, and I ſhall be call'd plain Mrs. *Worthy.* Then, where's the Diſtinction between me and my Brother's Wife: And who in their Senſes would part with twenty thouſand Pounds, to be nothing but what one was before? My Lord can make me a Woman of Quality, and intitle me to treat all below me with Contempt. That carries a valuable Conſideration—— Methinks, there is an Air in the very Footman of a Woman of Quality. He approaches with ſuch profound Submiſſion! And in a Tone ſo ſoft——*Did your Ladyſhip call, Madam?* Whereas, now, my blundering Raſcals come trotting up to my Noſe, with a *Dud you want me, Forſooth?* ——Ha! *Lord Pharaoh-Bank.*

Enter Tally.

Tally. I hope you'll pardon this abrupt Intruſion, Madam. It is intirely chargeable on the Impatience of my Love. Command my Abſence, I beſeech you, if I break in upon your more diverting Thoughts.

Wid. I had no Amuſements, my Lord, but what ought to give way to better Company.

Tally. You do me a particular Honour in that Diſtinction.

Wid. If I had not ſome Skill in the Choice of my Acquaintance, I ſhould be ſtifled with Impertinence. The firſt Leſſon I teach my Servants, is, to diſtinguiſh between Perſons of Rank, and the Droſs of Human-kind. I am pleas'd to find my Inſtructions are not loſt upon' em, by admitting one of your Lordſhip's Figure upon ſuch eaſy Terms.

Tally. Such an Approbation from a Lady of your good Taſte, cannot fail of inſpiring me with a better Opinion of myſelf, and a Confidence of my not being unwelcome to my dear Widow. (*Kiſſes her.*) She kiſſes ſofter than a ſouthern Wind!

Wid. Pugh! I hate to be complimented with Fragments of another's Wit, my Lord. It argues a Decay of Charms in the Perſon you addreſs.

Fainwell *peeping.*

Tally. I own it is a Fault, Madam. Your Ladyſhip has Beauty enough to inſpire the dulleſt Genius with ſomething new.

Fain. (*Aſide.*) You mean, ſhe has Money enough to inſpire you with Impudence.

Tally. Apollo and the Muſes dwell upon theſe Lips. Another Kiſs, and I ſhall be—— *Wid.*

Wid. A Poet.

Tally. Whatever you would have me. [*Kiſſes her.*

Wid. Say you ſo, my Lord? I have an odd Whim come into my Head—Will you give me a Proof of my Power, my Lord? I want an Elegy.

Tally. On a departed Monkey, or a favourite Kitten, I preſume.

Wid. No, upon a living Subject.

Fain. (*Aſide.*) A pretty new Invention, to bury People before they are dead.

Tally. A living Subject! An Elegy upon a living Subject!

Wid. You are not inſpir'd yet, I find, my Lord. I mean, a Characteriſtick of human Life; dead, and yet exiſting.

Fain. (*Aſide.*) Myſtery!

Tally. Popery, downright Popery! May the Genius of *England* defend us.——Let me ſee! What dead Folks have we among the Living?——There's a diſbanded Officer—An old Beau—A broken Tradeſman—A degraded Parſon—A *Quondam South-Sea* Director—An Eunuch—An, an, an old Maid.

Wid. You have hit it, my Lord.

Tally. Then crown my Succeſs with another Draught of Nectar.   [*Kiſſes her.*

Fain. (*Aſide.*) How warmly the Rogue kiſſes! He makes Love with as much Aſſurance, as if he had two Bottles of *Burgundy* in his Belly, and a real Title to ſupport his Impudence.

Wid. I proteſt, one ſhou'd take your Lordſhip for a Soldier; for you attack a Woman, as they do a fortify'd Town.

Tally. Love and War agree in every Point, my dear Widow; the Blockade of a Town reſembles an obſtinate Woman, and a phlegmatic Lover, who reſolves to weary her into Compliance. A Kiſs now and then from a diffident Lover, is like ſtealing a March, and ſurprizing the Enemy, by a circumſpect General. But eager and repeated Kiſſes, are, like Storming, more glorious to the Aſſailant.

[*Embracing and kiſſing her in a Rapture.*

Fain. (*Aſide.*) Theſe Rogues happen into good Company ſometimes, one may know by their Gleanings of Wit.

Wid. Oh gad, my Lord, what do you mean, by ruffling one at this Rate?

Tally. Judge my Meaning, by the Quickneſs of my Pulſe,
the

The ARTIFICE.

the Throbbing of my Heart, and Trembling of my Limbs! The unqueftionable Proofs of Love, and eager Wifhes for Poffeffion——Come, come! Thou art no Stranger to a Lover's Meaning!—My Life, my Soul! Let us improve this Dawn of Pleafure. [*Embracing her.*
Wid. As how, my Lord?
Fain. (*Afide.*) Sure fhe wou'd not have him tell her in plain Terms.
Tally. P'fhaw! for a Woman of thy Experience to afk that Quesftion!—Come, come, the Sight of the Bedchamber will refrefh thy Memory. [*Pulling her.*
Wid, Pifh?—Nay, fy—Be civil, my Lord.
[*Seems to ftruggle.*
Fain. (*Afide.*) Humph!—If it come to *pifh* and *fy* already, another Volley of Kiffes, and fhe furrenders at Difcretion.
Tally. Nay, ftruggling is your Sex's Privilege. You wifely know Refiftance but inflames Defire.
Wid. I proteft, I'll cry out, my Lord.
Tally. With all my Heart. Your Servants know their Duty better than to come, if you do.——Honeft *Jeffery* has taken care of that. [*Afide.*
Fain. How fecure the Rogue thinks himfelf! [*Afide.*
Tally. I will pofitively enjoy thee this Night—Honourably, if you pleafe.
Wid. Or not at all, my Lord, if you were the firft Man of Quality in *England*!
Tally. Send for the Parfon this Minute then.
[*Kiffes her again.*
Wid. Oh Gad! You ftop one's Breath——You are the moft impatient Man!
Tally. Impatient, quotha! Who can behold thefe dear Eyes without Impatience for the Bleffing?——
Wid. Well, my Lord, let us fign Articles :—And then—
Tally. I'll give thee a *Charte-Blanche.* Make thy own Terms; fo that I may this Night take Poffeffion of thefe Arms.
Wid. Well, fince your Lordfhip will have it fo——
Fain. Nay, you mou'not go in, an yow were ten Mafter *Worthefs*— (*In* Jeffery's *Voice.*) (Fainwell *within, in his own Voice.*) I tell you, I had your Lady's Commands to wait on her, and muft, and will go in : So, fweet Mr. *Jeffery Crumplin,* by your Leave.

The ARTIFICE.

Fainwell *rushes in, in his own Dress.*

Wid. Oh Gad! that's Mr. *Worthy's* Voice! What can he think, when he sees one ruffled in this Manner!——I'm surpriz'd——Did not I hear my Clod-hopper's Voice, in a resisting Tone, Mr. *Worthy*?

Fain. I was so far out of my Countryman's good Graces, that he would neither bring in my Name, nor permit me to enter.

Tally. (*Aside.*) That was in Favour of me. *Jeffery* is a Man of Honour, I find——But who's this Mr. *Worthy*? Disappointment catch him, for coming so *Mal a-propos.*

Wid. That Fellow the most impenetrable Sot!—Why did not you break his Head, Mr. *Worthy*?

Fain. That's a Liberty, Madam, no Man ought to take in your House, 'till you have made him Master of it—Were I that happy Person—— [*Takes hold of her Hand.*

Tally. (*Stepping in between them.*) You'd kick every-body out of it, I suppose?

Fain. That gave me just Provocation, Sir.

[*Steps in between.*

Wid. If they should quarrel now!—Mr. *Worthy*, pray let me speak a Word with you——Do you know who this Gentleman is?

Fain. Very well, Madam.

Tally. Then if you know me, you know your Distance.

[*Steps between again.*

Fain. So well, Sir, (*goes between 'em*) that were you not protected by this Lady's Presence, there should be just the Distance from hence to the Street between us.

Tally. How Sir? [*Stepping up to him.*
Fain. Through the Window, Sir. [*Pushes him away.*
Tally. You dare not talk thus elsewhere.
Fain. You dare not give me an Opportunity. [*In his Ear.*
Wid. Dear Mr. *Worthy*, for your own Sake, consider what you do—He is a Man of Quality; and for ought I know, a Privy-Counsellor—— [*Aside to* Fainwell.

Fain. To nothing above a Gang of Pickpockets, I'll answer for him. Hark ye, *Tally*; how long have you worn this Surtout of Honour, I beseech you? In what Reign were you created a Baron, pray?

Tally. Humph! He knows me, I find---My Business is done here.

Wid.

The ARTIFICE.

Wid. My Stars! Is he not a Man of Quality?

Fain. Yes, yes, Madam, I'll give you his Titles in a very few Words.——He is a Baron of *Fair-Chance* and Vifcount of all the *Pharoah-Tables* in and about *London*. He has a Pack of Cards for his Coat of Arms, quarter'd with Knaves; and falfe Dice, in a Field of Impudence.—His Creft is a Fool; his Supporters are *Parolie Traitla va.*

Tally. (*Afide.*) The Rogue has blazon'd me!—But I muft carry it off as well as I can.——I hope you'll prove this Sir,

Fain. Oh! inftantly, Sir.——*Sam*!

Enter Sam.

Fain. Call a Conftable.

Wid. Not for the World. I beg I may have no more Buftle in my Houfe.

Fain. You underftand me. [*Whifpers to* Sam.

Sam. Perfectly well.——Will your Lordfhip pleafe to walk this Way——What think you, my Lord, of a Pot of Porter, to drink to our better Acquaintance?

[*In a fcreaming tone.*

Tally. A Pox of Ill-luck!——I may find a Time, Sir—

[*Exit.* with *Sam.*

Fain. Not to cheat me of my Money Sir,——Ha, ha, ha!

Wid. I hope you are not miftaken in the Man, Mr. *Worthy.*

Fain. I'm glad *You* were not, Madam.

Wid. Which is intirely owing to your timely Difcovery, or I had been undone.

Fain. For which, give me leave to fay, you might have thank'd your own Vanity. Nothing but a Lord wou'd go down!—I admire, a Woman of your Difcretion, and a Widow too! should prefer empty Title to real Pleafure, and mere Shadow to conjugal Affection. [*Embracing her.*

Wid. A Fiddle of Affection, Mr. *Worthy*; I tell you, I have been lac'd very tight once in my Life; but having made my Fortune, and got my Liberty, if ever I try again the Matrimonial Bodice, the Lace fhall be tagg'd with a Title, I affure you.

Fain. Ah! that will make a Noife in the World; but your Pleafure, like a Squib, will vanifh in the Bounce, ha, ha, ha!—To give Twenty Thoufand Pounds for the bare
Name

Name of my Lord's Lady, whilſt Ten to One, but your Chamber-maid ſupplies your Ladyſhip's Place in his Arms, aud rattle about Streets in her *Berlin*, ſupported out of your Ladyſhip's Fortune.

Wid. You ſeem well acquainted with the Map of this World.

Fain. Perfectly, Madam; and have made this Obſervation, That Women who love to indulge their Vanity, and yet hope for their Dividend of Pleaſures, are acting as inconſiſtent a Part, as they who give a Looſe to their Fancy, and at the ſame Time think to preſerve their Reputation. ——I tell you, Madam, a Man of Quality will no more throw all his Love upon a Wife, than a Farmer will ſow all his Land with the ſame Grain. The only Way to engroſs your Joys is to marry one of us Country-Gentlemen.

Wid. To be rival'd by *March-Beer, Tobacco*, and *Fox-hounds.*

Fain. Even thoſe are preferable to Cards, Dice, and a Wench, as you wou'd have experienc'd had not I come in.

Wid. So! now will he value himſelf upon my Deliverance. (*Aſide.*)—Well, well, Mr. *Worthy*, ſince this Fellow proves a mere *Plebian*, he is a worthleſs Raſcal; but if he had really been a Lord, what is now Impudence, wou'd only have been Violence of his Love.

Fain. Humph! a very pretty Diſtinction!——No, Madam, I deny that Poſition——Love is ſoft and gentle, as the Morning-Sun in Autumn, mellowing Inclination by Degrees; but its Twin-Brother, like a Foot-Pad, knocks you down, and rifles you at once.—*He* was impatient for your Money only, Widow——*I*, for this dear Perſon.—Now, why can't you like me as well as a Lord?

Wid. Like you! For what?

Fain For what! Why, for an unalterable, faithful, conſtant, doating——

Wid. Hold, hold, Sir. Your Epithets are running away with your Meaning.—But to prevent your explaining it, I muſt tell you, that the very Name of Matrimony with a Commoner, will flatten our Converſation, and make us look very ſimple.

Fain. Ay! but there is ſomething ſo expreſſive in that Simplicity, that it gives a deeper Impreſſion than all the Gildings of Rhetorick. Ah! my dear Widow, wou'd you but

but return my Love, how many *Cupids* fhou'd I behold dancing in thefe Eyes! Nay, and you fhou'd fee ftrange Things before Morning.——

Wid. Sha! you talk foolifhly.

Fain. That's inherent to a Lover.

Wid. And fo you'd have me a Fool too, to keep you in Countenance. A very wife Foundation for the Fabrick of Matrimony.——No, no, I tell you once for all, though I do like your Person, you and I muft never be conjur'd into the Circle of a Wedding-Ring.

Fain. And no other Circle will do my Bufinefs.——I'll try if fhe has really a Liking for my Perfon. [*Afide.*

Wid. Well! what, have I put you in the Dumps, now? Are you confidering what Death will revenge you of an ungrateful Miftrefs? Ha, ha!

Fain. No, Faith, Madam; I'll live to be reveng'd, and balk your Vanity——

Then farewell Love,
Farewell Love, and all foft Pleafure,
Honour calls, and we muft part. [*Sings in a carelefs Manner.*

Wid. You are the merrieft Lover at parting!

Fain. I am of *Ben*'s Mind, Madam; refolve to be merry, though the Ship were finking. And fince I muft never hope to call you mine, I here difmifs all the Retinue of a formal Lover. Such as Vows, Ogles, Sighs, Dreams, Vifions, Sonnets, Gingles, Epigrams, Couplets, with a long &c.—Thus, with infinite Struggles, I hope to entertain as mean an Opinion of Matrimony, as your Ladyfhip, in a very little Time.

Wid. Oh! that he had a Title to fupport this Humour; he fhou'd find, I have no mean Opinion of Matrimony.
[*Afide.*

Fain. And, for the future, fhall look upon the Parfon's Patchwork, like a Pilgrimage to *Mecca*, or *Jerusalem*, fit only for the Superftitious, and People who have periodical Inclinations, to fill up the Vacancies of human Life with a huge Caravan of Children; a long Journey; dirty Road; through the Turnpikes of Jealoufy, Anxiety, Sufpicion. Animofity, pinching Cares, and a Thoufand other Inconveniencies.—By the way, you have travell'd the Stage, and, I fuppofe, know what I fay to be true.

Wid. Ha!——All is not right within this Breaft. I begin

begin to perceive his Indifference gives me Pain. [*Aſide.*
Fain. I fancy the only Object to give one a Surfeit of Matrimony, wou'd be to ſee a Pair of diſtemper'd Creatures in the Corner of a Room, in cloſe Conſpiracy to deceive one another; very ſincerely promiſing mutual Love for Fifty Years enſuing; when, upon Trial, a Month's Fruition makes either a Caterwauling Correſpondence, or a more peaceable and elegant Way of ſeparate Beds.—— She ſeems nettled, I'll proceed. (*Aſide.*)——With this Thought I comfort myſelf: And here, Madam, bid Matrimony and you eternally, Farewell.——*Who wou'd be let for Life.* [*Sings and hums that Tune.*
Wid. Eternally!——I wiſh I had never ſeen this Fellow.——Lord, how my Heart ſinks. [*Aſide.*
Fain. *Come all ye Winds, come all away,*
And briſkly in our Canvaſs play;
Waft me gently o'er the Main;
Farewell, Widow! Farewell, Pain!
Lara. dera, lara, dera, lal, lal, la!
[*In the Tune of* Over the Hills and far away.
Wid. You are exceeding gay, Sir.
Fain. Tous jour Gay, as the *French* ſay. I always meet the Frowns of Fortune thus.——The Jade may jilt, but never inſlave me.——But, to be ſerious, To-morrow, Madam, I embark for the *Indies.* It will be a ſecret Pleaſure to me, if you'll permit this Paper Room in your Cabinet. It is my laſt Will and Teſtament. If I miſcarry in the Voyage, that will intitle you to Forty thouſand Pounds, my Uncle's Death inrich'd me with in *Jamaica*; whither I am bound. This is a Proof of my Eſteem, though you have forbid my Love. [*Gives her a Paper, and takes up a Book from the Table, and ſeems to look in't.*
Wid. This is an Act ſo ſingular, ſo full of Generoſity, that it almoſt lays me under a Neceſſity of making you ſome Return.
Fain. Very ſingular, Faith, if ſhe knew all. [*Aſide.*
Wid. Forty Thouſand Pounds!—Why, one Quarter of that Money, would buy a Barony.
Fain. Quarter me, if I wou'd lay it out that Way, if I had it. [*Aſide.*
Wid. Or, ſuppoſe you ſhou'd ſell Part of your Eſtate in in, in——*Gloucestershire?*

Fain.

Fain. Ay ! or any other Shire. [*Aſide.*
Wid. A Patent wou'd be no difficult Thing to obtain.
Fain. No ! but the Money to pay for it wou'd. [*Aſide.*
Ha !———What's here, *The Pleaſures of a Single Life?* Luckily encounter'd !———
Wid. P'ſhaw ! a Fiddle of *Single Life* !
Fain. Nay, ſince you have impos'd the Study, Madam, you muſt give me Leave to con my Leſſon. [*Seems to read.*
Wid. Pugh ! now, I'm ſerious, you are turning every Thing to ridicule.———About this ſame Patent, I ſay ;— Suppoſe you ſell Part of your Eſtate.
Fain. Faith, Madam, my Eſtate is like a Wife, intai!'d ; and my Father made me ſwear, never to levy a Fine upon any Conſideration, but making a Lady a Jointure. So that it is like to be mine for Life.———But, I know, this ſudden Pretence of yours, is only to try the Strength of my Reſolution.———You are not in earneſt.
Wid.. Well, purſue your Voyage to *Jamaica* ; ſell your Effects ; return and purchaſe a Barony ; which you may eaſily do, in Eight or Ten Months, and you ſhall ſee if I am in earneſt, or not.
Fain. Eight, or Ten Months ! Ha, ha, ha ! Men love not now, Child, the Patriarchal Way. No, no, I wou'd not truſt to a Woman's Promiſe Eight or Ten Hours.— Marry me before I go, and then——
Wid. O ! then you won't go at all.
Fain. Juſt the ſame as if you do not marry me.
Wid. But what a ridiculous Figure I ſhall make, after ſo many Declarations againſt *Plebeianiſm,* when I ſhall be wiſh'd Joy by that vulgar Epithet——Mrs. *Worthy?*
Fain. If that be an Objection, I'll give you my Honour, you ſhall never be call'd Mrs. *Worthy*—(*Takes hold of her Hand, then ſnatches it away.*)—O, the Devil ! that Touch has thaw'd all my Reſolution, and Love and Folly begin to pour in like a Deluge : But when I think of thoſe terrible Words, *You and I muſt never be conjured into the Circle of a Wedding-Ring.*
Wid. This is nothing to the Barony. Look-ye, Mr. *Worthy,* your Generoſity has made this Moment yours? but if you don't take me at my Word, Conſideration may ſpoil my Gratitude.
Fain. Nay, I'm to be taken in the Moment too. Therefore,

fore, if you'll flip on your Hood and Scarf, and ftep into a Hackney-Coach with me, and drive to the *Fleet,* where we may be tack'd together by a Spiritual Journey-man. without a Licenfe, or the Knowledge of either your Servants or mine ; I promife you, as foon as the Ceremony is over, I'll on Board ; make what Hafte the Wind and Waves will permit ; Difpatch my Affairs with the utmoft Expedition ; and with the firft Ship, return to thefe dear Arms. 'Till when, 'till when, thy Widow's Name be worn. The World fhall be infenfible of my Happinefs, 'till it ring with thy Honour.

Wid. Aad you'll perform this ?
Fain. Moft religiously. *[Embraces her.*
Wid. But———
Eain. Nay, no more Fairy Fancies : Give real fubftantial Pleafure. We Country-Gentlemen are fo used to Surloins of Beef, that we fhall ftarve on the Whipt-Cream of Airy Promifes.——*Take me, take me, whilft you may.* (*Sings, then runs and catches her in his Arms.*) This Moment, whilft my Hopes are high ; whilft Imagination reprefents a Groop of Pleafures. Thou'lt find thy Account in't, I warrant thee, Widow !
Wid. Oh ! I can refufe the dear Man no longer.—— Well, wait in a Coach at the Corner of the Street, and I'll be with you in the Compafs of a Wifh. [*Exit.*
Fain. Ha, ha, ha ! fhe's caught by *Jupiter.*

Enter Sam.

Sam. Joy to you, Sir ! I over-heard the Bargain.
Fain. Not a Word in the Family.
Sam. Not for the World, Sir.
Fain. Wait you at my Lodging, with all Things in Readinefs for Confummation.
Sam. Never fear my Part of the Bufinefs, Sir.
Fain. What have you done with his Lordfhip?
Sam. Reduc'd him to a Commoner again, Sir ; but the Fellow is a reafonable Creature ; provided you'll forgive him, he'll obey your Commands.
Fain. Very well ! Away, and call me a Coach.
Sam. Yes, Sir, yes.——— [*Exit.*
Fain. Egad, I've earn'd her Fortune by mere Dint of Policy.———Thus,

When

The ARTIFICE.

When Truth, *and* Love, *to win a* Woman *fail,*
A well laid Plot, *and* Artifice *prevail.* [*Exit.*

SCENE *changes to the Street, before* Watchit's *Door. He in Armour, with a Blunderbufs on his Shoulder, which he often makes ready to fire.*

Wat. I fhall pepper this Dog, if he comes in my Way.—Hark! Sure I heard fomebody tread.——No, 'twas nothing but the Wind, I believe—'Tis very cold——I fhall catch my Death; but it is better to die once for all, than to live upon the Rack. What had I to do with a Help-Mete, when I was no Mete-Help for her? S'Death, to be bubbled in my old Age; to father Children that I never got, and leave my Eftate to a Mungrel Race, half Fifh, half Flefh, a Piece of Prieft Craft! I have had, as it were, by Inftinct, a Sort of Averfion to that Kind of People from my Cradle. Ah! honeft *John Dryden,* I fhall never forget a Paffage of Thine.——

Priefts of all Religions.——

Who comes there? Stand, or you're a dead Man.

Enter Demur, *who draws, ftrikes up* Watchit's *Piece, and difarms him.*

Dem. How! Villain——I'll fee you fairly trufs'd up, if I live.

Wat. 'Ounds, who are you, Sir? and what makes you fauntering here, at this time of Night? you are a Rogue, Sirrah, and I'll fecure you.—Watch, Watch, Watch.

Dem. That pretence fhan't fave your Bacon, you old Villain you. Watch. Watch.

Enter Sir John, *with his Sword drawn.*

Sir *John.* What's the Matter here? Ha! Doctor *Demur?* You are not hurt, I hope!

Wat. Doctor *Demur*! Who the Devil's he? a Patch of the Law? or a Carcafe-mender? I expected a Botcher of another Kind.—— [*Afide.*

Enter Conftable and Watch.

Dem. No, not hurt, Sir *John*; but I was like to have a Brace of Balls in my Guts.

Conft. Who call'd Watch?

Dem. I did, Sir; here's a Rogue attack'd me on the King's Highway, with a Defign to rob, and murder me, I fuppofe.

Wat.

Wat. I did, Sir; this ſtrapping young Dog difarm'd me, with Intention to enter my Houſe *Vi &' Armis*; plunder, and abuſe me——— [*They both ſpeak together.*
Conſt. Your Houſe! Where do you live, Sir?
Wat. What's that to you, Sir?———A Conſtable may cuckold an Alderman. I don't deſire any of you Nightwalking Sparks ſhould know my Houſe! [*Aſide.*
Conſt. A plain Caſe, a plain Caſe! he's aſham'd of his Habitation; away with him.
Sir *John.* Ay, ay, Mr. *Conſtable,* he's a Rogue! This is a worthy Gentleman, a Doctor of the Laws.
Conſt. Yes, yes, Sir; I know Doctor *Demur* to be as honeſt a Man, as any in the whole *Temple,* and ruins as few, I believe. We'll ſecure him, Sir.
Dem. Do; I'll have him examin'd before a Juſtice of the Peace in the Morning.
Wat. The Devil! this is a Trick to get me out of the way; and whilſt I'm detained by theſe Scoundrels, that Dog of a Fryar will lie at Rack and Manger with my Wife. Pray hear me, Mr. *Conſtable.*
Conſt. Yes, yes, Sir, you ſhall be heard before you go to *Newgate.*—You're a fine old Duke to come to the Gallows at theſe Years. Come, bring him along.
Wat. Sir, I ſay I'll go before a Juſtice to Night, and will have my Wife with me too. Zounds, I cou'd tear my Fleſh.—Oh! *Tim!* *Tim!* that ever thou ſhould'ſt marry?
Exit, *forc'd out by the Conſtables,* &c.
Sir *John.* This ſhou'd be *Fainwell*'s Uncle, by his talking of his Wife; and certainly miſtook you for one of her Gallants.
Dem. Odſo! I have heard *Fainwell* ſpeak of him. If it ſhou'd be him, we ſhall have good Diverſion. Where are you going, Sir *John*?
Sir *John.* I am ſent for by my Brother *Ned*; who, I am told, lies dangerous ill at the Widow *Hedleſs*'s.
Dem. 'Tis thither I'm going; I'm glad I met you: I hope it is for your Advantage.—I'll follow you, Sir.
Sir *John.* Haſte ſhou'd excuſe Ceremony, Doctor. [*Exit.*
Enter Conſtable and Watch, with Mr. Watchit *and his Wife, and* Lucy; *meeting Sir* Philip Moneylove.
Conſt. Come, come, bring them along to the Round-Houſe.

Mrs.

The ARTIFICE.

Mrs. *Wat.* Whither, cruel Man, muſt I be haul'd out of my Bed at this unſeaſonable Hour?

Conſt. Only to the Watch-houſe, Madam.

Wat. To the Watch-houſe! to the Devil, Sir! I'm a Gentleman, and won't be abus'd. Carry me before a Juſtice inſtantly.

Sir *Phil.* What's the matter here?

Conſt. Oh, Sir *Philip*! Here, here's a Juſtice of Peace for you. This old Man, Sir, aſſaulted Doctor *Demur.*

Wat. You lye, Sir! he aſſaulted me, Mr. *Juſtice.*——

Sir *Phil.* Hold, hold, Sir; I can't hear you in the Street. My Couſin *Heedleſs* lives the next Door, carry your Priſoners thither, *Conſtable*; you know the Houſe, I ſuppoſe.

Conſt. Yes, yes, very well, Sir. Come, come, bring 'em along.

SCENE *the Inſide of Mrs. Heedleſs's Houſe.*

The Back-Scene draws, and diſcovers Ned Freeman *and* Louiſa, *juſt married;* (*the Parſon making his Exit*) *and Sir* John *and* Demur; Louiſa *throws her Arms about* Freeman's *Neck.*

Lou. Now I'm happy. Now thou'rt mine again!
Look up, my Love! my *Freeman*!
My Joy! my Soul! my Huſband!
Take, take me in thy Arms; and ſay,
Thou doſt forgive me; or I'm ſtill moſt wretched.

Ned. Ha! Why this Joy? from whence theſe Raptures,
When Life is on the Wing; and Death purſues it
With an Eagle's Swiftneſs?

Lou. Far be that Thought! far as my wiſhes, ſend it!
I hope to hold it many happy Years:
Thou art not poiſon'd;

Sir *John.* You're in no Danger, I aſſure you, Brother; it was only your Surprize diſordered you.

Ned. Give me leave to tell you, Brother, the Diſorder I find myſelf in cannot proceed from Surprize alone.

Sir *John.* Something there was; but far from being fatal; the Doctor aſſur'd me, it wou'd have no other Effect than making you a little ſick for the preſent.——

Ned.

Ned. And, I affure you, Sir, that I am not to be trick'd, Sir. (*Draws.*) Cancel the Deed this Moment, or———
Sir *John.* (*Draws.*) That, and my Life fhall go together.
Lou. Ah! (*Shrieks.*) Murder! Murder!
[Demur *draws, and parts them.*
Enter Sir Philip, Watchit, *Mrs.* Watchit, Lucy, *Conftable and Watch.*
Sir *Phil.* Ha! Murder! I charge you in the King's Name to keep the Peace, Mr. *Conftable.*—What do I fee! Mr. *Freeman* and the mad Knight !———What would you murder your Brother, Sir. Secure him, Conftable—I have been looking for you, Mr. *Freeman,* all the Town over.— D'ye hear, ftep to my Houfe, and bid my Daughter come to me this Minute. [*To one of the Watchmen, who* Exits. Hark-ye, Mr. *Freeman* ; was not there fomething to be done at my Houfe to Night?
Ned. I thought fo, Sir, but was unluckily prevented.—
Wat. This is the Rogue, that took me up, Mr. *Juftice.*
Dem. Did not you bid me ftand, Sir? and did not I difarm you of that Blunderbufs in the Conftable's Hand, you old Thief, you?
Wat. Thief! I fcorn your Words, Sir; I was upon my Guard.———
Sir *Phil.* Guard of whaf, Sir?
Wat. Why, a Breach that's made in my Citadel here.
[*Pointing to his Wife.*
Sir *Phil.* Ha, ha, ha! By whom, pray?
Wat. Afk her that ; fhe can tell you.
Lucy. Yes, Sir, my Lady can tell you, what melancholy Days, and wretched Nights———
Wat. I'll wretched Nights you, Huffey!
[*Holds up his Cane.*
Sir *Phil.* Hold, Sir ; do you confider where you are?
Wat. Yes, and what I am too.
Sir *Phil.* And what may that be, I pray?
Wat. A Cuckold, Sir———
Dem. If you are fure of that——Why—the Law is open, Sir.
Wat. Ay! fo open, that it has fwallow'd both Juftice and Confcience ; and yet is as Hollow as ever.
Sir *Phil.* Ha, ha, ha ; but how came you arm'd? and to infult this honeft Gentleman?
Wat.

Wat. Have a care what you fay, Sir; he'll bring his Action againſt you for Scandal.—But I took him for juſt ſuch another honeſt Gentleman; a Botcher of Conſciences. One that has a better Knack at making Sin than forgiving it.—My Wife knows what I ſay to be true; and my Intention was to have ſent a Brace of Balls Hue-and-Cry thro' his Body, in Purſuit of his Continency.

Dem. Oh Lord! Oh Lord! Murder a Man for lying with your Wife!——Why, you ſhou'd take the Law of him.

Wat. That the Lawyers might murder my Eſtate; no, I thank you; I'm for the ſhorteſt way; I'd rather hang at *Tyburn*, than in one of your Courts.———

Mrs. *Wat.* Have you Witneſs of what you ſay, my Dear?

Wat. Yes, yourſelf, my dear Devil———

Mrs. *Wat.* I deny it; produce your Evidence!

Wat. Oh Impudence! Sir, pray give her her Oath and ſend her to the Devil at once——Did not you tell your ghoſtly Father, Miſtreſs, that a Fryar enjoy'd you every Night? Deny that, if you can! Nay, and even when I was in Bed with you too! And that ev'ry Door in the Houſe open'd as ſoon as he approach'd it! for which you believ'd him a Conjurer? A Pox on the Wizard, and the Circle too, I ſay—Now, Gentlewoman, can you ſafely take your Oath this was not your Confeſſion!

Mrs. *Wat.* I can ſafely take my Oath, I go in Danger of my Life with you.

Wat. No, no, 'tis I go in Danger of my Life, Miſtreſs—

Mrs. *Wat.* That ſhall be try'd; for know, Sir, I can bear theſe baſe Inſults no longer—I muſt not go abroad— Not ſo much as to Church; nor ſee any Company at Home; not a Relation in Breeches; and whenever you take a Whim in your Head to go Abroad, I muſt not lie in my Bed, tho' you have the Key of the Door in your Pocket. Nay, in ſhort, I muſt not ſleep, leſt I ſhou'd cuckold you in a Dream.

Sir *Phil.* Ha, ha, ha.

Mrs. *Wat.* A Woman may be made a Fool on, if ſhe will; but you ſhall find, Mr. *Watchit*, I have Friends that won't ſee me abus'd. *Lucy*, call me a Chair—I'll clear myſelf, I warrant you.

Wat.

Wat. Huffey, ftir if you dare. (*To* Lucy.) No, Madam, you fhall clear yourfelf here, if you can.

Sir *Phil.* I wou'd advife you, Sir, to agree with your Lady.—Mr. *Conftable*, you may leave your Prifoners with me. [*Exit Conftable*, &c.

Dem. This is a Caufe for the Civil Court.

Mrs. *Wat.* I have fomething to offer under the Cognizance of Common Law; have not we an Act againft Priefts, that belong to no Ambaffadors?

Dem. Yes, Madam, it's Death for fuch to live in *England*; and it's pity that Act is not put in Execution.

Mrs. *Wat.* Then, I here deliver up this Gentleman to you, Sir.

Wat. What, do you mean to hang me for a Prieft, Miftrefs? Am I a Prieft?

Mrs. *Wat.* So you pretended when you took my Confeffion; Cou'd you imagine, I did not know you? Yes, and refolv'd to fit you for your Jealoufy. And now this good Company fhall judge, if I don't bed every Night with a Fryar; and pray you, *Snub*, what Door in our Houfe keeps fhut, when you approach, and bid it open?
[*In a drolling Manner.*

Dem. Ha, ha, ha! You are bit, old Gentleman.——I fuppofe you'll afk my Pardon now, Sir? Ha, ha ha.

Wat. The Devil fneer you.—How have I expos'd myfelf! Ah! *Tim! Tim!* Thou art but a Fool of a wife Man! [*Afide.*

Enter Mrs. Heedlefs.

Sir *Philip.* Oh! Coufin *Heedlefs!* you'll forgive my taking up your Houfe here———

Wid. My Servants told me the Reafon.—You are welcome, Sir *Philip.* I hate the fight of him; but it's no Time to tell him fo now.——Well! I have made no ill Bargain. If this Spoufe of mine fhou'd never return, this Writing intitles me to all his Eftate in *Jamaica.*—If he lives to come back—I fhall be a Woman of Quality! and our Laws make farther Provifion for me, if he dies. I wifh all Widows were as wife as myfelf. Coufin *Olivia*, your Servant.

Enter Olivia.

Oliv. How go Matters here? Dear Coufin, inform me.

Wid. As you wou'd have 'em, I believe; for the Parfon
was

The ARTIFICE. 367

was fent for; and methinks, one may read Matrimony in Mr. *Freeman*'s Face already.

Sir Phil. Ho! Are you come. [*Seeing* Olivia.
Oliv. Did you fend for me, Sir?
Sir Phil. Ay, ay, come hither, Child.—Mr. *Freeman*, we had as good make an End of the Bufinefs now; and this good Company will make up a Country-Dance—— Here's my Girl. Coufin *Heedlefs* will fend for a Parfon.
Oliv. Oh miferable! What do I hear?
Sir Phil. The Bufinefs will foon be done.
Ned. My Bufinefs is done, Sir.
Sir Phil. But not with my Daughter, Sir.—Come, hang Thinking; fend home the *Dutch* Woman, They are heavy dull Jades. Here's a Girl of the true *Englifh* Breed, that will make you as merry as a Cricket, when the Parfon has faid Grace, Boy.
Ned. I tell you, Sir *Philip*, I have more Occafion for the Hangman's Halter, than the Marriage Noofe.
Sir Phil. What, before you are married? Pifh, Pifh! that's impoffible. But were there not certain Articles to be performed on your Part to Day?
Ned. I thought fo Yefterday, Sir.
Sir Phil. Yesterday, Sir? Zounds! What do you mean, Sir?
Sir John. Why, in fhort, Sir, this Lady has ftept in between my brother *Ned*, and your Daughter, and fupply'd her Place; that's all, Sir.
Oliv. O bleffed Sound. [*Afide*.
Sir Phil. Ha, ha, ha! What have you another Play to act, Sir *John*?
Sir John. No, Faith, Sir *Philip*, the Play is ended; and with your Leave, this Lady and I will fpeak the Epilogue.
[*Takes hold of* Olivia's *Hand*.
Sir Phil. Stark mad, by *Jupiter*. Hold, hold, Sir, this Lady does not underftand Epilogues, nor Prologues neither. (*Takes her from him.*) Do you think I am to be fool'd, Mr. *Freeman*?
Lou. No, Sir; but I think you muft look out fharp for another Son-in-Law, Sir *Philip*; for I am on the right fide of the Hedge, now.——We are married, Sir.
Sir Phil. Indeed, is fhe in earneft, Mr. *Freeman*?
Ned. Yes, Faith, I can fee no Jeft in't; and I'll tell you
another

another Secret; I have given my Brother every Foot of my Eſtate.———

Sir *Phil.* Really!

Dem. Really, Sir *Philip*. I drew the Deed.

Sir *Phil.* Why, then it was the worſt Deed he ever did in his Life; and if it be true——I wiſh you Joy, Sir *John*.

Sir *John*. To convince you, Sir, there's the Papers.
[*Gives him Papers.*

Sir *Phil.* Humph!——'Tis even ſo,——I wiſh you Joy with your *Dutch* Vrow, Mr. *Freeman*,——I do, Faith, Minheer.

Mrs. *Wat.* My Lover married! Nay, then I'm glad we were no better acquainted. [*Aſide.*

Wid. I wiſh you Joy, Madam. [*To* Louiſa.

Lou. It is not in the Power of Fortune to give me more. I hope, my Dear, you are pretty well again.

Ned. Humph, my Sickneſs will continue longer than ſhe imagines. (*Aſide.*) You aſſure me I'm in no Danger of leaving the World, Madam; I wiſh you cou'd tell me how to live in't———

Lou. Oh, truſt to Love, my Dear.

Ned. And ſtarve, my Dear! [*Walks from her.*

Wat. How ſhall I be able to look my Wife in the Face again?

Mrs. *Wat.* Methinks, *Lucy*, your Maſter ſeems to have an Air of Penitence.

Lucy. He does, indeed, look penitential, Madam.

Sir *Phil.* I've been conſidering you from Head to Foot, Sir *John*; and, upon my Soul, I think I never ſaw you look ſo well in my Life: Tho', to ſay Truth, I always thought you a fine Gentleman.—'Till he was diſinherited. (*Aſide.*)——*Olivia*, come hither, Child! Give me thy Hand; it was ever my Reſolution, that thou ſhould'ſt go with the Eſtate; and therefore, Sir *John*, ſince you've got one, e'en take t'other. (*Throws her to him.*)—There, now do your Endeavour to make me, within Ten Months, a Grandfather.———

Sir *John*. On my Knees I thank you. This Preſent is more Welcome, than what my Brother gave me.

Ned. Return my Deed then; I did not give it you: You trick'd me out of it; remember that, Brother.

Sir

The ARTIFICE.

Sir *John.* Out of nothing but my own, Brother; but half my Eſtate is at your Service. Your Generoſity to this Lady commands that.

Sir *Phil.* Say you ſo, Sir? Then your Generoſity ſhall command but half my Daughter's Portion; mark that.

Lou. I bar that Injuſtice; the Fortune's all his own; Nor do we need your kind Indulgence, Brother——

Ned. No!—Egad, I'm glad to hear that! [*Aſide.*

Lou. Yours was the Plot that made my *Freeman* mine; and Heaven rewards you for't, with your Eſtate; and puts it in my Pow'r to raiſe your Brother above the Reach of Want. Know, then, my Father left me his only Heir, and Miſtreſs of forty thouſand Pounds.

Ned. Ha! Say'ſt thou?

Lou. I knew not where to find thee; but reſolv'd to live unmarried for thy Sake—— But, upon Sir *John*'s Letter, haſten'd to prevent thy Breach of Faith. 'Tis done; forgive the Artifice, and all my Fortune's thine.

Ned. Forgive thee! What, forty thouſand Pounds, and aſk Forgiveneſs! One quarter of the Money would purchaſe a Pardon for all the Sins of thee, and thy Poſterity! I affirm, no Woman can be guilty of any Fault, that has forty thouſand Pounds.——But few of the Sex can boaſt ſuch Conſtancy. How ſhall I thank thee for this exceſſive Goodneſs? Brother! Let me thank you too. Had I known your Inclination for this Lady, you ſhould have had no Rival here. [*Claps his Hand on his Breaſt.*

Sir *Phil.* And if he had not got the Eſtate again, he ſhould have had no Father here. (*Clapping his Hand on his Breaſt.*) Come, come, 'tis all well, and the *Man has his Mare again*——What are you muſing on, Sir? (*To* Watchit.) Prithee be chearful Man—Suppoſe you were a Cuckold, the Fault's not yours, nor your Wife's neither: No doubt but you was born when *Mars* and *Venus* were in Conjunction; and if ſo, who can withſtand their Fate?

Omn. Ha, ha, ha, ha.

Dem. Ha, ha; but this Gentleman is in no Danger. ——Come, come, Sir, take your Lady and make much of her; give her her own Liberty; confide in her Honour, and that way preſerve her Virtue.

Ned. I'm glad the old Cuff does not know me again.
[*Aſide.*

Mrs. Wat. Let him ceafe to be jealous, and when I give him real Caufe, let him expofe me—What fay you, *Mumps*? Shall I enjoy the Liberties of an *Englifh* Wife?
Wat. An *Englifh* Wife, that's a large Latitude, *Pud*! But I agree to it; come, bufs, and Friends then! (*Kiffes her.*) So now;
I'll from this Moment banifh all my Cares,
With all my Locks, and Bolts, and Iron Bars.

Enter Fainwell *and* Sam *finging, the laft with a Bottle and Glafs in his Hand.*

Wid. Blefs me! What, do I fee my Rafcal drunk?
Sir *Phil.* Ha, ha, ha, *Jeffery* in his Cups?
Fain. I'm refolv'd to be merry to Night, be-mefs, Sir.—
[*Sings.*
Sing Ola wa, let us be merry———
Sam. *O nilly wa, let us be merry.*
Fain. *And drink the King's Health in racy Canary.*
Sam. *Ya hony Lee.*———
Wid. I'll honey Lee you, Sirrah——[*Runs to beat him.*
Fain. Hold, hold, my Dear; tho' I allow'd you to beat me, when you was my Miftrefs, the Cafe is alter'd now you are my Wife.———
Wid. Wife!
Fain. I am no longer *Jeffery*! but your Lord and Mafter.———
Wid. Ruin'd paft Redemption! Oh! oh! oh!
[*Burfts into Tears.*
Fain. No, no, my Dear, I'll fo hug, love, and bufs thee, that thou fhalt own to Morrow Morning thy Money well laid out. [*Goes to embrace her.*
Omn. Ha, ha, ha, ha.
Wid. Stand off; I never can forgive your putting fuch a Trick upon me, Mr. *Worthy*!
Fain. Mr. *Fainwell*, if you pleafe, my Dear. You fhall find me a Man of Honour. You know it was part of our Agreement, you fhou'd not be call'd Mrs. *Worthy.*
Wid. Not *Worthy*! Oh Heavens! then I have married a down-right Scoundrel! Oh! undone, undone; get out of my Sight. Oh! oh!
Fain. Get out of thy Sight! No, no, I'll get into thy
Arms,

The ARTIFICE.

Arms, my Girl: where I'll convince thee, that I am a Gentleman, of a better Family than your Sham-Lord.
[*Whispers* Sam, *who* Exits.
Wat. That he is, I affure you, Widow; for he is my Nephew.

Sir *Phil.* A very good Metamorphofis! You are an excellent Actor, Sir.

Fain. Every Man in his Way, Sir.

Sir *Phil.* Is your Vanity come to this! Faith, you have made but a blind Bargain of it, Coufin.

Fain. You had lik'd to have couzen'd her into a blinder Bargain——Hark-ye, Sir *Philip*, what was you to have had, if this noble Lord of your Dubbing, had been in my Place?

Enter Sam *and* Tally.

Sir *Phil.* What do you mean by alking that Queftion, Sir? Do you think I was to be brib'd?

Fain. So this fame Gentleman fays, Sir; to the Tune of Three Thoufand Pounds.——Is it not true, *Tally?*

Tally. To a Tittle, Sir——

Sir *Phil.* Why, you, you, you impudent Son of a Whore; were not Seventeen enough for you?

Wid. Not if he had been what you reprefented him, Sir. But I have nothing to thank your Friendfhip for.

Sir *Phil.* A Fig for your Reflections; nothing wou'd go down with your Vanity, but a Lord, forfooth: and fince no Lord of the King's making would be troubled with you, I made one on purpofe for you. Look-ye, 'tis my Opinion, ev'ry Man cheats in his Way——And he is only honeft, who is not difcover'd. [*Exit,*

Omn. Ha, ha, ha, ha.

Fain. I believe, Sir, I have a Guinea of yours.—— It is too much, to take both your Money and your Miftrefs; there, Sir; (*Gives him a Guinea.*) Now, Sir, I prefume your Abfence will be very agreeable to this Company.

Tally. With all my Heart, Sir.——And I am glad I'm come off fo well. [*Exit.*

Ned. Come, come, Madam, I think you have 'fcap'd very well, confidering all. You might have been undone: The Prevention of which is owing to Mr. *Fainwell.* There's nothing in a Title——Believe me, there are more heavy
Hearts

Hearts in Coaches with Coronets behind 'em, than you'll find in the Hacks, take 'em as they run, from the *Royal Palace* to the *Royal Exchange*.

Sir *John*. I'm of my Brother's Opinion, Madam ; Mr. *Fainwell* bears the King's Commiffion ; and tho' he is but a Subaltern, you have Fortune enough to buy him a Regiment ; and a Colonel's Lady is as good as my Lord's.

Wid. Well, fince it is no better, 'tis well it's no worfe ; ——But don't you think, Sir *John*, a Thoufand Pounds, rightly plac'd, wou'd not get him knighted ?

Fain. Ha, ha, ha ! We'll confider of that to Morrow Morning.

Wid. I hope you'll forgive the Blows, I———
Fain. And promife never to return 'em too.
Wat. Nephew, I wifh thee Joy with all my Heart.
Fain. I thank you, Uncle.

Sir *John*. I'm fo much indebted to you, that I love you now, methinks, in fpight of Principle.

Ned. My Principle, dear *Jack*, is the fame with thine. I did not think it prudent to contradict my Father ; but no Man fhall do more in Defence of his Country, or pay his Taxes more chearfully. Come to my Arms.

Sir *John*. To my Heart.   [*They embrace.*
Ned. Now every Man to his Mate ; and let's have a Country-Dance.   [*Goes to* Louifa.

Sir *John*. Come, Mr. *Watchit*, take your Wife, and let me advife you, if fhe has any Faults, hide them from the Publick :

For He *or* She, *who drags the* Marriage Chain,
And finds in Spoufe *Occafion to complain*,
Should hide their Frailties with a Lover's Care,
And let th' ill-judging World conclude 'em Fair ;
Better th' Offence ne'er reach the Offender's Ear.
For they who fin with Caution, *whilft* conceal'd,
Grow impudently *carelefs, when* reveal'd.

FINIS.

www.ingramcontent.com/pod-product-compliance
Lightning Source LLC
Chambersburg PA
CBHW031421230426
43668CB00007B/386